THE IDEA OF BIBLICAL POETRY

THE IDEA OF BIBLICAL POETRY
PARALLELISM AND ITS HISTORY

JAMES L. KUGEL

New Haven and London   Yale University Press

Published with the assistance of the Frederick
W. Hilles Publication Fund of Yale University.

Designed by Nancy Ovedovitz and
set in Times Roman & Four Quarters Special Hebrew type.
Composition by Four Quarters Publishing Company,
Guilford, Connecticut.
Printed in the United States of America by
Vail-Ballou Press, Binghamton, N.Y.

Library of Congress Cataloging in Publication Data

Kugel, James L.
  The idea of biblical poetry.

  Includes index.
  1. Hebrew poetry, Biblical—History and criticism.
2. Hebrew language—Parallelism. 3. Bible. O.T.
Psalms—Criticism, interpretation, etc.—History.
I. Title.
BS1405.2.K83   221.4'4   80–25227
ISBN 0–300–02474–6
      0–300–03101–7 (pbk.)

10 9 8 7 6 5 4 3 2

CONTENTS

PREFACE

The present study consists of two fairly distinct undertakings, two books, one might say. The first, represented by chapters 1 and 2, is an attempt to arrive at some comprehensive notion of biblical parallelism, a stylistic feature characteristic of what is generally considered the "poetry" of the Bible. The second, longer part is a history of ideas about parallelism—and biblical poetry generally—from antiquity to the present. Although the relatedness of these two topics is obvious, they are by rights not only considered separate subjects but even belong to separate disciplines, respectively modern biblical criticism (and hence to Semitic linguistics, archaeology, and ancient Near Eastern history) and the history of exegesis (with its connections to the history of religions and European intellectual history). It might be well before beginning, then, to explain how these two studies came to be one.

On the simplest level it was a marriage of convenience. To write a history of parallelism's exegesis it is surely necessary to begin with some solid notion of the concept itself, to investigate—and where necessary, to question—the best current understanding of parallelism in Hebrew and cognate literatures; and since arriving at this sort of understanding is no easy task, the initial exposition of such a history risks being long; indeed, a small book in itself. Conversely (and to state matters more in keeping with the actual sequence of events), one who sets out to investigate the phenomenon of parallelism and then finds his results somewhat at variance with prevailing views might naturally be drawn to trace the history of the concept, if only to show why his view of things, if correct, had not been advanced before, or, if it had, why it had subsequently been rejected or forgotten.

Such is the genesis of the present work. But if I have nevertheless gone ahead to unite these two studies within a single binding, it is in the hope that readers will find them in some measure mutually illuminating, and that indeed some "higher unity" may emerge from this combination of disciplinary interests. So at least has it been for the author: in a dozen specifics, as well as in the overall view of parallelism and biblical style presented in this book, the insights of past commentators have illuminated my own path. Perhaps—such is my hope, in any case—a perusal of ideas about biblical poetry culled from centuries past will prove worthwhile to other biblical critics, even to the stoniest positivist of the modern school.

Mingled with this hope is my own deeply felt sense of this history's incompleteness. It has often occurred to me that a proper treatment of my subject might only be undertaken by a committee of seasoned scholars (whom, in moments of difficulty, it has been my particular pleasure mentally to appoint) rather than by one such as myself; if I have nonetheless gone ahead to investigate the whole, detailed history of an idea, rather than to concentrate on a single aspect or period, it has been in the belief that nothing less than a full survey, however inadequate, was required by the view of Hebrew style espoused herein.

This project was begun under the auspices of the Society of Fellows, Harvard University. I am grateful to the society and to the Andrew Mellon Foundation, the Danforth Foundation, and the Ingram Merrill Foundation for their help in carrying it to its completion.

Chapters 1–5 appeared, in primitive form, as my dissertation, *Biblical Parallelism and Its Early Exegesis* (1977). A version of the present chapter 5 also appeared in *Studies in Medieval Jewish History and Literature*, Harvard University Press, 1979. An abbreviated version of chapters 1 and 2 was presented as a series of lectures at the Spanish and Portuguese Synagogue, New York City, in 1977. Chapters 3 and 4 were delivered as a lecture at Harvard, "Rabbinic and Patristic Ideas about Biblical Poetry" in November of 1978.

Of the many people who have generously given of their time to help me, I am particularly grateful to Isadore Twersky, Eric Werner, Solomon Feffer, Dan Pagis, and Samuel Levin for suggestions and help with the earliest drafts of the present study. To my teacher, John Hollander, special thanks are due. Many friends and colleagues have provided suggestions for subsequent drafts, and I am thankful to Michael Fishbane, Brevard Childs, Dominique Bourel, Moses Berger, David Stern, James Lehmann, and Bernard Septimus for their help. Throughout I have been extremely grateful for the suggestions and collaboration of my wife, Rachel.

I should like as well to use this occasion to express formally my gratitude to those who first guided me in the study of Hebrew texts and Jewish thought, and particularly to A. Lopes Cardozo, Arthur Green, Aryeh Frimer, and Isadore Twersky. Above all I am grateful to my father and teacher, John Hans Kugel, in whose memory the present volume is inscribed.

A note on transcriptions: Hebrew words that appear frequently in the body of the text (*māšāl*, *šîrâ*, and others) have been transcribed into Latin characters. Transcriptions have also been used where it is judged they will be useful to a reader who does not understand Hebrew, for example, in discussions of phonological features. Elsewhere Hebrew characters have been used, followed by English translation. In the transcription of names, I have generally followed conventional spellings; thus Sa'adya (and not Se'adya), Kimḥi (and not Qimḥi). The same is true for the spelling of commonly transcribed words: *torah* instead of *tôrâ*. Arabic words and book titles, even when cited from the texts written in Hebrew characters, have been transcribed into Latin characters. In places where scientific transcription is not required, Hebrew and Arabic ʾ and ʿ are represented by ʼ.

BIBLIOGRAPHICAL ABBREVIATIONS

ANET   J. B. Pritchard, *Ancient Near-Eastern Texts Relating to the Old Testament* (Princeton, N.J., 1969)

b.   precedes tractate of Babylonian Talmud; b. *Suk.* = Babylonian Talmud tractate Sukkah; b. BQ = Babylonian *Baba Qamma*

BASOR   *Bulletin of the American Schools of Oriental Research*

BJRL   *Bulletin of the John Rylands Library*

BZAW   *Beihefte zur Zeitschrift für die alttestamentliche Wissenschaft*

CBQ   *Catholic Biblical Quarterly*

CTA   A. Herdner, *Corpus de tablettes en cunéiformes alphabétiques* (Paris, 1969)

DBS   H. Cazelles, *Dictionnaire de la Bible, Suppléments* (Paris, 1966–)

EJ   *Encyclopedia Judaica*

EPH   L. Alonso-Schökel, *Estudios de Poetica hebrea* (Barcelona, 1964)

HTR   *Harvard Theological Review*

HUCA   *Hebrew Union College Annual*

j.   precedes tractate of the Jerusalem Talmud

JANES   *Journal of the Ancient Near Eastern Society of Columbia University*

JAOS   *Journal of the American Oriental Society*

JBL   *Journal of Biblical Literature*

JNES   *Journal of Near Eastern Studies*

JNSL   *Journal of Northwest Semitic Languages*

Joüon   P. Joüon, *Grammaire de l'hébreu biblique* (Rome, 1947)

JPOS   *Journal of the Palestine Oriental Society*

JQR   *Jewish Quarterly Review*

JSJ   *Journal for the Study of Judaism*

JSS   *Journal of Semitic Studies*

JTS	*Journal of Theological Studies*
M.	precedes tractate of the Mishna
MGWJ	*Monatschrift für Geschichte und Wissenschaft des Judentums*
MT	Masoretic Text
OTI	O. Eissfeldt, *The Old Testament: An Introduction* (New York, 1965)
PEPI	S. Gevirtz, *Patterns in the Early Poetry of Israel* (2nd ed., Chicago, 1973)
PG	J. P. Migne, *Patrologiae cursus completus*, series graeca (Paris, 1857–66)
PL	J. P. Migne, *Patrologiae cursus completus*, series latina (Paris, 1844–64)
Psalms I, II, III	M. Dahood, *Psalms I, II, and III* (New York, 1966, 1968, 1970)
PsIW	S. Mowinckel, *The Psalms in Israel's Worship*, vols. 1 and 2 (New York, 1962)
RSP	J. Fischer, ed., *Ras Shamra Parallels* (Rome, 1972–)
SB	E. Werner, *The Sacred Bridge* (New York, 1959)
SP	R. Lowth, *The Sacred Poetry of the Hebrews* (Boston, 1829)
SVT	Supplements to *Vetus Testamentum*
UF	*Ugarit Forschungen*
UT	C. Gordon, *Ugaritic Textbook* (Rome, 1965)
VT	*Vetus Testamentum*
YGC	W. F. Albright, *YHWH and the Gods of Canaan* (London, 1968)
ZAW	*Zeitschrift für die alttestamentliche Wissenschaft*

ONE

THE PARALLELISTIC LINE: "A IS SO, AND *WHAT'S MORE*, B"

1

The songs and psalms of the Bible were not written in quantitative meters, as were the songs of the ancient Greeks, nor do they have regular rhyme or alliterative patterns, as do the songs of many other peoples. Rather, the basic feature of biblical songs—and, for that matter, of most of the sayings, proverbs, laws, laments, blessings, curses, prayers, and speeches found in the Bible—is the recurrent use of a relatively short[1] sentence-form that consists of two brief clauses:

אשרי איש ירא את ה' במצותיו חפץ מאד

Happy the man who fears the Lord, who greatly delights in his commandments. *Psalm 112:1*

The clauses are regularly separated by a slight pause—slight because the second is (as above) a continuation of the first and not a wholly new beginning. By contrast, the second ends in a full pause. The structure might thus be schematized as

_____ / _____//

with the single slash representing the pause between the clauses (short) and the pair of slashes representing the final pause (long).[2] Here and there ternary sentences

_____ / _____ / _____//

also occur, but the binary form is definitely the rule in Hebrew and ternary the exception.

Often, the clauses have some element in common, so that the second half seems to echo, answer, or otherwise correspond to the

---

1. This basic fact about biblical songs is often overlooked or taken for granted, yet it is most significant; see on this point the commentary of the (medieval) Tosafot on b. *Baba Batra* 14b; Judah Alharizi singles out the "poetic" books of the Bible as having פסוקים קצרים וקלים [verses that are short and simple]; on both see chapter 5.

2. That is, it would be punctuated by a period or a semicolon in English. There are not a few lines where this full pause is nevertheless not "final"; see below.

first. The common element is sometimes a word or phrase that occurs in both halves, or the same syntactic structure, or commonly paired concepts ("by day . . . / by night . . . //"), or some similarity in the ideas expressed. For example, Psalm 94 begins:

אל נקמות ה' / אל נקמות הופיע //

הנשא שפט הארץ / השב גמול על־גאים //

ער מתי רשעים ה' / ער מתי רשעים יעלזו //

יביעו ידברו עתק / יתאמרו כל פעלי און //

God of retribution, Lord / God of retribution, appear! //
Rise up, earth's ruler / give the arrogant their due //
How long shall the wicked, Lord / how long shall the wicked rejoice? //
They brag, speak arrogance / all the evil-doers do act haughtily //[3]

The common element in the first verse is the repetition of the phrase "God of retribution." In the second, each half begins with an imperative addressed to God ("rise up . . . / give . . . //"). The third verse repeats a phrase, just as in the first. The fourth verse describes successively aspects of the evildoers' arrogant behavior.

Though Psalm 94 is an extreme example, it illustrates the general tendency of this biblical style to establish, through syntax, morphology, and meaning, a feeling of correspondence between the two parts. For that reason the style is called *parallelism*. The name has in the past proven somewhat misleading, for some students of the phenomenon have understood the term to imply that each half must parallel the other in meaning, or indeed that each word of the first must be matched by a word in the second. As will be seen, such complete correspondence is relatively rare.

2

The clauses of a parallelistic verse have been referred to by a bewildering variety of names: hemistichs, stichs, versicles, cola, bicola, half-verses, or (as we shall most often call them) A and B.[4] It is not known how they were referred to in biblical times; the earliest

3. While the meaning "salvation" for נקמה has clarified many previously puzzling texts, Dahood is correct (*Psalms II*) in asserting retribution as the theme here. See his p. 347 for the possibly implied "how long" in v. 4.

4. Terminology is important. Obviously stich and hemistich analogize parallelism to poetry; colon and bicola were terms used in Greek rhetoric (i.e., prose as well as poetry). When Robert Lowth called his discovery "parallelismus membrorum" he was certainly aware that *membrum* was the standard Latin translation of Greek *colon* in all writings on rhetoric, but his term has since been grievously

postbiblical references speak only of "the beginning" and "the end" of a verse. Perhaps they did not need a name, for this two-part form, A + B, was as much a habit of mind as a formal prescription. And it was on everyone's lips, commoners' and kings'; rumors and facts, cures, rules of conduct, rules of thumb, things one heard and things one might make up spontaneously[5]—all were framed in parallelisms. Indeed, this is the first thing to be grasped about parallelism: it was an extraordinarily versatile and popular form of expression, one that almost anyone could use almost anywhere. Parallelistic lines appear throughout the Bible, not only in "poetic" parts but in the midst of narratives (especially in direct discourse),[6] in detailed legal material concerning the sanctuary and the rules of sacrifices, in genealogies, and so forth.

The relationship between the two parts varies. In verses such as those seen in Psalm 94 one finds a very obvious correspondence. Indeed, in many psalm verses the second half seems nothing more than a restatement of the first in different words:

אהללה ה' בחיי / אזמרה לאלהי בעודי //

I will praise the Lord in my life / I will sing of my God while I live //
Psalm 146:2

At the same time one finds an almost equal number of lines in which the feeling of correspondence between A and B is so slight as to disappear entirely:

חנה מלאך־ה' סביב ליראיו / ויחלצם //

The Lord's angel stays about his worshippers / and [i.e., so that he] delivers them //
Psalm 34:8

ברוך ה' / שלא נתננו טרף לשניהם //

Blessed is the Lord / for he did not make us fall prey to their teeth //
Psalm 124:6

Not only do these latter verses lack the sort of correspondence-establishing elements seen earlier, they do not even seem to have a clear break dividing the verses in two (and in any case the "halves" are somewhat lopsided).

The majority of parallelisms in the Bible fall between such

---

misunderstood to mean "the parallelism of all the members [= words] of A with all the members of B"! Cf. *YGC* p. 5n. On the equivalence colon = member = clause for Lowth, see A. Baker, "Parallelism: England's Contribution," *CBQ* 35 (1973): 430.

5. See John Gray, *The Legacy of Canaan*, *SVT* 5 (Leiden, 1965): 304.

6. On this and the following, see chapter 2.

extremes. Here, by way of illustration only,[7] are some of the commonest ways in which the meaning of A and B are related in one book of the Bible, the Psalter:

Mere Comma

There are many verses in which A and B have no real semantic parallelism at all, sentences in which the medial pause is a mere comma separating units of roughly equal length:

חזקו ויאמץ לבבכם / כל המיחלים לה' //

Be strong and let your hearts be firm / all you who trust in the Lord //
Psalm 31:25

בינו נא זאת שכחי אלוה / פן אטרף ואין מציל //

Understand this, forgetters of God / lest I ravage and none escape //
Psalm 50:22

ה' אלהים צבאות / עד מתי עשנת בתפלת עמך //

Lord God of Hosts / how long will you be angry at your people's prayer? //
Psalm 80:5

Among specific subtypes of such "mere comma" lines, let us note:

Citation

ואני אמרתי בחפזי / נגרזתי מנגד עיניך //

I said in my dismay / "I have been driven from your sight" //
Psalm 31:23

וידברו באלהים אמרו / היוכל אל לערך שלחן במדבר //

And they spoke against God [and] said / "Can God spread a table in the desert?" //
Psalm 78:19

למה יאמרו הגוים / איה אלהיהם //

Why should the nations say / "Where is their God?" //   Psalm 79:10

Sequence of Actions

גפן ממצרים תסיע / תגרש גוים ותטעה //

You brought up a vine from Egypt / you banished nations and planted it //
Psalm 80:9

המה ראו כן תמהו / נבהלו נחפזו //

When they saw, they were astonished / they panicked and took flight //
Psalm 48:6

---

7. What follows is certainly not intended as a catalogue of different types of parallelism, on which practice see following.

הודיעני ה' קצי / ומדת ימי מה היא / אדעה מה חדל אני //

Show me, Lord, my end / and what is the measure of my days / [then] I
will know how fleeting I am //　　　　　　　　　　　　Psalm 39:5

Various subordinations

יהי חסדך ה' עלינו / כאשר יחלנו לך //

Let your love, Lord, be upon us / since we hope in you //　　Psalm 33:22

אם תחנה עלי מחנה / לא יירא לבי //

If a camp encamp about me / my heart shall not fear //　　　Psalm 27:3

Moreover, the forms and degrees of semantic parallelism vary. One
finds, for example:

Commonly paired elements establish parallelism[8]

יומם יצוה ה' חסדו / ובלילה שירה עמי //

By day the Lord sends forth his love / and *by night* his song is with me //
　　　　　　　　　　　　　　　　　　　　　　　　　　Psalm 42:9

אלהים שמע תפלתי / האזינה לאמרי פי //

Oh God *hear* my prayer / *hearken* to the words of my mouth //
　　　　　　　　　　　　　　　　　　　　　　　　　　Psalm 54:4

יברכך ה' מציון / וראה בטוב ירושלם / כל ימי חייך //

May the Lord of *Zion* bless you / and [i.e. so that you] enjoy[9] *Jerusalem's*
goodliness / your whole life //　　　　　　　　　　　　Psalm 128:5

Repeated element(s)[10]

בך בטחו אבתינו / בטחו ותפלטמו //

In you our forefathers trusted / they trusted that you would save them //
　　　　　　　　　　　　　　　　　　　　　　　　　　Psalm 22:5

כי חנם טמנו לי שחת רשתם / חנם חפרו לנפשי //

Secretly they hide their death-trap for me / secretly they lie in wait for
me //　　　　　　　　　　　　　　　　　　　　　　　　Psalm 35:7

---

8. On "fixed pairs" see chapter 1, section 7.

9. Probably *raʾōh* (infinitive) is to be read for MT imperative *rĕʾēh*. For *yqtl*
followed by the same probable infinitive with just this expression, cf. Eccles. 2:1
אנסך בשמחה וראה בטוב; also Eccles. 9:11 שבתי וראה. Note that (contra Dahood)
ראה ב– is not the idiom here, but ראה (ב)טוב ("enjoy"). Cf. Pss. 4:7, 34:9, 13; Job
7:7, Eccles. 2:1, 3:13, also the variant ראה כי טוב ("be very pleased") as in Gen.
1:4, 10, etc. See my "Adverbial Use of *Ki Tob*," *JBL* 99 (1980): 433–36.

10. On repetitive parallelism in Hebrew and Ugaritic, see section 7.

ראוך מים אלהים / ראוך מים יחילו / אף ירגזו תהמות //

When the waters saw you, God / when the waters saw you they
shook / yea, the depths were agitated //   Psalm 77:17

עד אנה ה' תשכחני נצח / עד אנה תסתיר את פניך ממני //

עד אנה אשית עצות בנפשי / יגון בלבבי יומם / עד אנה ירום איבי עלי //

How long, Lord, will you completely forget me? / How long will you hide
your face from me? //

How long will I keep sorrow in myself / pain in my heart [all] day? / How
long will my enemy triumph over me? //   Psalm 13:2–3

Each term of A paralleled in B

ה' שמך לעלם / ה' זכרך לדר ודר //

YHWH is your name eternally / YHWH your appelation forever //
       Psalm 135:13

All of B in apposition to part of A[11]

יכרת ה' כל שפתי חלקות / לשון מדברת גדלות //

Let the Lord cut off all lips of falsehood / a tongue speaking untruths //
       Psalm 12:4

תסתירני מסוד מרעים / מרגשת פעלי און //

You shield me from the council of the wicked / from the company of evil-
doers //   Psalm 64:3

AB / B'C //[12]

יקרא אל השמים מעל / ואל הארץ לדין עמו //

He calls to the Heavens above / and to the earth to judge his people //
       Psalm 50:4

ויהפך לדם יאריהם / ונזליהם בל ישתיון //

He turned their Nile[s] to blood / and their waters, lest they drink //
       Psalm 78:44

"Blessed" + Attribution[13]

ברוך ה' / כי שמע קול תחנוני //

Blessed is the Lord / may he hear the sound of my plea //   Psalm 28:6

11. On this pattern see M. Dahood, "Ugaritic-Hebrew Syntax and Style" *UF* 1
(1969): 27–28.

12. It is common practice to represent terms of a single line with the letters A, B,
C, etc. and terms that parallel them within the same line with the notation A', B', etc.

13. This was to become the Rabbinic ברכה; see W. S. Towner, " 'Blessed be
Y . . .' The Modulation of a Biblical Formula," *CBQ* 30 (1968): 386–99.

ברוך אלהים / אשר לא הסיר תפלתי / וחסדו מאתי //

Blessed is God / that he did not turn aside my prayer / nor his love from
me // Psalm 66:20

A is statement, B question

כי אין במות זכרך / בשאול מי יורה לך //

In death none can call on you / in the netherworld who will praise you? //
Psalm 6:6

אלהים בקדש דרכך / מי אל גדול כאלהים //

God, your dominion is in Heaven / what power is as great as God? //
Psalm 77:14

3

This is, of course, only a sampling—but a somewhat polemical one,
designed to bring home a central theme: the ways of parallelism are
numerous and varied, and the intensity of the semantic parallelism
established between clauses might be said to range from "zero
perceivable correspondence" to "near-zero perceivable differentiation" (i.e., just short of word-for-word repetition). Now how one reads
and interprets a line depends to a great extent on one's expectations,
that is, on the notion of parallelism one brings to each verse. It is here
that the term "parallelism" has proven somewhat misleading. For
example, in approaching Psalm 145:10

יודוך ה' כל מעשיך / וחסידיך יברכוכה //

All your works praise you, Lord / and your faithful ones bless you //

it is easy to see how B parallels A in form and in meaning. But what of
the slight differences? "Faithful ones" (those characterized by חסד,
"bestowed love") is a more specific notion than "all your works,"
angels, men, and beasts.[14] Similarly "praise" (acknowledge, thank),
though a frequent apposite of "bless" in the Bible, is a somewhat
different, more general form of "powerful speaking" than its pair.[15]

14. מעשיך really means "offspring" or "creatures" here. Cf. Pss. 8:7, 103:22,
104:24; Prov. 31:31 (!); Job 14:15, 34:19. חסידיך may denote a special group or sect.
See J. Coppens, "Les psaumes des hasidim" in *Mélanges André Robert* (Paris,
1956), pp. 214–24, an evolutionary view of the term's use; also *PsIW* 1:8, 103, etc.
15. On this general point see J. Muilenberg, "Hebrew Rhetoric: Repetition and
Style," *SVT* 1 (Leiden, 1953): 97–111.

Furthermore, B's syntactic variation, "subject—verb," is opposed to
the "verb—subject" of the A half. These are hardly overwhelming
differences, and in view of the obvious parallelism of meaning, it is
only natural to consider them "elegant variations" on a single idea.
They are, it seems, a natural consequence of having to say *the same
thing* in different words. Thus it is that discussions of parallelism
generally stress similarities, especially semantic. In one critic's (not
atypical) formulation, the ancient Hebrew "expresses his thought
twice in a different manner. . . . He repeats and repeats."[16] But this is
to miss the point of a great many parallelistic lines, indeed a majority.
About this particular verse one might ask: what *is* that same idea that
is being repeated? Is it: "Everyone praises / blesses you"? Then why
should the second half have introduced so specific a term as חסידיך,
"your faithful ones," (and not, e.g., "the whole earth," "all the
world," or the like)? Furthermore, as even our brief survey of
parallelism suggests, there are quite a few lines in which B is clearly a
continuation of A, or a going-beyond A in force or specificity. And
this, it is suggested, corresponds to the expectations the ancient
Hebrew listener, or reader, brought to every text: his ear was attuned
to hearing "A is so, and *what's more*, B is so." That is, B was
connected to A, had something in common with it, but was not
expected to be (nor regarded as) mere restatement.

The medial pause all too often has been understood to represent a
kind of "equals" sign. It is not; it is a pause, a comma, and the unity of
the two parts should not be lost for their division. Indeed, its true
character might be more graphically symbolized by a double arrow—

All your works praise you Lord ⟷ and your faithful ones bless you

for it is the dual nature of B both to come *after* A and thus add to it,
often particularizing, defining, or expanding the meaning,[17] and yet
also to harken back to A and in an obvious way connect to it. One
might say that B has both *retrospective* (looking back to A) and
prospective (looking beyond it) qualities.

Now by its very afterwardness, B will have an *emphatic* character:
even when it uses the most conventional synonyms or formulae, its
very reassertion is a kind of strengthening and reinforcing. But often
this feature (found in all apposition) is exploited: the meaning of B is
indeed more extreme than A, a definite "going one better." Thus,
when Job begins his complaint (3:3)

16. J. Pederson, *Israel: Its Life and Culture* (London, 1926), p. 123.
17. See on this Muilenberg, "Hebrew Rhetoric," 98.

יאבד יום אולד בו / והלילה אמר הרה גבר //

Perish the day I was born in / and the night it was said, "Let a boy be conceived" //

he does not mean the second half to be merely an independent version of the first, but something more emphatic: "My whole life is a waste! Blot out the day of my birth, *in fact*, go back to the very night I was conceived and destroy it." Of course the parallelism of A and B is clear. But saying they "mean the same thing" is hardly exact.

The much explicated Isaiah 1:3 is another example:

ידע שור קנהו / וחמור אבוס בעליו //
ישראל לא ידע / עמי לא התבונן //

If biblical parallelism were merely a repetition, the meaning of this verse would be: an ox knows its owner, and an ass its masters' trough; Israel does not know, my people does not understand. Any reader would, of course, be aware that some sort of unflattering comparison is being made. But if, in place of mere restatement, one allows B some independent existence, this series of clauses presents itself as a kind of progression. How is the first clause different from the second? The same verb, "know, obey,"[18] governs both halves. The animal of the first was hardly considered the most praiseworthy of beasts: nevertheless "ox" is in several significant respects considered superior to its frequent pair, "ass."[19] More important, parallel to the "owner" of the first is "masters' trough" in the second. The cumulative effect of these differences is the establishment of a climactic descent: "An ox knows its owner, and *even* an ass"—who may not be very obedient or attentive—at least knows where to stand to be fed, i.e., knows "his masters' trough; but Israel does not know,"—or obey, even this much; in fact—"my people does not understand at all."[20]

18. "Obeys" or "is attendant to" is what is meant in the first verse-half. For this meaning cf. 1 Sam. 2:12, Hos. 5:4, Prov. 1:29, 2:5; Job 18:21, 21:13. In Near Eastern treaty language, "know" was regularly used in the sense of "acknowledge as sovereign." See H. B. Huffmon, "The Treaty Background of Hebrew *Yadaᶜ*," *BASOR* 181 (Feb. 1966): 31–37.

19. In ritual purity, and in matters dependent on it, such as redemption. While שור and חמור are an oft-repeated, merismatic pair in the Bible, they are no more interchangeable in parallelism than in real-life agriculture. Here, however, the text is probably speaking of the simple matter of obedience; the ass's inferiority in this respect is well-known.

20. That this meaning is emphatic (hence, "at all") is stated in the *hitpaᶜel* itself. Elsewhere, when *ydᶜ–byn* is not meant as a climactic descent, one finds the normal *hifᶜil* form, thus Isa. 43:10, 44:18. Whether the infix-*t* has durative force (as Gen.

Sometimes, especially in proverbs and sayings, finding the precise connection between two apparently unrelated parallel utterances is the whole point:

טוב שם משמן טוב / ויום המות מיום הולדו //

Better a name than good oil / and the day of death than the day of birth //

Eccles. 7:1

The first half of Ecclesiastes' verse is difficult to argue with: who would deny that a man's reputation is more important than any material possession? And sound adds its approval to sense, for the verse-half is a near-perfect chiasmus, especially if one recalls the doubled š hides an elided n: tôb šēm min šemen tôb. The second half, however, seems eminently arguable: birth is always a happy occasion, and death always occasion for mourning—so in what sense could the latter be considered "better"?

In precisely the same sense. For the trouble with precious oil (as Ecclesiastes mentions later, 10:1) is that it is extremely fragile and spoils easily. What is of obvious value one day is completely worthless the next. The value of a name is quite the opposite: intangible, it is thus protected from the physical decay of the world. Now the newborn child is like the precious oil in that he is entirely physical[21]—no qualities, no character, in fact, *no name*, at least not for a while. As he grows he gains these less tangible attributes; then, as he ages, his physical existence begins to decay. On the day of his death, all that will remain is the intangible, the šēm; that day will be "better" in that on it the process of building the name (which only began at birth) will be complete.

The proverb exists in the form "A is so and B is so." But its "and" is not a simple connective. The two halves are a single conceit— "Since (the unarguable) A is so, therefore (the initially very arguable) B is so," "Not only A, but even B," "Just as A, so B also," etc. There was no need to state their relationship; it is implied in the form itself.[22]

Now it may be that we have some clue as to how this subtle

6:9), or imitative, or some other nuance is not as important as the emphasis it implies.

21. R. Gordis also suggests the two are associated because oil is useful on babies. *Koheleth: the Man and His World* (New York, 1968), p. 267.

22. One might single out the *waw* ("and") as implying comparison, the so-called *waw adaequationis*, but then that is the whole point: A . . . / weB . . . // is the form. There are , however, parallelisms of obviously comparative intent in which the *waw* is absent, e.g., Prov. 11:22. Moreover, comparison is far too narrow a concept: see below, n. 32.

relationship of B to A was seen in biblical times, especially where it is most common, in proverbs. For one characteristic most often associated with Hebrew proverbs is the quality of "sharpness." Thus Proverbs 26:9

חוח עלה ביד שכור / ומשל בפי כסילים //

A thorn comes by chance into the hand of a drunkard / and a proverb (*māšāl*) into the mouth of fools //

The sense of this verse is: you may hear fools citing words of wisdom, but they have gotten them without understanding their real meaning, by chance, like a burr that sticks into the hand of a groping drunkard. The proverbist's image is, however, significant: he associates *māšāl* (a proverb, or perhaps more generally, a parallelistic line)[23] with something sharp. A similar image appears in Ecclesiastes 12:11:

דברי חכמים כדרבנות / וכמשמרות נטועים בעלי אספות //

The words of the wise are like goads / and like nails firmly planted are those used in assemblies //[24]

דברי חכמים (words of the wise) is a (late) pair of *māšāl* (cf. Proverbs 1:6). Here again, then, these brief, proverblike utterances are sharp. The recurrent phrase *lĕmāšāl wĕlišnînâ* (Deut. 28:37, 1 Kings 9:7, Jer. 24:9, 2 Chron. 7:20) is an idiom meaning "as a byword or proverb" (especially as a warning); the second noun is from the root *šnn*, which means to be sharp or pointed. Now one might conclude from this that *māšāl* was "sharp" in that it spurred to action or pricked the conscience of the listener. But if this meaning is at all present, it is apparently an adaptation of an attribute of *māšāl* already

---

23. See chapter 2, n. 15.

24. Again, let us read B against A. The sharpness of דרבנות ("goads," from *drb* "be sharp," cf. Arabic *ḍariba*) exists in potential; it needs an object, something to be goaded. משמרות נטועים, "stuck-in nails," are already having their sharpness put to advantage; this is the nuance B adds. The somewhat obscure phrase בעלי אספות thus represents "words of the wise" that have found their mark, either because they have been incorporated in established collections (אספות), or because academy teachers (בעלי אספות) with many students are certain of having their words understood and preserved properly. On the latter point see J. Goldin on העמידו תלמידים הרבה in "The End of Ecclesiastes," in A. Altmann, *Biblical Motifs* (Cambridge, 1966), p. 135 (it is a pity he did not connect his remarks with this verse!) and in general Gordis, *Koheleth*, pp. 353–54 and 411. The superiority of teacher-to-student transmission over learning from the written word alone—על פי סופרים ולא על פי ספרים—remained a central Jewish tenet: see Profiat Duran, מעשה אפד (Vienna, 1865) pp. 20–21. On the existence of wisdom schools: J. P. J. Olivier, "Schools and Wisdom Literature" *JNSL* 4 (1975): 49.

known. For *ḥîdâ*, which seems to come from another root meaning "sharp,"[25] is also paired with *māšāl*. Whatever a *ḥîdâ* is (it is often translated as "riddle") its sharpness has nothing to do with spurring to action: as Samson's *ḥîdâ* (Judg. 14:14) and Sheba's (1 Kings 10:1) show, it was a test of wits or verbal showmanship of some sort.

Instead, the sharpness of *ḥîdâ* and *māšāl* is more likely the quality already described, the delight in creating a B half which both connects with, and yet cleverly expands, the meaning of A. "Sharpness" represented the potential subtleties hidden inside juxtaposed clauses. This is in any case what we shall mean by the term on the following pages; it is the highest advantage taken of parallelism, one might say the genius of the form.

4

That genius was not well understood by the modern expositors of parallelism, however.

Robert Lowth is the man generally credited with the discovery of biblical parallelism. His study *De sacra poesi Hebraeorum* . . . (1753, revised somewhat 1763) coined the phrase *parallelismus membrorum* ("the parallelism of the clauses")[26] and established the general lines of the modern critical approach to parallelism in the Bible. A most perceptive and sensitive writer on biblical style, Lowth nevertheless misstepped in insisting—and this is in many ways the most historically significant part of his exposition—on classifying different sorts of parallelism into broad "types." He distinguished three: synonymous, antithetical, and synthetic parallelism. This classification, far from illuminating, simply obscured the potential subtleties of the form: everything now fell into one of three boxes.

It was soon recognized[27] that the third, at least, was defective, a sort of catchall; but the first two terms are still alive today. Now the trouble with "synonymous" as a classification is that it leads to the view that B is essentially a restatement of A (though to judge by his examples, Lowth himself may not have had so narrow an idea in

25. On the affinity of verbal roots with $R_2 = R_3$ (i.e. *ḥdd*) and those with $R_2 = y$ or w (*ḥidah*, [denominative?] *ḥwd*), J. Kurilowicz, *Studies in Semitic Grammar and Metrics* (Warsaw, 1972) pp. 10–12.

26. See above, note 4.

27. See George Buchanan Gray, *The Forms of Hebrew Poetry* (London, 1915), pp. 49–52.

mind).[28] Parallelism, then, became "saying the same thing twice"; classified as "synonymous parallelism," our verse from Isaiah becomes only "An ox knows its owner, and an ass its masters' food trough,"[29] without any sense of the whole. What the synonymous reading, a drastic sort of leveling, lacked was a recognition of the fact of B's *afterwardness*. It conceived of the two as happening simultaneously, and consequently failed to see that B *must inevitably be understood as A's completion*;[30] A, and what's more, B; not only A, but B; not A, not even B; not A, and certainly not B; just as A, so B; and so forth.

Lowth's "antithetical" parallelism was a distinction without a difference. It was another way for B to pick up and complete A. Just as "synonymous" is inappropriate, so is "antithetical." Indeed, it was in order to preserve the synonymity of "synonymous" that antithetical parallelism was devised; it drained off a whole class of parallelism in which B's differentness from A was all too obvious.

Now the relationship of A to B in Lowth's antithetical examples, e.g.,

נאמנים פצעי אוהב / ונעתרות נשיקות שונא //
Proverbs 27:6

is not merely "antithetical." Saying this only repeats the synonymous reading's error, for here too A and B would then become independent (opposite) versions of "the same idea," rather than a single statement. But single statement they are. A translator might render the relationship A:B here as:

Just as a friend's barbs are sincere / so are an enemy's kisses false //[31]

28. T. H. Robinson, "Hebrew Poetic Form: the English Tradition" *SVT* 1 (1953): 130.

29. See, for example, the discussion of this very verse as "synonymous" in R. K. Harrison, *Introduction to the Old Testament* (Grand Rapids, Mich., 1969), p. 965; also the translation in L. I. Newman and W. Popper, *Studies in Parallelism* (Berkeley, Calif., 1918).

30. Here mention should be made of the major work on the subject of completion, B. H. Smith's *Poetic Closure* (Chicago, 1968). Note especially "Puns, Parallelism and Antithesis," pp. 166–71.

31. The precise meaning of נעתרות is somewhat in dispute, suggestions as widely divergent as "profuse" and "ferocious" having been put forward. Obviously the word is intended to contrast with נאמנים, as the parallel morphology indicates. But perhaps the latter ought to be taken not (as it often is) as "long-lasting," but in the equally acceptable sense of "faithful," "reliable," yielding, approximately, the first half of

or even more explicitly, in the spirit of "You know A, now understand B" (already seen in Eccles. 7:1)

> You know how a friend's reproaches ring true / understand how an enemy's praise should be taken for falsehood //

Of course, none of this spelling out of the relationship A:B is necessary in Hebrew: it is implied in the form.[32] But in the light of it, "antithetical" is shown to be a misleading concept.

In none of Lowth's examples of antithetical parallelism did B differ from A by being a negative complement, but this rather common sort of parallelism has, since Lowth, been associated with the antithetical category, and compounded the problem. Hebrew is fond of using negatives to reinforce: עם נבל ולא חכם "foolish and not-wise people," Deut. 32:6; חשתי ולא התמהמהתי "I hurried and did not linger," Psalm 119:60. As in these, so in longer phrases

פורה ה' נפש עבדיו / ולא יאשמו כל החסים בו //

The Lord redeems the life of his servants / and those who trust in him will not be condemned //   Psalm 34:23

the negation does not create contrast, but agreement. Here is nothing antithetical whatever.[33]

---

our translation: "Just as criticisms received from a friend (lit. "the woundings of a friend") are reliable. . . ." As for the second half, the common mistranslation of נעתרות as "abundant" is based on Ezek. 35:13, where the same root עתר parallels the root גדל. But תגדילו עלי בפיכם clearly means something like "blaspheme" in the context. It probably represents גדל = "twist" (Akk. *gidlu* "cord," Arab. *gadala* "twist a cord," Aram. גדל "twist," Heb. גדילים [Deut. 22:12] "twisted threads," and cf. Psalm 12:4 [גדלות // חלקות] and esp. *Psalms I* p. 73 for other examples and references). Our root עתר therefore probably means twisted or false—the perfect opposite of נאמן.

32. C. A. Briggs's new category, "emblematic parallelism," was intended to cover verses in which obvious comparison, "Just as A, so B," exists (he cites Psalm 42:2, "As a deer thirsts after springs of water, so do I thirst after you"), but he probably would not recognize its existence in such verses as this one. And indeed, focusing on comparison is only to express in translation a specific possibility of the form's general principle. As our second translation shows, comparison (or rather, equation) is only a category of the more generalized phenomenon, "A, and what's more, B." Indeed, we might also have said: "Better a friend's reproaches, in that they are sincere, than an enemy's praise, which is always falsehood"—cf. the previous verse (Prov. 27:5), "Better is open criticism than hidden love."

33. See also K. Koch, *The Growth of the Biblical Tradition* (New York, 1969) p. 94, on Prov. 10:1. M. Held correctly describes the "synonymous" role of such negations; see his "The Action-Result (Factitive-Passive) Sequence of Identical Verbs," in *JBL* 84 (1965): 282, n. 71.

Why Lowth should have imposed this classification system onto biblical parallelism is a question that will be explored in a later chapter. But for now let it suffice to note that despite obvious flaws his system has proven extraordinarily tenacious. Overall, it has had a disastrous effect on subsequent criticism. Because of it, synonymity was often imposed where it did not exist, sharpness was lost, and the real nature of biblical parallelism was henceforth condemned to a perpetual "falling between two stools." As the insightful Hebraist Karl Budde noted at the turn of the century (but how little his words have been heeded!):

> By distinguishing three kinds of parallelism, synonymous, antithetic, and synthetic, as well as by the very name "parallelism," he [Lowth] contributed at the same time to encourage too narrow a conception of the phenomenon. Nor is it any advantage to complete the scheme. . . . The variety of possible relations between the *stichoi* [verse-halves] is endless.[34]

5

As was noted briefly in section 3, B often demonstrates an obvious and conscious decision *not to parallel*. Thus, while it is easy to point out that the verse

אברכה את ה' בכל עת / תמיד תהלתו בפי //

Let me bless the Lord at all times / continuously [let] his praise [be] in my mouth //   Psalm 34:2

has certain points of correspondence ("all times" matches "continuously," "bless" and "praise" are related), the less obvious differentiation should also be underlined. For the second clause could have read: "Let me praise God continuously." The fact that it does not, but that the word-order is inverted, the objective genitive "his praise" replaces the verb-object sequence, and the element "in my mouth" is introduced (conveying the same first-person element as the verbal prefix in A), all evidence the very obvious intention of the Psalmist to say something that, in form at least, is rather different from the first half of the verse.

---

34. J. Hastings (ed.), *Dictionary of the Bible* (New York, 1902) 4:4. For the most recent (and impressive) attempt to "complete the scheme," see S. Geller, *Parallelism in Early Biblical Poetry* (Harvard Semitic Monographs 20; Missoula, Mont., 1979) pp. 30–52.

Now there is nothing astonishing in this observation *per se*—for so long as some semantic parallelism is established between A and B, there is no harm in variety, indeed, it apparently saves the verse from the potential monotony of more obvious forms of restatement. Yet such may not be the best understanding of this phenomenon, *differentiation*, for it is important to view it from the standpoint of the sentence as a whole. To the extent that B identifies itself as A's "mere parallel," it asserts A = B; while to the extent that it differentiates itself from A in meaning and morphology, it asserts A + B to be a *single statement*. B becomes A's complement or completion. Differentiation, in a word, *integrates* the sentence, asserts its unity. It may avoid repetition or monotonous restatement, but to say only this is to miss part of the point.

A number of phenomena may be grouped under the general heading of differentiation. The first involves morphological differentiation of verbs. As was seen in section 3, sometimes B's verb is clearly subsequent to A's in time, thus:

גפן ממצרים תסיע / תגרש גוים ותטעה //

You brought up a vine from Egypt / you banished nations and planted it //
Psalm 80:9

There are many such verses in which a sequence of activities is implied:[35] indeed, one finds in the Psalter the same use of the so-called *waw*-consecutive form found in the narrative books:

ויגער בים סוף ויחרב / ויוליכם בתהמות כמדבר //
ויושיעם מיד שונא / ויגאלם מיד אויב //
ויכסו מים צריהם / אחד מהם לא נותר //

And he breathed[36] on the Reed Sea and it dried / and he marched them through the waves as through desert //
He saved them from the enemy's hand / and redeemed them from the foe's hand //
And the waters covered up their enemies / not one of them was left //   Psalm 106:9-11

From this use of parallelism it is but a short hop to another, in which the apparent coordination of two actions (A happened . . . / and [then] B . . . //) really stands for a subordination:

---

35. See also below, chapter 2, section 1.
36. Elsehwere נער means "speak words of reproach," but here it is preferable to concretize the act of speaking.

צרה ויגון אמצא / ובשם ה׳ אקרא //

When sorrow and pain I find / on the name of the Lord I call //

Psalm 116:3-4

It is sometimes difficult to know how much subordination, and what sort, is implied, for Hebrew is notoriously reticent in this regard:

אלהי בך בטחתי / אל אבושה / אל יעלצו אויבי לי //

I trust in you, my God / let me never be disappointed / nor my enemies exult over me //   Psalm 25:2

The above translation duplicates that reticence, but what was intended (and understood) might better be rendered: "God in whom I trust, let me not . . .," "Because I trust . . . I will not . . .," or even "God, I have trusted you that I will not be disappointed. . . ."

Particularly noteworthy in this last verse is the alternation between the suffix (*qtl*) and prefix (*yqtl*) forms (viz. the Hebrew "perfect" and "imperfect," as they have imperfectly been called). Such alternation in Hebrew is difficult to justify consistently on grammatical grounds, but in cases such as this one it does seem to indicate a particular intermeshing of actions—i.e., asserts their interrelatedness, in the same way as subordinating phrases assert interrelations in English.[37] The two contrasting forms strike the ear as complementary. These nuances have in the past sometimes been mistranslated as a past-present or past-future distinction, or (when this was patently prohibited by the meaning) simply overlooked.[38] But interrelation and complementarity are often the whole point. Thus Psalm 92:5

כי שמחתני ה׳ בפעלך / במעשי ידיך ארנן //

must really be understood not as a temporal or aspectual contrast, but as the sort of intermeshing represented in English by a subordination,

Since you gladden me with your deeds / in your creations I exult //

The point is that here once again part of B works in the opposite direction of the paralleling: for all the obvious semantic parallelism (שמחה and רננה are both used for "songs of gladness,"[39] similarly "deeds" parallels the meaning of "creations" [or "actions"]), B's

---

37. See A. Blommerde, *Northwest Semitic Grammar and Job* (Rome, 1969) pp. 34–35; also Joüon, par. 112k-m; 113f-h, o (pp. 300–06).

38. M. Buttenweiser understood at an early date the precative *qtl* in his "The Importance of Tenses for the Interpretation of the Psalms" (*HUC Jubilee*, 1925, p. 109), but failed to focus on the phenomenon of alternating forms.

39. *Psalms III*, pp. 219, 271.

completion of A, rather than reiteration of it, is asserted in the contrasting verb forms. Such contrasts are extremely common:

טרף נתן ליראיו / יזכר לעולם בריתו //

Giving[40] food to his worshippers / he keeps his covenant forever //
Psalm 111:5

The effect is sometimes difficult to render. Consider, for example, the opening of Moses' Song (Deut. 32:1)

האזינו השמים ואדברה / ותשמע הארץ אמרי פי //

Listen, Heavens, and let me speak / and hear, O Earth, my words //

We are probably faithful to the meaning in translating the B-verb as an imperative, as if the text said שמעי. But the form תשמע is an assertion of B's *lack* of parallelism, intermeshing the three verbs almost as if they were sequential.[41] Here then is another form of differentiation, emphasizing B's going beyond A.

It is striking what a regular feature of parallelism verb alternation is.[42] Interestingly, a number of scholars have shown the use of aspectual alternations[43] of the same root in parallel halves, e.g.

נשאו נהרות ה' / נשאו נהרות קולם / ישאו נהרות דכים //

The floods lift up, O Lord / the floods lift up their voice / the floods lift up their roar //
Psalm 93:3

ותאכל את תהום רבה / ואכלה את החלק //

And it devoured the great depths / it devoured the ploughland //
Amos 7:4

אהבי ורעי מנגד נגעי יעמדו / וקרובי מרחק עמדו //

My friends and companions stand aloof from my affliction / those closest to me stand far off //
Psalm 38:12

To understand these alternations as supplying "variety" seems

---

40. Not a repointing to *nōtēn* but an attempt to convey intermeshing.

41. It ought to be compared to such A + B phrases as רפאני וארפא which certainly does not mean "Heal me and I will be healed" (implied sequence) but "Heal me, let me be healed," or, more faithful to the spirit, "Heal me and make me healthy." On this cf. M. Held, "The Action-Result . . .," 272–82.

42. See *Psalms III*, p. 363, and Blommerde, *NW Semitic Grammar*, pp. 34–35 for references. Dahood's "Grammar of the Psalter" (ibid., 420–24) lists more than 100 verbal alternations in the Psalms. See also *UT*, p. 123–24.

43. For other alternations, such as thematic (*qal-nifʿal, qal-piʿel*) see *Psalms III*: 414; M. Held, "The Action-Result . . ."; M. D. Cassuto in *Tarbiz* 14 (1943): 9–10; M. Held, "QTL-YQTL" in *Studies in Honor of A. A. Neuman* (Leiden, 1962), pp. 281–90.

STUDIES IN HEBREW WORD PATTERNS

Patrick D. Miller, Jr.

Union Theological Seminary in Virginia
Richmond, VA 23227

While the study of word pairs and word patterns in Hebrew reaches back even before Lowth's lectures on poetry in 1753, it has intensified considerably since the discovery of the Ugaritic texts and the recognition of both shared and distinctive word patterns in Hebrew and Ugaritic poetry. There is no need to rehearse here the history of this research. Avishur has summarized that with relatively full bibliography in his article in *Semitics*.[1] The result of these investigations is to make the reader of biblical and extrabiblical texts more aware of both the traditional material and patterns available to the writers of prose and poetry as well as the creativity of the poet, especially in shaping a poem or lines of poetry in different ways as individuality and the traditional are blended together in the poetic composition.

The brief study that follows seeks to explore further some of the patterns that appear in the poetic use of word pairs to see how and why the poet shapes poetic lines in the way that we receive them.[2] My interest in these pages is the investigation of two phenomena that appear with some regularity, not to establish or uncover fixed patterns, for such do not exist except in the broadest sense, but to illumine some of the compositional aspects and processes of both prose and poetry by focusing on a few examples that are sometimes paradigmatic and sometimes unique. The two phenomena are: (A) uses of a series of *three or more* words in parallelism, syndetic parataxis, and construct relationships (two examples); and

---

[1] Y. Avishur, "Pairs of Synonymous Words in the Construct State (And in Appositional Hendiadys) in Biblical Hebrew," *Semitics* 2 (1971–72) 17–81. To that should be added among other articles Avishur's studies in *UF* 7 (1975) 13–47; 8 (1976) 1–22.

[2] For a different sort of study with the same goal in mind see the writer's "Poetic Ambiguity and Balance in Psalm xv," *VT* 29 (1979) 416–24.

(B) common pairs or series of words that are used more than one way in the same composition (seven examples). Both of these phenomena have been studied to some degree before, but they merit more attention if one would understand the stylistics of biblical Hebrew.[3]

A. Series of three or more words.

1. *yātôm, 'almānāh, gēr*

One of the more familiar series of terms that are frequently used in relationship to each other is the grouping "orphan," "widow," and "sojourner." Other terms are used in sequence or parallel with one or more of these terms, but there are a significant enough number of cases of the three together in both prose and poetry to recognize here a pattern, a compositional triad that functioned in various ways.

There are thirty cases (Exod 22:20–21, 23; Deut 10:18; 14:29; 16:11; 24:17, 19, 20, 21; 26:12, 13; 27:19; Isa 1:17, 23; 9:16; 10:2; Jer 7:6; 22:3; 49:11; Lam 5:3; Ezek 22:7; Zech 7:10; Mal 3:5; Ps 68:6; 94:6; 109:9; 146:9; Job 22:9; 24:3; 31:16–17).[4] In twenty-four of these texts *yātôm* is in the A position or first position whether in poetic parallel (Isa 1:17, 23; 9:16; Jer 49:11; Lam 5:3; Ps 68:6; 109:9; 146:9; Job 24:3) or conjunction (Exod 22:20–21, 23; Deut 10:18; 20, 14:29; 16:11; 24:17, 19; 21; 26:12, 13; 27:19; Jer 7:6; 22:3; Ezek 22:7). In six instances (Isa 10:2; Zech 7:10; Mal 3:5; 94:6; Job 22:9; 31:16–17) *'almānāh* is first or the A word in prose and poetry. Eighteen of these twenty-four cases of *yātôm* and *'almānāh* as a word pair also include *gēr* as a third member of the group (Exod 22:20–21; Deut 10:18; 14:29; 16:11; 24:17, 19, 21; 26:12, 13; 27:19; Jer 7:6; 22:3; Ezek 22:7; Zech 7:10; Mal 3:5; Ps 94:6; 146:9). In sixteen of these eighteen cases, of the three terms appearing together or in sequence to each other, the pair *yātôm* and *'almānāh* are held together while *gēr* appears either before the other two words (thirteen times) or after them (Deut 10:18; Zech 7:10; and Mal 3:5). On six occasions (Deut 10:18; Exod 22:20–21;

---

[3]Cf., e.g., the discussions of S. Gevirtz, *Patterns in the Early Poetry of Israel* (Chicago: University of Chicago, 1963) 38–40, 44.

[4]The LXX of Jer 5:28 has *cheras* for MT *'ebyônîm;* and the *'wlm* of Prov 23:10 in parallel to *yetômîm* is frequently emended to *'almānāh* on the basis of the other examples of this pairing as well as the parallel to the verse in the *Wisdom of Amenemope.*

Ezek 22:7; Mal 3:5; Zech 7:10; Ps 146:9) *gēr* is separated in some fashion from the other two which are held together as a pair. In only two cases does *gēr* break the pairing of *yātôm* and *'almānāh*, and in both cases there appears to be a reason.

The two examples from the Psalms are instructive in this regard. Ps 146:9 reads as follows:

> *yhwh šōmēr gērîm*
> *yātôm wᵉʾalmānāh yᵉʿôdēd*

The subject of the first colon is replaced in the second colon by the expanded pair. The subject *yhwh* requires only one object word. The traditional patterns precluded using either *yātôm* or *'almānāh* by itself in this colon whereas *gēr* often functioned more loosely in relation to the others and fit naturally in the first colon. In similar fashion the use of either of the two terms in the following colon called for its usual paired term thus precluding the presence of a subject word. The traditional patterns of use for these three words thus led to a termination in v 9b of the sequence of cola (5!) beginning with *yhwh*. That was no longer possible once either *yātôm* or *'almānāh* was used after *gēr*.

Ps 94:6 breaks the usual order, as I have indicated:

> *'almānah wᵉgēr yahᵃrōgû*
> *wîtômîm yᵉraṣṣēhû*

But in this case assonance probably suggests *gēr* plus *hārag* (the repetition of *gimel* and *reš*). The colon then requires one of the other two for length; *'almānāh* and *yātôm* together would be too long. When *'almānāh* is used with *gēr, yātôm* is pluralized to help balance the cola in terms of length.

As for the other case where *gēr* breaks the pairing of *yātôm* and *'almānāh*, Deut 24:17, again an explanation seems possible. There are ten cases of the use of this triad in Deuteronomy and two instances in prose sermons in Jeremiah (7:6 and 22:3). In all these uses except Deut 10:18 the series is *gēr* + *yātôm* + *'almānāh*. In the Jeremianic examples there is no conjunction between *gēr* and *yātôm* as is the case in Deut 24:17. This last instance is a case of parallelism in which the usual Deuteronomic order is maintained with *gēr yātôm* providing the object of the prohibition in the first colon and *'almānāh* providing the balancing object in the second colon. The result is a neatly balanced bicolon:

$$lō' tatteh mišpāṭ gēr yātôm \quad (8)$$
$$w^elō' taḥᵃbōl beged 'almānāh \quad (9)$$

In summary, the following conclusions may be noted about this triad:

a) A clear Deuteronomic cliche is recognizable in the sequence *gēr w^eyātôm w^ealmānāh*, there being one exception[5] out of ten instances and one case where the order is preserved even in parallelism.

b) The Deuteronomic cliche enables one to use the triad in Jer 7:6 and 22:3 as one piece of evidence for arguing that the prose discourses in which they appear are Deuteronomistic.

c) The series has two words, *yātôm* and *'almānāh*, as a fixed pair with the third word *gēr* as quite flexible and not fixed.

d) There is a definite A and B order preferred, but it can be reversed.[6] Breaking up this sequence happens only two out of thirty times and then for particular reasons and only by the third term (*gēr*). Sometimes *yātôm* and *'almānāh* may be parallel in lines rather than cola, e.g., Job 31:16–17.

2. *dāgān, tîrôš, yiṣhār*

This triad is a very clear series of three words that are regularly used in relationship with one another. The first two are the most common, appearing forty and thirty-eight times respectively. They appear as a pair twenty-nine times and in conjunction (Gen 27:28, 37; Num 18:12; Deut 7:13; 11:24; 12:17; 14:23; 18:4; 28:51; 33:28; 2 Kgs 18:32; Isa 36:17; Jer 31:12; Hos 2:10, 24; 7:14; Joel 2:19; Hag 1:11; Ps 4:8; Neh 5:11; 10:40; 13:5, 12; 2 Chr 31:5; and 32:28) or in parallel (Isa 62:8; Hos 2:11; Joel 1:10; Zech 9:17). In one other case, Hos 9:1–2, the words appear in close relationship to each other in successive lines of poetry. Thus in over three-fourths of the occurrences of these two words they are used as a pair. In twenty-nine out of the thirty instances *dāgān* is the A word and *tîrôš* the B word. Only Num 18:12 is an exception. The order of the word pair, therefore, whether in parallel or in conjunction, in poetry or in prose, is quite fixed.

The word *yiṣhār* is used twenty-three times in the Bible. Only in Zech 4:14 does it appear without one or both of the preceding

---

[5] *The* reversal of order in placing *gēr* after the first two in Deut 10:18 may be because the word about the *gēr* is then elaborated in the following verse.

[6] The two examples in Ugaritic texts (*CTA* 16.6.49–50 and 17.5.8) have the order *ytm//almnt* in the first case and *almnt//ytm* in the second case.

words. Nineteen of the twenty-three uses have all three words. Again except for Num 18:12 the order is always *dāgān, tîrôš, yiṣhār*. In two cases (Joel 2:24 and Neh 10:38) *yiṣhār* appears in second position with *tîrôš*. It never appears only with *dāgān*. These two instances where *dāgān* is not included may be explained at least in part on the basis of the fact that all three terms are used elsewhere in the passage (Joel 2:19 and Neh 10:40), though one would normally expect that where two out of three words are used they would be *dāgān* + *tîrôš* as in Hos 2:10 and 11. *yiṣhār* thus belongs completely to this series of three. And while *dāgān* and *tîrôš* may on occasion appear alone or in parallel to another word, it is clear that the dominant use of all three of these words is in a series of three and sometimes two.[7]

One encounters in these three terms, therefore, a clear series as a part of the traditional stock of words and phrases available to poet and narrator. They had a fixed order that was varied only rarely and then apparently because of use of the triad elsewhere in the text. Two of the terms are used regularly together, like *yātôm* and *'almānāh*. The third, unlike *gēr*, may be said to occur only in juxtaposition with the other two (or on occasion one of them). The composers paid attention to the traditional patterns for these terms, varying them only rarely when repetition suggested it (Num 18:12 remaining the lone exception). None of these terms formed a series of any frequency with any other word.

B. Word patterns used more than one way in the same poem (or prose text)

Gevirtz has discussed this phenomenon briefly in his monograph[8] in the context of accounting for changes in the usual A–B order of word pairs. He cites several examples of a change in the customary order because the poet is using the same word pair a second time. For example, *'ereṣ* (A) parallel to *'āpār* (B) in Isa 34:7b, the usual order, are reversed in v 9. Or *yayin* (A) parallel to *šēkār* (B) appear in that order in Isa 28:7a but reversed in the

---

[7]LXX and Syriac have *yiṣhār* represented in their translations. It is unclear whether the original text included it or it came in because of the frequency of the triad.

[8]S. Gevirtz, *Patterns in the Early Poetry of Isarel*, 36–40.

immediately following line in v 7b. The same thing happens with these words in Prov 31:4, 6.[9]

The artifice of the poet and the individuality of his or her use of traditional patterns is readily seen when one examines on a broader scale the way in which word pairs are used more than once in the same text.

1. *dāgān, tîrôš,* and *yiṣhār*

This example has been discussed above and only a summary is necessary here. There are four instances where two or three of these are used more than once in a single text. In three cases (Hos 2:10, 11, and 24; Joel 2:19 and 24; and Neh 10:38 and 40) three of the terms are used in conjunction at one point in the text and two of them at another point. When this happens, the usual order *dāgān, tîrôš,* and *yiṣhār* is not held as rigidly. One may have either A + B, or B + C. In one text, Genesis 27, the pair *dāgān wᵉtîrôš* appears twice, once in poetry (v 28) and once in prose (v 37). The composers, therefore, take a fairly fixed series and use possible variations in that series when they need to use it more than once. The series can be more flexible than usual on these occasions.

2. *ḥereb* and *rā‘āb*

This pair, often with *deber* added either before or after but only once (34:12) in between *ḥereb* and *rā‘āb*,[10] is very common in Jeremiah (5:12; 11:22; 14:12, 13, 15 [2x], 18; 15:2; 16:4; 18:21; 21:7, 9; 24:10; 27:8, 13; 29:17, 18; 32:24, 36; 34:17; 38:2; 42:17; 44:12 [2x], 13, 18, 27). In only *two* instances is the fixed order, *ḥereb* (= A word) and *rā‘āb* (= B word) broken. One of these is 14:16 and the reason is surely because the pair is used five times in one brief passage. Variation is provided in two ways. At the beginning (v 12) *deber* is added to the sequence as is done commonly elsewhere. At the end the order is broken and *rā‘āb* is placed before *ḥereb*. The other instance of reverse order is 18:21, which is an example of a poetic phenomenon noted by Gevirtz. The usual order of a word pair may be reversed when an additional element is added to the word that usually comes first. In

---

[9]Ibid.

[10]As As in the cases of *gēr* and *yiṣhār* discussed above, *deber* is the more fluid member of the trio. It is used less often, and its position is flexible.

this case *rāʿāb* becomes the A word when *ḥereb* becomes *yᵉdê ḥereb:*

> *lākēn tēn ʿet-bᵉnêhem lārāʿab*
> *wᵉhaggīrēm ʿal yᵉdê ḥereb*[11]

3. *ṣābāʾ* and *haššāmayim*

In Isa 34:4 this pair is used twice. The first occasion is the common and expected construct p hrase *ṣᵉbāʾ haššāmayim.* Then the poet breaks that apart immediately in the next line and uses the two elements in parallel:

> *wᵉnāgōllû kassēper haššāmayim*
> *wᵉkol-ṣᵉbāʾām yibbôl*

The two words also provide a rather subtle word play for the poet. The poem begins (v 2) with an announcement of Yahweh's fury against the nations, i.e., "all their host" *(ṣᵉbāʾām)* so that "all their hosts" refers to the armies of the nations and the hosts of heaven at one and the same time. Then in v 5 where the imagery of Yahweh's sword is developed the poet says:

> For my sword has become sated
> in the heavens *(baššāmayim).*

A similar poetic variation of this word pair is found at the beginning of Ezra's prayer (Neh 9:6). Verse 6b reads:

> *ʾatt ʿāśîtā ʾet haššāmayim*
> *⸱ šᵉmê haššāmayim wᵉkol-ṣᵉbāʾām*
> You have made the heavens,
> the heaven of heavens and all their host.

Then in v 6d in the final colon Ezra speaks of "the host of heaven worshiping you."[12]

---

[11]This series is also used frequently in Ezekiel which shows somewhat more flexibility in order, though here also the normal order is *ḥereb* in the first position and *rāʿāb* in second position, with *deber* as a variant in first or third position, except for 7:15 where it appears in the middle. This is probably because of the fact that the series appears twice in the same verse. Repetitive usage in 6:11–12 also accounts for the placing of *deber* in third position in v 11 and first position in v 12.

[12]For other examples of the breakup of the construct *ṣᵉbāʾ (haš)šamayim* into *(haš)šāmayim* parallel to *ṣᵉbāʾām* see Isa 45:12 and Ps 33:6. In Gen 2:1 the two words appear in collocation or conjunction, but *hāʾāreṣ,* which is an even more common parallel to *haššamayim,* is inserted between them. Thus: *wayᵉkullû haššāmayim wᵉhāʾāreṣ wᵉkol-ṣᵉbāʾām.* One should compare also Ps 148:1–4.

4. *yōš^ebê hā'āreṣ*

This very common phrase (e.g., Exod 23:31; Num 32:17; 33:52, 55; Jos 9:24; 13:21; Jer 1:14; 25:29, etc.) can be broken up in different ways. One may find *hā'āreṣ* parallel to *yōš^ebê* or *yōš^ebeyhā* (e.g., Ps 107:34; Jer 12:4; Isa 24:1). Or the latter phrase may be in collocation with *hā'āreṣ* either in conjunction (e.g., Jer 25:9; Ps 75:4) or in some syntactical relationship (e.g., Mic 7:13, Isa 24:5).

Hos 4:1–3 provides an excellent illustration of the poet/prophet using this constuction in two different ways as a vehicle for combining indictment and announcement of judgment in a judgment speech. The indictment in v 1 begins:

> *kî rîb lyhwh*
> *'im yôš^ebê hā'āreṣ*
> For Yahweh has a lawsuit
> with the inhabitants of the land.

The rest of vv 1 and 2 then spell out the bases for Yahweh's lawsuit. Then in v 3 the prophet announces

> *'al-kēn te'^ebal hā'āreṣ*
> *w^eumlal kol-yôšēb bāh*
> Therefore the land mourns (or "is dried up"),
> and all who dwell in it languish.

The object of the lawsuit is repeated in the announcement but the construct phrase is now broken up into parallel words.

An even more elaborate variation on this word pair occurs in Isa 24:1ff., which describes the desolation of *hā'āreṣ*. The poem begins by placing *hā'āreṣ* and *yōš^ebeyhā* in parallel in v 1. Then in v 5 they are used in a different syntactical relationship:

> *w^ehā'āreṣ ḥān^epāh taḥat yōš^ebeyhā*
> The earth lies polluted under its inhabitants.

Finally v 6 provides two parallel lines with varying uses of this word pair:

> *'al-kēn 'ālāh 'āk^elāh 'ereṣ*
> *wayye'š^emû yōš^ebê bāh*
> *'al-kēn ḥārû yōš^ebê 'ereṣ*
> *w^eniš'ar '^enôš miz'ār*
> Therefore a curse consumes the *earth,*
>   and *its inhabitants* bear their guilt,
>   therefore *the inhabitants of the earth* are scorched,
>   and few people are left.

In none of the examples in this poem is the word pair used in the same way twice.

5. ḥeblê māwet

This expression appears as a construct subject in the first colon of Ps 18:5. Then in the next line (v 6) the *ḥeblê* is used in the first colon as the construct element with another word while *māwet* is used in the second colon as the absolute word with another construct element. The poetic artistry is further seen in the fact that both expressions in v 6, *ḥeblê šᵉôl* and *môqᵉšê māwet* mean the same things as *ḥeble māwet* in v 5. The two verses are as follows:

> 5) ᵃpapûnî ḥeblê māwet
>   wᵉnaḥᵃlê bᵉlîyaʿal
> 6) ḥeblê šᵉôl sᵉbābûnî
>   qiddᵉmûnî môqᵉšê māwet
>
> The *cords of death* encompassed me,
>   the torrents of destruction assailed me;
> the *cords* of Sheol surrounded me,
>   the snares of *death* confronted me.

6. Words for sin in Psalm 51

This most familiar of the pentitential psalms uses the vocabulary of sin extensively. Robert Boling has analyzed carefully the patterns of words for sin in the psalter as they appear in parallel with one another.[13] Building on his analysis one may see how the poet holds to the traditional order in which certain word pairs appear but is able to vary the order in the psalm as a whole by using different pairs. The list of words for sin in this psalm is as follows:

	A word	B word
v 4	ʿāwōn	ḥaṭṭāʾt
v 5	pᵉšāʿîm	ḥaṭṭāʾt
v 6	ḥṭʾ (vb)	ʿśh raʿ
v 7	ʿāwōn	ḥēṭʾ
v 9	ḥṭʾ (vb)	kbs (vb)
v 11	ḥᵃṭāîm	ʿᵃwōnōt
v 15	pōšᵉʿîm	ḥaṭṭāʾîm

---

[13]R. Boling, "Synonymous Parallelism in the Psalms," *JSS* 5 (1960) 221–55.

One notes immediately that all seven of these verses include some nominal or verbal form of the root *ḥṭʾ*. The possible monotony of such repetition is broken several ways:

a) Counting singular and plural forms five different words from the root *ḥṭʾ* are used in the seven verses.
b) Counting singular and plural six different words are used in parallel with these forms of *ḥṭʾ*.
c) Despite the general tendency of *ḥṭʾ* words to function as B words in parallelism, the prophet has been able to vary the order by a careful choice of parallel words. In vv 4, 5, 6, and 15 the *ḥṭʾ* words are in B position. This is what one would expect in the light of Boling's demonstration that *ʿāwōn* and *pešāʾ/pōšeʿîm* are regularly A words in parallel with nominal forms of *ḥṭʾ*. Vv 6, 9, and 11, however, have forms of *ḥṭʾ* in A position. The poet creates this constant variation by choosing different parallel words. For while *ʿāwōn* is regularly an A word, *ʿawōnāh* is regularly a B word. So it is used in v 11. And while *nominal* forms of *ḥṭʾ* are regularly B words, *verbal* forms of *ḥṭʾ* are regularly A words. So the poet uses verbal forms in vv 6 and 9. The result is a psalm in which one is overwhelmed with the poet's sense of sin but not dulled by a monotonous repetition. A rich mixture of vocabulary around the thematic *ḥṭʾ* element and using traditional word pairs in their usual order gives variety and spontaneity to what could otherwise be a boring and rigid recital.

7. Words for creation in Isaiah 45

Gevirtz has pointed to the frequency of the scheme A//B//C//B in poetic uses of series of three words. One example he cites is Isa 45:7 where we have the sequence *yāṣar//bārāʾ//ʿāśāh//bārāʾ*.[14] While that analysis is correct, we may observe that elsewhere in the poem the pairs *yāṣar//bārāʾ* and *ʿāśāh//bārāʾ* are used.

> 12) *ʾanōki ʿāśîtî ʾereṣ*
>   *weʾādām ʿāleyhā bārāʾ tî*
> I *made* the earth;
>   humankind upon it I *created*.

[14]Gevirtz, *Patterns in the Early Poetry of Israel*, 44.

Then in v 18:

bôrē' haššāmayim
hû' hā'elōhîm
yōṣēr hā'āreṣ we'āśāh
hû' kônenāh
lō' tōhû berā'āh
lešebet yeṣārāh

The pair bārā' and yāṣar in reverse order from v 7 govern this verse, appearing twice in parallel and in the same order. Again the poet has used a rich mixture of pairs, putting them together, breaking them apart, rearranging them, and adding other elements— all to give individuality and demonstrate poetic craftsmanship in using the traditional compositional materials to convey the message and reality that he or she is constrained to set forth.

Many similar and different examples could be given,[15] but these at least serve to illustrate with regard to word pairs used in series of three and in different ways in the same text how tradition and individuality come together in the composition of biblical prose and poetry.

[15]For example, the use of hārôn 'ap and 'ebrāh in conjunction and in parallel in Isa 13:9 and 13 or the use of peša' and ḥṭ' in Ps 25:7 and 18, on which see Boling, "Synonymous Parallelism," 231.

contradicted by the very repetition of the verbal root; instead, something closer to completion or complementarity seems to be their role, the integration of A and B into a single whole. So similarly, when the verbs are quite distinct and not even conventional pairs:

הסירותי מסבל שכמו / כפיו מדוד תעברנה //

I removed his shoulder from toil / his hands were freed from the basket //
Psalm 81:7

כי אבי ואמי עזבוני / וה' יאספני //

Even if my father and mother abandoned me / still the Lord would care for me //
Psalm 27:10

one nevertheless finds the same *qtl-yqtl* alternation. A translator must proceed with caution, given the actual subordinating function of such alternation described above. But clearly there are some alternations to which subordination cannot be ascribed. Instead (and, one might say elsewhere, *in addition to* subordination), it is differentiation that is intended, contrasting B's verb to A's and (therefore) emphasizing the unity of A + B.

Differentiation is also behind the frequent use of chiastic[44] word order in parallelistic lines, e.g.

על שחל ופתן תדרך / תרמס כפיר ותנין //

On lion and snake you tread / you crush lion-cub and serpent //
Psalm 91:13

Of course chiasmus is a well-known trope of Greek and Latin literature, and has been all too readily assimilated to such biblical uses as the above since the days of the Church Fathers (see chapter 4). But chiasmus in Hebrew, while it undeniably provides the same aesthetic pleasure as in European languages, ought rightly not to be separated from the context of parallelism itself. That is, where it appears in Greek or Latin more or less "out of the blue," in Hebrew it is truly a concomitant of the binary structure of parallelistic sentences, and it therefore represents a decision *not to parallel* the word order of A. Now again, several writers[45] have noted the use of

44. On this see M. Dahood, "Ugaritic-Hebrew Syntax and Style," *UF* 1 (1969): 24; J. W. Welch, "Chiasmus in Ugaritic," *UF* 6 (1974): 421–36; Dahood, "Chiasmus in Job," in H. N. Bream, ed. *A Light unto My Path*, (Philadelphia, 1974), pp. 119–30; "Chiastic Word Patterns in Hebrew" *CBQ* 38 (1976):303–11. An extensive bibliography is to be found in Welch, "Chiasmus," ns. 1–10.
45. Dahood, "Chiastic Word Patterns," p. 303; A. R. Čeresko, "The A:B:B:A

chiasmus in successive clauses containing identical words or roots, as in these verses from Ezekiel:

הנה לאש נתן לאכלה / את שני קצותיו אכלה האש //

If it is given to the fire to consume / its two ends the fire will consume //
Ezek. 15:4

ונתתי לכם לב חדש / ורוח חדשה אתן בקרבכם //

I will give you a new heart / and a new spirit will I put in your midst //
Ezek. 36:26

The functional similarity of chiasmus to *qtl-yqtl* alternation (and in fact, in the latter example, its combination with it) is clear. Indeed, chiasmus is but one form of varied word order in parallelism; it ought not be separated from less symmetrical forms of differentiated word order,[46] such as

כי השקיף ממרום קדשו / ה' משמים אל ארץ הביט //

For he peers from the heights of Heaven / the Lord from sky to earth looks down //   Psalm 102:20

הנתן שלג כצמר / כפור כאפר יפזר //

He gives snow like wool / frost like ashes he spreads //
Psalm 147:16

In all such cases it is B's complementing of A that the chiasmus effects, and consequently the unity of the two-clause combination.[47]

Another form of differentiation is between singular and plural forms. Sometimes this differentiation is explicitly the point:

טוב מעט לצדיק / מהמון רשעים רבים //

Better is the little of one righteous man / than the plenty of many evil men //   Psalm 37:16

Word Pattern . . ." *UF* 7 (1975): 84–90; L. Boadt, "The ABBA Chiasm . . . in Ezekiel" *VT* 25 (1975): 44.

46. So Welch, "Chiasmus," p. 422. Here mention ought to be made of a related phenomenon, the word pattern ABCB, in which a second term appears twice in consecutive clauses. Thus: "Be fruitful and multiply / swarm on the earth and multiply in it //" (Gen. 9:7), with ורבו repeated; "Who fashions light and creates darkness / makes peace and creates discord //" (Isa. 45:7), with ובורא repeated; "Listen and hear my voice / harken and hear my speech //" (Isa. 28:23), ושמעו repeated. See *PEPI*, p. 44; B. Porten and U. Rappaport, "Poetic Structure in Gen. 9:7," *VT* 21 (1971): 363–69. But this is but one pattern in which actual repetitions occur. See below, section 6; also cf. Job 13:7, 38:17, and many others. Note also Čeresko, "A:B:B:A Pattern," 86; Dahood in *UF* 1:15.

47. See on this F. I. Andersen, *The Sentence in Biblical Hebrew* (The Hague, 1974), pp. 119–23.

Other times the intention is less certain:

לב נבון יבקש דעת / ופני כסילים ירעה אולת //

The heart of a sage seeks out knowledge / while the mouth of fools fosters
stupidity //   Prov. 15:14

Moses ibn Tibbon, a medieval Jewish commentator and translator,
observed about this verse: "The text says 'the heart of a *sage*' and not
'sages,' and says 'the mouth of fools' and not 'a fool' in order to
indicate the scarcity of the former and the abundance of the latter.
There are many such verses [that contrast the singular and plural] in
Proverbs, and they all have the same point [which was stated
explicitly in Eccles. 7:29], '[Only] one man among a thousand have I
found.' "[48] But sometimes no intention can be attributed to the text
other than the desire to differentiate by making B *not parallel* in every
detail:[49]

וכל קרני רשעים אגדע / תרוממנה קרנות צדיק //

All the horns of the wicked I will cut / but the horns of the righteous will
be exalted //   Psalm 75:11

(where not only does one find the same singular-plural differentiation,
but also the alternation: קרני–קרנות).

מהרו שכחו מעשיו / לא חכו לעצתו //

They hurried to forget his deeds / and did not attend to his counsel //
                                                                                Psalm 106:13

To these may be added several other peculiar forms of differentiation, including:

1. apposition of a word with a possessive suffix in A with an article in
B, and vice versa:[50]

שקר הסום לתשועה / וברב חילו לא ימלט //

The horse is no salvation ("is false for saving") / and by the might of *his*
force one will not escape //   Psalm 33:17

---

48. M. ibn Tibbon, פירוש לשיר השירים (Lyck, 1874), pp. 5–6.

49. Sometimes an abstract noun will parallel a concrete, e.g., Psalm 25:19 ("my
enemies . . . / violent hatred . . . //"). Dahood describes this (*UF* 1:32; *Psalms III*,
pp. 411–12) but his examples are sometimes questionable; see also W. van der
Weiden, "Abstractum pro concretum . . ." *Verbum Domini* 44 (1966): 43–52.

50. On this see chapter 2, section 6, on "telegraph style"; also *Psalms III*, p. 429,
C. H. W. Brekelmans in *Ex Oriente Lux* 17 (1963): 202–06. Note also Albright on
the alternation חיתו ארץ and חית הארץ in Gen. 1:24–25 in "The Refrain 'And God
Saw . . .' " *Mélanges A. Robert*, p. 24.

ידרך ענוים במשפט / וילמד ענוים דרכו //

He directs the humble into justice / and teaches the humble *his* way //

Psalm 25:9

2. changes from one grammatical person to another:[51]

ישקני מנשיקות פיהו / כי טובים דדיך מיין //

Let him give me of his kisses to drink / better is your love than wine! //

Song of Songs 1:2

3. omission of pronominal suffix in one verse-half when present in the other:

ואתה שנאת מוסר / ותשלך דברי אחריך //

But you despise (my) teaching / and cast my words behind you //

Psalm 50:17

בן חכם ישמח אב / ובן כסיל תוגת אמו //

A wise son makes a father glad / but a foolish son is his mother's sorrow //

Prov. 10:1

4. prepositional alternation[52]

לא תשבע עין לראות / ולא תמלא אזן משמע //

The eye is not satisfied with [ל] seeing / nor the ear filled up with [מ] hearing //

Eccles. 1:8

5. omission of prepositions, conjunctions, interrogative particles, negations and other particles from one clause:

כי לא לנצח ישכח אביון / תקות ענוים תאבד לעד //

The poor will not be forgotten forever / [nor] the hope of the needy be eternally dashed //

Psalm 9:19

6. the differentiating "all":[53]

כי ישר דבר ה' / וכל מעשהו באמונה //

For upstanding is the Lord's word / and all that he does [is done] in faithfulness //

Psalm 33:4

---

51. See R. Gordis, *Song of Songs and Lamentations* (New York, 1974) p. 73. This is a regular feature of postbiblical ברכות, and see above, n. 13. Dahood remarks on the alternation "Your servant . . . me . . ." as well as "my self [נפשי] . . . I . . ." See *Psalms III*, p. 374.

52. Dahood in *UF* 1:30. Note also the opposite case, use of the same preposition with obviously different meaning: כי חוק לישראל הוא / משפט לאלהי יעקב // "Israel's [ל] law it is, a statute from [ל] the God of Jacob" (Psalm 81:4).

53. See below, section 9.

Now as noted, some differentiation is implicit in the very idea of parallelism: "the same thing in different words" means shunning actual repetition, and presumably this might also include avoiding a monotonous consistency in verbal themes, or other morphological features. Yet the examples adduced are difficult to explain on the grounds of "elegant variation" (as this feature of style is known in English prose). As was noted above: if avoidance of repetition were the point, why does one find *qtl-yqtl* differentiation of the *same verbal root*, or actual repetition of the same words in the very verses which illustrate some other differentiating feature? If "elegant variation" were the point, would it not operate first and foremost on the level of *lexis*? Instead, what differentiation seems to be about is the "afterwardness" of B. B follows A, and its containing differentiated verbal themes or other morphological and syntactic differentiations seems designed to draw attention to this circumstance, "A is so, and what's more, B." The foregoing examples are decisive in the domain of morphology and syntax in the same way that sharpness, afterwardness, overt subordination, and the like are decisive in semantics.

6

Parallelism as a general phenomenon can be found in a variety of literatures, prose and poetry; it has been analyzed as a form of "coupling," which one critic sees as the principle behind nearly all poetic structure.[54] It is not surprising, then, that parallelism as an organizing principle exists in literatures unrelated to Hebrew, for example, Chinese and Japanese.[55] The *runon kerto* of Finnish has often been compared to biblical parallelism,[56] as has the use of

54. S. R. Levin, "The Conventions of Poetry" in S. Chatman, *Literary Style* (1971), and Levin, *Linguistic Structures in Poetry* (*Janua Linguarum* no. 23, 's-Gravenhaage, 1962), pp. 30–41. Parallelism is also discussed by Roman Jakobson, "Linguistics and Poetics," in T. Sebeok, *Style in Language* (Cambridge, 1960), p. 369; R. Austerlitz, "Parallelismus," in *Poetics* (Warsaw, 1961): 439–43; Jakobson in *Language* 42 (1966): 399–429. Note, however, that "parallelism" in these and similar treatments is used in the most general sense; thus M. Riffaterre, "Describing Poetic Structures" in J. Ehrmann, *Structuralism* (New York, 1970), p. 189, "The recurrence of equivalent forms, *parallelism*, is the basic relationship underlying poetry." The parallelism involved in the biblical phenomenon "parallelism" is, as we shall see, rather more specific.

55. See Newman and Popper, *Parallelism*, pp. 68–74, 75–76; also T. M. Tschang, *Le parallélisme dans le vers du Chen King* (Paris, 1937).

56. See W. Steinitz, *FF Communications No. 115* (Helsinki, 1934). See also

parallelism in Old Turkish poetry,[57] Mongolian,[58] Rumanian,[59] and
Sanskrit.[60] But because biblical parallelism is more than paralleling,
the value of such comparisons is somewhat circumscribed. Far more
interesting to the biblical scholar are cognate comparisons, evidences
of parallelism or something like parallelism in texts produced in other
Semitic languages, or in non-Semitic civilizations with which ancient
Israel might have had direct or indirect contact.[61]

Until the end of the eighteenth century, all that was known about
ancient Israel and its neighbors came from the Bible and a few other
scattered accounts; but beginning at that time, archaeology began to
reveal something more of the region's history. The first decipherment
was of Old Persian (by G. F. Grotefend in 1802), a discovery that led
to the further decipherment of Elamite and Akkadian. In 1877, E. de
Sarzac unearthed the first remains of Sumerian civilization, and this
and subsequent finds provided further information about the origins of
Near Eastern literatures.

Since the nineteenth century, then, it has been observed that a form
of parallelism existed in hymns, proverbs, and epics from different

---

G. B. Gray's discussion of the *Kalevala* in *The Forms of Hebrew Poetry* (reprinted
New York, 1972), p. 38, and Newman and Popper, *Parallelism*, pp. 61–68. In that
they focus on the mere fact of paralleling, such comparisons are superficial.
Furthermore, the analogy is complicated by the presence of a definite alliterative
pattern in Finnish, as well as a kind of meter. See P. Kiparsky, "Metrics and
Morphonemics in the Kalevala" in D. C. Freeman, *Linguistics and Literary Style*
(New York, 1970), pp. 165–81. Note also Austerlitz on the use of parallelism in Ob-
Ugric (a Finno-Ugric language) in "Ob-Ugric Metrics" *Folklore Fellows Communi-
cations* 174 (Helsinki, 1958).

57. See V. M. Žirmunski, "Ritmiko-sintaksičeskij parallelizm . . . drevnoturkskogo"
in *Voprosy jazykoznanija* 13 (1964), p. 4.

58. N. Poppe, "Der Parallelismus in der epischen Dichtung der Mongolen" *Ural-
Altaische Jahrbücher* 30 (1958): 195–228.

59. L. Ionescu, "Parallelismul in lirica populara" *Revista de etnografie si folclor*
2, pp. 48–68.

60. J. Gonda, *Stylistic Repetition in the Vedas* (Amsterdam, 1959). R. C. Culley,
Oral Formulaic Language in the Biblical Psalms (Toronto, 1967) pp. 128–29, and
P. B. Yoder, "A-B Pairs and Oral Composition" *VT* 21 (1971): 482 cite the
parallelism of the Todas of South India, discussed by M. B. Emeneau, "The Songs of
the Todas," *Proceedings of the American Philosophical Soc.* 77 (1937): 543–60,
and "Oral Poets of South India," *Journal of American Folklore* 71 (1958): 312–24.

61. We shall not treat here the question of the origin of parallelism in the Ancient
Near East, other than to note its presence in the very oldest texts available. In
addition to its universal rhetorical appeal (see above notes), parallelism in the Near
East may be connected with merismus and inclusion, on which see A. Massart,
"L'emploi en égyptien de deux termes opposés" in *Mélanges A. Robert*, pp. 38–46,
as well as A. M. Honeyman, "Merismus in Biblical Literature" *JBL* 71 (1952).

parts of the Near East; in fact, it was argued, parallel clauses in some texts were even delineated in the writing, by means of spacing and/or a vertical "verse-divider" mark (in Akkadian) and the so-called "verse-points" in Egyptian.[62] Perhaps stimulated by the gains in archaeology, writers about parallelism turned their attention to resemblances between Hebrew and the oldest strands of Arabic literature. Following the work of I. Goldziher,[63] Gray and Newman adduced the resemblance of saj' ("unmetered poetry," sometimes rhymed, it was early on regarded as the prototype of later poetic forms)[64] to biblical parallelism. D. H. Mueller had already shown the existence of bits of parallelism in the Qur'an.[65]

But it is the use of parallelism in Ugaritic texts which, because of Ugarit's temporal (fourteenth century B.C.)[66] and geographic (on the north Syrian coastline not far from Latakia) proximity to the Bible's homeland, has invited the closest comparisons with biblical usage. Common vocabulary and motifs, and even what may be a case of full-scale literary borrowing,[67] all argue the close relationship of Ugaritic

---

62. The verse points were a New Kingdom invention, but the principle of division into parallel clauses, each half forming a unit of grammar, rhetoric, and thought, is certainly older. See J. L. Foster, "Thought Couplets in Khety's 'Hymn to the Inundation,' " *JNES* 34 (Jan. 1975): 14–15. These names—"verse-points," "verse-dividers"—are misleading in that they prejudge the function: punctuation, rather than a division into "verses" (on the unspoken analogy of modern practice with poetry), seems to be the point. In the same way the Masoretic *ṭe'amim* are somewhat mistakenly called "notes" (see chapter 3). Ugaritic only rarely contains such marks: see W. J. Horwitz, "A Study of Ugaritic Scribal Practices," *UF* 5 (1973): 165–73.

63. *Abhandlungen zur arabischen Philologie* (Leiden, 1896); he already had made comparisons with Hebrew "poems" such as the Balaam oracles (p. 42).

64. See R. A. Nicholson, *A Literary History of the Arabs* (London, 1930), p. 74. Sa'adya Gaon (or, more likely, one of his students) describes *saj'*, *ḫuṭba*, and *rajaz* as precursors of poetry, and it is possible that he regarded some parallelistic portions of the Bible in the same light; see below, chapter 3, and N. Allony (ed.), ספר האגרון (Jerusalem, 1968), pp. 79–81. Note also that the first chapter of Moses ibn Ezra's treatise on poetry (*Kitāb al-muḥāḍara wal-mudākara*) is devoted to *ḫuṭba* and its relation to verse. A. F. L. Beeston's "Parallelism in Arabic Prose," *Journal of Arabic Literature* 5 (1974): 134–46, notes: "*Saj'* in its original connotation was rhymed but not dominantly parallelistic. For the pre-Abassid period, therefore, *saj'* and the *khutba* style have to be regarded as distinct phenomena" (p. 143).

65. Newman and Popper, *Parallelism*, p. 102.

66. As is often quite correctly pointed out, while the dating of the Ugaritic tablets is rather certain, the texts thereon recorded are most likely older and perhaps represent a tradition (oral?) stretching back many centuries.

67. See T. H. Gaster, "Psalm 29," *JQR* 37 (1946): 54–67; F. M. Cross, "Notes on a Canaanite Psalm in the OT," *BASOR* 117 (1950): 19–21; also D. N. Freedman

and Hebrew writings,[68] and Ugaritic texts have, for nearly half a century, provided valuable insights into all aspects of biblical studies. At the same time, Ugaritology has come into its own as a discipline, as each year new texts and artifacts have filled in the picture of this complex ancient society.

Three aspects of Ugaritic style are particularly striking to the student of biblical parallelism, and each merits mention here. They are: the frequency of three-clause sentences; the very common appearance of repeated words or phrases in consecutive clauses; and the existence of a stock vocabulary of pairs of words—proper names and their epithets, standard synonyms or antonyms, commonly paired ideas—which are found again and again in consecutive clauses. For while none of these features is absent in Hebrew style, their appearance in, as it were, exaggerated form in Ugaritic has cast a new light on biblical style and current critical approaches to it.

The latter two features have been discussed at length, but before examining some of the current theories it will be worthwhile to make one brief observation about the three-clause sentence in Ugaritic. The basic binariness of the Hebrew parallelistic sentence contributed mightily to the idea of parallelism: the apparent symmetry of so many lines, in which term answered to term, seemed to bespeak some system of symmetry or symmetrizing. Now while three-clause sentences illustrate some of the features of parallelism, the basic idea of B "answering" A, "corresponding" to it, is confuted by the presence of the newcomer, C. What is it doing there? The putative rhythm of statement-restatement, statement-restatement, is broken by the ternary line. In Hebrew such breaks could be viewed as emphatic, intermittent spots of underlining which pleasantly broke the monotony or formed an emphatic closure—much as ternary rhymes are interspersed among the prevailing couplets in the verse of Dryden and Pope. With Ugaritic, however, this notion must be reexamined. For here, binary and ternary sentences freely alternate without apparent order or purpose—so much so that, still today, dividing the words of Ugaritic texts into clauses and the clauses into sentences remains a most speculative endeavor. In Ugaritic, at least, there is nothing fundamental about the parallelistic "couplet." Indeed, in contemplating even a short passage from the Ugaritic myths, with the

---

and C. Franke Hyland, "Psalm 29: A Structural Analysis," *HTR* 66 (1973): 237–56. B. Margulis argues against the prevailing view: "The Canaanite Origin of Psalm 29 Reconsidered," in *Biblica* 51 (1970): 332–46.

68. On this subject in general consult the articles in *RSP*.

characteristic interspersing of two- and three-clause sentences and smattering of repetitions and stock pairs:

> ydn [dn]il ysb palth / bṣql yph bpalt / bṣ[q]l yph byġlm //
> bṣql y[ḥb]q wynšq / aḥl an bṣ[ql] //
> ynpᶜ bpalt bṣql / ypᶜ byġl ur //
> tispk yd aqht ġzr / tštk bqrbm asm //
> ydnh ysb aklth / yph šblt bak[l]t / šblt yp[h] bḥmdrt //

Dan'el investigates, goes around the parched land / he sees a plant in the parched land / he sees a plant in the scrub //

He embraces the plant and kisses [it] / "Ah me, for the plant //
May the plant flourish in the parched land / may the herb flourish in the scrub //
May the hand of the hero Aqhat gather you / may it put you in the granary" //

Dan'el investigates, goes around the consumed land / sees a grain-ear in the consumed land / a grain-ear he sees in the blasted land //

CTA 19 II 61-70

a student of biblical parallelism is inevitably moved to question the idea of symmetry and balancing clauses. Do not these lines suggest a somewhat different function for repetition and restatement, an emphatic, elevating function quite independent of symmetry, parallelism, or even poetic structure?

7

The first of the two main features of Ugaritic parallelism to attract wide attention was its use in successive clauses of two synonyms or otherwise closely associated words or concepts. It was seen briefly in our sampling of biblical parallelism above (section 2), thus:

יומם יצוה ה' חסדו / ובלילה שירה עמי //
By day the Lord sends forth his love / and by night his song is with me //[69]
Psalm 42:9

Day and night are, obviously, a logical pair. By placing them at the beginning of consecutive short clauses, a correspondence is created, and the clauses as a whole—which are otherwise rather dissimilar—acquire a feeling of balance that is aesthetically pleasing.

---

69. On ṣwh see *Psalms III*, p. 259. His explanation of שירה as "vision" is hardly to be preferred to "song," and cf. Psalm 119:54.

It is striking how much the parallelism of Ugarit resorts to precisely this tactic:

ks yiḫd [il] [b]yd / krpn bm [ymn] //
He takes a cup in his hand / a flagon in his (right) hand //

CTA 15 II 16–18

tšt išt bbhtm / nb[l]at bhk[l]m //
Fire is set in the house / flame in the palace //

CTA 4 VI 22–23

where *ks-krpn* (cup-flagon), *yd-ymn* (hand-hand; the second, as in Hebrew, does not necessarily specify "right hand" but is an elegant synonym), *išt-nblat* (fire-flame) and *bht-hkl* (house [= also temple, palace]-palace) are all frequently paired. Thus it is not uncommon, as above, to find two pairs in a single line.

Not only is the phenomenon of pairing common to Ugarit and the Bible, but often the very same words are used in both. Thus:

אך אלהים ימחץ ראש איביו / קדקד שער מתהלך באשמיו //

But God will beat his enemies' head / the [hairy?] pate of him who goes counter to him //   Psalm 68:22

ytbr ḥrn rišk / ʿttrt šm bʿl qdqdk //
May Ḥrn break your head / ʿttrt šm bʿl your pate //

CTA 16 VI 54–57

כמעט אויביהם אכניע / ועל צריהם אשיב ידי //

At once I would humble their enemies / and on their foes turn my destruction //   Psalm 81:15

Mnm ib ypʿ lbʿl / ṣrt lrkb ʿrpt? //
What enemy rises against Bʿl / foe against the Cloud-rider? //

CTA 3 IV 48

The recurrence of such pairs of words was striking to Ugaritic scholars, and it was not long before there was established a vocabulary of "fixed pairs" common to Hebrew and Ugaritic: "earth-dust," "enemy-foe," "cup-goblet," etc.[70] By now hundreds have been

---

70. For earliest treatment see Virolleaud in *Syria* 14 (1933); H. L. Ginsberg and B. Mazar in *JPOS* 14 (1934): 248–49, thereafter *JPOS* 15 and *Orientalia* 5 (1936). U. Cassuto was one of the earlier researchers into pairs (see *The Goddess Anath* [Jerusalem, 1971], pp. 25–31), also M. Held in *Leshonenu* 18–19 (1952–54): 144–60. For lists of pairs see Dahood in *RSP* 1 (1972): 71–382 and 2 (1973): 1–39; also Dahood *Psalms III*, pp. 445–56, and *PEPI*, p. 101. An important article was E. Z. Melamed, "Hendiadys in the Bible," *Tarbiz* 16 (1945), later "Break-up of Stereotypical Phrases," in Ch. Rabin, *Studies in the Bible* (Jerusalem, 1961), pp.

catalogued, and these have proven immensely useful, not only in clarifying lexical obscurities but as a guide in problems of textual emendation.[71]

As far as the workings of parallelism are concerned, the function of such fixed pairs is obvious. They strongly establish the feeling of correspondence between A and B. Indeed, the more stereotypical the pairing, the greater the bond;[72] with the most frequently used pairs, the appearance of the first in itself creates the anticipation of its fellow, and when the latter comes it creates a harmonious feeling of completion and satisfaction.[73] In another way the pairs themselves may bring out the "what's more" relationship of B to A, for, as has been pointed out, the second word of the pair sequence is most often the rarer and more literary term; when both terms are common, the second is sometimes a going-beyond the first in its meaning.[74]

A number of critics have described the pairs as "clichés" and "stereotypical formulae."[75] Such judgments should not, however, lead readers to impose modern-day notions of originality on ancient

---

115–53. Note also G. E. Watson, "Fixed Pairs in Ugaritic and Isaiah," *VT* 22 (1972): 460–67, and Y. Avishur, "Stylistic Features Common to Phoenician Inscriptions and the Bible," in *UF* 7 (1975): 13–47, and 8 (1976): 1–22. C. F. Whitley, "Some Aspects of Hebrew Poetic Diction," *UF* 7 (1975): 493–502 is an important corrective to the "Break-up" idea.

71. See J. Talmon, "Synonymous Readings in the Textual Tradition of the Old Testament" in Ch. Rabin, *Studies in the Bible*, pp. 335–83.

72. This point has been clouded somewhat by the spreading practice of scholars to refer to any parallelism of two words that is duplicated elsewhere in the Bible or Ugaritic as such a "fixed pair." Obviously some sort of distinction, albeit not foolproof, should be made between an apposition that occurs frequently and one that appears only two or three times. (Dahood proposed substituting "parallel" pair for "fixed" pair to avoid implying their *order* was fixed, but this will not help our problem.) Furthermore, some things that are called "fixed pairs" seem more like logically connected concepts than full-scale "literary clichés." Here again, *repeated* use should be the key. As Yoder notes ("A-B Pairs," 473), it is not the semantic closeness of the terms that should be regarded in discussions of pairs, but the frequency of the pairing.

73. See on this point Smith, *Poetic Closure*, p. 137.

74. See R. G. Boling, "Synonymous Parallelism in the Psalms," *JSS* 5 (1960): 221–55. On numerical parallelism, an obvious kind of going-beyond, see section 8. The order of the pairs is not always fixed in Hebrew (P. C. Craigie, "A Note on Fixed Pairs . . .," *JTS* 22 [1971]: 140–43), nor in Ugaritic (Dahood, *RSP* 1, p. 77). Note also that Hebrew sometimes pairs the same *ideas* as Ugaritic but uses different terms (e.g. ḥrṣ = זהב). Both practices indicate that the pairing, not the fixity, was what was central about fixed pairs.

75. *PEPI*, pp. 9–10.

texts. As an examination of even medieval poetics will reveal,[76] premodern songs and poems did not aim at setting out new comparisons and images, but reworking traditional themes and standard language into new formulations: originality consisted of the new variations within a conventionalized framework. But more than this, it is an error to see the pairs themselves as the essence of the line. On the contrary, the pairs often function to bring into equation the *other* words of the line—words that are rarely connected, or in any case words whose apposition is the whole point. It was noted in our earlier example,

יומם יצוה ח' חסדו / ובלילה שירה עמי //

By day the Lord sends forth his love / and at night his song is with me //

Psalm 42:9

that the two clauses have little parallelism beyond the pair-words, and this is sometimes just the point: the pair-word in B provides the retrospective element that establishes a feeling of continuity and completion, while the rest of the verse-half is prospective, carrying the meaning forward:

והוכן בחסד כסא / וישב עליו באמת //

In love a throne is prepared / so that one may sit *faithfully* upon it . . . //

Isa. 16:5

In such verses this "rest of the line" is essential and the pair-words may be seen as a mere tip-of-the-hat to parallelism.[77] Thus, a standard trope of beginning in the Bible is the summoning of the audience's attention, and it is here that one frequently finds the pair "listen . . . / hear . . . //":

האזינו השמים ואדברה / ותשמע הארץ אמרי פי //

Listen O Heavens while I speak / and hear, Earth, my words //

Deut. 32:1

76. See D. Pagis, שירת החול ותורת השיר (Jerusalem, 1970), pp. 110–15. About biblical style and fixed formulae, consult Culley, *Oral Formulaic Language*.

77. Hence Melamed is quite wrong in suggesting that this last verse means, "A throne has been prepared in faith and truth in David's tent, and a judge will sit on it" ("Hendiadys" 180). This is an example of the "distribution" misreading, which will be discussed in section 8. Similarly he is puzzled by Mic. 7:20, חסד / תתן אמת ליעקב // לאברהם . . . // which he wishes to translate "Give faith and truth to Jacob (= Israel = Abraham)," and goes on to assure the reader that the absence of Isaac is not to be wondered at! But the point is that B goes *beyond* A—indeed, the whole verse (not cited by Melamed) makes this clear: "May you give faithfulness to Jacob, even love to Abraham, as you swore to our ancestors in days of old"—Jacob a long time ago, and Abraham at the very beginning of our history.

שמעו שמים והאזיני ארץ / כי ה' דבר //

Hear O Heavens, listen Earth / for the Lord is speaking //　　Isa. 1:2

שמעו דבר ה' קציני סדם / האזינו תורת אלהינו עם עמרה //

Hear the word of the Lord, rulers of Sodom / listen to the teachings of our God, people of Gomorrah //　　Isa. 1:10

שמעו מלכים האזינו רזנים / אנכי לה' אנכי אשירה //

Hear O kings, listen princes / I of the Lord, oh I shall sing //

Judg. 5:3

שמעה תפלתי ה' / ושועתי האזינה //

Hear my prayer, O Lord / and listen to my cry //　　Psalm 39:13

שמעו זאת כל העמים / האזינו כל ישבי חלד //

Hear this, all peoples / and listen all dwellers on Earth //

Psalm 49:2

שמעו זאת הכהנים / והקשיבו בית ישראל / ובית המלך האזינו //

Hear this, O priests / and hearken, house of Israel / hear, O you of the royal palace //　　Hos. 5:1

שמעו חכמים מלי / וידעים האזינו לי //

Hear my words, wise men / and you knowing ones, listen to me //

Job 34:2

Now in all of these, to focus on the fixed pair is to consider precisely the part of least interest to the listeners.[78] It is, as stated, a trope of beginning and utterly predictable. The use of pairs does not mean the *clauses* are equivalent, and what is interesting in these lines are the subtle variations—including, of course, *who* is being summoned and in what order: Heaven and Earth, kings and noblemen, nations and people. These are what tell the story.[79] This point is important, for in the enthusiasm following the discovery of the pairs, the differences between A and B have sometimes been overlooked. Let one example stand for many: the war boast of Lamech (Gen. 4:23–24). One student of the pair phenomenon[80] has sought to explain the passage as "synonymous" parallelism; this leads him to suppose that the line

כי איש הרגתי לפצעי / וילד לחברתי //

78. See *PEPI*, p. 27; Cassuto, *Goddess Anath*, p. 38. Gunkel is also weak on this point; see *The Psalms: A Form Critical Introduction* (Philadelphia, 1967), p. 11.

79. Moreover, the fact that "hear" and "listen" sometimes occur in the *same* clause indicates that they are not merely the tool of parallelism, nor were they specially created to meet its "demands." See below.

80. *PEPI*, pp. 25–34.

which he translates "For I have slain a man for my wound, even a boy for my hurt," refers to a single incident, and that "man" and "boy" are, in fact, a "pair," i.e., references to one and the same person. He finds this man-boy pair a "deliberate rejection of the traditional 'man—son of Man [sic]' parallelism" which must, therefore, be explained as a striking attempt to underscore the youth of the "upstart would-be hero." The writer is so caught up in the synonymity of word pairs that he sees them even where they do not exist.

Of course there is no need for any of this, and even he finds troubling the question "Why should Lamech boast of having slain a boy, a child?" Actually, the passage should read:

עדה וצלה שמען קולי / נשי למך האזנה אמרתי //
כי איש הרגתי לפצעי / וילד לחברתי //
כי שבעתים יקם קין / ולמך שבעים ושבעה //

'Ada and Ṣilla hear my voice / women of Lamech listen to my words //
I would kill a man for [i.e., to avenge] my wound / in fact a boy for a bruise //
If [as is said][81] Cain is avenged seven-fold / then Lamech seventy-seven! //

The *qtl* forms of the second line are conditionals, not past (cf. Gen. 42:38, Judg. 9:9 and ff.) as they are usually mistranslated; initial *kĭ* may be an indicator for this conditional sense.[82] "Man" and "boy," far from being synonyms, instead work to create a "sharp" crescendo of unequal retribution: I would kill a man for only wounding me, in fact, an innocent boy (there is no reason to suppose the child is the inflictor of the wound—if Lamech is such a fierce warrior the image is on the contrary somewhat trivializing and difficult to imagine) to avenge a bruise; Cain's retribution is already grossly, proverbially unfair—but mine will be far worse![83]

---

81. Gen. 4:15.

82. Cf. our earlier example (p. 19) of Psalm 27:10, כי אבי ואמי עזבוני "Even if my father and mother abandoned me . . ."

83. A particularly apposite comparison is with Jacob's (proverbial) characterization of Simeon and Levi (Gen. 49:6):

כי באפם הרגו איש / וברצונם עקרו שור //

The whole passage might be rendered: "Simeon and Levi are brothers, weapons of violence are their rightful possession[?]; into their company let me not come, nor let me stay in their fellowship; for in their anger they *would* kill a man, and in a good humor, hough an ox." Here we have the same *qtl* form to indicate the conditional, and the same initial *ki* to underscore this meaning. The sharp punchline is much the same in its effect as in the Lamech boast: "The people of these tribes are so violent

Where do the pairs come from? Initially this subject suffered from
some wishful thinking on the part of writers who wished to see in the
"pair" phenomenon the "regular stock in trade of the Canaanite
poets,"[84] specially created to serve the poetic device of parallelism.
This judgment is only partially correct. It is true that the recurrence of
certain pairs—"house-palace," "earth-dust"—suggests something of
a literary stereotype, and their frequency is consistent with what was
noted above concerning premodern fondness for oft-repeated, solemn-
izing formulae. But one ought not to conclude more than the evidence
warrants. Hebrew and Ugaritic, like most languages, had their stock
of conventionally associated terms, of synonyms and near-synonyms,
and of antonyms and near-antonyms. Some of these were regularly
paired to make a single merismatic phrase:[85] "day and night" meant
"all the time," "silver and gold" meant "everything of value," "ox
and ass" meant "beasts of burden," etc. Other pairs, while not
merismatic in a strict sense, are nevertheless frequently used in a
single phrase—"love and faithfulness," "teaching and law," etc.
Indeed, some such words, like תושב ("resident"), never occur singly
in the Bible.[86] The use of such pairs as stock phrases in the form
X + Y argues against the notion that they were created for the
purposes of parallelism—indeed, the opposite seems far more likely,
that the stereotypical formula X + Y was subsequently broken down
into parallel halves "X . . . / Y . . . //" This is further evidenced by
the breakdown of names and patronymics (another X + Y) into
parallel "Name . . . / Patronymic . . . //"[87] Again, the fact that some
of the "pairs" consist of nothing more than conventionally interchangeable concepts, synonyms and near-synonyms, is witnessed by
textual variants within the Masoretic Text (or between the MT and
other texts or versions) which consist precisely of the substitution of
one such "word-pair" for another. Thus, there is nothing "poetic" or

---

that when angered they will not flinch at murder; and even when they are feeling
kindly, what do they do? Go out and cripple an ox!" Dahood's suggestion
"circumcision blades" (!) for מכרתיהם (*CBQ* 23 [1961]: 54) is based on the common
faulty assumption that this verse refers to the Shechem incident in Gen. 34. Actually,
it is a tribal saying without historical reference—the *qtl* verbs are not "past" at all. (If
not, to what historical incident does the "ox" refer?!)

84. H. L. Ginsberg, "Rebellion and Death of Baʿalu," in *Orientalia* 5 (1936):
171–72.

85. A. M. Honeyman, "Merismus in Biblical Literature," *JBL* 71 (1952): 11–18.

86. Melamed, "Hendiadys," 175.

87. See on this *PEPI*, pp. 50–52; in general, Melamed, "Break-up of . . ." in Ch.
Rabin, *Studies in the Bible*, pp. 115–53. There are many instances of such name-
patronymic pairings, e.g., Num. 23:18, 1 Sam. 10:11, 20:1.

literary in the pairs per se, any more than there is in "far and near," "law and order," "bag and baggage," etc. in English. What is "poetic" is the breaking up of such proverbial pairs, or, more generally, of any conventionally associated concepts into adjacent clauses to establish the interclausal connection and the feeling of closure.

Finally, it should be noted that there is no evidence to show that these pairs functioned as "oral formulae" comparable to those described by Milman Parry and Albert Lord in the poetry of ancient Greece or modern south-Slavic epics.[88] As remarked earlier: the function of the pairs is no different from the use of similar syntactic structures, alliteration, etc.—all establish the sense of correspondence between A and B. The fact that certain pairs recur may indicate that they had achieved a certain formulaic popularity, or perhaps simply that they expressed a concept adaptable to a wide variety of lines. But in no way does their presence in a line suggest the line was the extemporaneous production of "poet-performers" who composed "on their feet."[89] Indeed, what we know of the genre of biblical proverbs and various Psalm-types hardly supports such "oral theory." It would stretch the limits of credibility to argue that, for example, the alphabetical acrostics of the Psalter or Lamentations were composed by poets "on their feet," yet here we have the same pairs:

מלכותך מלכות כל עלמים / וממשלתך בכל דור ודר //

Your kingdom is a kingdom of *all eternities* / and your dominion is in *every age* //   Psalm 145:13[90]

וישמח עליך אויב / הרים קרן צריך //

The *enemy* rejoices over you / your *foe* is triumphant //   Lam. 2:17

And so an "oral theorist" would have to dismiss these as learned adaptations of an originally oral device, presumably because they had acquired a certain formulaic ring, a literary resonance. But the same motive could be attributed to *all* their uses. *Formulaic language is not necessarily spontaneously composed language.* No doubt some of the Bible's parallelistic passages were composed spontaneously in front of their intended audience, and perhaps even some of the lines exhibiting stereotypical pairs are among them. But parallelism is a far less exacting requirement than the meter of Greek epics—indeed, as will be seen, it is not a comparable "requirement" at all. There is no

88. See A. Lord, *The Singer of Tales* (Cambridge, 1960), and *PEPI*, pp. 10–14. Also Yoder, "A-B Pairs," 470–89; Dahood in *RSP* 1, p. 75.

89. *PEPI*, p. 10.

90. On this pair see *PEPI*, pp. 36–37.

reason, logical or empirical, to associate the frequent use of such pairs with spontaneous composition, still less to search out their origins in the conditions of oral poetry.

The other very prevalent form of parallelism found at Ugarit involves taking a word or phrase from A and repeating it in B. An example of this practice was already seen in Psalm 94:3:

עד מתי רשעים ה' / עד מתי רשעים יעלזו //

How long shall the wicked, Lord / how long shall the wicked rejoice? //

and this particular verse represents a relatively common configuration of the Ras Shamra texts,[91] in which a vocative ("Lord") interrupts the thought before completion: in B (or B + C) it is repeated and finished:

lk labk yṣb / lk l[a]bk wrgm / ṯny lk[rt adnk] //
Go to your father, Yṣb / go to your father and speak / repeat to Krt your lord //   *CTA* 16 VI 27–29

But this is only one use to which repetition is put in parallelism. Also common are repetitions with two complete thoughts, e.g.,

ימינך ה' נאדרי בכח / ימינך ה' תרעץ אויב //

Your hand, Lord, is glorious in power / your hand, Lord, crushes enemies //   Exod. 15:6

or repetitions without any intervening word:

לפני ה' כי בא / כי בא לשפט הארץ //

Before the Lord who now approaches / now approaches to rule the land //
                                                           Psalm 96:13

yqḥ il mšt⁽ltm / mšt⁽ltm lriš agn //
El takes two kindlings / two kindlings from the top of the fire //
                                                           CTA 23:35–36

Repetition is sometimes combined with pair-words in Hebrew:

אנה הלך דודך / היפה בנשים //
אנה פנה דודך / ונבקשנו עמך //

Where has your love gone / most beautiful of women? //
Where has your love turned? / [Tell us] that we may look for him with you //   Song of Songs 6:1

91. Lowth discussed this and other repetitive patterns in *SP*, pp. 158–59. It had been described earlier by the medieval commentator Rashi, as well as his grandson, Rashbam. See chapter 5, section 1.

Sometimes the repetition takes place within a single clause:[92]

לא לנו ה' לא לנו / כי לשמך תן כבוד //

Not to us, O Lord, not to us / but to your name give glory //

Psalm 115:1

and sometimes the repetition stretches beyond the individual line:

רבת צררוני מנעורי / יאמר נא ישראל //
רבת צררוני מנעורי / גם לא יכלו לי //

"Much have they oppressed me from my youth" / —come now, Israel, say //

"Much have they oppressed me from my youth / yet they have not overcome me" //   Psalm 129:1–2

and all these patterns have been duplicated in the Ugaritic texts. Now these, and other repetitions,[93] may be mere variations on a single principle, though the peculiar prominence of the interruptive vocative suggests this may indeed have been a particular *type*, a sort of formula[94] (but note the use of interruptive vocatives without repetition, as in Psalms 50:22, 127:2). However, it is probably unwise to see this formula as the archetype from which the others "developed," as one writer has proposed.[95] Indeed, the whole notion of an "original" form of repetitive parallelism is highly questionable.

The resemblance of certain repetitive structures in the Bible with Ugaritic repetitions is so close as to indicate beyond reasonable doubt an organic connection. Now because repetition had been found, inter alia, in texts of reputed antiquity in the Bible, and because the Ugaritic texts were ascertainably old, an attractive hypothesis

92. See Y. Avishur, "Addenda to the Expanded Colon," *UF* 4 (1972): 4, where he divides the verse so as to put the repetition in different verse-halves, and cf. his treatment of Psalm 57:2. He thus sacrifices relative equality of line-length to the parallelistic use of repetition. I believe he is wrong (as obviously the Masoretes also would). As we have seen, there is no need for obvious paralleling in every line, and furthermore many Ugaritic lines illustrate repetitions within the same verse-half or third; cf. in Hebrew Judg. 5:3. Moreover, repetition is found to operate in more than adjacent clauses (see example of Psalm 129 below). This topic will be discussed more fully in section 10.

93. See above, page 5; also Muilenberg, "Hebrew Rhetoric," 107; S. E. Loewenstamm, "The Expanded Colon in Ugaritic and Biblical Verse," *JSS* 14 (1969): 179, Y. Avishur, "Addenda," 1–10. S. E. Loewenstamm, "The Expanded Colon Reconsidered," *UF* 7 (1975): 261.

94. See E. L. Greenstein, "Two Variations of Grammatical Parallelism," *JANES* 6 (1974): 87–104.

95. Loewenstamm, "Expanded Colon in Ugaritic," 195.

presented itself: traces of this "repetitive parallelism" in Hebrew are confirmation of a text's antiquity and may, in fact, become the basis for dating different parts of the Bible.[96] This practice, "stylistic sequence dating," was set forth by W. F. Albright and some of his students;[97] according to his theory, repetitive parallelism gradually gave way to paranomasia (as in the blessings of Jacob, Gen. 49). This shift in Hebrew aesthetics was carried out over some period of time, so that where one finds repetition in untrammeled abundance, as in the Song of Deborah, one may suppose the text represents the oldest stylistic layer, derived from the ancient, "pan-Canaanite" style:

Judg. 5:6	// ... בימי יעל / בימי שמגר בן ענת /
Judg. 5:7	// ... שקמתי אם / עד שקמתי דבורה /
Judg. 5:12	// עורי עורי דבורה / עורי עורי דברי שיר
Judg. 5:20	// ... ממסלותם נלחמו / מן שמים נלחמו הכוכבים /
Judg. 5:21	// נחל קישון גרפם / נחל קדומים נחל קישון
Judg. 5:23	// ארו ארור ישביה /ה'/אורו מרוז אמר מלאך
	// לעזרת ה' בגבורים / כי לא באו לעזרת ה'
Judg. 5:24	// מנשים באהל תברך / תברך מנשים יעל / אשת חבר הקיני
Judg. 5:27	// בין רגליה כרע נפל / בין רגליה כרע נפל שכב
	// באשר כרע / שם נפל שדוד
Judg. 5:30	/ שלל צבעים לסיסרא / שלל צבעים רקמה
	// צבע רקמתים לצוארי שלל

This theory is not entirely convincing,[98] however, for the reason that other instances of "repetitive parallelism" have been discerned in a wide variety of texts, including those of reputedly late periods. The latter, including the "Songs of Ascents" (Pss. 115–29) and other parts of the Psalter, have been described as "archaizing" by proponents of the Albright thesis;[99] later instances of the repetitive style are supposedly characterized by "a formal and stilted repetitiveness"[100] not present in the old style. But this position is

96. W. F. Albright had re-recognized repetitive parallelism (following Lowth, who described it as a species of synonymous parallelism, and C. A. Briggs, who called it "step-like" parallelism) and proposed a hypothesis about its early date ("The Earliest Forms of Hebrew Poetry," *JPOS* 2 [1922]: 69–82) in the decade before Virolleaud, Ginsberg, et al. began to describe the uses of parallelism and repetition in Ugaritic. Their articles thus seemed to come as a confirmation of the Albright thesis.

97. See *YGC*, chapter 1.

98. See John Gray, *Legacy*, pp. 303–05.

99. See, e.g., *Psalms III*, pp. 194–95.

100. F. M. Cross and D. N. Freedman, *Studies in Ancient Y. Poetry* (Ph.D. diss., Baltimore, 1950), pp. 23–24.

difficult to maintain. In addition to texts in the Psalms and the Prophets, one may adduce examples from the very latest elements of the canon:

הבל הבלים אמר קהלת / הבל הבלים הכל הבל //

Vanity of vanities, says Qohelet / vanity of vanities, all is vanity //

Eccles. 1:2

It is particularly prominent in the Song of Songs,[101] e.g.,

1:15   הנך יפה רעיתי / הנך יפה עיניך יונים //

4:8   אתי מלבנון כלה / אתי מלבנון תבואי /

4:9   לבבתני אחתי כלה / לבבתני באחד מעיניך /

If this repetitive style indeed is to be explained where it is most abundant, factors other than age ought to be considered—including geography. For the fact is Ugarit bears two quite distinct relations to biblical Israel: it is older, and it is farther north. In some discussions, the former is assumed to be the only relevant consideration: what one finds in Ugaritic is older than Hebrew, hence it is the ancestor of what exists in Hebrew.[102] But its differentness may be explained in the other way as well: it was written in another territory, in a language akin to, but distinct from, Hebrew.[103] Indeed, geography accounts for marked differences in vocabulary and usage even within Hebrew, i.e., between the Hebrew of Northern and Southern provenance; so that if a fourteenth-century "far-Northern" text matches in some feature a later biblical one, it may not be proof of the latter's age, but only its northern provenance.[104] Conversely, the durability of certain Ugaritic

---

101. Albright, in a later article ("Archaic Survivals in the Text of Canticles," *Hebrew and Semitic Studies* [*Driver Festschrift*] [Oxford, 1963]) argued that this book, while containing irrefutable Iranian loan-words that suggest a late date (fourth to fifth century B.C.), contains "material" (i.e., whole verses) "from the last centuries of the second millennium, and perhaps even older, [which] persisted into the fifth-fourth centuries B.C., when it was presumably collected by an unknown amateur." While not impossible, there is something disturbingly circular about this hypothesis: (1) repetitive parallelism is an indication of a text's antiquity because it is found in our most ancient texts; (2) it is found in the undeniably late Song of Songs; (3) therefore, the Song of Songs contains "archaic material."

102. See D. A. Robertson, *Linguistic Evidence in Dating Early Hebrew Poetry* (SBL Dissertation Series, Missoula, Montana, 1972).

103. Ch. Rabin, "The Origins of the Subdivisions of Semitic," in *Hebrew and Semitic Studies* [*Driver Festschrift*] (Oxford, 1963), p. 110; also *UT* 5.13, p. 30.

104. Thus Robertson (n. 102) concludes on the basis of his criteria that Job is one of the oldest texts in the Bible (p. 54); Dahood, on the basis of comparison of its fixed pairs with Ugaritic, argues its Northern provenance (*RSP* 1, p. 81).

elements[105] argues that if a biblical text *differs* in some fundamental pattern from Ugaritic, it may not be a case of the one evolving away from the other, but of both having a common ancestor from which they had diverged along geographic lines long before.

Finally, care should be taken to distinguish what seem to be patterns or formulae (like, as noted, the interruptive vocative) from mere repetitions.[106] For while all sorts of repetitions can be found in Ugaritic and the Bible, the mere fact of repetition should not be equated with poetic convention. Repetitions have been invented and reinvented a thousand times in the songs and poems of every people, prized not for their usefulness in the -specific requirements of parallelistic style, but for the sense of return and completion on which every poetry thrives.[107]

About the nature of biblical parallelism the Ugaritic evidence underscores the dual nature of B, which, it has been seen, typically contains retrospective and prospective elements. For in much repetitive parallelism this is quite obviously the whole point: when B begins again like A and either finishes what was left incomplete or provides a new completion, it is, quite undeniably, both harking back and moving forward. Furthermore, the Ugaritic use of both conventional word-pairs and repetition of phrases, either the two together or separately, in binary or in ternary units, and now and then interrupted by a single clause lacking any semantic parallelism with its neighbors:

a[tt tq]ḥ ykrt / att tqḥ btk / ġlmt tšʿrb ḥzrk //
tld šbʿ bnm lk / wtmn tttmnm lk //
tld yṣb ġlm / ynq ḥlb a[t]rt / mṣṣ ṭd btlt //
The wife you take, O Krt / the wife you take to your house / the woman you bring to your courts //
May she bear you seven sons / yea eightfold may she bear you //
May she bear a boy yṣb / who will suck the milk of Aṭrt / nursing on the breast of the virgin (ʿAnat) //

CTA 15 II 21–27

underscores the fact that paralleling is not a dependable, structural constant, but a fairly dependable, variously manifested, feature of style. In this sense, as one writer noted in his study of Ugaritic style,[108] one of the lessons of Ugarit is that far too much has been

---

105. See on this point *Psalms III*, p. xxiv–v; Dahood cites B. A. Levine, "Ancient Survivals in Mishnaic Hebrew" (Brandeis University dissertation, 1964).

106. Loewenstamm's categories are in this respect worthwhile, though his developmental use of them seems, as noted, risky.

107. See Levin, *Linguistic Structures.*

108. G. D. Young, "Ugaritic Prosody," in *JNES* 9 (1950): 133.

made of parallelism in the Bible. It is less consistent, less structural, than Lowth and his followers have implied.[109]

8

One possible tactic in reading biblical parallelism is that which Theodore of Mopsuestia (fourth to fifth centuries) called "distribution."[110] In this reading, parallelism is "seen through" and the elements of A and B are recombined to make a single complex utterance. That Lowth also was aware of this possibility is apparent in his reading of, for example, Song of Songs 1:5

שחורה אני ונאוה בנות ירושלם / כאהלי קדר כיריעות שלמה //

I am black and comely, women of Jerusalem / like the tents of Qedar, like the tent-dwellings of Solomon //

which Lowth understood to mean, "I am black as the tents of Qedar but beautiful as the tent-dwellings of Solomon."[111] The same sort of "redistribution" is often performed by modern comentators, though not in any systematic way. Thus, D. N. Freedman says of Psalm 135:5,

כי אני ידעתי כי גדול ח' / ואדנינו מכל אלהים //

For I know that YHWH is great / our lord is [greater] than all the gods //

We observe that the poet has successfully rearranged the words of a simple declarative statement to produce a poetic couplet. Written as prose the sentence would be: "For I know that our Lord YHWH is greater than all the gods."[112]

S. Mowinckel, writing about Psalm 90:16

יראה אל עבדיך פעליך / והדרך על בניהם //

Let your work be shown to your servants / and your glory to their sons //

makes this observation:

> According to the rules of the "thought rhyme" [= parallelism] in Hebrew poetry, there is no question here of two different things, as if "thy servants" . . . may see his "work," but "their sons" see his

---

109. See chapter 2.
110. *Diaeresis* ("dividing in two"); see chapter 4, section 6.
111. *SP*, p. 161. Cf. Origen, Midrash R., Rashi ad loc.
112. D. N. Freedman, "Prolegomenon," in G. B. Gray, *The Forms of Hebrew Poetry* (New York, 1972), p. xxx.

glory; the two parts express the same thought: let thy servants and their sons see thy work and thy glory, i.e., thy glorious work of salvation; let the present, as well as the coming generation, experience thy grace and thy salvation.[113]

Similarly, in Psalm 72:1

אלהים משפטיך למלך תן / וצדקתך לבן מלך //

God give your statutes to a king / and your righteousness to the son of a king //

he sees a single request, for statutes and righteousness.

These all represent a somewhat more subtle misunderstanding of parallelism. Unlike the "synonymous" reading, they grant that B *is* somewhat different from A, e.g., the variation "work"/"glory"// is a significant one and not merely a casting about for similar concepts. But by recombining the two into a single statement, they lose the whole "what's more" of B. Obviously, this matters not a little to our Psalmist: "Let your active-force[114] be made manifest to your servants, yes, and your majesty even to their children!" Similarly: "For I know YHWH is great, in fact, our Lord is greater than all gods!" (The example from the Song of Songs is somewhat more subtle, because it involves the unification in B of apparently disparate concepts in A, a truly "sharp" accomplishment: I am black and I am beautiful, yes, black as the proverbially black tents of Qedar and beautiful as the proverbially beautiful tent-dwellings of Salma. Lowth correctly identified the comparative intention of this verse, but what he missed was the whole genius of its being stated in this precise form.)

Behind this reading lies the assumption that the biblical writer started off with a single sentence and then, via distribution, made it into two parallel halves. Redistributing them into a single assertion intends to find out what was "really" meant. This is a crude idea at best, for the parallelistic form itself communicates part of the meaning, the "what's more," and without it the new version falls flat. But more than that, redistribution sometimes forces the commentator to equate or combine elements that are uncombinable, or at least better left uncombined. Thus, W. F. Albright has remarked on instances of "self-contradictory description" in Ugaritic and Hebrew parallelism, in which the second half-verse "seems to correct" the first:

113. S. Mowinckel, *PsIW* 2, p. 102.
114. A bit more faithful to פעליך than "works."

For instance, the first half line says that a god "drank wine from a cup of gold," the next half-line that he "drank it from a flagon of silver." A variation on this theme is that a god is given "a cup in one hand, two flagons in both hands." Obviously, he could not have held both simultaneously. Evidently these poets, following ancient stylistic tradition, were unconsciously trying to create a vague, changing outline in order to make the picture shimmer, so to speak, in the mind of the listener. Whether this stylistic device made the resulting text sound more sacred, or simply more poetic, we cannot say because we cannot fully penetrate this mentality.[115]

By way of disagreeing with this last judgment, it is appropriate to adduce here another feature common to the Bible and Ugaritic parallelism, the numerical saying:[116]

שלשה המה נפלאו ממני / וארבע לא ידעתים //
דרך הנשר בשמים / דרך נחש עלי צור //
דרך אניה בלב ים / ודרך גבר בעלמה //

There are three things too wondrous for me / and four I do not know //
The way of the eagle in the sky / the way of a snake on a rock /
the way of a ship at sea / and the way of a man with a woman //
Prov. 30:18–19

תחת שלוש רגזה ארץ / ותחת ארבע לא תוכל שאת //
תחת עבד כי ימלוך / ונבל כי ישבע לחם //
תחת שנואה כי תבעל / ושפחה כי תירש גברתה //

For three things the earth groans / and for four it cannot endure: //
For a slave who rules / for a fool who's had his fill //
For the hated wife when she is sought / and for a handmaid who is heir to her mistress //
Prov. 30:21–23

These two phenomena, "self-contradictory discription" and the numerical saying, are in principle one and the same: the modern misunderstanding of them derives from the idea that A and B "mean the same thing," for we have lost the biblical habit of reading B as A's completion. Their relationship here is really "A, and what's more, B," "A, and as a matter of fact, B." "There are three things I do not understand, indeed four things," and in this particular proverb the fourth is definitely in an emphatic position. The same is true of "one

115. W. F. Albright, *History, Archeology, and Christian Humanism* (London, 1965) p. 95. Cf. *PEPI*, p. 21; F. M. Cross, "Prose and Poetry in the Mythic and Epic Texts from Ugarit," *HTR* 67 (1974): 7–8.

116. See W. M. W. Roth, "The Numerical Sequence X/X+1," in *SVT* 12 (1962): 300–11.

cup . . . two flagons"—no impossibility, just a vivid instance of the "I'll go you one better" mentality of parallelism. This is even true of "a cup of gold . . . a flagon of silver." For here B is a flowery "yea" version that goes beyond what A stated (it is important to recall that "flagon" is the somewhat rarer, literary term in Ugaritic).[117] None of these expressions is "primitive" or "protological."[118] What makes them seem so is the notion that A and B are simultaneous, hence able to be redistributed into a single statement. To be sure, a cup cannot simultaneously be gold and silver, any more than the number of things can be simultaneously three and four. But that is just the point: B always comes after A, not simultaneously.

What, then, do such lines mean? Was the cup made of *both* gold and silver? Did he actually pick up one cup, or two?! There is a basic ambiguity in any "what's more": for this copula can represent a true addition ("A is so, and what's more, B," that is, both A and B are so); or an equation ("A is so, yes, B is so," that is, A *or* B is so, it does not matter which), or a "going one better" ("A is so, nay, B is so," that is, in fact B is so). Now such ambiguity will not survive redistribution, which always demands a choice. Thus, Albright's example,

ירה ליתר תשלחנה / וימינה להלמות עמלים //

She reached her hand to a tent-peg / and her [right] hand to a worker's mallet // Judg. 5:26

might imply one implement, and it might imply two.[119] Retelling the story in another form (see Judg. 4:21) requires deciding which, but, in the form above, neither possibility is to be ruled out a priori.[120]

Usually the context clarifies which "what's more" is to be preferred, when clarification is necessary. Thus, in Prov. 30:18 "Three things . . . four things" we do not understand B as an addition to A (making a total of seven) but a stronger version of A; this reading is reinforced by the parallelism "are too wondrous for me / . . . I do

117. See Boling, "Synonymous Parallelism," 221.

118. Albright, *History, Archeology* p. 95.

119. The hapax הלמות, usually taken as "hammer" on the basis of *hlm*, might conceivably be some other pounding or flattening instrument; יתר means not only "tent-peg" but "stick" or possibly even "shovel" (Deut. 23:14). Equation is thus not to be lightly ruled out.

120. If it were clear that the apposition יד-ימין was always equative, then one might well insist that only one implement was seized; and indeed, this may have been clear at the time. However, some have argued that יד means "left hand" in certain cases (see C. Stuhlmueller in *CBQ* 29 [1967]: 196, n. 25), and if this is so, addition may have been intended.

not know //" and, of course, by the subsequent fourfold list. At the same time, the numerical parallelism of 1 Sam. 18:7—

הכה שאול באלפו / ודוד ברבבתיו //

Saul has killed his thousands / and David his ten-thousands //

is ambiguous. If the "what's more" is left completely unstressed, equating "thousands" and "ten-thousands," then little harm would be done by the redistribution "Saul and David have killed by the thousands and ten-thousands." But such a redistribution is far from obvious—perhaps the women who sang this chant in David's honor intended to praise him *even beyond Saul* in military prowess, that is, intended the "what's more" of the numerical parallelism in its full force. In any case, this is how the jealous old king understands it: "And Saul became very angry, and the thing was evil in his eyes, and he said: 'They have given to David "ten-thousands," but to me they gave only "thousands." ' "[121]

We are probably right to read as "additional" the Ugaritic parallelism

lqḥ imr dbḥ bydh / lla klatnm //
He took a lamb [as] sacrifice in his hand / a kid in two hands //

CTA 14 III 159–161

i.e., to understand that both a kid and a lamb were sacrificed, on the basis of "one hand / both hands." But what of the following:

[b]hty bnt dt ksp / hkly dtm ḫrṣ //
My house I build of silver / my mansion of gold //

CTA 4 VI 36–38

Certainly house/mansion is one and the same building: but is the apposition silver/gold to be understood as meaning "silver and gold," "silver, nay gold," or "precious metal" (silver or gold, it does not matter which)? No doubt a denizen of Ugarit would roar with laughter over such a question, for the significant content is clear enough, the ambiguity is only a formal one. The point, he would say, is not

---

121. Gevirtz (*PEPI*, pp. 15–24) is wrong—absurdly so—to deny the historicity of Saul's "what's more" understanding of this refrain. This is the whole point of the story! (Instead, he attributes this reading to a later "prose" author who was "seeking to explain the rift that occurred between" Saul and David.) On the contrary, this exemplum of Saul's jealousy has all the ring of authenticity. Incidentally, the author of Ben Sira (Ecclesiasticus), surely no slouch in the ways of parallelism, endorses the "what's more" reading of this verse in 47:6, "Therefore the women sang about him and praised him with 'ten thousand.' "

whether *and* means "plus," "nay," or "or," but that B *goes beyond* A, completes it, as much in "mansion" as in "gold."

The impulse to "redistribute" brings parallelism's ambiguity to the fore—sometimes irresolvably—and at the same time obscures the essence of the form. Indeed, the same impulse lies behind the analysis of two non-synonymous pair-words X . . . / Y . . . as "really" being nothing more than the breakup of the pat phrase X + Y.[122] Reconstructing their deconstruction—another form of "redistribution"—is a risky affair at best, for it denies B any possibility of contrast, and in any case always distorts part of the meaning.[123] Thus, while it is wrong, as Mowinckel asserts, to read Psalm 90:16 "Let your work be seen by your servants and your glory on their children" as implying a distinction (let one group be shown one thing and let another group be shown another), his distribution-reading is equally deceiving. "Let thy servants and their sons see thy glorious work of salvation" is simply not what it says, and it is a denial of the form. "What's more," in whatever sense or strength, is always part of the meaning.

9

An extremely common semantic relationship already seen is the setting of the entire B-clause in apposition to part of the A:

יכרת ה' כל שפתי חלקות / לשון מדברת גדלות //

The Lord destroys all lips of falsehood / a tongue speaking untruth //

Psalm 12:4

Here "lips of falsehood" (= speakers of falsehood) is paralleled by the entire B-half. The same sort of apposition occurs frequently:

זכרו נפלאתיו אשר עשה / מפתיו ומשפטי פיו //

Recall the wonders he worked / his signs and the laws of his mouth //

Psalm 105:5

In such verses, and indeed in any verse in which a single word or phrase does double duty (i.e., is stated in one half and merely implied

122. See Melamed, "Break-up," and especially n. 77 above. Note also C. F. Whitley, "Some Aspects of Hebrew Poetic Diction," p. 493.

123. A similar error is the "redistribution" of elements of repetitive parallelism, where eliminating repetitions simply means breaking the whole force and suspension of the line. Thus Loewenstamm reconstructs Psalm 77:17, ראוך מים א' ראוך מים יחילו, אף ירגזו, as "The waters trembled when they saw you." Similar is his (borrowed) summary of Judg. 5:12—"Deborah's awakening is nothing else than an awakening to song" ("Expanded Colon in Ugaritic," 186.)

in the other) a potential imbalance is created: one side will be longer than the other. It is noteworthy, therefore, that in many verses (like the preceding) this potential imbalance is rectified by the addition of a term or terms in B:

לאסר מלכיהם בזקים / ונכבדיהם בכבלי ברזל //

To bind their kings in chains / and their nobles in shakles of iron //
Psalm 149:8

תסתירני מסוד מרעים / מרגשת פעלי און //

Keep me from the company of the wicked / from the gathering of those who do evil //
Psalm 64:3

G. B. Gray called this general phenomenon "compensation," and more recently Cyrus Gordon has written about it under the name "ballasting." Under either name, what is meant is the tendency of the B-clause to compensate for some missing element by adding something new, or by paralleling a small term in A with a larger term in B. Thus our line

ידע שור קנהו / וחמור אבום בעליו //

An ox knows its owner / and an ass its masters' trough //

has the single verb "knows" do double duty. The phrase "owners' trough" may thus be seen to compensate in length for the space left empty in the B half by the absent verb. Such "compensation" is often found, though it should be pointed out that it is no fast rule. A large number of noncompensations may be found, for example our

יודוך ה' כל מעשיך / וחסידיך יברכוכה //

All your works praise you, Lord / and your faithful ones bless you //

for equivalent line length is a consistent, but not infallible, form of correspondence between A and B. In some sections, "uncompensated" lines seem to be the norm, such as in the so-called "qînâ" meter characteristic of Lamentations and other sections.[124]

But it must be noted that in this whole question of compensation and "ballast variants" there is a rather misleading assumption about intention. Behind these phrases lurks a prejudgment of purpose: the *extra* element in B *compensates* for something that is missing, and what is added is merely ballast. Were the need not there, the compensatory phrase presumably would not have been written. But on the contrary, as has been seen, the phrase "masters' trough" is the

---

124. First discussed by K. Budde, "Das hebraeische Klagelied," *ZAW* 2 (1882). See chapter 7.

linch-pin of a climactic descent; were it not there—were the wording instead, "An ox listens to its master, and an ass obeys its owner"— that descent would surely be less forceful. It is reasonable to suppose that in many cases, including this one, the "compensation" came before the need to compensate, that the verb "knows" was made to apply to both clauses precisely so as to allow the phrase "masters' trough" to appear in B and yet maintain the balance in line length.

ירבר עמים תחתינו / ולאמים תחת רגלינו //

He subdues peoples beneath us / and nations beneath our feet //
Psalm 47:4

Is the phrase "beneath our feet" mere ballast, or was a counterpart for "subdues" omitted in B so as to allow this more graphic going-beyond A's "beneath us"? What of:

כי בחנתנו אלהים / צרפתנו כצרף כסף //

You have sifted us, O Lord / you have refined us as a silver-refiner //
Psalm 66:10

or

היינו חרפה לשכנינו / לעג וקלם לסביבותינו //

We have been a [source of] mockery to our neighbors / jeering and embarrassment to those around us //   Psalm 79:4

or

כי אתה תקותי אדני / ה' מבטחי מנעורי //

For you are my hope, my lord / O Lord, my reliance since my youth //   Psalm 71:5

The whole notion of "ballast" or "compensation" asks us to decide about the Psalmist's intention in these lines—it is an impossible question to answer in most cases, and a foolish one to ask.

This is especially true in the use of the word *kol* ("all") in Hebrew parallelism. For it is a fact that one of the most characteristic ways that B is made to go beyond A is through the use of *kol* as a reinforcement.[125] Sometimes, of course, there can be no question of "ballasting":

125. When this word appears singly in a parallelistic pair, it is most often in the B-clause. Thus, a survey of the first book of the Psalter (Pss. 1–41) reveals that the word *kol* is used alone in B forty-three times, as opposed to twenty-one times in A. Of course it is an important and flexible differentiating tool in either verse-half (section 5).

יראי ה' הללוהו / כל זרע יעקב כבדוהו //

Worshippers of the Lord, praise him / all the seed of Jacob, honor him //
Psalm 22:24

But quite often *kol* does appear in such a ballasting situation:

וינחם בענן יומם / וכל הלילה באור אש //

And he led them in a cloud by day / and all the night in a fiery light //
Psalm 78:14

כי ישר דבר ה' / וכל מעשהו באמונה //

For straight is the word of the Lord / and all his doing in faithfulness //
Psalm 33:4

לשמע בקול תודה / ולספר כל נפלאותיך //

To make heard the sound of praise / and to recount all your miracles //
Psalm 26:7

זה עני קרא וה' שמע / ומכל צרותיו הושיעו //

Whenever a poor man cries the Lord hears / and delivers him from all
his sorrows //
Psalm 34:7

לדעת בארץ דרכך / בכל גוים ישועתך //
יודוך עמים אלהים / יודוך עמים כלם //

To make known your dominion on earth / amongst all nations your
salvation //
Peoples will praise you, God / peoples will praise you every one //
Psalm 67:3

ימלא פי תהלתך / כל היום תפארתך //

My mouth is filled with your praise / all the day with your lauding //
Psalm 71:8

It would be wrong to dismiss these as "ballasting"; to do so is the
equivalent of the *metri causa* argument in metered poetry. For
whatever purpose, the B-clause's *kol* brings with it a feeling of
inclusiveness that puts it beyond A. Indeed, one can see that the B-
clause *kol* sometimes became something of a reflex:

משמים הביט ה' / ראה את כל בני האדם //
ממכון שבתו השגיח / אל כל ישבי הארץ //
היצר יחד לבם / המבין אל כל מעשיהם //

From the sky the Lord looked down / he saw all mankind //
From the place of his dwelling he peered out / at all the dwellers on
earth //
He made their hearts together / and understands all their deeds //
Psalm 33:13–15

10

We have noted in the preceding pages the workings of parallelism in individual lines taken from the Psalter and other books. While some lines are highly parallelistic, in others the resemblances between A and B are slight. "Semantic parallelism"—which is really an abbreviated reference, for rarely is semantic parallelism found without some accompanying parallelism of grammatical forms, syntax, and line length—characterizes some lines, while in others the parallel elements are limited to these lesser domains of morphology, syntax, and phonetics, resemblances which tend to be less striking. Indeed, there are not a few lines such as we have already seen in which approximately equal length is the sole element on which to pin the principle of parallelism between clauses.

If one wishes to say that it is this *principle of parallelism* that lies behind the structure of all lines, one will be hard pressed to explain why parallelism in some lines is so full and striking, while in others it is so slight, virtually nonexistent.[126] Indeed, the whole notion of syntactic, morphological, phonetic, etc. parallelism is a relatively recent critical creation,[127] which, however valid, seems to have been devised in the necessity of salvaging the principle of parallelism for lines where semantic similarities were obviously lacking. It is one thing to point out such attenuated forms of parallelism as a critic; it is quite another to imagine the Psalmist, having in mind the *principle of parallelism*, coming up with a composition such as Psalm 23:

ה' רעי / לא אחסר //
בנאות דשא ירביצני / על מי מנחות ינהלני //
נפשי ישובב / ינחני במעגלי צדק למען שמו //
גם כי אלך בגיא צלמות / לא אירא רע //

כי אתה עמדי / שבטך ומשענתך המה ינחמני //
תערך לפני שלחן נגד צררי / דשנת בשמן ראשי / כוסי רויה //

126. "Variety" is a possible answer, but it will not account for the fact that some Psalms (as the aforementioned Psalm 94) are so consistently semantically parallelistic and binary, while others are neither most of the time.

127. Lowth seems to have intended parallelism as more than a semantic phenomenon (see chapter 6); however, those who followed him and elevated *parallelismus membrorum* to a structural feature were concerned only with semantic parallelism. Even Mowinckel still speaks of "thought-rhyme" as the governing principle. Important steps away from this analysis are the articles of Holladay, Kosmola, and A. Ehlen, "Poetic Structure of a Hodayah" (Harvard Ph.D. dissertation, 1970).

אך טוב וחסד ירדפוני כל ימי חיי / ושבתי בבית ה' לארך ימים //

1. [Since] the Lord is a shepherd for me / I [will][128] lack nothing //
2. In verdant fields he grazes me / at tranquil streams he waters me //
3. He revives my being / he leads me to generous pasture as befits his name //
4. [So that] even when I enter a valley of deathly dark / I fear no ill //

5. Surely you are with me / your staff and your leaning-stick[129] are what guide me //
6. You provide me generous food in the midst of adversity /[130] in fact you grant me comfort / abundance is my portion //
7. Only well-being and kindness pursue me[131] my life long / and I will stay in the Lord's house for the length of time //

Certainly no one could argue that symmetry has governed the Psalmist's choices; but even parallelism, of which line 2 is a standard example, is strangely muted in most lines. Could a normal listener, unschooled in the doctrine of morphological parallelism, even be aware of a correspondence in the halves of line 3? Line 4? Two verses, 6 and 7, illustrate the *yqtl-qtl* alternation described earlier. One must ask oneself how this, as indeed other forms of differentiation, squares with the principle of parallelism; for here the intent is obviously not the avoidance of too close a resemblance between verse-halves—the two "halves" are different enough as it is! On the contrary, the use of *similar* forms is what the principle of parallelism seems badly in need of here. A dozen changes suggest themselves that would make any of the lines more parallelistic: could not 3 and 5 be rearranged so as to be less 'lopsided'? Instead of "my cup overflows" in 6, could not a phrase corresponding to "in the midst of adversity" have been

128. It is on the ambiguity of present-future that this and subsequent verbs play, for while the "sheep" speaker utters everything in the present, the description of resurrection and eternal life (which, contra Dahood, begins only in the third line) ought to be mentally translated as future. The subject of this psalm is Divine beneficence in earthly and eternal life. Note also that I have indicated a major break at line 5, with the abrupt shift to second person.

129. Given the heavy metaphorizing, we should perhaps read something into this pair—"punishment" and "support" or "words of rebuke and comfort," a standard duality as in, e.g., Deut. 32:1–4. For "guide" with enclitic *mem*, *Psalms I*, p. 147.

130. These are not our idioms, so literal translation is absurd. The first clause should be compared to Psalm 78:19, where "in the desert" corresponds to "despite [in the face of] my enemies"; both represent Divine help as more than just "getting by." Similarly oil was a *figura* of comfort; see Psalm 132:2. Abstinence from oil accompanied fasting not only in talmudic times but in the Elephantine (fifth century B.C.) community; see *ANET* 491.2.

131. That is, "My only pursuers are well-being and kindness."

adduced? In all, the presence of paralleling has such a decidedly haphazard flavor that there is something absurd in thinking of it as the organizing principle of this psalm.

One should like to advance something more basic, like the "binary form," as its organizing principle. Yet the blocks of words involved are of such irregular length that the "binary form" becomes a self-deception: it implies a regularity in clause length that is simply not there. Consider the aforementioned "lopsided" lines, or the contrast in the clause length of the first and last lines (four words vs. twelve!). Moreover, line 6 is clearly ternary: certainly the "binary form" cannot be organizing the principle of lines that are not even binary.

What is the essence of biblical parallelism? From the beginning our whole presentation has been pitched against the notion that it is actual *paralleling* of any sort that is the point. Save for this last discussion of Psalm 23, our argument has not been based on lack of regularity carried over groups of lines (a phenomenon well known to students of parallelism), but on evidence taken from *within* single parallelistic lines. Sharpness, sequences of actions and cause-effect sequences, differentiation, differences in the *other* words in "fixed pair" parallelism, B's going beyond A in repetitive parallelism, the nonsynonymity of numerical and "self-contradictory" parallelism, the "B-clause *kol*"—each is, in its way, an argument against fixing on the similarity of A and B as central. This is not to say that paralleling is not important—of course it is, it is the most striking characteristic of this style. But focusing on it is just somewhat beside the point.

What then is the essence? In asserting the primacy of our form

$$\underline{\hspace{3cm}} / \underline{\hspace{3cm}} //$$

we are asserting, basically, a sequence: first part—pause—next part—bigger pause (and only secondarily the rough limits on the length of the clause and their approximate equivalence). But even this sequence is a bit of a shorthand for the real point, for what those pauses actually embody is the *subjoined, hence emphatic,* character of B. The briefness of the brief pause is an expression of B's connectedness to A; the length of the long pause is an expression of the relative disjunction between B and the next line. What this means is simply: B, by being connected to A—carrying it further, echoing it, defining it, restating it, contrasting with it, *it does not matter which*—has an emphatic, "seconding" character, and it is this, more than any aesthetic of symmetry or paralleling, which is at the heart of biblical parallelism.

To state the matter somewhat simplistically, biblical lines are parallelistic not because B is meant to be a parallel of A, but because B typically *supports* A, carries it further, backs it up, completes it, goes beyond it. This is a slight, but very important, nuance, for it will explain why paralleling is so inconsistent, so *untended*: it was not in itself the point. And this will explain how this basically emphatic sequence could be further abstracted to the series of pauses _____ / _____ // which, as we have seen, was adapted to such unemphatic configurations as "since A, therefore B," "if A, then B," "A happened, and B happened," and so forth—variations that are often disturbingly unparallelistic, but whose filiation with emphatic "seconding" is clear.

Thus, for example, we have treated the question of ternary lines somewhat casually because the difference between binary and ternary lines *is not crucial*, and this again points up the wrongheadedness of focusing on parallelism. It does not matter whether

יברכך ה׳ מציון / וראה בטוב ירושלם ; כל ימי חייך //

May the Lord of Zion bless you / [so that] you enjoy Jerusalem's goodliness ; your whole life //   Psalm 128:5

is a two- or three-membered verse, that is, whether we pause after ירושלם or not, and the lack of clear semantic support for this pause, and for others, so indicates. This is to say as well that it does not matter that, if it is read as binary, the line is "lopsided." It has sufficient parallelism to establish B as a "seconding" of A, that is, to establish the sequence _____ / _____ //. So even in a clearly defined tercet,

רוממו ה׳ אלהינו / והשתחוו להר קדשו / כי קדוש ה׳ אלהינו //

Exalt the Lord our God / and bow down to his holy mountain / for holy is the Lord our God //   Psalm 99:9

the sequence _____ / _____ / _____ //, while longer, is not different in kind. That is why the binary and ternary lines can alternate freely in Hebrew and Ugaritic; neither overall line length, nor symmetry of paralleling, is the point.

It should be noted here what this pause-sequence eliminates and what, as a consequence, we do not find in the Psalter or elsewhere. We do not find:

_____ // _____ //

that is, two complete, utterly independent, yet in some respects parallel utterances, such as the following composites:

טוב להודות לה׳ // טוב ללכת אל בית אבל //

It is good to praise the Lord. It is good to go to the house of mourning.

Psalm 92:2, Eccles. 7:2

שירו לה׳ שיר חדש // סורו ממני כל פעלי און //

Sing another song of the Lord. Turn from me, all evildoers.

Pss. 96:1, 6:9

כי בחר ה׳ בציון // ה׳ ידע מחשבות אדם //

Yea, the Lord has chosen Zion. The Lord knows a man's thoughts.

Pss. 132:13, 94:11

יומם השמש לא יככה // בלילה שירת ה׳ עמי //

The sun will not strike you by day. By night the Lord's song is with me.

Psalm 121:6; as per Psalm 42:9

These "lines," though illustrating semantic parallelism, pair words, repetitions, etc. are absurdly inappropriate—for it is not B's mere parallelism to A that is crucial, but it is what this parallelism *means*, B's subjunction.

It should also be noted that if parallelism were the whole point, we should be forced to divide Psalm 123:3:

חננו ה׳ / חננו כי רב שבענו בוז //

Have mercy, Lord / have mercy for we are greatly shamed //

and not as we do (see above, note 92):

חננו ה׳ חננו / כי רב שבענו בוז //

Have mercy, Lord, have mercy / for we are greatly shamed //

and we should be dismayed by lines like:

שמעו שמים והאזיני ארץ / כי ה׳ דבר //

Hear heavens and listen earth / for the Lord speaks //　　　　Isa. 1:2

שמעו מלכים האזינו רזנים / אנכי לה׳ אנכי אשירה /

Hear kings, listen princes / I of the Lord, oh I shall sing /　　　Judg. 5:3

וערבה לה׳ מנחת יהודה וירושלם / כימי עולם וכשנים קדמניות //

May the offering of Judah and Jerusalem please the Lord / as in the days of old and years gone by //　　　　Mal. 3:4

where the means of parallelism are obviously being flaunted, squeezed together into a single verse-half and apposed to a B which has no semantic or syntactic parallelism with it. But on the contrary, it is B's subjunction that is the whole point. For, to recapitulate: the parallelistic style in the Bible consists not of stringing together clauses that bear some semantic, syntactic, or phonetic resemblance, nor yet of "saying the same thing twice," but of the sequence _____ /

_____ // in which B is both a continuation of A and yet broken from it by a pause, a typically emphatic, "seconding" style in which parallelism plays an important part but whose essence is not parallelism, but the "seconding sequence."

How is B's subjunction to be accomplished? The dangers are, on the one hand, the lack of a clear break between A and B, causing the two to merge into a single assertion; and on the other hand, the lack of a clear connection between the two, so that A + B become isolated, independent assertions.[132] Their separation (or, rather, separability) is largely a matter of syntax. In establishing their connection, grammatical and semantic elements both have a crucial role. The typical "A, and what's more, B" (to second, support, carry further) is abstracted to our pause sequence, adaptable to different subordinations and other syntactic variations. Some of the phenomena described in the preceding pages may now be understood more fully—functionally—as the means by which B's subjunction is expressed:

1. *Incomplete B completed by reference to A*—i.e., ellipsis in B (most typically, the subject or verb appears in A and is implied in B; a noun appears in A and is referred to pronominally in B; all of B is in apposition to a single term in A; etc.)—all these are forms of dependence that ally B to A. Note especially the "differentiations" definite article–possessive suffix, and no article–possessive suffix (above, pp. 21–22). This elliptical line (what G. B. Gray called "incomplete parallelism without compensation" and which had been identified with laments and dirges) is sometimes carried out consistently in whole compositions, e.g. Psalm 114 (no lament, by the way!).

2. *Incomplete A completed by B*—this is rarer, because of the danger of A and B running together, but see for example Psalms 27:3, 94:3, 115:1 discussed above. In this pattern the "interruptive vocative" is an important option: its interrupting provides the break between A and B, allowing A to be incomplete without any danger of running together. Another frequent recourse is the inversion of normal word order, which tends to isolate the aberrant clause:

בחצצרות וקול שופר / הריעו לפני המלך ה' //

With psalmody and trumpet-sounds / make music before the Lord the king //   Psalm 98:6

---

132. It is on this latter "danger" that *māšāl* is often built: the point in Eccles. 7:1, 12:11, Prov. 26:9 seen above is to establish the elusive connection *which we know must exist*, for we understand the principle of the form.

Working with either of these "incomplete" patterns, or with the "A is so, and B is so," are:

3. *actual repetition of a term in B*;

4. *"pair-words,"* associated concepts, semantic, syntactic, morphological parallelism (all asserting B's identity or association with A);

5. *sequentiality, subordination expressed or implied (qtl-yqtl)*; and

6. *unusual word order, chiasmus, etc.* (marks either A or B— usually B—as the pair, template or correspondent of the other).[133]

Equally important is the other pause in our sequence, the final "//." What makes it final? It is precisely the fact of B's connection with A, and hence its relative disjunction with what follows it, that "//" represents; a kind of closure. By identifying itself as A's conclusion— reasserting it, "going one better," providing an anticipated (and often, grammatically necessary) completion—B has a closural quality that allows it to break discourse into fairly short units, organizing the flow of clauses into twos and threes. Many writers have remarked on the end-stopped quality of the Psalms and other compositions. Perhaps the strongest demonstration of this feature is the curious case of Psalm 68, which W. F. Albright suggested, is actually no "psalm" at all but a list of first lines of different songs that became included in the Psalter quite by accident—a kind of table of contents masquerading as a psalm![134] It matters little whether Albright is right: the fact that such a theory could even be credibly put forward testifies to the great disjunction between the lines of this psalm; and, on the other hand, the fact that this degree of disjunction was singled out only thirty years ago as somewhat egregious should indicate that disjunction itself is no

133. This last item is particularly significant. A recent study has shown that verbal sentences in Lamentations evidence a significant divergence from normal prose syntax (D. R. Hillers, "Observations on Syntax and Meter in Lamentations," in H. N. Bream, et al., *A Light unto My Path* [Philadelphia, 1974], pp. 265–70), and no doubt the same could be demonstrated for the Psalter and other books. But in addition to marking the style as "special," variations in normal word order often serve a precise function: they qualify the medial pause, either strengthening a potentially weak pause by inverting syntax, or, where A would otherwise contain a complete thought and B consist only of a prepositional phrase or some other apparent afterthought, by suspending some essential from A—subject, or verb, or both—thereby binding A to B. Edward Greenstein remarks on this (in his "Some Variations"; see also his "One More Step on the Staircase" *UF* 9 [1977]: 77–86), though his notion of what will and will not "cue" the listener to "suspend processing" (ugh) seems somewhat arbitrary.

134. W. F. Albright, "A Catalogue of Early Hebrew Poems (Psalm 68)," *HUCA* 23 (1950–51): 1.

stranger to the style of the Psalter. (Further instances will be seen below.)

How is such (sometimes ferocious) "end-stopping" achieved? That is, what means are used to mark B (or C) as final? Here again, paralleling is not the point, but one way of reaching the point—the sense of completion provided by parallelism is provided as well by the other observed phenomena: actual repetitions, contrasting verb forms, chiasmus, the B-clause *kol*, overt and implied subordinations (If A / then B //; just as A / so B //; and so forth). All enable B to close with a click—though sometimes more loudly than others.

Of course, we should not go too far. There *is* an obvious delight in symmetry in many lines. Parallelism is not simply a means of realizing the form _____ / _____ // but its archetype, and is prized in and of itself. The fact of B's subjunction will hardly explain the obvious care taken to make B correspond in length to A, a tendency that, if not consistent, is nevertheless manifest in, for example, the ill-named phenomenon of "compensation." Our point is hardly that parallelism does not exist, but that care must be taken to see it in the proper terms, as part of a larger, overall rhetorical structure. For paralleling itself is not the essence of the (now let us say "so-called") parallelistic line, and will not explain the evidence we have adduced.

Here another brief observation is in order. It was asserted that the two basic characteristics of Ugaritic parallelism are repetition and the use of fixed pairs. It is striking how similarly the two are used. Both appear as spots of resemblance, points of connection between clauses. Yet how different the two are theoretically! The one is the very essence of what has been conceived of as parallelism—the "same idea" expressed in different words—and the other the very thing such parallelism seems bent on avoiding, repetition! The fact that the two are used interchangeably in Ugaritic is a striking demonstration that it is not "paralleling," elegant variation, saying the same thing in different terms, or the like that stands behind their use. The purpose of parallelism and repetition is one and the same—to establish the connection between (syntactically) separate entities, to subjoin.

At first blush, this may seem to be a rather minor distinction: whether parallelism is the "essence" of the form, or whether the "essence" of the form has frequent recourse to parallelism, the result is that *most* lines, the vast majority, of the Psalter and other books are characterized by some parallelism between their clauses. Admitting that parallelism was prized and cultivated for itself further weakens the distinction. But the point is this: not only is the "sequential" explanation better able to account for the asymmetries mentioned earlier (symmetry was not the point, only *enough* symmetry to establish the connection) and to account, as well, for the various "what's more" relationships outlined in the foregoing pages, but it will establish the connection between parallelistic lines and not-very-parallelistic lines, encountered both in books like the Psalter and in the Pentateuch and Prophets, and it will aid in illuminating the structure of the Qumran hymns and other postbiblical prayers and songs. To compare small things with great, it is a bit like the Copernican explanation of the earth's rotation about the sun: it is not the observed phenomena that change but our understanding of what motivates them and, consequently, of their connection with things apparently outside them.

If the various sorts of "what's more" relationships the B-half can illustrate have been presented somewhat insistently in the foregoing pages, it is not because "what's more" expresses the relationship between *every* A and B. "What's more" is in itself an inexact version of the concept of subjunction. But it has been stressed in the belief that this approach ultimately leads to a proper orientation toward *all* lines. In this sense, the foregoing presentation of the characteristics of the parallelistic line has been programmatically anti-Lowthian.

Lowth himself was a biblical commentator and exegete of rare sensitivity and ability; he possessed the courage to follow his thinking beyond the canons of the day, and was also a gifted and persuasive writer. Yet one must wonder how it was that a phenomenon so striking and fundamental as his *parallelismus membrorum* could have been overlooked by so many generations of earlier commentators and critics, clerics, preachers, scribes, and scholars of different religions and backgrounds and periods. And the answer, as will be seen, is that in a very real sense *parallelismus membrorum* was not so much a discovery as an invention. Lowth[135] mistook parallelism for the *whole idea* of this biblical style, then gave the impression of a system operating in what is, really, not systematic at all. As we have seen above, "synonymous" parallelism is rarely synonymous, and there is no real difference between it and "antithetical" parallelism—the whole approach is wrongheaded. All parallelism is really "synthetic": it

---

135. And more than Lowth himself, his followers. See chapter 6.

consists of A, a pause, and A's continuation B (or B + C). As far as
structure is concerned, there is no significant difference between

שירו לה' שיר חדש / כי נפלאות עשה //

Sing another song of the Lord / how he has worked wonders //

Psalm 98:1

and

שירו לה' שיר חדש / שירו לה' כל הארץ //

Sing another song of the Lord / sing of the Lord all the earth //

Psalm 96:1

שירו לה' שיר חדש / תהלתו בקהל חסידים //

Sing another song of the Lord / [sing] his praise in a company of the
faithful //   Psalm 149:1

and

שירו לו שיר חדש / היטיבו נגן בתרועה //

Sing another song of the Lord / play a goodly tune //   Psalm 33:3

And, on the other hand, the differences between them are hardly
expressible with Lowth's categories. Biblical parallelism is of one
sort, "A, and what's more, B," or a hundred sorts; but it is not three.

That Lowth's general approach, and even his tripartite scheme,
have survived to exercise such influence is no doubt attributable in
part to the vigor of his presentation and the thoroughness of his
investigation into other aspects of biblical style. Yet, in a more general
way, it reflects an overall attitude toward the biblical text that is far
older than Robert Lowth. It is connected to the notion of biblical
poetry, to which we now turn.

TWO

POETRY AND PROSE

1

Biblical parallelism—and still more so the "seconding sequence" which is at its heart—appears in a great variety of contexts. While it is concentrated in the so-called "poetic" books, it is to be found almost everywhere. No one would doubt, for example, the parallelism of:

וה' פקד את שרה כאשר אמר / ויעש ה' לשרה כאשר דבר //

And the Lord remembered Sarah as he had said / and the Lord did for Sarah as he had spoken //

or

צחק עשה לי אלהים / כל השמע יצחק לי //

God made me cause of laughter / all who hear will laugh at me //

קומי שאי את הנער / והחזיקי את ידך בו //

Come, pick up the lad / take firm hold of him //

אל תשלח ידך אל הנער / ואל תעש לו מאומה //

Do not harm the boy / do nothing to him at all //

כי ברך אברכך / והרבה ארבה את זרעך //
ככוכבי השמים / וכחול אשר על שפת הים //

I will surely bless you / and surely multiply your seed //
As the stars of the sky / and as the sand upon the shore //

but these occur not in the Psalms, but in the Genesis account of the career of Isaac (vv. 21:1, 6, 18; 22:12, 17, respectively). Many other verses in this same account, containing less obvious semantic parallelism but clearly built on our "pause sequence," could have been adduced. For, in fact, the Pentateuch is full of such lines—not only single verses here and there (especially in direct discourse), but whole sections. Take, for example, the account of the birth of Moses (Exod. 2:1–7):[1]

---

1. Conceptually, this part of the tale begins not in 2:1 but in the preceding verse (1:22), and in this respect the traditional paragraphing is misleading. For the whole

וילך איש מבית לוי / ויקח את בת לוי //

ותהר האשה ותלד בן / ותרא אתו כי טוב הוא //

ותצפנהו שלשה ירחים / ולא יכלה עוד הצפינו //

ותקח לו תבת גמא / ותחמרה בחמר ובזפת //

ותשם בה את הילד / ותשם בסוף על שפת היאר //

ותתצב אחתו מרחק / לדעה מה יעשה לו //

ותרד בת פרעה / לרחץ על היאר //

ונערתיה הלכת / על יד היאר //

ותרא את התבה בתוך הסוף / ותשלח את אמתה ותקחה //

ותפתח ותראהו את הילד / והנה נער בכה //

ותחמל עליו ותאמר / מילדי העברים זה //

The verse-halves have some correspondence-establishing elements:
bêt lēwī . . . bat lēwī; *wattişpĕnēhû . . . haşşĕpînô*; *wattāśem . . .
wattāśem*. But the verse-halves are generally sequential; where B has
an independent verb of its own, it does not echo A's action, but moves
on to the next item. This makes for a less emphatic, less closural,
style—yet such was seen in the last chapter to be perfectly at home in
the Psalter. Furthermore, note here how these coordinated sequences
of A and B are nevertheless tied together in their meanings:

> A Levite man went out / he took a Levite woman //
> The woman conceived and bore a son / she saw how good he was[2] //
> She hid him three months / she could not hide him more //
> She got him a *gomeh*-box / she smeared it with pitch and slime //
> She put the boy in it / she put [it] in the reeds by the river //
> His sister stood far off / to find out what would happen to him //
> Pharoah's daughter went down / to wash by the river //
> Her maidens were walking / alongside the river //
> She saw the box amid the reeds / she sent her maid to take it //
> She opened it and saw the child / and look! a crying boy //

---

premise of the story is Pharaoh's decree that all male children be cast into the Nile;
the mother of Moses devised a way of obeying the letter of the law and yet not
thereby drowning her own child (her hope, as v. 4 indicates, was indeed that someone
would find the basket and save the child). A similar error rests in the faulty division
of Gen. 2:1 from the preceding verse, 1:33—here the sixth day, unlike the others,
should conclude: "And it was evening, and it was morning, the sixth day, and the
heavens and the earth stood completed, and all their host." (This is how the LXX
breaks the section into paragraphs.)

2. This is how we must translate the text as is; one cannot but wonder, however,
how this טוב standing alone was understood or intended—and in view of the common
idiom ראה כי טוב it might be suggested that the הוא of our text represents a later
accretion (see chapter 1, note 9).

She had pity on him and said / "This is one of the Hebrew children." //

It is not common to think of narrative passages such as this one as poetry. But it would be difficult on the basis of any objective criteria to distinguish the structural organization of this passage from that of certain narrative parts of the Psalter:

ויכעיסו במעלליהם / ותפרץ בם מגפה //
ויעמד פינחס ויפלל / ותעצר המגפה //
ותחשב לו לצדקה / לדר ודר עד עולם //
ויקציפו על מי מריבה / וירע למשה בעבורם //
כי המרו את רוחו / ויבטא בשפתיו //
לא השמידו את העמים / אשר אמר ה׳ להם //

They angered [him] with their unfaithfulness / and a plague fell upon them //
Pinhas arose and slew [?] / the plague was stopped //
It was accounted to his merit / from age to age, forever //
And they angered [him] at Meriba's waters / on their account he did ill to Moses //
For they embittered his spirit / and he spoke rash words //
They did not destroy the peoples / as the Lord had told them //

Psalm 106:29–34

Structurally the passages are identical. The only difference is that the latter appears in a traditionally "poetic" book.

We have discussed "seconding" as essentially an emphatic form, and as such it is hardly limited to the normal purview of poetry. It seems to be something far more basic, a "reflex of the language," which turns up in every conceivable context—in laws:

לא יהיה כלי גבר על אשה / ולא ילבש גבר שמלת אשה //

Let not a man's garment be on a woman / nor let a man wear a woman's dress //   Deut. 22:5

and in the hazy area separating law and saying:[3]

שפך דם האדם / באדם דמו ישפך //

Who sheds man's blood / by man his blood is shed //   Gen. 9:6

Is Eve's restatement of the Divine prohibition concerning the Tree of Omniscience:

לא תאכלו ממנו / ולא תגעו בו //

Do not eat of it / do not [even] touch it //   Gen. 3:3

3. See on this point S. McEvenue, *The Narrative Style of the Priestly Writer* (Rome, 1971), pp. 70–71 n.

a case of this "natural reflex" running away with itself?[4] In fact, even
in such a sentence as Samuel's:

ויאמר שמואל אל כל ישראל הנה שמעתי בקלכם לכל אשר אמרתם
לי ואמליך עליכם מלך

And Samuel said to all Israel: "Surely I have listened to your voice [i.e.,
obeyed your wishes], *as to all that you have told me*, and appointed a king
over you."   1 Sam. 12:1

the italicized phrase, which is of a purely emphatic character, is
nothing but parallelism "in the rough."

The point might be made most strongly by considering the text of
the well-known "Moabite Stone," a memorial basalt stele written in a
Canaanite dialect close to biblical Hebrew and erected in Moab
around 830 B.C. It recounts the accomplishments of King Mesha^c and
is noteworthy here precisely because it is not a "literary" or even
epistolary text. It is highly unlikely that its words were framed to
facilitate memorization, that it was ever to be read ceremonially,
sung, or anything similar. It was a memorial inscription, written to
survive to future generations and preserve the king's name. An
interesting feature of the stone is that the major pauses (= sentences)
are indicated by vertical lines in order to facilitate reading. The first
four lines read:

אנך משע בן כמש(ית) מלך מאב הד
יבני | אבי מלך על מאב שלשן שת ואנך מלכ
תי אחר אבי | ואעש הבמת זאת לכמש בקרחה | במ( )
שע כי השעני מכל ה( )לכן וכי הראני בכל שנאי |

I [am] Mesha^c son of Chemosh[yat], king of Moab, the Dibonite.
[pause] My father reigned over Moab thirty years and I have
reigned after my father. [pause] And I made this high-place to
Chemosh in Qarḥoh [a victory high-place?] because he saved me
from all the kings and because he made me triumph over all my
enemies.

Here is a structure that is somewhat reminiscent of biblical "poetry":
the indicated pauses fall at intervals corresponding to the (short) line

4. The original prohibition (Gen. 2:18) did not involve *touching* the tree, only
eating. The midrashists saw in this the snake's cleverness, for by demonstrating
himself that touching the tree was not fatal, he was able to induce Eve to eat; it also
became a model of the dangers of adding unnecessary extensions to the Divine
commandments. See S. Schechter (ed.), *Abot de R. Natan* (New York, 1967), p. 4;
Midrash R. Section 19 (4) of Genesis; cf. L. Ginzberg, *Legends of the Jews*
(Philadelphia, 1913), 1, p. 73.

lengths of, say, the Psalter, and the lines cited subdivide into rough halves. Indeed, we even have a certain parallelism of meaning:

כי השעני מכל ה(מ)לכן / וכי הראני בכל שנאי //

Because he saved me from all the kings / and made me triumph over all my enemies //

Of course it is not a "poem," but this is just the point: the same traits that seem to characterize Hebrew "poetry" also crop up in what is clearly not poetry.[5] These are not like accidental rhymes, or the poor beggar's alexandrine, "Prenez pitié d'un pauvre aveugle s'il vous plaît"—for they are, on the one hand, far more common than mere accident would explain, and on the other, they are not consistently present in what is considered biblical "poetry."

Many have sensed in Hebrew "prose" a structuring and organization which, if it falls short of the strictly parallelistic and binary lines seen earlier (chapter 1, section 1) in Psalm 94, is nevertheless undeniably there.[6] Its very intermediateness is what is troubling: if it is meant to be seconding, why is it not more striking? And if it is not, why does it seem to be trying? As a one-line example, one might cite the opening of the Tower of Babel story (Gen. 11:1):

ויהי כל הארץ שפה אחת ודברים אחדים

And so it was the whole land was [of] the same language and the same words.

The reader senstitive to biblical style cannot but feel something rhetorically pleasing in the presence of the last two words, which turn an otherwise straightforward ＿＿＿＿＿＿＿＿＿＿ into a ＿＿＿＿＿ / ＿＿＿＿＿＿ //. For the last two words, whatever they may clarify or add, also clearly parallel the meaning of the previous two: // אחרים / אחת // שפה / דברים. Yet the pause thereby created is off center and the paralleling incomplete. How easy it would have been for the text to add ודברים אחדים לכל תבל ("and the whole earth shared the same

---

5. In place of the Meshaᶜ stone other examples might have been taken, e.g., the Yavneh Yam ostracon lines 10–13 (see J. C. L. Gibson, *Textbook of Syrian Semitic Inscriptions* [Oxford, 1971], p. 28). On poetic features in the Tel-el-Amarna letters see section 4. The metricist E. Sievers recognized the difficulties in distinguishing "prose" from "poetry" in Hebrew, and even wrote about the Meshaᶜ inscription, but his approach was too polarized: see on this T. H. Robinson, "Principles of Hebrew Poetic Form," *Festschrift A. Bertholet* (Tübingen, 1950), p. 443.

6. See McEvenue, *Priestly Writer*, pp. 49–50, 185–86.

words") or the like! To repeat, is it parallelism? Where does art leave off and "native rhetoric" begin?

Much of the Bible lies in this rhetorical "intermediate kingdom." As an extended example, consider a legal passage such as Num. 5:12–15:

דבר אל בני ישראל / ואמרת אלהם //

איש איש כי תשטה אשתו / ומעלה בו מעל //

ושכב איש אתה / שכבת זרע //

ונעלם מעיני אישה / ונסתרה והיא נטמאה //

ועד אין בה / והיא לא נתפשה //

ועבר עליו רוח קנאה / וקנא את אשתו והיא נטמאה //

או עבר עליו רוח קנאה / וקנא את אשתו והיא לא נטמאה //

והביא האיש את אשתו אל הכהן / והביא את קרבנה עליה //

עשירת האיפה קמח שערים / לא יצק עליו שמן / ולא יתן עליו לבנה //

כי מנחת קנאת הוא / מנחת זכרון מזכרת עון //

Speak to the Israelites / saying to them: //
Any man whose wife strays / and acts unfaithfully to him //
So that a man lie with her / a carnal union //
And it is hidden from her husband / and her impurity is dissimulated //
There is no witness against her / and she was not caught //
But a suspicion enters his mind / and he suspects of his wife that she has become impure //
Or a suspicion enters his mind / and he suspects his wife but she has not become impure //
Then the man shall bring his wife to the priest / and shall bring a sacrifice on her behalf //
A tenth of an ephah barley-flour / on which no oil is poured / and on which no spice is placed //
Yea, a suspicion-offering it is / a symbolic[7] offering symbolizing a sin //

Clearly, these long, technical sentences are not much like the Psalter's. Yet if one were looking for semantic parallelism and other sorts of correspondences, they could be found in every "line": *dabbēr* / *ʾāmartā* //, *tisṭeh* / *māʿălâ* // (note here also the *yqtl-qtl* alternation, and the alliterative *tisṭeh ʾištô* paralleling *māʿălâ . . . māʿal*); *šākab* / *šikbat zeraʿ* //; *neʿ lam* / *nistĕrâ* //; *ʾên* / *lōʾ* //; *rūaḥ qinʾâ* / *qinnēʾ* // (twice); *hēbîʾ* / *hēbîʾ* //; *lōʾ yiṣōq* / *lōʾ yittēn* //; *minḥat qĕnāʾōt* / *minḥat zikkārôn* //. Beyond these, the seconding structure of each sentence is so insistent (and consistent) as to

---

7. That is, symbolizing a sin that in fact might have not taken place. For this meaning cf. the parallel use of זכרון with אות in Exod. 13:9. The phrase זכרון תרועה (Lev. 23:24) is used in rabbinic literature for a Sabbath New Year on which the shofar may not be sounded but only "mentioned." Cf. Isa. 57:8.

constitute a "poetic" regularity. Note furthermore the refrainlike ending in lines 4 to 7. This is not "poetry," but as the psalmist himself says,

זמרות היו לי חקיך / בבית מגורי //

Your laws were my songs / in my dwelling place //   Psalm 119:54

Laws were known by heart, repeated—and musically rendered.[8] How were they structurally different from poetry?

This last verse—or rather its structure—brings up another point. We have cited strictly parallelistic and binary psalms such as our *locus classicus*, Psalm 94. It is these that give us the notion that the Psalms have some structural regularity, "lines," as well as some rough idea of their length. But how to delineate these lines in the absence of such strictness is a problem that, on close analysis, is insoluble (for, as will be seen, there is no independent metrical principle in Hebrew). In our discussion of Psalm 23 (chapter 1, section 10), we divided lines on the basis of the "seconding sequence" alone. But this created "lines" varying between four words and twelve words, seven (Masoretic) syllables and twenty-six! Is the sense of regularity produced by the pause sequence stronger than the feeling of irregularity in such extremes of brevity and length? Nothing tells us that in recitation or musical performance, our extraordinarily long lines 6 and 7 were not rendered as two rather than one—indeed, it seems highly probable that they were, for in alphabetic psalms (where line delineation is a certainty) we have verses like

לעולם ה' / דברך נצב בשמים //

לדר ודר אמונתך / כוננת ארץ ותעמד //

Forever, Lord / your word stands as the heavens //
From age to age [is] your faithfulness / you who founded earth to endure //

                                        Psalm 119:89–90

in which clear parallelism spans what are undeniably two lines; and there are quite a few lines in this psalm (like 119:54 above) in which there is no semantic pause, no parallelism, no "sequence" at all.[9] In other words, while "seconding" and parallelism are fairly consistent features, they are not infallibly present; and where lineation is clearly defined by alphabetical acrostics, sometimes parallelism overlaps

---

8. See the Mishnaic injunction cited in b. *Megilla* 32a, discussed below, chapter 3, section 4.

9. It has made scribes and commentators since Origen (see below, chapter 4) wonder what actually constitutes a "line" in this psalm.

these units or is missing entirely. Thus, there is no reason to assume unquestioningly the traditional equation, parallelistic pair (or even seconding sequence) = poetic line. Regular lineation (that is to say, resolution of the phonic material into roughly equivalent lengths) can be performed on *any* text in recitation—it need not correspond to units delineated by grammar, alliteration, or whatever. If we wish to base our lineation in the Bible on such structural features, we shall come up with "lines" of widely diverging lengths, even within a single composition (witness our treatment of Psalm 23), and we shall run counter to the evidence before our eyes in alphabetic acrostics like Psalm 119. Uncomfortable as such a conclusion is, we must admit that while lineation in some psalms is, on the basis of parallelism, clear, in most it is an act of analogizing from clear lines to not-so-clear, and in some cases it is altogether impossible.

Let us at this point consider the structure of two psalms, both labeled "song of ascents," and, presumably, of similar genre:[10]

שמחתי באמרים לי / בית ה' נלך //

עמדות היו רגלינו בשעריך ירושלם / ירושלם הבנויה / כעיר שחברה
לה יחדו //

ששם עלו שבטים / שבטי יה עדות לישראל / להודות לשם ה' //

כי שמה ישבו כסאות למשפט / כסאות לבית דוד //

שאלו שלום ירושלם / ישליו אהביך //

יהי שלום בחילך / שלוה בארמנותיך //

למען אחי ורעי / אדברה נא שלום בך //

למען בית ה' אלהינו / אבקשה טוב לך //

1. How I rejoiced to hear them say / "We shall go to the Lord's House" //

2. Our feet were standing within your gates, Jerusalem / the built-up Jerusalem / indeed, a city completely joined //[11]

---

10. Scholars have long noted the structural contrast between the strict parallelisms of Psalm 132 and other "songs of ascent," and it may well be that this is a somewhat older psalm that was associated with the pilgrim songs either by editors or the pilgrims themselves: on the other hand, the "Northern" features catalogued in this and other songs of ascent by Dahood point to some communality. In any case, common origin or even precise genre equivalence is not essential to our point, that two songs within the same group (and, presumably, of the same use and life-setting) could be so structurally dissimilar.

11. Understanding the *k-* here as asseverative. For our translation of יחדיו "completely," cf. Psalm 33:15 (parallels כל).

3. Standing where there had ascended tribes / the tribes of Israel's assem-
    blies[12] / to praise the Lord's name //
4. And yes, where they had sat [upon] judgment thrones / the thrones of
    the House of David //

5. They prayed for Jerusalem's well-being / that those who love you
    might prosper //
6. "May there be well-being in your walls / prosperity in your citadels" //
7. [So] for my kin and my companions / let me wish well-being upon
    you //
8. And for the House of the Lord our God / let me pray for your every
    good //

Psalm 122

זכור ה' לדוד / את כל ענותו //

אשר נשבע לה' / נדר לאביר יעקב //

אם אבא באהל ביתי / אם אעלה על ערש יצועי //

אם אתן שנת לעיני / לעפעפי תנומה //

עד אמצא מקום לה' / משכנות לאביר יעקב //

הנה שמענוה באפרתה / מצאנוה בשדי יער //

נבואה למשכנותיו / נשתחוה להדם רגליו //

קומה ה' למנוחתך / אתה וארון עזך //

כהניך ילבשו צדק / וחסידיך ירננו //

בעבור דוד עבדך / אל תשב פני משיחך //

1. Be mindful of David, O Lord / all his sworn obligations //[13]
2. That which he pledged to the Lord / vowed to Jacob's Strength //
3. Let me not go back to my tent-dwelling / nor lie on resting-couch //
4. Nor grant sleep to my eyes / or to my eyelids slumber //
5. Until I find a holy-place for the Lord / a dwelling for Jacob's
    Strength //
6. As far as Ephrata they heard / even in Śĕde Yaᶜar they know //[14]

---

12. Amending שבטי העדות לישראל, a construct chain with genitive *lamedh* as in,
in fact, לבית דוד in the next line.

13. Perhaps this old crux ought to be associated with the ancient word for "to
swear legally" as attested, inter alia, in the Ten Commandments (Exod. 20:16). This
sense accords well with the next line, and the overall theme of the psalm is precisely
the mutual oaths and obligations of Israel's God and the Davidic line.

14. This translation supposes an original *šamᶜunnah*, etc. with energic *nun* (see
R. J. Williams, "Energic Verbal Forms," in *Studies in the Ancient Semitic World*
[Toronto, 1970], pp. 75–85) with the MT's *waw* either an inversion of object suffix
hu (for combination of this object with energic *nun* see, e.g., Deut. 32:10) or *mater
lectionis* wrongly added after the *nun*. Involved as this is, I prefer this reading to the
(standard) translation of these verbs as first person plural; but it is proffered without

7. [Saying] "Let us go to his dwelling / worship at his footstool" //
8. Arise, O Lord, to your place / you and the ark of your might //
9. Let your priests be dressed in righteousness / and your devoted ones sing out: //
10. "For the sake of [your oath to] your servant David / do not disappoint your annointed [king]" //

Psalm 132:1–10

Both compositions would readily be classified as "poetic"—yet how different their structure! Few psalms in the Psalter could be more regular than 132: almost every line is a perfect, binary, semantically corresponding pair. Psalm 122 is certainly not lacking in parallelistic elements, but these do not create much of a feeling of symmetry, or even regularity; the lines are far less end-stopped, and the correspondences *between* lines are sometimes stronger than those within them. Even to speak of "lines" in this psalm is something of a liberty, for one might well treat both lines 2 and 3 as being *each* two lines (cf. the lineation of the MT). The style tightens somewhat in lines 5 to 8, but the first four lines are loose, almost conversational. In fact, lines 2 to 4 constitute a single, flowing sentence, ornamented with a few repetitions.

The fact that some psalms are so semantically parallelistic and others so little, the fact that our pause sequence emerges naturally from most lines but in some is clearly an imposition—and the fact that these extremes of laxity and strictness in organization are found within compositions of presumably the same genre—all argue that there is nothing essential about the features cited. They are hardly a structural constant, a sine qua non of biblical "poetry," but something at once less consistent and more widespread than any of the organizing characteristics of Western poetry.

---

overwhelming conviction. F. M. Cross reads the apparent feminine object as referring to the Ark, ארון, "treated both as masculine and feminine in classical Hebrew" (*Canaanite Myth and Hebrew Epic* [Cambridge, 1973], p. 94n.); cf. his remarks there about Ephratah (pp. 94n–95n) and Sede Ya'ar (pp. 96–97). Note also the following "sharp" reading: "The gorges of these great theologians are often crammed with God's Name, but his mercy and his works are found among humble folks. That is the meaning of these words I have often noticed in the Psalter, 'Until I found a place for the temple of the Lord, an habitation for the mighty God of Jacob. Lo we have *heard* of the same at Ephrata, and *found* it in the wood.' The clergy [associated with Ephrata], and others like them, speak readily of God, and His name is often in their mouths; but lowly men [i.e. those who live "in the wood"] have Him truly in their hearts." William Langland, *Piers Ploughman* (fourteenth-century England), book 10. See the translation of J. F. Goodridge (Baltimore, 1966), p. 114.

2

There is no word for "poetry" in biblical Hebrew. There are a great number of genre classifications in the Bible—words for different types of psalms, hymns, songs and choral arrangements; proverbs, sayings, wordplays; curses, blessings, prayers; histories, tales, genealogies; laws, cultic procedures; speeches, exhortations of moral intent; oracles, predictions, orations of consolation or rebuke—but nowhere is any word used to group individual genres into larger blocs corresponding to "poetry" or "prose." Indeed, where lists of genres exist—as in Proverbs 1:1–6 or Ben Sira (Ecclus.) 47:17—the absence of such groupings comes into bold relief. There is, in fact, no word to describe parallelism per se,[15] and parallelism and its absence are nowhere distinguished: if an opposition was made, as in 1 Kings 5:12 or Ecclus. 44:5, it was between sung and spoken (or written) genres (i.e., שיר or מזמור vs. משל), all of them, however, parallelistic to some degree.

Thus, to speak of "poetry" at all in the Bible will be in some measure to impose a concept foreign to the biblical world. Obviously, there is some ground for this imposition: we have a notion of what poetry's thematic, generic, and organizational characteristics are, and where we find these in the Bible we are certainly justified in viewing them through our native terminology. But this identification is seductive: one ought to consider well the assumptions that accompany it.

The first has already been alluded to: one of the most common formal characteristics of poetry is its regularity, its establishing of some sort of pattern of units—lines—whose characteristics are continuously reproduced. With only certain well-defined variations, one expects the same line of dactylic hexameter in line after line of

---

15. It is possible that the word *māšāl* originally designated many things written in the closural style of biblical parallelism, rather than specifically meaning "proverb" or "saying." Akk. *mašalu* is connected to both "similar" and "half"; an attractive hypothesis is that the name comes from the structure itself, in which B is similar to A in some respect, or simply in that it is A's pair. (The notion that a *māšāl* is so called because it is a simile or likeness to something in real life seems erroneous, for there are many imageless *mĕšālim*, including some identified as "ancient" in the Bible [1 Sam. 24:13, Ezek. 12:22]). The phrase *śĕʾēt māšāl* may have been used in Num. 23:7, 18, etc. and Job 27:1, 29:1 to mean "speak in the parallelistic style." (Medieval Hebrew poets like Falaqera and Alharizi used the same phrase to introduce metrical epigrams in their *maqāmāt*.) But if this meaning is preserved in *śĕʾēt māšāl*, it seems to have disappeared from the regular use of *māšāl* at an early period.

the *Aeneid*: if one were to read a line with an extra foot, or an inappropriate foot (e.g., an iamb) or even an inappropriately placed foot (a spondee in the fifth foot), the line would immediately be perceived as a violation of the pattern, a "break" in the meter. A thirteen-syllable alexandrine would be equally out of place in classical French poetry; so would a nonalliterating (or wrongly alliterating) line in *Beowulf*.

No similar prescription attends prose; yet, as has been noted often, prose is highly structured (indeed, the periodic sentences of classical Greek rhetoric were characterized by parallelism of clause length and syntax very similar to that found in the Bible).[16] Even today, the modern writer of English prose has a variety of model utterances or "frames" before him as he writes: he makes his choices from among well-established alternatives. His sentences will interrupt and continue in patterns familiar to the reader, they will pile up adjectives in twos and threes, connect clauses in well-worn patterns of subordination—and all this will be done with an eye to variety and balance, and in such a way as to emphasize what the writer considers most important. Prose, it has been observed, is quite different from ordinary discourse: it is "common speech on its best behavior." The precise patterns and rhythms change from language to language and from period to period, but they are nonetheless real, and observable.

This is as much as to say that the regularity perceivable in some parts of the Bible ought not automatically to be identified as poetic. For in using this term, biblical critics have unconsciously assumed something about the Bible (and, more recently, about parallelism) that, on inspection, will simply not hold true. There is in the Bible no regularizing of a consistency comparable to those familiar to us from Western poetics. Parallelism, or even seconding, is slightly less than consistent: it is a frequent, but not infallibly present (or absent) form of heightening adaptable to a wide variety of genres. The equation parallelism = poetry has led critics both to overlook parallelism in "unpoetic" places—in laws, cultic procedures, and so forth, and especially in *single lines* that come to punctuate, emphasize, or sum up less formally organized discourse; and, on the other hand, to attribute to biblical parallelism a consistency it lacks.

3

We should be justified in balking at the notion of biblical poetry if only

16. See on this A. Baker, "Parallelism: England's Contribution to Biblical Studies" in *CBQ* 35 (1973): 436.

for the distortion it has created in the modern understanding of parallelism. But the damage is far more widespread.[17] The whole idea that parts of the Bible are written in meter, and the hundreds of trial scansions and textual emendations it has engendered, is a concomitant of this notion. This "metrical hypothesis" has been around since the first century A.D., and, as will be seen in subsequent chapters, its elaboration has played an important role in the history of parallelism's exegesis.

To a certain extent, of course, the lines of Job, the Psalter, and other books *are* regular. For parallelism, as we have seen, functions in part via correspondences between A and B (or sometimes A, B, and C), and this includes a rough equivalence of clause length, however measured. Not only will syntactic similarities create metrically similar verse-halves (whether one counts the total number of syllables, long syllables, stressed syllables, or number of words) but, as we have seen, in some cases of syntactic inequivalence, Hebrew lines maintain the balance of clause length through the use of the (inaptly named) "ballast variants." More than this, as will be shown, terseness and compression of style accompany parallelism in a great many cases. This terseness makes for very brief, semantically stripped clauses which, though not metrical,[18] often contain no more than four or five major words and thus make for a certain regularity of length in clause after clause and (where lines are binary) line after line.

From earliest times, this consistency was identified by those steeped in the Greek meters as a comparable organizing system (it was on this that the claim of biblical poetry originally rested). But the "meter" of the Bible differs from these other meters in that it is only part of a complex of equivalences. Moreover, it is indisputably true that even the most parallelistic sections of the Bible have a markedly

---

17. Cf. in a related matter the observation of S. Mowinckel (*PsIW* 1, p. 12): "It is in fact surprising that a cultic interpretation of the Psalms has not been suggested long ago. The traditional Jewish and Christian interpretation, however, took it for granted that the Psalms were originally private, individual poetry. . . . Exegesis was concerned to discover what events in David's private or public life had occasioned a particular psalm." That is to say, the Psalms were misread because they were identified with the inspired, personal lyrics of Greek and other literatures.

18. That is, with no visible pattern (X number of syllables, stresses, etc. per clause or line) or any attempt to equalize obvious aberrant (yet equalizable) lines— nothing, in short, not explainable by parallelism itself and this "terseness." (See below.) It is a lack of clarity about what does and does not constitute meter that causes many a modern discussion to founder.

different "aesthetic of regularity" from that observable in metrical poetry: they simply did not demand the same consistency.[19]

It requires a healthy imagination, to say the least, to believe that the lines delineated by the pauses in Psalm 23 are metrically equivalent, no matter what sort of meter is involved. And so the metrical hypothesis has survived by turning its attention away from such compositions and concentrating on more regular passages.[20] But here comes the same problem of consistency in different garb: at what point of irregularity does a meter cease to be a meter? Why do some psalms begin metrically and then violate the very regularity they seem to be built on? In the regular Psalm 103, one suddenly has the extraordinarily long clauses of verse 17:

וחסד ה' מעולם ועד עולם על יראיו / וצדקתו לבני בנים //

And the Lord's mercy is everlastingly upon his worshippers / and his righteousness on [their] children's children //

What delight in even rough metrical equivalence can be perceived in the exceptionally long line of Psalm 136 (whose lines are, however, undisputably delineated by the antiphonal refrain):

את הירח וכוכבים לממשלות בלילה / כי לעולם חסדו //

The moon and the stars as governing bodies at night / for his lovingkindness is forever //   Psalm 136:9

Even in so consistently binary a song as that of Deuteronomy 32, there intrude (from a metrical standpoint) the ternary lines 14 and 39, and though most verse pairs are of quite regular length, some (e.g., 16)

---

19. It is striking how little appeal regularity seemed to hold for biblical authors. There are, for example, a few compositions like Psalm 107, in which repeated lines function as a sort of refrain. But at what intervals? Not, as a Westerner might expect, at every four lines, or every six, chopping the text into regular blocks: but *here and there*, at lines 8, 15, 21, and 31, creating "stanzas" of eight, seven, six, and ten lines respectively. How difficult would it have been to make this approximate equality "perfect"? And what does this say about biblical aesthetics? See, on another aspect of this point, J. Goldingay, "Repetition and Variation in the Psalms," *JQR* 68 (1978): 146.

20. A favorite text is Lamentations, because its alphabetical acrostics clearly delineate lines, but even here the contradictions are formidable. How is one to argue the metrical equivalence of lines in the same poem which, by one metricist's own count, vary between twelve syllables and twenty-four? How, in Prov. 31, can a line of twelve syllables be the metrical equivalent of a line of twenty-two syllables, or, in Psalm 25, nine syllables vs. thirty-two?! (D. N. Freedman, "Acrostics and Metrics in Hebrew Poetry," *HTR* 65 [1972]: 367–92. Note that Freedman's system is based entirely on the notion of syllabic equivalence—he does not postulate an accentual meter or metrical feet which might otherwise vitiate the obvious inequalities).

are shorter than the rest. For this song, of greater regularity than many
in the Bible, is still not "metrical" in the usual sense. All too often
those who have so described this and other parts of the Bible have had
no real acquaintance with metrics; but on the contrary, metricists who
turn their attention to the Bible tend rather to follow the conclusion of
B. Hrushovski: "These basic units [parallel verses] are not equal; all
attempts to correct the text in order to achieve strict numbers make no
sense from any textual point of view."[21]

As our history of parallelism's exegesis will show, it is the notion of
"poetry" in the Bible that has been a major confusing factor in the
question of meter. For centuries semantic parallelism was recognized
here and there in the Bible, but its connection with the more basic
seconding structure of most lines was misunderstood; it was mistaken
for a poetic ornament, like the figures of classical Greece, used now
and again to beautify and adorn. Meanwhile, the approximate
regularity of the sentences in some songs fed the notion of biblical
poetry; egregiously unmetrical songs were simply ignored.

Interestingly, even the discoverer of parallelism did not put an end
to the metrical hypothesis, for Robert Lowth did not believe his
parallelismus membrorum was the basis of biblical poetry's
organization:

> But since it appears essential to every species of poetry that it be
> confined to numbers, and consist of some kind of verse (for indeed
> wanting this, it would not only want its most agreeable attribute, but
> would scarcely deserve the name poetry) in treating of the poetry of
> the Hebrews, it appears absolutely necessary to demonstrate, that
> those parts at least of the Hebrew writings which we term poetic are
> in metrical form.[22]

He went on to argue that because of all the unknowns in Hebrew
pronunciation, this meter was forever lost; nevertheless, one could
infer its existence from the general "conformation of the sentences."
The exact wording of this passage is crucial:

> But although nothing certain can be defined concerning the meter of
> the particular verses, there is yet another artifice of poetry to be
> remarked of them when in a collective state, when several of them
> are taken together. In Hebrew poetry, as I before remarked, there
> may be observed a certain conformation of the sentences, the

21. "On Free Rhythms in Modern Poetry," in T. Sebeok, *Style in Language*
(Cambridge, 1960), p. 189.

22. *SP*, p. 31.

nature of which is, that a complete sense is almost equally infused
into every component part, and that every member [= clause]
constitutes an entire verse. So that as the poems divide themselves
in a manner spontaneously into periods [= sentences], for the most
part equal; so the periods themselves are divided into verses, most
commonly couplets, though frequently of greater length. This is
chiefly observable in those passages which frequently occur in the
Hebrew poetry in which they treat one subject in many different
ways, and dwell upon the same sentiment; when they express the
same thing in different words, or different things in a similar form of
words; when equals refer to equals, and opposites to opposites; and
since this artifice of composition seldom fails to produce even in
prose an agreeable and measured cadence, we can scarcely doubt
that it must have imparted to their poetry, were we masters of the
versification, an exquisite degree of beauty and grace.[23]

Lowth here anticipates what he is to describe in detail in his
nineteenth lecture, *parallelismus membrorum*. Note, however, its
function in his reasoning: Hebrew poetry, to be worthy of the name,
must have meter. That meter is lost. Nevertheless, we can see
evidence of its presence in that not only are the "periods" (sentences)
for the most part equal, but that they themselves subdivide into verses
(clauses), most frequently pairs, *as delineated by parallelism*.
Parallelism thus reveals the structure of Hebrew meter. In itself, as
Lowth notes, parallelism is not poetic, for one finds it imparting an
"agreeable and measured cadence" even in prose. But the point is that
by paying attention to the parallelism one can clearly delineate the
periods and verses into which the words fall and these, by their
general "conformation," will bear witness to the workings of the
unknown meter.

Since Lowth this point has been obscured, for parallelism is now
widely taken as a kind of substitute meter, a structure-giving
regularity whose role in biblical Hebrew is comparable to that of
meter in ancient Greek. But certainly the discoverer of parallelism
would not agree: he rightly said that it occurs "frequently," but surely
knew that neither parallelism nor even the division of sentences into
binary units was any constant. It is precisely this point that I have
been at some pains to demonstrate.

Chapter 7 will survey the major metrical theories that have been
advanced since the resurgence of metrical speculation in the
nineteenth century. But let one conclusion be stated in advance: none

23. *SP*, p. 34–35.

of these theories will ever work to an acceptable degree, because biblical authors had an entirely different notion of their compositions than that imputed to them by later criticism. The off-and-on, more-or-less regularity of their "seconding" sentences, the intermingling of semantic, syntactic, and purely phonetic consistencies, was all the regularity they needed.[24] *We* need more, because we believe these are biblical "poems," and this belief entails some notion of poetic structure.

Lowth's presentation of paralleism, at once insightful and yet conservative in the claims it made, was nevertheless the prisoner of the notion of biblical "poetry." As a result, a sick symbiosis has grown from it. Some have continued in his belief that Hebrew poetry is metrical. At the same time, even those who reject this path have not been led to question the idea of biblical poetry, for Lowth's discovery has become, in their eyes, a substitute for meter. Thus, while some poetry is written "in meter" (or "in rhyme"), biblical poetry is written "in parallelism."[25] Presented differently, Lowth's discovery might

24. Here one encounters the frequent objection that the fact of their being sung, or being set to instrumental accompaniment (as witnessed by many passages), requires one to suppose some structural regularity, some *system*, in the words of the Psalms, etc. To this whole question of music we shall turn in the following chapter. For now let it suffice to observe that this argument is quite mistaken. As noted above, *any* text—the U.S. Constitution, the Manhattan telephone book, the warranty of a clock-radio—can be sung or set to music. Indeed, a proof of this in the present case is close at hand: in the course of a year the entire Pentateuch—its genealogies, sanctuary measurements, and inventories, and so forth, as well as its songs—plus liberal selections from the histories, Prophets, and hagiographa, are all musically rendered in the regular synagogue service.

25. T. H. Robinson, "Basic Principles of Hebrew Poetic Form" (*Festschrift A. Bertholet* [Tübingen, 1950]): "If the form be non-metrical, it may still be a form, with definite rules which the poet observed. . . . Parallelism is not merely a matter of style, any more than is the alliteration of Anglo-Saxon verses. It is the principle which controls the form which every line of Hebrew poetry takes, and though in our existing poems it may exhibit various types, and even be, in its strictest sense, absent from individual lines, yet the outward form which it produces is still there, and unless there is some trace of it we cannot speak of a passage of Hebrew being poetic at all." But the difference between parallelism and Anglo-Saxon alliteration is precisely that the latter *is* always there. Robinson's last sentence is an admission that parallelism is "in its strictest sense, absent from individual lines," that is, it is the predominance of parallelism in a passage that qualifies it as poetry, rather than the presence of parallelism in each line. (By "outward form" he means, presumably, the binary structure—but even this is no sine qua non, as we have seen.) Had he cast his eyes to some of the clear parallelism-amid-"prose" seen above, or to the intermediate, quasi-parallelistic passages of the sort to be examined below, he would have come up still more strikingly against our problem.

long ago have led critics away from the metrical hypothesis entirely
and brought about a reexamination of the nature of the texts
themselves: what is the difference between what is called biblical
poetry and biblical prose?

4

In various ways, the Bible's disquieting refusal to present some
clearly defined "poetic structure" has been reflected in the rhetorical
and stylistic theories of the last hundred years. This is true even of
metrical speculation: Eduard Sievers eventually concluded that most
of the Bible was "poetry," and this led him to extend his scansion
system to such "prose" books as Genesis and Exodus. The same is
true of the more recent metrical theories of Arvid Bruno. George
Buchanan Gray, who also believed, with somewhat less conviction, in
biblical meter, nevertheless wondered if some intermediate category
might be created between prose and poetry to describe the evidence of
parallelism he found unmistakable in biblical narrative:

> Had then the ancient Hebrew three forms of composition—metrical
> poetry and plain prose, and an intermediate type differing from
> poetry by the absence of metre, and from prose by obedience to
> certain laws governing the mutual relations between its clauses—a
> type for which we might as makeshifts employ the terms unmetrical
> poetry or parallelistic prose?[26]

More recently, observations of the sort that prompted this remark
have led critics to suppose that the Bible contains "poetic fragments"
left over from a now-lost poetic version of the biblical histories.[27] For
example, John Gray writes:

> It may well be that we have the trace of an original saga in the
> revelation to Abraham in Gen. 12:1–3, which is in verse:

לך לך מארצך וממולדתך ומבית אביך

אל הארץ אשר אראך

ואעשך לגוי גדול ואברכך

ואגדלה שמך והיה ברכה

ואברכה מברכיך ומקלך אאר

---

26. G. B. Gray, *Forms of Hebrew Poetry* (repub. New York, 1972), p. 46.

27. See, e.g., *YGC*, pp. 30, 33; J. L. Myers, *The Literary and Linguistic Form of the Book of Ruth* (Leiden, 1955); O. Loretz, "Poetische Abschnitte im Rut-Buch," *UF* 7 (1975): 580–82, and even L. Alonso-Schökel in "Poésie Hébraique" (DBS) 52–53.

(וְנִבְרְכוּ בְךָ כֹּל מִשְׁפְּחֹת הָאֲדָמָה)

The verse form seems to take us back to a very early stage in the tradition . . . primitive patriarchal or tribal sagas in verse after the style of the Krt text of Ugarit.[28]

Now there is little doubt that Israel did have some saga texts that have not survived.[29] But to see in every instance of parallelism in Genesis another fragment of some "long-lost original" seems all too convenient. Nor will this account for the less obvious, but still more common, forms of "seconding" in Genesis, nor indeed for parallelism in far later narrative books of the Bible. Furthermore, one wonders why an ancient, sacred, "poetic" text would be abandoned and recast as "prose"—and this at a time when reading and writing were still relatively rare commodities! Certainly literary history of later periods abounds in examples of the precise opposite.

The "lost poetic version" theory is really just another way of dealing with the same problem noticed by Gray and Sievers. Even if it could explain some instances of parallelism within prose, it can hardly make a dent in the overall phenomenon, whose extent has been masked until recently by a reluctance to look deeply into the structure of biblical "prose" sentences.

The issue is most obvious, and most troublesome, in the prophetic books, particularly Jeremiah and Ezekiel. Readers familiar with Kittel's *Biblia Hebraica* or other editions which attempt to distinguish typographically between prose and poetry know the confusing mishmash which this attempted distinction can produce: the text lurches from prose into poetry and back to prose, sometimes within a single sentence. In the case of Jeremiah, critics since B. Duhm have recognized different "sources" or "types" of texts within the book—viz., (1) "poetic" oracles and sayings, (2) biographical prose, and (3) "rhetorical" prose discourses.[30] The last category, which is often compared to the style of the book of Deuteronomy,[31] is characterized now and again by some of the same things attributed to "poetry"—paralleling, balancing clauses, fixed pairs, *yqtl-qtl* alternation, and the like. Editions and commentators that distinguish between "prose" and "poetry" are frequently troubled by this third class of utterance in Jeremiah. Take, as a by no means isolated example, Jeremiah 30:6–11 as it appears in Kittel:[32]

---

28. John Gray, *Legacy of Canaan* (Leiden, 1965), p. 308.
29. See Eissfeldt, *OTI*, pp. 132–34.
30. See on this John Bright, *Jeremiah* (New York, 1965), pp. lx–lxxv.
31. But see ibid.
32. Bright's edition follows Kittel's division.

⁶שַׁאֲלוּ־נָא וּרְאוּ אִם־יֹלֵד זָכָר
מַדּוּעַ רָאִיתִי כָל־גֶּבֶר יָדָיו עַל־חֲלָצָיו כַּיּוֹלֵדָה
וְנֶהֶפְכוּ כָל־פָּנִים לְיֵרָקוֹן: ⁷הוֹי
כִּי גָדוֹל הַיּוֹם הַהוּא מֵאַיִן כָּמֹהוּ
וְעֵת־צָרָה הִיא לְיַעֲקֹב וּמִמֶּנָּה יִוָּשֵׁעַ:
⁸וְהָיָה בַיּוֹם הַהוּא נְאֻם ה' צְבָאוֹת אֶשְׁבֹּר עֻלּוֹ מֵעַל צַוָּארֶךָ
וּמוֹסְרוֹתֶיךָ אֲנַתֵּק וְלֹא־יַעַבְדוּ־בוֹ עוֹד זָרִים: ⁹וְעָבְדוּ אֶת ה'
אֱלֹהֵיהֶם וְאֵת דָּוִד מַלְכָּם אֲשֶׁר אָקִים לָהֶם:
¹⁰וְאַתָּה אַל־תִּירָא עַבְדִּי יַעֲקֹב נְאֻם־ה' וְאַל־תֵּחַת יִשְׂרָאֵל
כִּי הִנְנִי מוֹשִׁיעֲךָ מֵרָחוֹק וְאֶת־זַרְעֲךָ מֵאֶרֶץ שִׁבְיָם
וְשָׁב יַעֲקֹב וְשָׁקַט וְשַׁאֲנַן וְאֵין מַחֲרִיד:
¹¹כִּי־אִתְּךָ אֲנִי נְאֻם־ה' לְהוֹשִׁיעֶךָ
כִּי אֶעֱשֶׂה כָלָה בְּכָל־הַגּוֹיִם אֲשֶׁר הֲפִצוֹתִיךָ שָּׁם
אַךְ אֹתְךָ לֹא אֶעֱשֶׂה כָלָה וְיִסַּרְתִּיךָ לַמִּשְׁפָּט וְנַקֵּה לֹא
אֲנַקֶּךָּ:

It is easy to see why 30:8 suggested "prose" to editors and commentators, especially with its "rubric" beginning. Still, there is a certain parallelistic balance in:

אשבר עלו מעל צוארך / ומוסרותיך אנתק //
ולא יעברו בו עוד זרים / ועברו את ה' אלהיהם //
ואת דוד מלכם / אשר אקים להם //

I will break the yoke off your neck / and your shackles I will snap //
And no longer shall they serve foreigners / but they will serve the Lord their God //
And [serve] their Davidic king / whom I shall appoint for them //

And on the other hand, what of the adjacent "poetry"? Here, as elsewhere, typography is deceptive: for example—

ואתה אל תירא עבדי יעקב / נאם ה' / ואל תחת ישראל //

But you, do not be afraid, Jacob my servant / says the Lord / nor be dismayed, Israel //

This is hardly a regular three-membered verse. The first clause is long enough to be subdivided, and probably would have been were it not for the fact that "says the Lord" would then also have to be subjoined to it, making a "tricolon," which would then leave an isolated but obviously paralleling "nor be dismayed Israel" to fend for itself. So instead we have the very long initial clause, the interruptive attribution, and a third clause which parallels the first. Is this poetry? And if so, what distinguishes it from the above "prose"? So it is that W. L. Holladay and others have rightly, and impressively, questioned the categorizations of certain sections of Jeremiah and other prophets.[33]

But the question is not so much *which* category is correct as it is *what* are the categories in the first place. This "rhetorical prose" of Jeremiah, Ezekiel, and Deuteronomistic passages of other books is indeed noticeably different from, say, the elliptical parallelistic lines of Job or Proverbs; it is different, though generally less noticeably, from the "poetic" oracles of the same Jeremiah, Ezekiel, et al. But what *is* it?

כי הרויתי נפש עיפה וכל־נפש דאבה מלאתי: 26על־זאת הקיצתי ואראה
ושנתי ערבה לי: 27הנה ימים באים נאם־ה' וזרעתי את־בית ישראל ואת־
בית יהודה זרע אדם וזרע בהמה: 28והיה כאשר שקדתי עליהם לנתוש
ולנתוץ ולהרס ולהאביד ולהרע כן אשקד עליהם לבנות ולנטוע נאם־ה':

Jer. 31:25(24)–28(27)

For I relieve the weary soul, and every longing soul I fulfill. 26. So I have woken up and seen, and my sleep was pleasing to me. 27. For the time is coming, word of the Lord, when I will sow the house of Israel and the house of Judah, the seed of man and the seed of beast. 28. And just as I have been zealous with them to rip and tear, to sunder, destroy and cause suffering—so will I be zealous with them to build and to plant, word of the Lord.

I have not wanted to prejudice the reading of the above typographically (Kittel treats it as prose), but certainly there are lines whose parallelism is unmistakable:

כי הרויתי נפש עיפה / וכל נפש דאבה מלאתי //

For I relieve the weary soul / and every longing soul I fulfill //

Indeed, Kittel himself does not hesitate to divide as poetry a very similar verse which, however, occurs in a "poetic" context:

כי השביע נפש שקקה / ונפש רעבה מלא טוב //

For he satisfies the longing soul / and the hungering soul he fills with
goodness //   Psalm 107:9

At the same time, the last verse of our passage, stated in almost any other form, would have been *more* parallelistic than it is. In its actual wording the two parallel units of this verse are far too long to

33. W. L. Holladay, "Prototypes and Copies: A New Approach to the Prose-Poetry Problem in the Book of Jeremiah," *JBL* 79 (1960): 351–67; "The Recovery of Poetic Passages of Jeremiah," *JBL* 85 (1966): 401–35; also idem in *VT* 12 (1962): 494 and *VT* 16 (1966): 53–64; Hans Kosmala, *VT* 14 (1964): 423; *VT* 16 (1966): 152.

fit even the broad limits seen in the Psalter, and the catalogue of
five verbs of destruction is apposed to two verbs of building. Why
could it not have said

> As I have been zealous with them to destroy / so will I be zealous with
> them to build //
> As I have uprooted and torn / so will I plant and make flourish //

were parallelism the desired end?

Most surprising are critical assessments such as the following:

> It must be admitted that the prose of Jeremiah—particularly that
> of the prose discourses . . . —is not, at least to our taste, the best
> of which the ancient Hebrew was capable. It is a rather inflated
> style. It lacks the terse stylistic economy of the classic prose of
> the "Golden Age" (tenth century)—such as we find, for example,
> in the stories of Saul and David in the books of Samuel—and is,
> if not without a certain rhetorical eloquence, repetitious and
> wordy and, moreover, loaded with stereotyped expressions.[34]

Elsewhere the same author expresses astonishment that "some of
the noblest passages in the book (the Temple Sermon in VII 1–15
and the New Covenant passage in XXXI 31–34, to mention only
two) are couched in this rather pedestrian 'Deuteronomistic' style."[35]
But this is hardly believable. Certainly one capable of the highest
use of the Hebrew language would not elsewhere frame his message
in a "repetitious and wordy" manner if that was, indeed, how this
style was perceived. And should a critic claim, as some have, that
these "prose sermons" are not the work of the prophet himself but a
reconstruction made by his disciples,[36] let it be admitted that any
Tel Aviv high school student today would be capable of turning the
"Temple Sermon" into strict parallelisms. It is a most incredible
thesis to suggest these verses were once in a higher, more pleasing
form, but in the process of being "remembered, understood and
repeated" fell into a prolixity utterly out of keeping with the
original. On the contrary, "terse stylistic economy" tends to be
remembered exactly—in fact, where it is originally absent the
memory, or tradition, tends to invent it. Even if Jeremiah's exact
words had been forgotten, certainly something similarly pithy would

34. Bright, *Jeremiah*, p. lxxv.
35. Ibid., p. lxxi.
36. Ibid.: "Though the prose tradition of Jeremiah doubtless had its origin in his
preaching, it does not record that preaching verbatim, but rather as it was
remembered, understood and repeated in the circle of his followers."

have replaced them—*if that had been their form.* Instead of the
"poor style" of these passages, it is the commentator we must fault,
and the whole set of assumptions he brings to bear in this stylistic
assessment.[37]

Over the past century, more and more texts of all sorts have been
recognized as poetic and "quasi-poetic." Form criticism has pointed
up structural patterns in oracles and genealogies; testaments, cultic
sayings, and the like[38] have fallen within the purview of biblical
"poetry." The stereotyping that once limited poetry to those genres
which had ready Occidental poetic correspondents has had to
recede in the face of hard examination. But this has left present-day
students in a quandary. A recent study is forced to wrestle with the
poetry-prose distinction, and its struggle is revealing:

> Every poetic text in the Bible is built on these two prosodic
> structures, rhythm and parallelism. Yet it must be noted that one
> does in some places find parallelism alone (without meter) or
> meter alone (without parallelism). There are especially many of
> this latter sort. Our criterion for classifying a text as poetic will
> be the presence of at least one of these two fundamental conven-
> tions. . . . We do sometimes find [in prose] verses or whole
> sections capable of being divided into more or less "balanced"
> units [in which] the principle of poetic meter, i.e. the existence of
> verse halves of an equal number of "lifts," is also apparent. . . .
> Yet we have decided *not* to include these passages [among the
> "poetry"] not only because in metered prose there is not the
> same measure of exactitude and regularity as in poetry . . . but
> also because there is no escape from the many textual emenda-
> tions necessary to achieve a reasonable measure of rhythmical
> harmony within prosaic parts.[39]

37. On the whole matter of "stereotyped expression" see chapter 1, section 7. In
some books, many such "stereotypes" (apart from their obvious aesthetic appeal) are
in fact internal citations, or allusions to well-known oracles, proverbs, or laws. R.
Gordis discusses this phenomenon in *Koheleth: The Man and His World* (New
York, 1968), and in his *Poets, Prophets, and Sages* (Bloomington, Ind., 1971), pp.
104–59.

38. See Eissfeldt, *OTI*, 64–86.

39. R. Sappan, *Typical Features of the Syntax of Biblical Poetry in its Classical
Period* (Ph.D. dissertation, Jerusalem, 1975; in Hebrew), pp. 59–60. Another recent
study of syntax, F. I. Andersen's *The Sentence in Biblical Hebrew*, speaks of an
"epic prose" in the Bible which is sometimes characterized by "the use of the same
vocabulary (repetitive parallelism), or it may use conventional synonyms (synonymous

If this seems not a little inconsistent, the author should not be faulted for more than showing the inappropriateness of the categories he wields—"parallelism" (too narrowly understood), meter, and most of all, "poetry."

Prophetic books, as noted, pinpoint the problem, for it is here that one encounters passages of intermittent semantic paralleling and artful repetitions amidst other lines lacking any obvious desire to parallel or even employ the terse style that often accompanies parallelism. One recent study of unusually systematic methodology[40] has pointed out the multifarious paralleling that exists within a passage normally called "prose" in Jeremiah. The case is well made—but then the author goes on to urge the passage henceforth be regarded as "poetry"! This is most emphatically *not* the point. For despite all the correspondences and paralleling he adduces, one is left with the validity of the original observation which classified it as *different* from the pithy, highly parallelistic "poetry" of Jeremiah. Certainly the style is less intense, less symmetrical, less semantically parallelistic—why? Doubtless not because parallelism is so exacting a "form" that it can be achieved only now and again! Though he will answer in the negative, one might pause at the question his own study raises in this author's mind: "In looking for poetry with such means as I have here suggested, will we not find that we can make 'poetry' of any given passage of Hebrew?"[41]

Another writer, having treated the Septuagint version of the list of nations in Jeremiah 25:18–26 (=LXX 32:4–12) as a poetic text, notes:

> Objections may be raised regarding the reconstruction of a prosaic list of nations in a form which suggests poetic composition. It should be noted, however, that lists do appear elsewhere in poetic contexts, such as the list of Moabite cities in Jer. 48:21–24 . . . Moreover the [surrounding] prose context in which th[is] list of nations is found contains evidence of an original poetic tradition.[42]

---

parallelism), which often come in an established sequence" (p. 43). He asserts that Genesis "is neither poetry nor prose, but epic composition containing both poetic devices and extended rhetorical structures" (p. 124). At the same time he notes: "The addition of an equivalent clause in apposition may be used in [non-epic] prose to underscore an important point. The effect is real, but incidental."

40. W. L. Holladay, in *JBL* 85 (1966): 401–35.

41. Ibid., pp. 433–34.

42. D. L. Christensen, *Transformations of the War Oracle in OT Prophecy* (Harvard Dissertations in Religion, Scholars Press, Missoula, Mont., 1975), pp. 200–01.

Note that in this list it is not the presence of semantic parallelism that has suggested "poetry" to the author, but the balancing clauses and the syntactically similar handling of material in sucessive lines.

One recent article, focusing squarely on the problem of classification observes:

It is no more possible to draw a clear division between the characteristics of poetic style and prose than between "poetic" vocabulary and "prosaic" vocabulary. Poetry raises to the utmost the possibilities of normal speech: these verbal creations of the poetic idiom then turn back towards the language of artistic prose or of ordinary prose, or of conversational speech. . . . Stylistic devices . . . *by their frequency and their force,* are a sign of poetic language. Meeting them in prose, we feel an unexpected poetic resonance.[43]

The perceptions that stand behind these remarks are surely acute. Yet one is moved to wonder precisely how much "unexpected poetic resonance" is required before prose drifts into poetry. More pointedly, is the difference perceived here even one that properly corresponds to our normal distinction of poetry and prose? The same question emerges in regard to recent statistical analyses which seek to discriminate between poetry and prose by examining the density of various lexical, morphological or syntactic features: where the percentages are high, there is poetry; where low, prose. The conclusion that such studies tend to draw is that "the distinction is often quantitative rather than qualitative, and in terms of degree rather than kind."[44] But moreover this whole approach should suggest that there is nothing absolute about the stylistic poles distinguished— that, in this respect most of all, the very identifying of one extreme of parallelistic, terse, elliptical sentences as "poetry" and their opposite as "prose" is in some basic way misleading.

"Rhythmical prose," "now-lost poetic sagas," "unmetrical poetry," "parallelistic prose," "poetic resonance" are all symptomatic. At the root of these commentators' difficulty is the polarity itself, and it is a difficulty that will not go away. One writer, having noted in the

43. L. Alonso-Schökel, *s.v.* "Poésie hébraique," in *DBS* Fasc. 42, pp. 56–57 (emphasis added).

44. D. N. Freedman, "Pottery, Poetry, and Prophecy: An Essay on Biblical Poetry," *JBL* 96 (1977): 6. In addition to the studies by Y. T. Radday and others mentioned by Freedman, cf. studies of word distribution, sentence length, and the like, or investigations of syntax such as D. R. Hillers, "Observations on Syntax and Meter in Lamentations," in H. N. Bream, *A Light unto My Path* (Philadelphia, 1974), pp. 265–70.

Amarna letters verbal alternations of the sort "so familiar from
Ugaritic and biblical poetry," finds their presence in letters an
"invaluable witness to the diffuseness and serviceability of the
Canaanite literary idiom"—an observation that might, somewhat
uncharitably perhaps, be translated as: what's a poetic device doing in
some administrative correspondence?[45] Another writer finds parallelism so strongly rooted in Canaanite and Israelite poetry "that it
influenced even prose in the case of both, as may be observed,
especially in direct speech in the Old Testament and in the letters
from Canaanite rulers in the Amarna Tablets."[46] F. M. Cross
pronounces a genealogical inscription found at Tell Siran "a poetic
cliché, a triplet" in which one finds "parallel formulae which echo in
contemporary biblical literature."[47] Elsewhere he notes the mixing of
"prose" and "poetry" in Ugaritic, holding, for example, that
introductory phrases "sometimes . . . are in poetry, sometimes in
prose."[48]

M. Dahood wishes to use parallel pair words as a criterion for
poetry,[49] but the same pairs abound in Hebrew and Ugaritic "prose."
Cyrus Gordon, discussing clause length, notes: "There is an interplay
between prose and poetry. Even in an administrative text a scribe may
be impelled to make his last entry climactic."[50] Another writer
remarks: "The Phoenician inscriptions, and the El Amarna letters,
are non-literary creations, [but] from between th[eir] lines peek
fragments of poetry and proverbs, word- and expression-pairs and
special verb forms coming from the treasure troves of Canaanite
literature."[51] Another writer remarks on the "rhythmical or poetic
quality" of the narrative in Genesis 11, finding verse 1 "a well-formed
bicolon," verse 3 "two synonymous bicola," etc.[52] Examples could be
multiplied for pages.

45. S. Gevirtz, "Evidence of Conjugational Variation in the Parallelization of
Selfsame Verbs in the Amarna Letters," *JNES* 32 (1973): 104.

46. John Gray, *Legacy of Canaan*, p. 293.

47. F. M. Cross, "Notes on an Ammonite Inscription from Tell Siran," *BASOR*
212 (Dec. 1973): 12.

48. "Prose and Poetry in the Mythic and Epic Texts from Ugarit," *HTR* 67
(1974): 1.

49. Thus *RSP* 1, p. 74, n. 10; p. 80.

50. *UT*, pp. 133–34.

51. Y. Avishur, "Studies of Stylistic Features Common to the Phoenician
Inscriptions and the Bible," *UF* 7 (1975), 13.

52. I. M. Kikawada, "The Shape of Gen. 11:1–9," in J. Jackson, et al.,
Rhetorical Criticism of the Bible (Pittsburgh, 1974), p. 20. See also J. Muilenberg

5

If one puts aside the notions of biblical poetry and prose and tries to look afresh at different parts of the Bible to see what it is about them that distinguishes one from another, it will soon be apparent that there are not two modes of utterance, but many different elements which elevate style and provide for formality and strictness of organization. Consistently binary sentences, an obvious regard for terseness, and a high degree of semantic parallelism characterize some sections; less consistent (and less consistently semantic) parallelism is found in other parts; some narrative sections (as we have seen above) are basically built of short, simple clauses but lack correspondences between them; still others show little regularity in clause length and sentence structure. This represents a continuum of organization or formality, with parallelism of different intensity and consistency characterizing a great span of texts.

It may strike the reader as perverse to refuse simply to call the relative concentration of heightening factors "poetry" and their relative absence "prose." But the burden of proof falls on the other side. For the distinction between "poetry" and "prose" is, as noted, not native to the texts: it is a Hellenistic imposition based, at least originally, on the faulty notion that parts of the Bible were metrical (indeed, written in Greek-style hexameter and trimeter!). Although this original basis now seems absurd, the idea it supported has remained; and, like so many Hellenisms—for example, the equation of Hebrew *torah* with Greek *nomos*—it is only approximately true. To see biblical style through the split lens of prose or poetry is to distort the view; then even an awareness of parallelism will not much improve things, for it too will be distorted in the process.

---

on repetition as a characteristic that "extends beyond its expression in poetry," *SVT* 1 (Leiden, 1953): 100. Also symptomatic: "Elsewhere in the Bible there are curses by the handfuls, especially in Leviticus 26 and Deuteronomy 28. . . . At points the curses are metrical and form a grim ditty:

"The maid that you wed
You will ne'er take to bed.
You will build a fine home
But in exile you'll roam.
You will plant a vine,
But not drink the wine."

(from D. R. Hillers, *Covenant: the History of a Biblical Idea*, Baltimore, 1969, pp. 53–55).

The reason that commentators have, since Hellenistic times, been unable to pin down "seconding" and its epitome, the parallelistic pair, is that these do not correspond to anything in their native rhetoric. Biblical parallelism is not a meter, although *materiae metricae* are affected by it; it is not consistent enough to be compared accurately to any of our well-known structures. At the same time, it would be incorrect to call parallelism a rhetorical figure or trope—though, as we shall see, this was commonly done by the Church Fathers. It was more like *the* trope, the one shape of elevated speech, "A is so, [and] B is so." The more intense the correspondence between clauses, the more obvious the structuredness, hence the formality, of the style. Thus a terse, syntactically differentiated, parallelistic couplet:

צדיק כתמר יפרח / כארז בלבנון ישגה //

The righteous man flourishes like a palm tree / like a cedar in Lebanon he grows great //   Psalm 92:13

is the summum, the highest form of heightening. It stands out from among lesser approximations of this ideal, lines of less obvious semantic parallelism or closural "click." But the biblical skyline has buildings of all shapes and sizes; a stylistic analysis of a passage must properly take into account the relative intensity and formality of each line. For this reason too, the categories of prose and poetry imply too sharp, and total, a polarity: to use only these terms is to describe sections of the skyline as consisting either of "building" or "no building."

Of course, there is a case to be made for the use of the term "poetry" in regard to some parts of the Bible. It has, as noted, an approximate validity, and is sanctioned by a centuries-old tradition. But it is not a perfect fit; and since ancient Israel seems to have gotten along without any corresponding term, it might be better for modern critics to enclose the phrase "biblical poetry," at least mentally, in quotation marks. Indeed, as far as the study of biblical style is concerned, it might well have been better if Robert Lowth had chosen differently and declared *parallelismus membrorum* to be (as in Greek) a feature of prose style, that is, claimed (as some of his Jewish predecessors had) that poetry in ancient Hebrew simply does not exist. For he then would have been left free to observe different levels and intensities of parallel structure, and observe it not just where he felt "poetry" ought to be found,[53] but throughout the Bible. And it

53. Lowth of course saw his own achievement as that of having restored the Prophets—excluded since the early Church from the "poetic" corpus because they

would then have been clear that this biblical "prose," that is, "common speech on its best behavior," consists not (as in English) in the judicious arrangement of long and short sentences, the employment of familiar motifs of subordination, and so forth, but in variations on an ideal form, _____ / _____ //, variations whose formality, whose "structuredness," increases with the intensity of the correspondence established between the clauses. Although the term "prose" has its own disadvantages, its use would have at least clarified this one main point: passages are not either written "in parallelism" or "not in parallelism," but they are elevated with respect to the frequency and intensity of this idealized norm.

6

Allusion has already been made to the terseness that characterizes many of the same passages in which parallelism is most visible. For terseness too is a form of heightening in biblical style, indeed, one of the most striking and commonly used. It amounts to far more than the concision and compression of expression that one associates with poetry. It is more reminiscent of "telegraph style" ("Urge support tax reform package for increase housing starts 1980") or the elliptical language of some popular sayings ("Red sky at morning, sailor take warning"), in which some of the signposts of ordinary discourse have been stripped away.

In our presentation of the characteristics of the parallelistic line, we stressed the brevity of the clauses and their semantic simplicity. Three or four words per clause is common—often no more than a simple subject and predicate. This is a striking uniqueness, certainly as noticeable in its effect as the parallelism that usually accompanies it:

נטית ימינך תבלעמו ארץ / נחית בחסדך עם זו גאלת /

נהלת בעזך אל נוה קדשך //

שמעו עמים ירגזון / חיל אחז ישבי פלשת //

You-stretched your-hand earth swallowed-them / you-led in-your-love people that you-saved / you-direct in-your-strength to dwellings of-your-holiness //

Peoples heard were-excited / trembling seized dwellers of Pĕlāšet //

Exod. 15:12–14

---

did not suit Greco-Roman notions of artful creation—to their rightful place among the "poets." See his Lecture 20, "General Characteristics of the Prophetic Poetry," and esp. *SP*, pp. 168–70.

yet it tends to be overlooked or explained in some other way. (Indeed, the impression of metricality in many compositions comes from this feature which, if it is neither expressible in strict numbers or even a general rule, nevertheless imposes broad limits on the length and syntactic complexity of the clauses.)

Now terseness is hardly a characteristic of all seconding sentences, or even the most obvious semantic parallelisms, in the Bible. There are many lines, like Jeremiah 30:10 seen above (which, as far as seconding is concerned, ought to be broken

ואתה אל תירא עבדי יעקב נאם ה' / ואל תחת ישראל //

And you, do not fear, my servant Jacob, word of the Lord / nor be dismayed, Israel //)

which are clearly parallelistic and yet "unterse." Indeed, as is evident upon examination, paralleling and more generally seconding of all sorts function in sermonic discourses and other texts in units somewhat longer and wordier (and often, as above, less symmetrical) than in proverbs and some songs. The stylistic difference we feel so keenly between a passage like Numbers 5:12–15 (above) and Psalm 23 rests not on semantic parallelism or seconding, both of which are, if anything, more pronounced in the former, but on the terse "telegraph style" of the latter.

So it is evident that terseness ought to be treated on its own as a heightening feature of biblical style, separable (and often separate) from parallelism. At the same time it is important to treat it for what it is, a variously manifested standard. Studies of syntax,[54] or attempts to reduce terseness to metrical formulae, fail just as we should fail if we tried to express the principle governing the style of telegrams in formulae concerned with length alone ("no more than X words per sentence") or syntax: everything is variable, but the standard of terseness, like the telegram-taker's word count, exerts a constant pressure toward concision and ellipsis.

54. That of Sappan (*Typical Features*), while contributing valuable insights, suffers precisely from the narrowness of its focus (as well as its confusion of the poetry-prose question cited above). This leads him to such assertions as, "Almost all the syntactic phenomena that occur in prose are also found in poetry" (p. 3). Where he is strongest and most useful from our standpoint is in matters touching on differentiation, for in demonstrating the "distributional equivalence" at a "deep" level of semantically and morphologically differentiated elements, he shows this differentiation to be a kind of conscious tinkering—it is not their congruence that is coincidental, nor are parallel ideas put into equivalent forms, but "deeply" similar syntactic structures are differentiated as to their immediate constituents.

The latter is as significant as the former, for terseness is as much a matter of grammatical and other omissions as it is of overall clause length and syntax. This is most prominently true of the use of the definite article, *ha-*,[55] which is often omitted in terse texts—*šāmayīm* instead of *haššāmayīm*, *rašaᶜ* instead of *hārašaᶜ*. Thus:

שפטו דל ויתום / עני ורש הצדיקו //

Take-the-side of *the* needy and *the* orphan / *the* poor and *the* downtrodden protect /

Psalm 82:3

Often its absence seems to be compensated by using constructs or personal suffixes, thus:

אל תבטחו בנדיבים / בבן אדם שאין לו תשועה //

תצא רוחו ישב לאדמתו / ביום ההוא אבדו עשתנתיו //

Do not rely on officials / on any powerless human being //

When his breath departs he returns to *his* earth/ on that very day his projects disappear //

Psalm 146:3–4

where "his earth" seems to substitute for the more normal "the earth."[56]

Of course *ha-* ellipsis is allied with "differentiation" and with the establishment of patterns of apparent dependency between successive clauses.[57] The phenomenon of apparently random possessives in combination with this ellipsis is striking, especially in the so-called Wisdom books, as has already been seen in our verses:

---

55. The development of the definite article came relatively late in Northwest Semitic languages and took different forms. The position adopted by Albright (see, e.g., *JBL* 61 [1942]: 117; *JBL* 63 [1944]: 216) and some of his students (see F. M. Cross and D. N. Freedman in *Biblica* 53 [1972]: 418–19) has been to suggest that the relative newcomer *ha-* is rare in early "poetic" texts both because of the "conservatism" of poetic style and because the loss of case endings in Canaanite languages and the introduction of *ha-* had the makings of a "prosodic revolution" that was sporadically resisted for a while. But this historical explanation will not explain the ellipsis in late prophetic writings or indeed the latest parts of the canon, nor the *inconsistent* ellipsis of *ha-* in all periods. D. A. Robertson, *Linguistic Evidence in Dating Early Hebrew Poetry* (Ph.D. dissertation, New Haven, 1966), p. 5, n. 3, notes the frequent ellipses of את, the relative pronoun אשר, and the definite article, "all of which are rare in the greatest portion of biblical poetry of whatever date." Cf. Freedman, "Pottery, Poetry, and Prophecy," p. 7.

56. Here the fact of the loss of case-endings in Canaanite languages is perhaps not irrelevant. Cf. the seventeenth century English writing convention, "Richard his house," which misunderstands the genitive "Richard's house."

57. See above, p. 54.

טוב שם משמן טוב / ויום המות מיום הולדו //

Better a name than good oil / and the day of death than the day of *his*
birth /   Eccles. 7:1

בן חכם ישמח אב / ובן כסיל תוגת אמו //

Wise son makes father glad / but foolish son grieves even *his* mother //
                                                                       Prov. 10:1

Finally, one should note the difficulty in determining the extent of this
ellipsis, for in its elided form the definite article is not represented in
the consonantal text. Where the Masoretic vocalization indicates
such a definite article (thus, Psalm 146:7 נתן לחם לרעבים וג') we may
perhaps question the tradition, especially in the presence of widespread
ellipsis in the surrounding verses. In its unelided form, in any case,
ha- is often conspicuously absent. It occurs not once in the entire
Song of the Sea (Exodus15), only once in the first chapter of
Proverbs, and so forth.

Other forms of ellipsis have been mentioned in the previous chapter
and have received detailed consideration elsewhere.[58] They include:

1. Omission of indicators that would normally specify subordinations:

יקראני ואענהו / עמו אנכי בצרה //

When he calls me I answer him / with him am I in distress //
                                                                       Psalm 91:15

2. Omission of relative אשר:

אבן מאסו הבונים / היתה לראש פנה //

[The] stone the builders rejected / became the corner-piece //
                                                                       Psalm 118:22

3. Omission of personal suffixes with nouns, verbs, prepositions:

אודה ה' בכל לבב

I praise the Lord with all [my] heart . . .   Psalm 111:1

4. Ellipsis of particles:

מה אנוש כי תזכרנו / ובן אדם כי תפקדנו //

What is man that [or "yet"] you remember him / and [*what* is]a human
being, that you take note of him? //   Psalm 8:5

5. Ellipsis of "and"—occasionally in a single phrase, as perhaps "sun
moon" in Hab. 3:11 (though שמש may belong to the previous verse),

---

58. See *Psalms III*, "Grammar of the Psalter," and Dahood's student A. C. M.
Blommerde, *Northwest Semitic Grammar and Job* (Rome, 1969), pp. 34–35.

but more frequently omitted between clauses; see, for example, the song of Asaph (1 Chron. 16:8 ff.). Psalm 93 contains not a single "and."

6. Ellipsis of thematic connectives: The foregoing ellipses consist of the omission of expected morphological or syntactic indicators, or of the substitution of an unexpected one for the usual one. Another striking sort of ellipsis is that already discussed in the previous chapter, the leaving unstated of a rather complex relationship between clauses, as in our "sharp" reading of Ecclesiastes 7:1. This sort of terseness is evident as well in the lack of specified connection between successive lines of a given passage (chapter 1.10). Many psalms and songs seem to be more a collection of individual "one-liners" than unified compositions: even the famous shepherd imagery of Psalm 23, elaborated over several lines, is suddenly interrupted by "You spread a table . . . you annoint my head"—actions hardly appropriate for a shepherd to perform on behalf of his sheep! And when an interlinear connection is present, it is nevertheless usually couched in a style which seems to deny it:

האזינו השמים ואדברה / ותשמע הארץ אמרי פי //
יערף כמטר לקחי / תזל כטל אמרתי //
כשעירם עלי דשא / וכרביבים עלי עשב //

Listen O Heavens, and let me speak / and hear, Earth, my words //
Let my lesson fall as rain / my speech distill as dew //
Like storm-drops on grass / like soft drops on greenery //

Deut. 32:1–3

Moses' words are compared to waters that flow from Heaven to Earth: rain and dew are symbolic of Divine blessing,[59] and, more precisely, a *figura* of poetic speech (cf. Isa. 55:10–11). The third line above will thus be seen to culminate a single, elaborate metaphor: the grass and greenery nourished by rain and dew represent those who listen to "my words." But note how each line is *couched in separateness:* even the third, which in its sense follows directly from the second, has found new pair-words corresponding to the second's "rain" and "dew"[60] and the particle *k-* is repeated twice more—it is as if a whole new

---

59. Cf. *PEPI*, pp. 35–36.

60. I believe שעירם is here associated with סערה ("storm") because some of the prophetic discourse is to be דברי תוכחה ("reproach"); the ending is comparable to gentle dew (for the association of רביבים with dew, see Mic. 5:6, Psalm 72:6) in that it is נחמה, consolation. Both were standard prophetic genres. Cf. N. H. Snaith, "The Meaning of שעירם," *VT* 25 (1975): 116. For the connection between reproach and hard rain, cf. the folk etymology of rain יורה (Deut. 11:14) as "teacher" in b. *Ta'anit* 6a and Rashi ad loc.

comparison were being offered, instead of the original one elaborated.
Now of course this is connected to our form:

$$\underline{\hspace{2cm}} / \underline{\hspace{2cm}} //$$

The very essence of the second pause is that it makes for such end-
stopping. But there is more involved: the fact is that very often there *is*
little connection between one verse and the next, and when such
connection does exist, quite often it is left to the reader or listener to
figure it out.

The effect created by all these various ellipses is that of concision
and a certain gnomic quality. The absence of normal signposts
heightens attention and sets the discourse off as special and carefully
made:

אגר בקיץ בן משכיל / נרדם בקציר בן מביש //
Gathers in summer wise son / sleeps in harvest shaming son //

Prov. 10:5

כי הנה החשך יכסה ארץ / וערפל לאמים //
If the darkness cover earth / and mist nations //   Isa. 60:2

כי טוב זמרה אלהינו / כי נעים נאוה תהלה //
Greatly sing our God / sweetly hymn praise //   Psalm 147:1

איש אמו ואביו תיראו / ואת שבתתי תשמרו //
Each his mother and his father respect ye / and my sabbaths keep
ye //
Lev. 19:3

Note also that in these verses the "absence of signposts" extends
beyond ellipsis to include deviations in normal word order (see also
chapter 1, section 5). Thus the delayed subject and absence of articles
in the first verse above is typical of all *māšāl*. The second verse cited
omits articles in three out of four cases. The third inverts an order
found even in other psalms, and omits the particle *l-* ("of")[61] before
"God"; the last transposes the more usual "father and mother,"
locates the verbs at the end of the clause instead of the beginning, and
further departs from the norm with the emphatic initial "each." All of
these are a kind of "strangeifying"[62] that marks the language as
special.

61. In Dahood's catalogue of *lamedhs* (*Psalms III*, pp. 394–95) he misses this
meaning so important to the Psalter and common even outside it, thus Gen. 17:20,
20:2, Deut. 33:12, 13, etc.
62. What Russian Formalist criticism called *ostranenije* ("making strange"), a
feature of literary language in many traditions. See on this V. Erlich, *Russian
Formalism* (The Hague, 1955).

These phenomena are in themselves heightening features, but it is important to stress their natural alliance with parallelism's pause-sequence. For not only does this sequence insure comprehension in the absence of an otherwise expected element, but indeed the form itself permits ellipsis, nay encourages it, through such familiar patterns as "double-duty" verbs, implied interrogative particles and the like:

ידע שור קנהו / וחמור אבום בעליו //

Ox knows his master / and ass his masters' trough //

Furthermore, we have already stressed the connection between ellipsis of personal suffixes in one verse-half (while the suffix appears in the other) and the implication of dependency on which often rests the realization of our pause sequence.

In a similar way, parallelism is allied to syntactic simplicity. For example, with a sentence that is too complex to permit "seconding,"

ויטלו את הכלים אשר באניה אל הים להקל מעליהם

And they cast the baggage which was in the ship into the sea to lighten themselves   Jon. 1:5

it is possible to drop one of the clauses and so make the verse conform to the pause sequence,

ויטלו את הכלים אל הים / להקל מעליהם //

And they cast the baggage into the sea / to lighten themselves //

a sentence that might be compared with, say, Psalm 106:26:

וישא ידו להם / להפיל אותם במדבר //

And he raised his hand against them / to strike them down in the desert //

But, as well, some new, parallel element could be introduced:

ויקחו את הכלים / הארונות אשר באניה //
ויטלום אל הים / להקל מעליהם //

And they took the baggage / the crates which were in the ship //
And they cast them into the sea / to lighten themselves //

which would allow the sentence to break into two (simple) sets of pauses. The paralleling addition has, paradoxically, made the style seem more concise; so in a single line, such as the pattern analyzed as AB:BC

ויהפך לדם יאריהם / ונוזליהם בל ישתיון //

And he turned their Nile[s] to blood / and their waters lest they drink //   Psalm 78:44

parallelism turns one potentially long proposition to two short ones.

The above modification of Jonah 1:5 would certainly be at home in the Psalter, though it is not overwhelmingly parallelistic. Now we could further heighten it through more overt semantic parallelism:

ויקחו את הכלים באניה / כל ארון וארגז אשר בה //
ויטלום אל הים / וישליכום במצולה //
להקל מעליהם / ולחיותם בסערה //

And they took the baggage in the ship / every crate and box that was in it //
And they cast them to the sea / and they threw them into the deep //
To lighten themselves / and to keep them alive in the storm //

and still further with ellipsis, inversion, etc.—thus:

אל מים הטילו / וישליכו במצולות ים //

To waters they cast / and sent to [sea's] depths //

The point is again: there is no use in speaking of parallelism or its absence, for in "parallelism" what is crucial is B's seconding, closural, force; nor is parallelism solely responsible for the impression of formality created by a text.

7

In sum, what is called biblical "poetry" is a complex of heightening effects used in combinations and intensities that vary widely from composition to composition even within a single "genre." No great service is rendered here by the concept of biblical poetry, since that term will, if based on the various heightening features seen, include compositions whose genre and subject are most unpoetic by Western standards, and since it will imply a structural regularity and design that are simply not there. The extremes of heightened and unheightened speech in the Bible are visible enough. But the "middle ground" between these extremes is important, and will forever elude a biblical critic equipped only to recognize the maximum of heightening or its total absence. Moreover, such an approach appears to be unfaithful to the Bible's own rhetorical scheme of things. Biblical authors were certainly aware of heightening features, but (judging by the text themselves) they did not see them as requirements to be applied in prescribed strengths for particular genres and rigorously avoided for others. The rhetoric of the Bible is far simpler. It consists of a few characteristic features that, singly or in combination, mark a sentence as special, lofty, carefully made. Such sentences appear consistently, fairly regularly, or here and there. There is nothing more of a prescriptive nature to be said about biblical style—and yet everything remains to be said about single lines or individual compositions.

As for the specific stylistic trait we have been examining—biblical parallelism—it is, as we have seen, not merely paralleling, nor does it appear at a single level of intensity; nor, for that matter, is it consistently present or absent. At base an emphatic, rhetorical closure, it was capable of elaboration to increasingly high levels of symmetry and design, and frequently combined with other elevating features. Viewed for what it is and without preconception, biblical parallelism is so obvious, so clear! And yet our burden will be that from Antiquity to the present, it has not been so viewed. The history of its interpretation is an involved, and involving, story, and one that still profoundly affects our notion of the Bible's very nature.

THREE

RABBINIC EXEGESIS AND THE "FORGETTING" OF PARALLELISM

1

The heightening characteristics of biblical style, and parallelism in particular, were clearly not lost on the remnant of Israel that lived at the close of the biblical period. Prayers and songs going back to this period,[1] like indeed later Hebrew, Aramaic, and even Greek compositions[2] of various genres, show themselves to be the true heirs of biblical style, not only in their penchant for familiar forms of "seconding" but in their use of traditional pair-words, differentiation, repetition, verbal alternations, and ellipses—features that, as we have seen, accompany parallel style in much of the Bible. Nor ought one to see here an antiquarian revival. For the ways in which these compositions *differ* from, for example, their Psalter prototypes, precisely in the matter of parallelism,[3] argue that they are a development rather than an imitation of biblical stylistics, one that preserved some of the conventions of the latter and yet underwent an overall loosening of constraints and formulae, a phenomenon that in fact probably began in the latest stratum of biblical texts.[4]

1. For a small sampling of these, see Appendix. Note also these articles by A. Mirsky: ירושלים) השירה העברית בתקופת התלמוד, in ב', שנתון לדברי ספרות, (Jerusalem, 1966): 161–79; יריעות המכון לחקר השירה, ז' in מחצבתן של צורות הפיוט (Jerusalem, 1958), esp. 3–10; and הפיוט פרק ראשון בתולדות in שנתון לדברי ספרות: ירושלים ב'י'א'י (Jerusalem, 1977): 172–88.

2. See G. B. Gray, *The Forms of Hebrew Poetry* (New York, 1972), pp. 23–33; *PsIW* 2, pp. 117–20; also W. F. Burney in *JTS* 14 (1913): 414–24; W. Tannehill in *JBL* 93 (1974): 263–75. Cf. M. Black, "Formal Elements of Semitic Poetry," *An Aramaic Approach to the Gospels* (Oxford, 1946), pp. 105–17.

3. Mowinckel characterizes this as a "disintegration" of biblical style (*PsIW* 2, p. 133).

4. For example in Psalm 1, whose intermittent parallelism and "unterse" style is mirrored in the Qumran *hodayot* and in rabbinic prayers. For this reason its "poetic" status has often been questioned: see, e.g., B. Duhm, *Die Psalmen* (Freiburg, 1899), p. 1; Sievers, *Metrische Studien* (Leipzig, 1901), p. 500, and most recently, O. Loretz, "Psalmenstudien I," *UF* 3 (1971): 101—03.

At the same time that this "literary" activity continued, biblical exegesis proceeded apace, and it is here that the modern reader encounters a striking contradiction: for while in their own compositions the Rabbis showed ample awareness of the elements of biblical style, as exegetes they seem singularly blind to the same procedures.[5] Stated bluntly, the point is this: the ways of biblical parallelism are everywhere apparent in rabbinic prayers and songs: yet nowhere do the Rabbis speak of parallelism or acknowledge it in their explanation or interpretation of biblical verses, even when—to our eyes—it is so obvious that the greatest industry seems necessary to devise a reading that does *not* comment on it. The resolution of this apparent paradox is not difficult to find, but it is an important step in understanding what happened to parallelism after the close of the biblical period—why, specifically, it was "forgotten" by the Jews.

2

Faced with the most obviously parallelistic sort of line,

אהללה ה' בחיי / אזמרה לאלהי בעודי

I will praise the Lord in my life / I will sing to my God while I live //
Psalm 146:2

a commentator may deal with the question of meaning in one of two ways: he may either seek somehow to distinguish A from B by focusing on some real or imaginary nuance—and so dispel any apparent synonymity—or he may accept synonymity as *the whole point,* in which case he will have to dismiss any real differences of meaning as mere elegant variation, necessitated by the goal of restating a single idea in different words. In the former approach, the commentator would perhaps claim that "while I live" (above) means something other than "in my life"—life in the world-to-come, for example, or spiritual vs. physical existence. In the latter approach he would stress their equivalence, and this would probably lead him to discuss the parallelistic form or otherwise speculate on the purpose of such restatement.

Anyone familiar with rabbinic exegesis will recognize the former as its habitual *modus operandi*; but for readers unfamiliar with the

---

5. Pointed out by G. B. Gray, *Forms of Hebrew Poetry*, p. 27: "At the very time that the Rabbis were examining Scripture with eyes blind to parallelism, other Jews were still writing poems that made all the old use of parallelism." Not "other Jews"—the very same!

general phenomenon of midrash,[6] a few examples of this sort of approach to parallelistic texts will be helpful.

Example 1:

יורו משפטיך ליעקב / ותורתך לישראל //

Let them teach your statutes to Jacob / your teaching to Israel //

Deut. 33:10

A modern scholar might recognize the pairs "statutes . . . teaching" and "Jacob . . . Israel" as commonly associated items, and thus read B as a completion and strengthening of A, similar to, say, Psalm 81:4, "For a law of Israel it is, a statute of the God of Jacob." But *Sifre*, a midrashic collection on Deuteronomy, sees in this verse two distinct referents: "*Your teaching* indicates that there are two laws [the oral and the written]." That is, the use of "teaching," (after "statutes" had already been said) is understood as indicating a *second* body of laws. What might it be? Why, the group of laws handed down orally which, in the rabbinic view, came to complement the written ordinances of the Pentateuch. In such a reading B gains a raison d'être beyond its emphatic and elevating function: it indicates that the oral law was no less a Levitical duty than the written—and indeed (since these words are spoken by Moses) that the oral law is also Mosaic in origin.[7]

Example 2:

וה' פקד את שרה כאשר אמר / ויעש ה' לשרה כאשר דבר //

And the Lord remembered Sarah as he had said / And the Lord did for Sarah as he had spoken //

Gen. 21:1

---

6. On the "method of midrash" in general the best overall treatment is I. Heinemann's דרכי האגדה (Jerusalem, 1970). Happily, there are too many "bird's-eye views" of midrash in English to mention here; some are cited in M. P. Miller's excellent topical bibliography, "Targum, Midrash and the Use of the OT in the NT," *Journal for the Study of Judaism* 2 (1971): 29–82. On the earliest stages of midrashic exegesis, see M. Fishbane, "Torah and Tradition," in D. A. Knight, *Tradition and Theology in the OT* (Philadelphia, 1977), pp. 275–300; G. Vermes, *Post-Biblical Jewish Studies* (Leiden, 1975), pp. 37–49, 59–126; also his *Scripture and Tradition* (Leiden, 1961), pp. 67–126; J. Bowker, *The Targums and Rabbinic Literature* (Cambridge, 1969), pp. 3–28; and (despite many errors in Hebrew) D. Patte's provocative *Early Jewish Hermeneutic in Palestine* (SBL Dissertation Series, Missoula, Mont., 1975). Among special studies on rabbinic expression is W. S. Towner's form-critical analysis, *The Rabbinic "Enumeration of Scriptural Examples"* (Leiden, 1973).

7. For similar interpretations aimed at establishing the antiquity of oral law see Bowker, *Targums and Rabbinic Literature*, p. 41, n. 3.

This too is a fairly straightforward piece of parallelism: "did for" is perhaps a stronger or more direct verb than merely "remembered" (or "took note of"), but the similarity in meaning is unmistakable, particularly via the parallelism of "as he had said . . . as he had spoken." This same verse is treated in the Targum Yerushalmi (also called Targum Pseudo-Jonathan)—which may represent one of the earliest written layers of the midrashic approach—in the following manner:

> And the Lord remembered Sarah as he had said / And the Lord did for Sarah *as Abraham had spoken* to him in his prayer concerning Abimelekh //

This last is an allusion to the previous chapter, in which Abraham prays on behalf of Abimelekh and his wife. The midrashist understands that just as that prayer was effective for them, so was it effective for Sarah's barrenness. The result of this interpretation is that A and B now have entirely different meanings. In the first half of the verse God remembers Sarah in accordance with His *own* words; in the second half He acts on Sarah's behalf in accordance with *Abraham*'s words.

Example 3:

אל תשלח ידך אל הנער / ואל תעש לו מאומה //

Do not harm the boy / do nothing to him at all //   Gen. 22:12

Sometimes the midrashist will create additional material, especially direct speech, to "sharpen" an apparent emphatic construction. For the above verse the midrash elaborates: "Said the angel, 'Do not harm the boy.' Said Abraham, 'Let me extract a drop of blood then [and so at least perform a token of what I was commanded].' The angel replied, 'Do not cause the slightest blemish.' "[8] This reading, in other words, takes the seconding B clause and gives it additional and necessary significance by imagining an intermediate proposal short of actual physical harm, which the angel then also rejects. It is to be noted that here the midrash does no more than make explicit, by its invention, the "what's more" inherent in B.

Such invented dialogue to account for emphatic speech in the Bible is common. Surely the best known is the midrashic handling of an earlier verse in the same Isaac story, Gen. 22:2—"Take now your

---

8. *Genesis Rabba* 56:10. Here "nothing" (מאומה) is understood puningly as מומא ("blemish, fault").

son, your only one whom you love, even Isaac, and go to the country of Moriah." The midrash explains: "God said to Abraham, 'Be so kind as to take now your son.' He replied: 'But I have two sons [Isaac and Ishmael]—which one?' 'Your only child.' 'But each is an only child for his mother.' 'The one whom you love.' 'But I love both!' 'Even Isaac.' "

Example 4:

בסדם אל תבא נפשי / בקהלם אל תחד כבדי //

Into their company let me not come / and in their assembly let me not stay //   Gen. 49:6

Sometimes the midrashic distinguishing of A and B will hang on some lexical or thematic connection of the verse with another part of the Bible. Such is the case with this verse, uttered by Jacob about his two violent sons, Simeon and Levi. The midrashist comments: "*Their company* refers to the spies [sent by Moses to reconnoitre, Num 13:1-33] and *their assembly* to the band of Korah [who rebelled against Moses, Num. 16:1-35]." In other words, the midrashist sees in the apparent repetition a prophetic allusion to two separate incidents to be perpetuated by Jacob's descendents—neither of which, Jacob is saying here, he wishes to be connected with. But what is the basis for this association? The second half of the verse is connected with the Korah incident because the latter's band is said to have *assembled* against Moses and Aaron (Num. 16:3); Jacob's use of the root קהל is therefore allusive. Moreover, Korah himself is a Levite, and though his genealogy is traced back all the way to Levi (Num. 16:1), there it stops without adding "son of Jacob." Why? The midrashist explains (b. *Sanh.* 109 b) that it is because of Jacob's wish expressed in this testament, "and in their assembly let me not stay," that is, do not associate my name with theirs. Similarly, the spies of Num. 13:1, though presumably descended from Jacob, are not so designated; סוד ("company") is furthermore associated with them because of the word's more common postbiblical meaning of "secret"—viz., the shared knowledge the spies brought back with them from their mission and subsequently let out indiscreetly among the people (Num. 13:32). Thus, the apparently emphatic seconding in our original text is hermeneutically differentiated both on the basis of lexis (סוד becomes "secret") and textual reference (the spies and Korah).

Example 5:

מה אקב לא קבה אל / ומה אזעם לא זעם ה' //

How shall I curse what God has not cursed / and how shall I execrate what the Lord has not? //   Num. 23:8

An even more elaborate reading differentiates the obvious parallelism of these verse-halves. The word "execrate" (זעם), which also means "to be angry with," draws the midrashist's attention to an apparent contradiction in the "closed system of signs"[9] that is the Bible—for in Psalm 7:13 the text reads "God is angered each day," and in Psalm 30:6 it says "an instant [is] his wrath." Combining these two verses of apparently opposite tendency, the midrashist concludes that God is angered each day for only the tiniest instant; Balaam, he asserts, is said to "know the Exalted's knowledge" (Num. 24:15) in that he among mortals knows the precise instant of the day in which God is angry, and indeed had planned to curse Israel at this very moment in the hopes of associating the Divine anger with his own! However, knowing *this,* God is said by the midrashist to have restrained his wrath throughout the day, thus foiling Balaam's plan—which is why (our midrash concludes) the Balaam episode is referred to in Micah 6:5 as an instance of "the Lord's righteousness."[10] It will be noted that what the homily has done—inter alia!—is to separate the referent of Balaam's curse / execrate into two acts, cursing and being angry, so that a truly "sharp" distinction emerges from the midrashic scenario: "How can I curse what God has not cursed, how can I *even* be angry when the Lord has not been [all day]?"

These examples should illustrate sufficiently the rabbinic approach to the phenomenon of biblical style called parallelism. It is to be stressed that they are not isolated readings, but single instances chosen among thousands. Whether the distinctions are "real" or fanciful, based on lexical nuances, supposed etymologies, metaphorizations, or homiletical references to other parts of the Bible, the result is the same: B always means something beyond A.

Now here an obvious point must be stated: such a reading, whether grossly stretched or merely making explicit some "sharpness" already in the verse, is in any case opposed to awakening the reader's

9. The phrase is used by Patte, *Early Jewish Hermeneutic*, to describe the midrashic assumption of complete harmony between every part of the Bible and every other part, which (1) allows one to explain the meaning of one verse by another, no matter how distant, and (2) in fact requires such explanation in the face of apparent contradiction. For limits on this approach in matters of *halakhah*, see below.

10. This homily is found in b. *Abod. Zara* 4a and b.

attention to parallelism as a stylistic feature. How so? We saw, in Isaiah 1:3, that a parallelism-minded reading,

> An ox knows his owner / and an ass his masters' trough //

equates the two halves. The second means the same thing as the first. B's raison d'être, then, is not difficult to see; it is intended to repeat "the same idea." However, as soon as we read the two as a single, integrated sentence:

> An ox knows his owner / and *even* an ass his masters' trough //

the second half-verse has a new raison d'être; it becomes independent of the first because its meaning goes beyond the first. The fact of its parallelism is thus in danger of being obscured by the additional significance it has acquired. The situation is somewhat comparable to the formal requirements of poetry. An awkward poem, one that tramples rhythm and perhaps good sense in its struggle to rhyme, will have no difficulty in making the reader notice the fact of its rhyming; a more subtle poet will meet the requirements of form without letting them take over the poem, and unless we are looking for them, these formal elements will tend to recede. It is therefore hardly an exaggeration to assert that to the extent to which the Bible took "sharp" advantage of its own emphatic form, it helped diminish awareness of this formal element. But the rabbinic genius went beyond what most texts might conceivably intend in the way of sharpness. In effect, rabbinic exegesis simply does not recognize the possibility of restatement.

In fact, it is striking to what extent the seeking out of such differentiation is central to that whole search for nonapparent significance that is midrash. And so clearly is this *act of distinguishing* (rather than its fruits) the whole point that midrashic collections regularly record conflicting interpretations of the same verse. Thus for Genesis 21:1:

> And the Lord remembered Sarah as he had said / and the Lord did for Sarah as he had spoken //

Genesis Rabba assembles a whole host of new possible distinctions between A and B:

> R. Judah said: "And the Lord remembered Sarah as He had *said*" refers to promises introduced by the verb "say" [as Gen. 17:19]; "and the Lord did for Sarah as He had *spoken*" means promises introduced by "spoke" [as, perhaps, Gen. 15:18, introduced (15:1)

by רבר].[11] R. Nehemiah said ". . . as He had said" means as he had said by means of an angel; "as He had spoken" means He Himself [i.e., Gen. 18:10 vs. 17:16]. R. Yehuda said "And the Lord remembered Sarah . . . "—to give her a son, "And the Lord *did* for Sarah"—to bless her with milk to nurse that son. [as per Gen. 21:7] R. Nehemiah objected: Had anything been openly announced about her nursing yet? But [if you wish to base the distinction on "remember" vs. "do"] let this verse teach us that what God did for Sarah was return her to her youthful condition. R. Abbahu said: [first] He made her respected by all, so that none should deride her with "barren woman" [as presumably Hagar had in 16:4; then he gave her a son]; R. Yudan said: She lacked an ovary; the Lord [first] fashioned an ovary for her [and then gave her a son].[12]

All these ingenious interpretations accomplish the same thing—they give B some different meaning from that of A, and so demonstrate why both are necessary. Fulfilling this function is indeed the whole point. It does not matter on which particular words the distinction is hung, nor is there any further need to designate one as "correct."

3

But why not simply recognize the obvious parallelism for what it is? This question has a decidedly post-Lowthian ring, and certainly the first answer one might put forward is that parallelism is no more obvious than the "nuancing" approach of midrash; as we observed in our initial exposition of parallelism, much depends on the assumptions and expectations one brings to the text. Now "sharpness" is a real phenomenon of the Bible, especially in Wisdom texts. Very often B is a true going-beyond A in force or specificity, or indeed a contrasting statement. In either case, it is the distinction between A and B that is crucial, a sometimes most subtle nuance that makes B more than *res eadem bis inculcatur.* No doubt the compare-and-contrast of such texts' method formed the basis of text study in schools even before the close of the biblical period.[13] Thus, the reading of parallelism one

11. See Th. Albeck, *Genesis Rabba* (Berlin, 1929), p. 559 n.
12. The last three seem to take Gen. 17:16 "I will bless her and *yea* [Heb. גם, understood in rabbinic times as "also"] give you a son from her" as supplying the spoken promise to which our verse's "as He had said" refers, since clearly the "blessing" must be something other than the promised child.
13. See R. Bloch, s.v. "Midrash" in *DBS* 5:1269.

finds in the earliest sources of rabbinic writing is certainly a reflection of an older tradition of reading and indeed writing.

Furthermore, this reading is laterally connected to the rabbinic conception of the Bible's sanctity, and most notably to the principle of biblical "omnisignificance." For the basic assumption underlying all of rabbinic exegesis is that the slightest details of the biblical text have a meaning that is both comprehensible and significant. Nothing in the Bible, in other words, ought to be explained as the product of chance, or, for that matter, as an emphatic or rhetorical form, or anything similar, nor ought its reasons to be assigned to the realm of Divine unknowables. Every detail is put there to teach something new and important, and it is capable of being discovered by careful analysis. Thus, R. Akiba, a gifted exegete and homilist, is said to have learned from Nahum of Gimzo homiletical explanations even for the particle אֵת (a grammatical determinant indicating the accusative).[14] When, in accordance with normal Hebrew style, a "doubled verb" (that is, the required verb form preceded by its infinitive as a form of emphasis, e.g., Gen. 31:30, 40:15, Lev. 10:16) appears, it is not seen as merely an emphatic form: the Rabbis seek in the precise circumstances of its occurrence a clue to some further teaching. Thus, the doubled form of the verb "cut off" in Num. 15:31 is read as an allusion to the doctrine that not all are destined to be resurrected: "cut off in this world, cut off in the world to come" (b. *Sanh.* 64b). While excess in this approach was met with R. Ishmael's doctrine, "The Torah spoke as human beings do" (ibid.), this apparent concession to the exigencies of rhetoric and emphasis did not extend to parallelism. If a distinction was not to be drawn, there was nothing to say.

Now in this principle of biblical omnisignificance there is certainly a theological element. The words of the Pentateuch are, after all, instructions given to a prophet with whom God had spoken "mouth to mouth" (Num. 12:8). It is inconceivable that any of those words should owe their existence solely to chance, rhetoric, or for that matter some mechanical principle of parallelism. The purpose of the Torah is to teach; if a statement is parallelistic in form, that statement must be examined to reveal its full meaning—everything must be read, in other words, as potentially "sharp." And what is true of the Torah can hardly be less true of the Prophets, the inspired teachers whom the

---

14. b. *Hagigah* 12a and b. *BQ* 41b. Similarly Zechariah b. Ḥaqqaṣṣab is said to have deduced *halakhot* from the particle *waw* (M. *Sota* 5:1, *Ketubot* 2:9). See on this M. H. Segal, "Promulgation of the Authoritative Text," *JBL* 72 (1953): 37.

Torah itself prescribes (Deut. 18:18) as the arbiters of the later age, nor even of the Hagiographa.

A second force behind omnisignificance derives from the first and is, for want of a better word, temperamental. If the Torah teaches, it is our duty to learn. What one learns from it—it is true nowadays as ever—depends on what one looks for. The Rabbis, who of course knew the Bible quite well, were inclined to "attribute greatness" to God wherever they read his name (Deut. 32:4); what they looked for in the text was its highest reading. To say that this or that verse has been written for the purpose of parallelism ends discussion. It is really no different from arguing that this or that word of a poem appears *metri causa*; rabbinic exegesis shares with literary criticism the recognition that this argument is a dead end.

But the omnisignificance doctrine extends beyond reluctance to read B as a mere restatement or rewording of A: it includes a thoroughgoing lack of interest in any deducible principle of composition in the Bible, or in explaining peculiarities of expression stylistically. Such authorial concerns, which would involve the critic in viewing the text as if humanly composed, are just the sort of question ominsignificance ruled out. Every textual trait or peculiarity had to be examined as an individual case, in order to reveal what particular fine point of law or lore it was designed to communicate, rather than as an instance of some general stylistic or formal principle. Indeed, nothing was to be taken for granted, or to be explained as inevitable, only natural, or unavoidable, not even the fact that one sentence followed another.

So it was that *juxtaposition* was, wherever possible, read as significant—and this too worked against a structural reading of a normal binary sentence. For example, in the admonition (seen earlier) in Leviticus 19:3

איש אמו ואביו תיראו / ואת שבתתי תשמרו //

Each his mother and father respect ye / and my Sabbaths observe //

a modern critic could not but note certain parallelistic features—the parallel imperative plurals "respect" and "observe" in identical positions, the preceding objects each with a possessive suffix—whose symmetry, he would explain, makes the whole pleasing and memorable. As for their meaning, if the two verse-halves are not synonymous, they are at least quite similar: parallel specifics of the general commandment that just precedes them (Lev. 19:2), "Be holy because I am holy." The midrashic mentality, however, is quite otherwise. It sees the second half as *significantly juxtaposed* in order to set out the limits of the first; you shall respect mother and father so long as this respect does not cause you to violate the Sabbath. That is, it understands the last clause as "And you shall all keep my Sabbaths, parents and children" (b. *Yeb.* 5b). In other words, instead of a seconding commandment, parallel in syntax and similar in its sentiments, B is read as an integral part of A, a modification or definition of its applicability.

Later exegesis even expanded on the "sharp" reading of such juxtaposition. היקש ("comparison") is used in the Talmud[15] to describe the situation of, for example, the Passover law of Deuteronomy 16:3

Thou shalt not eat any leaven with it[16] / seven days thou shalt eat unleavened bread with it //

Of course the Talmud sees here not one commandment, but two: (1) No leaven may be eaten; (2) unleavened bread *must* be eaten (rather than, for example, seeing the second clause as a restatement of the first, viz., "Do not eat leaven; when, during the seven days, you want to eat bread, take care that it be unleavened"). And it goes even further—it understands from the juxtaposition that women, too, are required to eat unleavened bread (although they are normally exempt from this class of law, called "time-dependent positive commandments"). The fact that the positive commandment is juxtaposed to the negative indicates to the Talmud that the positive is meant to have as wide an applicability as the negative, and therefore women are included in it.

Similarly, two verses are called by the Talmud סמוכין ("juxtaposed") when the fact of their proximity becomes the basis for an interpretive point. Thus Exodus 22:17–18:

מכשפה לא תחיה / כל שכב עם בהמה מות יומת //

Thou shalt not suffer a sorceress to live / Anyone who lieth with an animal shall surely be put to death //

Simeon ben ʿAzzai deduces from the apposition of these laws that they are somehow similar offences. Consequently, since the penalty for the latter is known to be death by stoning, it may be inferred that the former is also punishable by stoning.[17] What is particularly interesting to us about this example is that the two verses may be read as twin

15. See b. *Pes.* 43b.
16. The paschal sacrifice.
17. See the discussion in b. *Yeb.* 4a.

halves of a parallelistic statement, where the alternation "not let live" and "surely die" seems particularly parallelistic. The same is true of other verses read in the סמיכות (juxtaposition) manner, e.g.,

> Let a man not take his father's wife / and let him not uncover his father's covering[18] //   Deut. 23:1

where the second clause is taken to refer not to the father's wife, but to a woman seduced by him (and is even extended, by the סמיכות method, to include a woman taken by force, because of the proximity of Deut. 22:28–29).[19]

Of course rabbinic exegesis involves far more than such creative reading of parallelism: the assumption of omnisignificance led to the greatest interpretive licence, later regulated by increasingly elaborate hermeneutical systems, from the seven rules of Hillel to R. Ishmael's thirteen principles and, still later, the thirty-two principles of Eliezer b. Yose ha-Gelili. Nor does omnisignificance alone explain the particular direction rabbinic exegesis took: certainly it is allied to, and dependent on, the principle of textual comparison, embodied in the גזרה שוה,[20] whose roots are ancient.[21] But so far as parallelism is concerned, the main points of the rabbinic approach have been set forth: whether lexically, thematically, or through cross-referencing

---

18. The second clause apparently has emphatic force, either comparative ("for to do so is the equivalent of exposing his father's nakedness") or additive ("in fact, let him in no way expose his father's nakedness").

19. See b. *Ber.* 21b, *Yeb.* 3b–4b; also *Pes.* 118a.

20. Because the word גזרה has the biblical meaning of "decree" (Dan. 4:4, 14 // פתגם) it has been suggested that this hermeneutical device was originally limited to the comparison of laws. Later, it came to have the broadest sort of application, though in legal matters certain restraints were imposed: the comparison must not be invented but based on authentic tradition (b. *Pes.* 66a), both passages must come from the Torah (b. *BQ* 2b) and the words compared must be מופנים ("available"), i.e., their presence in the passage is not necessary for any other purpose, and can best be explained as a specific indication that a comparison was intended. R. Akiba, who was a zealous picker-up of the slightest textual hints, disagreed with this last condition (j. *Yoma* 8:3); for his zeal in hermeneutics and conflict with R. Ishmael, see b. *BQ* 41b, *Sanh.*, 51b, 64b.

21. Thus, the so-called "Damascus Document" of the Qumran scrolls contains Sabbath strictures not found in later Jewish legal material: they are apparently all based on the ambiguous phrase דבר דבר in Isa. 58:13, which was interpreted by means of a גזרה שוה to refer to demanding payment for debts on the Sabbath, judging matters of property or gain, or speaking idle or vain words. (Based on uses of the word in Deut. 15:2, 17:8, and 32:47. See E. Slomovic, "Exegesis in the DSS," *Revue de Qumran* 25 [Dec. 1969]: 9–10; also L. Schiffman, *The Halakhah at Qumran* [Leiden, 1975], pp. 88–90.) On the meaning of this expression see G. Bregman, ("גזרה שוה מהי?"), *Sinai* 71 (1972): 132–39.

with some other part of the Bible, the most similar B was to be distinguished from its A. Moreover, even when A and B were clearly distinct in meaning, the fact of their parallel form was often obscured by some integrative reading.

Moderns who do not share the omnisignificance outlook may see in this reading only hermeneutical excess and the woolliest talmudism. But in fairness what has been implied several times heretofore should be stated outright; the midrashic reading of parallelism seems to have biblical roots, to be, in fact, a direct outgrowth of sharpness and sharpness's interpreters. Since Robert Lowth, critics have tended to an opposite excess, seeing parallelism as the whole point of verses, when most of the time such a reading is at least reductive and sometimes misleading. The midrashic approach at least began from a more reasonable premise, that parallelism was *not* the whole point— and if it carried sharpness beyond what conceivably could be intended in a normal text, well, so much the better, for as noted before, it was the rabbinic idea of the text's sacredness that permitted such readings.[22] At the same time, for the parallelistic connections between A and B there was always to be found some reason or other, so parallelism itself ceased to be a reason, and it was never so invoked. Certainly the Rabbis were aware that the "beginning" of a verse was often quite like its "end," and of course interpreted, as we have seen, by "juxtaposition" and by the explicit comparison of A and B. But as to pointing out reiteration, reassertion, the very fact of parallelism— why dwell on the reductive obvious? In rabbinic exegesis, parallelism per se did not exist.

This will explain the paradox with which we began: the Rabbis themselves wrote parallelistic prayers and aphorisms because such was, after all, the very visible method of the Psalter and other writings that were their models, whose verses interlaced their own,[23] and gave them their vocabulary and subject—and perhaps as well because the "seconding" impulse was a rhetorical reflex basic to Hebrew and other languages, a decorative, elevating trait implicitly recognized

---

22. This idea contrasts sharply with the Philonic and early Christian notion of the Bible's sanctity, on which see chapter 4.

23. That is to say, the medieval practice of such "interweaving" (שיבוץ) has rabbinic, nay biblical, roots—for it characterizes rabbinic prayer composition from the earliest periods, the Qumran *hodayot*, targum and midrash (where André Robert calls it the "style anthologique") and indeed sections here and there of Chronicles and even earlier biblical books. For an overview of the style of early rabbinic compositions see Ezra Fleischer, שירת הקודש העברית בימי הביניים (Jerusalem, 1975), pp. 23–46.

and used, if never explicitly described. In this sense, parallelism was never forgotten. But theirs were human texts. To the Holy Writ no such explanation, had it even occurred, would have been appropriate—and indeed, what need was there for it? The ways of wisdom consisted of looking deeply into things for their slight differences, their tiny nuances, allusions, hidden connections. This was manifestly how the cases in law courts were deduced by judges from cryptic statute, and was the method of Solomon in his Proverbs and David in his Psalms. Under such circumstances, he who sought to explain B's resemblance to A by so lame a principle as parallelism was little more than a fool.

While this is, in our view, the most significant force behind the Jewish approach to parallelism until the late Middle Ages, a few other factors also played a significant role: the musical elaboration of the textual accents ("*ṭe'amim*"), the decline of antiphony in the synagogue, stichography, and the invention of poetry.

4

The Bible contains many references to the public reading of various of its parts (e.g., Deut. 31:10-13) and it is probable that this "reading" contained some musical elements—that it was more a chant than a flat "reading voice." In this regard one ought to cite the famous injunction attributed to R. Yoḥanan in b. *Megilla* 32a:

> Anyone who reads from the Bible without a melody or recites the Mishnah without a tune, to him applies the verse (Ezek. 20:25) "And I also gave them laws which were not good."[24]

In what sense might God's laws be said to be "not good"?! Certainly nothing in the laws themselves could be so qualified; thus it is that R. Yoḥanan understands the adjective to refer to the manner of transmission. (It may also be that he connects this first half of Ezekiel's verse to the second half, not cited: "and statutes they will not live by." Through a grammatical ambiguity, this last clause might be understood "and statutes that will not abide with them," that is, they will be forgotten, for only the mnemonic reinforcement of music guarantees a text long life.)

Perhaps it is fruitless to speculate on what sort of chant was used.

---

24. Cf. b. *Sanh.* 99a and b, "Rabbi Akiba said [about regular study] 'Sing every day, sing every day!' " Note also the discussion of the mnemonic value of melody in B. Gerhardssohn, *Memory and Manuscript* (Uppsala, 1961), pp. 162–68.

The systems of cantillation now in use are all elaborations of relatively recent vintage. No doubt originally the mode of rendition varied widely by genre and from composition to composition within a single genre. Perhaps something like modes or maqāmāt[25] governed the chants and were adapted to the text or the occasion. Whatever the case, one can imagine that a relatively unadorned chant pattern prevailed for much of the narrative, legal, and prophetic material; psalmodic[26] rendering of the parallelism would carry the sense of regularity through the varying lines. The relatively florid musical effects at Israel's disposal were no doubt lavished on special songs like that of Deuteronomy 32 (divided into six parts, it was rendered by the Levites in the Temple). But even publicly "read" texts were probably chanted, for while present-day cantillation patterns of the Torah and the Prophets were a later development, they were probably not a completely fresh departure. In the current Yemenite or Bukharan Bible chants (far simpler than those of other Jewish traditions) one may be hearing a fossilization of what once was the common renditional mode—a simple and more fluid improvisational form.[27]

25. A set of conventions in traditional Arabic music determining scale, characteristic motives, and their placement within the scale and their sequence within the melodic structure; tempo; and the association of certain rhythms with certain themes or genres. There are no fixed melodies: maqāmāt are rather musical "modes" (comparable to the ragas of Indian music) which provide the basis for each improvised performance. Twelve to fifteen maqāmāt have been catalogued. Some writers have remarked on the correlation between certain maqāmāt and the cantillations used by various Eastern Jewish communities; see S. Idelsohn, "Die Makamen in der hebräischen Poesie," MGWJ 57 (1913): 314–25. Sa'adya discusses rhythmic modes in chapter 10 of Beliefs and Opinions, and describes (his own imposition) a system of eight modes used in the Temple (see E. Werner and I. Sonne, "Medieval Jewish Musical Theory," HUCA 16–17 [1941, 1942–43], pp. 551–52; cf. their mention in Bahya b. Asher's Torah commentary [H. Avenary, "Sa'adya's Psalm Preface and Its Musical Aspects," HUCA 39 (1968): 160–61]).

26. See SB, pp. 128–66, 347. Also, E. Werner, "The Church Fathers and Hebrew Psalmody," in Review of Religions (May, 1943): 340.

27. SB, pp. 427–28. This simplicity may also be reflected in the earliest known "punctuation" of a biblical text, which occurs in a Septuagint text of the second century B.C.; it is punctuated by spacing. See E. J. Revell, "The Oldest Evidence for the Hebrew Accent System," BJRL 54 (1971–72): 214–22. In another article, "Biblical Punctuation and Chant in the Second Temple Period," JSJ 7 (1976): 181–98, Revell postulates the existence of an early "Syro-Palestinian" accent system still reflected in the text's pausal forms, but not in the Tiberian accentuation marks themselves. His studies thus push back the putative origins of a punctuation "system," very simple in scope, to an early date, yet he is cautious about speaking of the "ancestors" of known systems; see especially "Biblical Punctuation," 197–98.

It is striking that even today the method of psalm rendition in the most ancient traditions of the Roman Catholic, Greek Orthodox, and Syrian churches, as well as certain Jewish communities, are quite similar: all use a basic monotonous "recitation note" that carries the bulk of each clause. The recitation note is introduced and ended by a brief melodic phrase, so that, in effect, each binary verse's beginning, middle, and end are melodically marked (ternary verses may either be treated melodically as binary or may contain two medial cadences). A similarly unornamented recitation doubtless underlies all biblical chant.

At a certain point this chant met up with the phenomenon called in Hebrew *ṭe'amim* ("accents"). Nowadays the word refers to a written system of graded pauses—a kind of punctuation of the text that indicates full stops, various short pauses, and run-ons. Originally, however, the term seems rather to have designated the oral parsing of the text into its sense units. Children learning to recite were taught where to pause and where to continue, and these same pauses could be indicated to the reader during public lection by means of various hand gestures (cheironomy).[28]

Gradually, the necessity for a fixed, written system to record established readings became obvious. Pauses were the arbiter of differences sometimes slight and sometimes crucial. For example, depending on where one pauses in the first part of Isaiah 1:5

על מה תכו עוד תוסיפו סרה

one may render "Why should you be further stricken, you will only continue to act sinfully," or "Why should you be stricken, you will only continue further to act sinfully."[29] A famous question revolves around the Masoretic division of Isaiah 40:3—

קול קורא במדבר פנו דרך ה'

---

28. On cheironomy, see b. *Ber.* 62a, and *SB*, pp. 107–10. That פיסוק טעמים, and הפיסוקים designated such sense division is clear from an examination of b. *Meg.* 3a, *Ned.* 37b, and j *Meg.* 4:1. See also b. *Qidd.* 30a, *Hag.* 6b, *Yoma* 52b. One early understanding of the biblical word טעם was "proper interpretation," hence the importance of Psalm 119:66 for such apocalyptic-interpretation sects as the Dead Sea Covenanters (see on this Paul E. Kahle, *The Cairo Geniza*, 2d ed. [Oxford, 1959], pp. 103–05); the Septuagint translates טוב טעם as *khrestoteta kai paideian* (kindness and education), the latter word perhaps representing a conflation of טעם and דעת. Such an understanding of טעם seems to underlie the talmudic expression.

29. For a talmudic example of how the *ṭe'amim* convey shades of meaning, see b. *Hag.* 6b. Rashi attempts to apply knowledge of the *ṭe'amim* to explicate Deut. 11:30.

According to the *ṭe'amim*, the verse should be understood not in the Christian manner, "The voice of him that crieth in the wilderness" (on this depends the identification with John the Baptist in Matt. 3:3), but, "A voice cries out: 'In the wilderness make a highway.' "[30] So even if one learned Scripture "with a melody," that is, with some sort of loose chant with a medial pause, potential ambiguities remained. Especially in legal matters, these little differences could be significant.

Three systems of annotating *ṭe'amim* onto written texts in Hebrew have been evidenced; they are known as the Palestinian, Babylonian, and Tiberian systems. The Tiberian, the most detailed and the most recent, is the system currently in use.[31] It was perfected by the Masoretes of Tiberias, who also developed the current vocalization of the biblical text—indeed, the two activities were seen as coordinate, both being notational systems clarifying potential ambiguities in the written transmission of the text.[32]

The workings of this system, and its development, are subjects far too complicated to be treated here,[33] but it is important to point out that this complexity developed only over a long period. The Tiberian system's antecedents are simpler, and the earliest written notation system may well have indicated no more than the middle and end of what we now call "verses," duplicating on the page the most basic act of punctuation accomplished vocally by the reader or reciter.[34] But gradually the notational system became far more complex. It was capable of distinguishing many grades of conjunction and disjunction and became, as we have seen briefly, the arbiter of the most subtle sorts of ambiguities in the written text. These of course also are communicated by reading or chanting: willy-nilly the reader orally parses whatever he recites. But what happened here went well beyond this "parsing." For just as the major disjunctions—ends of verses and major clauses within them—were orally marked by melodic elaboration, so now musical phrases apparently came to be fixed for lesser

---

30. See C. Westermann, *Isaiah 40–66* (Philadelphia, 1969), p. 37.

31. See on this *SB*, pp. 102–103, 410–28, and in general A. Dotan's article "Masorah" in *EJ* 16:1412–71.

32. Of the two activities, if one aspect is older it is probably the *ṭe'amim*; the Samaritan Pentateuch also has *ṭe'amim* and vocalization, but while the name of the vowel marks are Arabic, the *ṭe'amim* have Aramaic names (*EJ* 16:1433).

33. In addition to Dotan's "Masorah," see the articles collected in S. Z. Leiman (ed.) *The Canon and Masorah of the Hebrew Bible* (New York, 1974).

34. See above, n. 27. Some Psalter fragments with Palestinian punctuation (Cambridge MS. T-S 10, No. 52, 53, 54, 58) show only a few vowel signs and only one kind of accent. See Kahle, *Cairo Geniza*, p. 68.

disjunctive and conjunctive patterns not only to express the parsing which they themselves embodied, but to set one pattern off from another. The *ṭe'amim* thus became musical prescriptions—"the notes," as today's Bar Mitzvah boy will call them—denoting melodic phrases usually associated with only a single sign or sign-group.

Of course we do not know what the public rendition in the early days of the *ṭe'amim* (or before) sounded like. But the evidence from the *ṭe'amim* themselves (i.e., the relative simplicity of the Palestinian system), as well as from what seem to be the oldest surviving chant traditions,[35] suggests that as the systems of *ṭe'amim* grew more complex, they took the lead musically, and began to generate melodic creations beyond the immediate needs of parsing. The variety in the rendering specifically of these lesser conjunctions and disjunctions further supports this thesis.

Before the systematic development of the *ṭe'amim,* in the days of our "Ur-sprechgesang," a precise reader might draw out a syllable here or there to emphasize disjunction; perhaps even some sort of melodic phrase or trill was improvised. As with present-day psalmody, the final pause was doubtless marked melodically, as well as the main interior pause(s). Sense units were thus delineated orally just as they were in ancient written texts by "verse-dividers" or the vertical slashes seen above in the Mesha' Stone. But with the emergence of the written systems these musical markings became more elaborate, varied, and fixed: in time, a system of melodic prescriptions came forth. The *ṭe'amim* had become "notes."[36]

The significance for parallelism of the emergence of the *ṭe'amim* was not negligible. Within a parallelistic line, the generally binary structure, which under a loose and improvised chant had been obvious (the only melodically emphasized pauses falling at the middle[37] and end of each line) was now lost in a series of elaborations at minor pauses (the medial pause now became one of the most drab from the standpoint of melody): such regularity as existed in successive sentences was now obscured in the musical asymmetry. Moreover, there was a corresponding psychological effect, for now the written signs for the main pauses—the medial and the final—were but two

35. See n. 27.

36. The connection between *ṭe'amim*, specifically the Babylonian system, and the Greek neumes has long been known to scholars, and is discussed in *SB*, p. 110. Indeed, it is theorized that the Greek term comes not from *neuma* ("nod"), still less *pneuma* ("breath") but represents Semitic *nġm* (Heb. נעם), "play a tune, sing."

37. In the Yemenite chant the אתנח (caesura) still has "a special melody that seems almost to divide the verse"—J. Kafih, "נקוד טעמים" *Sinai* 29 (1951): 264.

among many. Every verse came with its own special series of signs, a
genetic code of different counters attached to each word or phrase (in
the Tiberian system). Their communality of structure was obscured
on the page and in the memory by the very obvious diversity.
Furthermore, the most obvious instances of parallelism were sometimes covered over by asymmetry and/or misparsing in the *ṭe'amim*.
For example, Balaam's opening *māšāl*:

מן־ארם ינחני בלק מלך־מואב מהררי־קדם

From Aram does Balak summon me / the king of Moab [summons me]
from the Eastern mountains //   Num. 23:7

is completely obscured by the asymmetry of the *ṭe'amim*, which parse
"Balak king of Moab" as a single phrase. Not only this, but the terse
consistent parallelism of passages such as Balaam's oracles (as a
whole) was no longer set off from its surroundings in such bold relief.
The same musical phrases were used throughout, and this served to
harmonize the text.

In this connection it should be noted that three books of the Bible,
Psalms, Proverbs, and Job, are annotated with a special system of
ṭe'amim. It is not known what the original purpose of this distinction
might have been. Parallelism in their lines made ambiguity less a
problem, so the complicated system of the other twenty-one books
was not necessary. But the fact that different symbols, peculiar to
these books, were developed not only in the (late) Tiberian system,
but also in the earlier and simpler Palestinian one, suggests that
perhaps a melodic distinction was also intended or reflected.[38]

The existence of this separate system was significant for the
recognition of parallelism, but not because the system itself showed
the parallelism in any obvious light—on the contrary, the *ṭe'amim* for
parallel phrases are not usually the same (how they were sung is
unknown, all current traditions being apparently of postbiblical
origin).[39] But the special *ṭe'amim* of *Sifrei ʾEmet,* as the books were

---

38. See W. Wickes, טעמי אמ׳׳ת (in English, Oxford, 1881), p. 9. He cites ibn
Bilaam's remark that the poetic system was instituted because the verses of these
books were so short, that is, he says nothing about their parallelism or their "poetic"
content. Cf. the remark in the (minor) collection, מדרש שיר השירים (ed. L. Grunhut,
Jerusalem, 1897), "And why are the *ṭe'am*[im] of these three books, Job, Proverbs,
and Psalms, the same? Because their punishments [i.e., of their authors, Job,
Solomon, and David] were equal," that is, the fall from high estate and eventual
restoration (page 9a). Here too there is no mention of poetry or song.

39. The twelfth-century traveler Benjamin of Tudela reports finding Levites in
Baghdad who still sang the Psalms in their original (Temple) manner. See Avenary,
"Sa'adya's Psalm Preface," 161.

called,[40] helped to foster the later reputation of these texts as "poetic"; in medieval Hebrew discussions of biblical poetry the names of Sifrei ⁾Emet are often cited, and no doubt the special ṭe'amim were in part responsible. (It is curious, for example, how rarely the book of Lamentations is mentioned in such discussions, though its parallelism is obvious, as is the alphabetical structure of the first four sections—a particularly "poetic" trait and one that continued into medieval religious poetry.)

The special ṭe'amim themselves were not always applied consistently. While the parallelistic "dialogues" of Job are differentiated from the "prose" introduction and conclusion by means of the special ṭe'amim, elsewhere the Masoretes were less systematic. Thus, when the same text appears in both a "poetic" book and elsewhere (e.g., David's Song, which is Psalm 18 and, slightly changed, 2 Sam. 22; or Psalm 105:1–15, which is 1 Chron. 16:8–22) the "poetic" ṭe'amim appear in the "poetic" book and the "prose" ṭe'amim in the "prose" book. That is, here the ṭe'amim do not appear to be proper to the character of the text itself.

Two final effects of the ṭe'amim should be noted. The first is that, in the minds of many, they became the structure of biblical texts. The medieval poet and scholar Yehuda ha-Levi's assertion that meter was foregone in Hebrew poetry in favor of the ṭe'amim[41] simply makes explicit an impression that no doubt lived unconsciously in the minds of Jews for generations before him, that the ṭe'amim represented some kind of systematic ordering underlying the text's form. Secondly, because the ṭe'amim decided where pauses fell, there was no reason for later scholars to arbitrate in these matters: they were already decided. Had the Tiberian system not gained such a total acceptance, the placement of the medial pause especially would have kept the question of structure alive, and perhaps would have encouraged a keener interest in the ways of parallelism. As it was, such questions were now closed. Where, as occasionally happened, the ṭe'amim contradicted the text's parallelism,

למה תשיב ידך / וימינך מקרב חיקך כלה //

Why should you withdraw your hand / and your right hand from amidst your breast remove? //   Psalm 74:11

(where the ṭe'amim place the main pause after "right hand"), and:

40. An acrostic of the first letters of Job, Proverbs, and Psalms.
41. See chapter 5.

אמר לה' מחסי / ומצודתי אלהי אבטח בו //

I call the Lord "my shelter," / and "my fortress" my God in whom I trust //   Psalm 91:2

(the *ṭe'amim* place the pause after "fortress"), the authority of the *ṭe'amim* overpowered parallelism and made it seem unimportant. Surely these, with the other factors discussed, aided in the "forgetting" of parallelism.

5

Many writers have suggested that parallelism itself was originated to meet the demands of musical performance, that the verse-halves "answer" each other because they were intended to be sung by choruses or soloists who would recite or sing them antiphonally. Antiphony in the Near East is certainly very old (it is mentioned for example, in Babylonian and Ugaritic writings).[42] Some Hebrew songs were clearly designed for a leader and chorus or two choruses (e.g., Psalm 136), while in others the antiphonal possibilities are certainly present. Deuteronomy 27:12 describes an antiphonal arrangement, though it is not clear if it was to involve singing.[43] The arrangement of Nehemiah 12:24 and 12:37–47 is clearly musical antiphony. Whether sung or spoken, antiphony itself might emphasize such parallelism as existed. Two individuals or choruses answering each other created a strong sense of balance in the text.

In rabbinic times, antiphony was common in the synagogue. At least four different antiphonal patterns are attested from rabbinic sources: (1) the responsive rendering of consecutive verse-halves or verses (which might be schematized as "Leader: A, Choir: B; Leader: C, Choir: D"); (2) antiphonal use of a refrain (Leader: A, Choir: B; Leader: C, Choir: B); (3) repetitive antiphony (Leader: A, Choir: A; Leader: B, Choir: B); (4) a combination of the first and third types (Leader: A, Choir: A+B; Leader: C, Choir: C+D).[44] These same

---

42. *SB*, p. 203. See Gilgameš Tablet 6, 180–85, Montgomery in *JAOS* 53: 99.

43. A consistent difficulty in this question is the meaning of the Hebrew word ענה, which conceals two historically different roots, the one corresponding to Arabic ʿ*ny*, the other to ġ*ny*; the first means, in Hebrew, "answer," the second, "sing." What is particularly confusing is that the second word meant "sing" in (among others) the specific sense of "to lead antiphony" (see Exod. 15:21); that is, the leader sang ענה (sense 2) and the chorus answered ענו (sense 1)!

44. These may be deduced from an examination of b. *Sota* 30b, j. *Sota* 5:6, *Mekhilta* 2 (Lauterbach ed., Philadelphia, 1933), pp. 7–8; and b. *Sukkah* 38a and b, 39a. The Samaritan *Memar Marqah* also describes the antiphonal rendering of

patterns seem to have continued afterward. Instructive are the arrangements described by Nathan ha-Babli (tenth century) in his description of the installation of the Exilarch:

> The leader of the congregation begins with "Blessed Who Spoke" and the choir sings in answer to each line "Blessed is He," and when he says Psalm 92 they answer [as a refrain] "It is good to give thanks to the Lord." Then everyone reads the morning psalms together, until they finish them. The *ḥazzan* stands and says the opening [verse] of "The breath of all Living" and the chorus sings in answer "shall bless thy Name." He says a line and the chorus sings [the last part] in answer after him, until they reach the קדושה [of יוצר אור; this part everyone participates in], the congregation say it softly and the choir out loud.[45]

If parallelism was brought out by antiphonal performance, its nature was particularly precious to that relatively common situation of a lead singer or singers fully familiar with the text to be sung, and a general chorus or congregation only partially familiar. For here the precise nature of this heightening device comes into its full value: the "seconding" of meaning makes it easier for the chorus to complete the verse responsively or repeat the second part after the leader. This is the last arrangement described by Nathan (above), and, indeed, it seems to be what Philo has in mind in his description of the Therapeutai in "The Contemplative Life":

Exod. 15: "The Prophet Moses sang the song section by section. When he finished each section, he would fall silent and all the Elders would respond with the verse 'I will sing to the Lord, for He has triumphed gloriously: the horse and his rider he has thrown into the sea.' Then all Israel would say, 'My strength and my song (זמרתי), and He has become my salvation' up to 'The Lord is a hero (גבור) of war; the Lord is his name.' They would then fall silent and the prophet Moses would begin to sing. In the same way Miriam would sing and say 'Sing to the Lord" along with the elders, and the women would say with the Israelites, 'My strength and my song' to the end of it. [She would say] 'For He has triumphed gloriously' and they would say about Pharaoh and his chariots, whose power was great against the Israelites, 'The horse and his rider He has thrown into the sea.' " See John MacDonald, *Memar Marqah* 1 (Berlin, 1963), pp. 37–38. The last sentence is apparently a play on *ramat* ("was great") and *rāmâ bayyam* "cast into the sea." On the general subject of antiphony see I. W. Slotki, "Antiphony in Ancient Hebrew Literature," *JQR* 26 (1935–36): 210–12. Two discussions of antiphony in the Hallel by Slotki are "Omnipresence, Condescension and Omniscience . . .," in *JTS* 32 (1931): 368–69, and "The Stichometry and Text of the Great Hallel," *JTS* 29 (1928): 260–68.

45. Reprinted in B. Halper, *Post-Biblical Hebrew Literature* 1 (Philadelphia, 1921), p. 37.

Then the President rises and sings a hymn composed as an address to God, either a new one of his own composition or an old one by poets of an earlier day. . . . After him all the others take their turn [in singing a hymn] as they are arranged and in the proper order, while all the rest listen in complete silence except when they have to chant the closing lines or refrains,[46] for then they lift up their voices, men and women alike.[47]

(Philo also specifies various singing arrangements used, "sometimes chanting together, sometimes singing antiphonally," and describes the rendition of Exodus 15.)[48]

But antiphony gradually disappeared from synagogue prayers and rendition of the Bible. Whether owing to a general decline in Jewish learning among congregants (making their participation lackluster and undesirable) or to the "monopolistic" ambitions of the ḥazzan (precenter), this disappearance became noticeable as early as the ninth century.[49] Musical rendering of the psalms and other parallelistic parts of the service became more and more the ḥazzan's exclusive property, and his dominance of the liturgy was fixed by the tenth or eleventh century.[50] Where antiphony had previously been the norm, solo performance now took over. Complementing this specialization was a general decrease in the amount of material musically rendered at all; what had been sung before was now sometimes spoken or whispered.

In this connection, a remark of Profiat Duran (late fourteenth century) is interesting, for it draws a stark contrast between the musical renditions of Christian psalm-singing and synagogal rendition of biblical passages according to the ṭe'amim:[51]

One consequence of this feature [ṭe'amim] is that you can hear a hundred people reading aloud a part of the text [of the Bible] as if it were one man reading: they all pause or continue their reading simultaneously. . . .[52] And if you listen to the sound of the songs of

46. Gk.: akroteleutia kai ephymnia. On these terms, see SB, p. 137.
47. Philo, text and tr. ed., F. H. Colson (Cambridge, 1960), pp. 163–65.
48. Ibid., pp. 164–68.
49. SB, p. 134.
50. SB, p. 185.
51. Incidentally, Duran attributes the invention of the ṭe'amim to Ezra, who (he says) wished to compensate for the Bible's being learned in book form rather than from the mouth of a teacher alone. מעשה אפד (Vienna, 1865), p. 21.
52. This idea was first stated by Yehuda ha-Levi in the Kuzari 2:76–77 (see Slonimsky ed. [New York, 1964], p. 127) and repeated after Duran by M. ibn Habib in דרכי נעם (see chapter 5).

other peoples you will find matters quite the contrary: they almost annihilate the words, so that virtually nothing may be understood of them but the sound and tonality—because they had no concern to do this [to make the words clear], but only to please the sense of hearing with the differences in pitch, harmony and the like.[53]

Antiphony survived in the Church while it all but disappeared from the synagogue—and this may be one reason Christians were, as we shall see, often more attentive to biblical parallelism. For there is some kinship between antiphony and parallelism, and responsive recitation and the like cannot but bring the parallel structure into clearer focus. To this extent, Jewish awareness of it in psalms and prayers was decreased by the decrease in antiphonal rendition in the synagogue service.

6

Antiphonal recitation falls clearly in the domain of what one modern critic has called "the poem in the ear."[54] For the awareness of parallelism what he calls the "poem in the eye"—what is seen on the page—is at least as significant. As we have already seen, texts of the ancient Near East were sometimes set off by the various punctuating devices in use—a dividing sign, or dots, or the use of special spacing. This last came to be used traditionally in certain parts of the Bible, and the history of its use is in some measure connected to awareness of *structure* in the most consistently parallelistic parts of the Bible. The spacing of verses or verse-halves is nowadays generally called "stichometry," but the term "stichography" is in fact more precise[55] and will be used here.

Stichographic arrangements are found here and there in the Dead Sea Scrolls, which are the oldest surviving biblical manuscripts. Thus, the document 4Q Ps.[b] (= the second Psalter Fragment found in Qumran Cave 4) is written in short, narrow columns consisting of a single verse-half per line. (Considering the size of the document and

---

53. מעשה אפר, p. 21.

54. John Hollander, *Vision and Resonance* (New York, 1975).

55. "Stichometry" was used in regard to the Bible in the "Stichometry of Nicephorus" and the like; apparently the word, originally coined to describe a function ("measuring," that is, listing verses) was expanded to describe the format of individual lines. An aggressively descriptive lexicographer might insist that matters be left as they are, but this seems to me too bookish a word to have developed a large and emotional constituency, and too bookish a word to be wrongly used.

its spacing, it seems unlikely the entire Psalter was contained in the original document,[56] and one wonders what the function of it may have been; the Psalms represented are 91–92, 94, 99–100, 102–103, 112, 116, 118). At the same time, 4Q Ps.[a] writes the Psalms without any line breaks, as in many modern Hebrew Bibles: this is, indeed, the arrangement of a great many of the Qumran psalms, [57] as well as the *hodayot* ("thanksgiving hymns") of the Qumran community members. Another common arrangement, which most clearly represents parallelism to the eye, is that of two separated clauses per line.[58] Sometimes, however, this arrangement fails to represent the line's semantic parallelism and simply apposes random chunks of words![59] This is a phenomenon repeated in later periods—indeed, it is true to a certain extent of current scribal convention governing the writing of Exodus 15 in Torah scrolls—and is a most interesting piece of evidence, for it probably indicates that stichographic arrangements even at Qumran were not designed to follow parallelism or singing arrangements, and therefore that stichography had already acquired another purpose beyond (and sometimes instead of) its verse-dividing, punctuating function: it was also a distinctive feature, marking passages as "special" or simply arranging them so as to make a pleasing design. This is confirmed by the continued use of similar spacing techniques in passages of lists, such as the kings of Canaan (Josh. 12:9) or Haman's sons (Esther 9:7–9), where no verse-halves are involved.

In this regard it ought to be noted as well that stichography at Qumran is not limited to the Psalms or other traditionally "sung" texts. Thus 2Q 18 contains a stichographic fragment of the wisdom of Ben Sira (Ecclesiasticus), a late collection of Wisdom sayings.[60] It is difficult to imagine that this book was ever intended for singing. The Ben Sira scroll of Massada is likewise stichographic.[61]

In sum, this earliest evidence of scribal practice shows that spacing was used in several ways to distinguish parallelistic passages, particularly the Psalms but also other texts. Whatever its original

56. P. W. Skehan, "The Qumran MSS. and Textual Criticism," *SVT* 4 (1957): 154.

57. See M. Baillet, J. T. Milik, and R. de Vaux, *Les petites grottes de Qumran* (Oxford, 1962), pp. 148–49.

58. Ibid.

59. See Skehan, "Qumran MSS.," p. 155.

60. Baillet, Milik, and de Vaux, *Petites grottes*, pp. 75–76.

61. Y. Yadin, *The Ben Sirach Scroll from Massada* (Jerusalem, 1965), p. 7.

purpose, by the time of the Dead Sea Covenanters this spacing had acquired a "distinctive" or decorative function quite apart from indicating parallelistic breaks, and it was used for spoken as well as sung texts; nor was it (as far as can be determined) de rigueur for any particular text or class of texts at this point.

Had stichography been used exclusively to emphasize parallelism, it might eventually have raised certain structural questions at a time when Jewish commentators were of a mind to answer them. (We have seen above how the whole problem of what is and is not "poetry" in the Bible has been put to modern-day commentators most dramatically, and irresolvably, by their own post-Lowthian zeal for representing *parallelismus membrorum* typographically.) But not only did the decorative use of stichography for lists becloud the issue, but the practice of stichography as a whole soon came to be governed first by convention and then by statute in such a way as to restrict its use and obscure its relationship to parallelism.

In talmudic times, as we may judge from even later practice, spacing was in wide use. A remark in b. *Pes.* 117a (cited in a debate about whether "Halleluyah" is one word or two) is instructive: "Rab said: I saw a Psalter in the house of my uncle in which 'Hallelu' was written on one side and 'yah' on the other." Apparently this (purely decorative) spacing of a single word was anomalous, but it is not unreasonable to suppose that this particular Psalter as a whole was in some way stichographic. But while stichography may well have been the rule in certain books, it was not *required*: the Talmud established special writing for only four small sections, the two lists mentioned above (Josh. 12:9, Esther 9:7–9), the Song of the Sea (Exod. 15), and Deborah's Song (Judg. 5).

In regard to songs the talmudic sources were, it is true, somewhat confusing. *Shabbat* 103b contains the brief observation: "If he [a scribe] wrote it [the Pentateuch] as the song, or if he wrote the song as the rest [of the text] . . . these [copies] must be put aside." But the statement is unclear: "song" might mean the Song of the Sea or song in general; in the latter case, it might include any unusual arrangement, as implied in b. *Menahot* 31b. The Talmud (b. *Megilla* 16b and j. *Megilla* 3:7) supplies the names of two different stichographic techniques. The terms used derive from two sizes of brick: אריח was a small brick, placed at intervals in a wall, and לבינה was the regular, larger one. The first technique is called "small brick over large brick, large over small" and indicates the interlocking construction usual with bricks and ashlar masonry:

that is, blocks of writing ("small bricks") alternate with the blank spaces in an interlocking pattern on the page.[62] The second pattern is called "small brick over small brick, large over large" and consists of two rows of writing separated by a row of blank spaces:

The remark of the Jerusalem Talmud, brought in the name of Rab, says: "The Song of the Sea and Deborah's Song are written small brick over large brick, large over small; the ten sons of Haman (Esther 9:7–9) and the kings of Canaan (Josh. 12:9–24) are written small brick over small brick, large over large, for anything so constructed cannot stand up." The Babylonian Talmud's version of the same remark (*Megilla* 16b) is brought in the name of R. Shila of Kefar Tamrita:

All the songs are written small brick over large brick, large over

---

62. This form of stichography is still found in the מקראות גדולות Bible printed in Venice in 1525, but generally one finds a somewhat more complicated system of alternating lines:

Mordechai Breuer, in a chapter-long study of the question in his כתר ארם צובא (Jerusalem, 1976), pp. 149–89, explains that the simpler form had to be dropped in view of scribal regulations governing the use of "open" and "closed" spaces in the Torah. With the adoption of the somewhat more complicated form above, the terms "large brick" and "small brick" were apparently reinterpreted to *both* refer to blocks of writing.

small, except for this song and the kings of Canaan, which are written small brick over small brick, large over large—what [he asked] is the reason? So that [this unstable construction, bricks directly atop each other instead of interlocking, portend that] their downfall come without any chance of rebuilding [Lev. 26:37].

This version is interesting because "all the songs" may have included "Ha᾽azinu" (the Song of Moses in Deut. 32).

These prescriptions were repeated, modified, and expanded somewhat by the late (eighth century?) tractate *Soferim*. It required that Deuteronomy 32 be written two verse-halves per line, and that the Song of the Sea and Deborah's Song be written "small brick over large brick," giving the exact details of the arrangement (*Soferim* 12:8–12). Furthermore, David's Song (2 Sam. 22 = Psalm 18) is mentioned, though, unlike the others, in this song "the Sages did not specify the measure" of spacing (13:1).

In actual practice, far more than the passages mentioned received stichographic treatment of some kind. Throughout the Middle Ages, it was common practice for Jewish scribes to use some sort of special spacing at least for the "poetic" books of Psalms, Proverbs, and Job (i.e., those with the special *ṭe'amim*), as indeed *Soferim* seems to urge (13:1); moreover, isolated songs like the Song of Asaph (1 Chron. 16:8–36), and occasionally Lamentations (whose alphabetical construction called out for graphic representation of some sort), as well as lists such as Eccles. 3:2–8, 1 Sam. 6:17, Ezra 2:3 ff., 1 Chron. 24:7 ff., 25:9–14, etc. received special spacing. For songs, the system of spacing was often that seen already in the Dead Sea Scrolls—two verse-halves per line, separated by a space; when a verse was parsed as having three members, the third was sometimes connected to the second and sometimes centered on the next line.

Why, then, did the Talmud go out of its way to specify the form of writing for the Song of the Sea and Deborah's Song? Because their arrangement was, so it seems, *unusual*; the norm was simply separating verse-halves by brief spaces, but in the case of these two songs, with their numerous three-membered verses, a visual jumble would result. The solution—the interlocking pattern—failed to represent parallelism as clearly, for each clause floated, as it were, in isolation, no closer to its related neighbor than to the next or previous verse; but it did make for a regular, pleasing pattern on the page. It should also be noted that many psalms pose a similar problem. Psalm 18 (= 2 Sam. 22) came to be written in the same interlocking system, and some medieval manuscripts use a version of it for all, or almost all, the Psalter.[63]

In the case of Deuteronomy 32 we have seen that its form was first *regulated* in the tractate *Soferim*. But it is found with special spacing even in the Dead Sea Scrolls (interestingly, a fragment of Deuteronomy 32 from Qumran Cave 4 is written sometimes with two verse-halves per line and sometimes one—perhaps, as P. Skehan theorizes, so as to be able to finish exactly at the bottom of the page).[64] Note that Gaster's Samaritan Torah scroll fragment likewise has Deuteronomy 32 written stichographically, but he notes, "The division did not always follow exactly the Jewish tradition. . . . The space in the middle is merely due to mechanical division."[65] Moreover, the form of Deuteronomy 32 varied widely even after *Soferim*. The manuscript Barb. Or. 161 (thirteenth century) treats it like the Song of the Sea, "small brick over large," except for a title flourish. Vat. Ebr. 5 (which has been dated 840) has a decorative ashlar pattern using single words. The ספר העתים, an eleventh–twelfth-century tract attributed to R. Yehudah b. Barzillai of Barcelona, prescribes the two-column format for Deuteronomy 32, suggesting that the two columns represent the two Levite choirs that used to render this song in the Temple.[66] Even within this form, the actual disposition of the verses varied widely.[67] In short, in spite of attempts to regulate the writing,

---

63. See, e.g., *Vat. Ebr.* 468 (1215?).

64. Skehan, "Qumran MSS.," p. 150 n.

65. M. Gaster, *A Samaritan Pentateuch* (London, 1907), p. 36.

66. See E. N. Adler, ed., "An Eleventh Century Introduction to the Hebrew Bible," *JQR* 9 (1897): 703–04. Note also that Yehuda describes האזינו, the Book of Psalms, Proverbs, and Job as all being written in the same manner. He does not, however, describe this style as "small brick over small," possibly because this description was reserved for lists in which the white space predominated over the writing, or possibly because, as we have seen, the Talmud associated this form with downfall. The first person to describe האזינו as having the form "small brick over small" was, according to Breuer (כתר, p. 180 n.), R. Nissim b. Reuben Gerondi in the fourteenth century. Breuer's discussion of this question is most informative, though he may be wrong to understand the Talmud and *Soferim* 1:11 as implying that האזינו does not fall into the category of שירה! Sometimes שירה refers specifically to the Song of the Sea, the שירה par excellence.

67. For photographs of different arrangements, see Y. Yeivin, *The Aleppo Codex of the Bible* (Jerusalem, 1968) and the discussion of האזינו in M. Gottstein-Goshen, "The Authenticity of the Aleppo Codex," in *Textus* 1 (1960). The Aleppo Codex's anomalous arrangement of two crucial verses is found, with a slight variation, in an eleventh-century Persian manuscript (British Museum Or. MS. 1467): the fact that its version of the line begins with a different גם suggests that this scribe was perhaps working from a list of first words (similar to that found in *Soferim*, for example)—

variety persisted for some time. When he came to the question of the writing of the Pentateuchal songs, Maimonides noted in his *Mishneh Torah*, "I have found great confusion in all the scrolls I have consulted in regard to this matter" (הלכות ספר תורה 8:4).

What did all this mean for the awareness of parallelism in the Bible? First it is to be noted that there are no premodern Hebrew Bibles that systematically attempted to represent *all* fairly consistent passages of parallelism, or even most, with special spacing: the Prophets are notably neglected.[68] The "poetic" reputation of Psalms, Proverbs, and Job (perhaps traceable to their special *te'amim,* or perhaps these are themselves symptomatic) caused them to be spaced specially throughout medieval manuscripts, and the use of a similar spacing technique in the writing of Arabic poetry[69] no doubt heightened this identification in the minds of Jews in Arab lands. There is much obvious paralleling in other books, but these were by and large neglected. Thus, even at this early point the whole question of "poetic structure" in the Bible had taken a somewhat misleading turn.

The actual manner in which verses were divided by the special spacing was often still more confusing. We have noted above that the manner of dividing the Song of the Sea (Exod. 15) still in use today sometimes distorts, rather than supports, such "seconding" as does exist, and the same may be said in general of scribal spacing of other songs, psalms, and proverbs. Some copyists' spacing is frankly random.[70] Others tried to follow the *te'amim* where possible, causing the space to fall at the major medial pause of the line. But this only approximately set off the parallelism (often as we have seen briefly, *te'amim* parse the sentence against its parallelism, and sometimes only one of several parallelistic pauses will be marked as major). Moreover, when the major pause (according to the *te'amim*) fell drastically to one side or other of the line, copyists sometimes disregarded it and set the space somewhere closer to the middle of the line; this is true of the Aleppo Codex Psalter and many later manuscripts. All this tended to do for the eye what the elaboration of the *te'amim* had done for the ear: what was originally designed (or so

---

indeed, such lists may be behind the contortions of the Aleppo Codex's own arrangement.

68. Jerome's remark (PL 28:825) that his special arrangement of the prophetic books ought not to be taken as an indication that they are poetry (on which see chapter 4, section 5) is intriguing: did he institute this stichography because he had before him stichographic texts, either Greek or Hebrew?

69. See chapter 5.

70. See, e.g., Deborah's Song or the Psalter in Vat. Ebr. 468.

we believe) to reflect the basically binary structure of certain books and passages became increasingly arbitrary, mysterious, and governed by not-always-explainable convention. At the same time it should be noted that some scribes occasionally departed from the *ṭe'amim* to represent the parallelistic structure instead: this is true today of most departures from the *ṭe'amim* in the conventional writing of Exodus 15 and Judges 5,[71] and true here and there of medieval Psalter manuscripts.

The last major development in this saga of parallelism and stichography came with the invention of movable type. Printing simply did not allow typesetters the same leeway as copyists had enjoyed in spacing out parallelistic passages. The commentary מנחת שי ("Gift Offering") by Yedidya Solomon Raphael b. Abraham of Norzi, which was completed in 1626, tells the story:

> It is said in Tractate *Soferim* that . . . an outstanding scribe should space out all the Psalms, Job and Proverbs, and so indeed did those who preceded us use to do. But since all the verses are not of equal length, and many a time one of them will run on into the territory of its fellow, thus confusing the readers and making the printers' task more difficult, therefore I have chosen to abstain from this practice and not make any distinction between these and other parts of the Sacred Scripture.[72]

Norzi's commentary, of tremendous influence in Masoretic details of all sorts, won the day in this matter as well; since his time Jewish printers have largely abandoned stichography in the Bible, save for some of the lists cited above and the four songs mentioned in *Soferim*. Of these, only one, Deuteronomy 32, is written in a form that truly represents parallelism visually, that is, with parallel clauses spaced on the same line; the other three are all written, as noted, "large brick over small," which isolates A and B without necessarily setting them opposite each other. Moreover, Deuteronomy 32 contains a three-membered sentence in verse 14, which upsets the balance of its two-column system; from verse 15 to verse 39 (where another three-clause sentence occurs) the verse-halves answer each other not horizontally but diagonally!

It is thus no exaggeration to say that stichography in the seventeenth century severed whatever frail connection it still had with

---

71. See Breuer, כתר, p. 186, who lists the variances with the *ṭe'amim* without, however, offering this explanation.
72. Introduction to the Psalter.

parallelism. No doubt the form of stichography found in the Dead Sea Scrolls is already somewhat conventionalized and, as noted, a decorative device; yet one might fairly see in this a reflection of a still earlier practice (witnessed in the scribal practice of other ancient Near Eastern texts) in which special spacing followed singing arrangements and/or parallelism.[73] These systems antedate the written *ṭe'amim* and indeed compensated for their absence. But as time passed the spacing grew more and more remote from actual parallelism and more and more entwined with the *ṭe'amim* and with the rules governing spacing (i.e., paragraphing) in the "prose" sections of the Bible. The "poem in the eye" was finally down to four songs in the whole Bible; in truth, down to only a few verses in only one of the four.

7

A final important development for parallelism and its understanding is the spread of the Greek notion, "poetry." With the entrance of Hellenic political power into the territory of Israel, first under Alexander and then with successive regimes of Ptolemies and Seleucids, Greek culture began to penetrate every aspect of Jewish life. Buildings were constructed in the Greek style, Greek first names replaced Hebrew ones, and the Greek language began to be spoken by Jews.[74] Among the many new items Hellenization brought with it was its own peculiar concept *poiesis*. What was this concept? The Greeks had used their meters for all sorts of compositions, but even before Alexander, the notion that poetry was a matter of subject and style rather than meter must have been current. Aristotle wrote:

> It is the way with people to tack on "poet" to the name of a meter and talk of the elegiac-poets and epic-poets, thinking that they call them poets not by reason of the imitative nature of their work, but indiscriminately by reason of the meter they write in. Even if a

73. See, e.g., Eissfeldt, *OTI*, p. 58.
74. Gradually, it came to dominate much of the Land of Israel. "Aramaic, we judge from the inscriptions, remained important during the first Christian centuries in Palmyra, Nabatea, and Babylonia, but practically nothing has survived in Aramaic from popular Palestine. On the contrary, the inscriptions show after the fall of Jerusalem almost as complete a victory of the Greek language in Palestine as in Rome" (E. R. Goodenough, *Jewish Symbols in the Greco-Roman Period* 2 [New York, 1953], p. 123). Citing this, Bowker says, "Many Jews, both in the Dispersion and in Palestine, knew Greek and nothing else" (*The Targums*, p. 3). See also M. Hengel, *Judaism and Hellenism* 1 (Philadelphia, 1974), pp. 58–61.

theory of medicine or physical philosophy be put forth in a metrical form, it is usual to describe the writer in this way; Homer and Empedocles, however, have really nothing in common apart from their meter; so that if the one is to be called a poet the other should be termed a physicist rather than a poet.[75]

Thus, even if the Bible had used something akin to Greek-style meters in the places where one finds parallelism, this generic notion might still have prevailed among Hellenized Jews and eliminated from the corpus of true "poetry" laws, sayings, and other unpoetic utterances. But of course Hebrew was not written in meter, and to Greeks or Hellenized Jews embued with the metrical idea, parallelism, "seconding," was too loose and easy a thing to render something a poem, or indeed to be perceived as *structure* at all. Were it not so, we should find statements that remark on the poetic rendering of genres that in Greek are normally "prose"—statements that "the Jews even write their laws in verse" or the like.[76] What happened instead was quite the converse: only those genres which in Greek would have been "poetic" were called poetry in the Bible. In fact, they were said to be metrical.[77] In describing Hebrew songs, even Jewish writers failed to recognize the native parallelism, and superimposed Greek terminology. Philo consistently did so, though he occasionally stresses the antique origin and great variety of the "meters," as if to hint that their exact structure is no longer understood:

> They have also writings of men of old, the founders of their way of thinking, who left many memorials of the form used in allegorical interpretation, and these they take as a kind of archetype and imitate the method in which this principle is carried out. And so they do not confine themselves to contemplation but also compose hymns and psalms to God in all sorts of meters and melodies [*pantoion metron kai melon*] which they write down with the rhythms necessarily made more solemn.[78]
>
> Poets of an earlier age . . . have left behind them hymns in many

---

75. Aristotle, *Poetics* 1447b.

76. Thus Thomas Hobbes: "And in ancient time, before letters were in common use, the laws were many times put into verse; that the rude people, taking pleasure in singing or reciting them, might the more easily retain them in memory." He then cites specifically Prov. 7:3, Deut. 11:19, 31:12 (*Leviathan* 2, chapter 26 [1651 ed. repr. London, 1929], pp. 209–10).

77. See chapter 4.

78. Philo, *Contemplative Life*, 29–30. This last phrase appears obscure. The general sentiment expressed in this passage is reminiscent of Eccles. 44:5.

measures and melodies, [hexameter] verses and trimeter, processional hymns, libation- and altar-hymns,[79] standing choruses, arranged in a way suitable for one or many turns.[80]

In Philo's Alexandria, and even within Judea, the Greek norms of poetry were thus simply transposed onto Hebrew texts of suitable genre. For some, as will be seen, the well-known songs of Moses and David were soon indisputably "hexameters." As for parallelism, if it was perceived at all, was it not now read in a Greek way, as a "color of rhetoric," or a manifestation of something like periodic style?[81] In a world conditioned by *poiesis,* parallelism became "prose."

Rabbinic circles, as we have seen, were not keen on investigating Scripture's use of parallelism, and it is certainly not surprising that one also finds no interest in the "meters" of biblical texts or inquiry into their poetic structure. But it is noteworthy that even the general idea of a "biblical poetry," clearly espoused by Josephus and others, is wholly absent from rabbinic texts. Nor indeed is there any apparent interest in comparing the ways of biblical prophets and singers with those of the poet. Surely Moses, David, Isaiah might have been described as "poets" (as indeed they later were by Christian writers), if only to extol their technical prowesses beyond those of ordinary singers (such an opportunity presents itself in, e.g., b. *Berakot* 10a). They were not. Significantly, the Greek *poietes* appears (as *poyyetan, payyetan,* etc.) in only a handful of rabbinic texts, and there without any indication that poetry is to be found in the Bible; at best, only the

---

79. See E. Werner, "The Conflict between Hellenism and Judaism," *HUCA* 20 (1947): 411.

80. Does this refer to a single chorus or to different, possibly antiphonal, choroi? (Philo uses different terminology for antiphony, so perhaps he means something specifically relating to the arrangement of the voices; some translators have taken the phrase as referring to physical movement of the choir. The passage is in *Contemplative Life*, 80.)

81. On this point see Aristotle's *Rhetoric*, 1409b–1410a. The entire section is important to an understanding of how a "Greek mind" might react to Hebrew parallelism if it perceived it. I shall only cite part: "The periodic style, which is divided into members, is of two kinds. It is either simply divided, as in 'I have often wondered at the conveners of national gatherings and the founders of athletic contests'; or it is antithetical, where, in each of the two members, one of one pair of opposites is put along with one of another pair, or the same word is used to bracket two opposites, as 'They aided both parties—not only those who stayed behind but those who accompanied them; for the latter they acquired new territory larger than at home, and to the former they left territory at home that was large enough' " (tr. by W. Rhys Roberts).

use of alphabetical acrostics bespoke the sort of structural arrangement that might be compared to a "poet's" work.[82]

Indeed, the whole idea of a poetry with some formal defining
feature emerged only gradually in Hebrew. At first, elevated post-
biblical compositions seem to follow the biblical scheme of things:
parallelism, terseness, and a fondness for gnomic, allusive diction
characterized the songs, prayers, and sayings of the talmudic period
and even afterward. It is most instructive to consider the close
relationship of some of these early prayers with the rabbinic (prose)
homily. The "poet" (*payyetan*) often composed liturgical material of
a highly exegetical character, loosely structured litanies, sometimes
arranged into alphabetical acrostics.[83] Later, rhyme was adopted as a

---

82. See on this L. Zunz, הדרשות בישראל (Jerusalem, 1947), p. 489, ns. 134 and
135. In *Ber. Rabba* 85 one finds the explicit opposition of *piyyutin* to words spoken
"through Divine inspiration"; this idea, more than anything else, militated against
the notion of biblical meters or "poetry" in general. Note in *Yalqut Shim'oni* Song of
Songs 983 (re. Song of Songs 1:10) the distinction between *torot* (here Scripture, and
perhaps also the Oral Law) and *payyetanim*. Cf. b. *Erub.* 21b (interprets "proverbs"
and "songs" of Solomon as extrabiblical), and the well-known prohibition (b. *Sanh.*
101a) of treating Song of Songs as an ordinary song. On alphabetical acrostics and
piyyut see *Song of Songs Rabba* 1 and *Eccles. Rab.* 1 (both re. Eccles. 1:13), and
Zunz, p. 183 and p. 489, n. 136. The word *piyyut* is also found in the Jerusalem
targum, of 2 Kings 3:15, and also 2 Sam. 6:16, the latter mentioned in the medieval
treatise אמרי שפר (See A. Neubauer, מלאכת השיר [Frankfurt, 1865], p. 25). Of
course, *piyyut* in the foregoing rabbinic passages has a far narrower range than
"poetry" (indeed, it seems to refer to *exegetical* poetry, or poetry with biblical
references, even centoization), but this is just the point. Similarly, *šîrâ* is not
"poetry," nor yet properly "song," but *song of praise or thanksgiving*, thus the
frequent formula שירות ותשבחות. See also J. Schirmann, "Hebrew Liturgical Poetry
and Christian Hymnology," *JQR* 44 (1953): 130–32.

83. On the emergence of *piyyut* consult A. Mirsky's articles (n. 1), Schirmann,
"Hebrew Liturgical Poetry," and E. Fleischer, עיונים בבעיית תפקידם הליטורגי של סוגי
הפיוט הקדום, *Tarbiz* 40 (1971): 73–95. Mirsky has shown the close connection of
some early liturgical pieces to midrashic homilies. As Schirmann points out, A.
Norden and others had observed that Church hymns originated not in imitation of
classical odes, but "in the old Greek homily which was often a kind of 'hymn in
prose'" (Schirmann, 149). Similar observations are made by J. Fontaine about the
overlapping of poetry and prose in the hymns and homilies of Ambrose ("Prose et
poésie: l'interférence des genres et des styles dans la création littéraire d'Ambroise de
Milan," in G. Lazzati, *Ambrosius Episcopus* 1 (Milan, 1976), pp. 124–70). The same
conclusions about the relationship of "prose" to "poetry" in the talmudic period
emerge from an examination of early *piyyut*, and indeed are further substantiated by
the use of parallelism in many of these prayers and songs and the view of parallelism's
nature outlined in the preceding chapters. Cf. the view espoused by Sa'adya or one of
his students (below, n. 85): "poetry" only begins in Hebrew with the institutionaliza-
tion of rhyme, then coexists for a while with the "high style" of parallelism and

regular feature of Hebrew songs and prayers, along with some attention to the length of rhyming lines, and this period (perhaps the fifth or sixth century) marks a significant step in the evolution of a clearly defined poetic form of discourse in Hebrew. At the same time, parallelistic compositions, often pastiches of biblical style, continued to be written, frequently for the same genres as those served by rhyming poems, and by the same writers.

Instructive about the relationship of parallelism to poetry is the case of R. Sa'adya Ga'on, a tenth-century Jewish scholar and poet who not only wrote liturgical poetry in the conventional rhymed style of his day but also composed prayers in an unrhymed, more biblical and clearly parallelistic idiom.[84] Now it appears from Sa'adya's preface to his Psalms translation as well as from the Arabic introduction to his ספר האגרון ("Poet's Dictionary") that he did not believe the Bible contained anything that could be classified as poetry. Poetry ($ši^cr$) seems to have implied to him a composition with some systematic arrangement, typically rhyme. (Similarly, a fragment attributed to Sa'adya or one of his students characterizes the parallelistic compositions of the early liturgist Yose b. Yose as one form of "poetic prose," specifically *ḥuṭba*, a highly parallelistic Arabic style used in sermons, which in turn is distinguished from ordinary prose by its being "constructed in [poetic] lines but unrhymed."[85] Thus Sa'adya (and probably others), who knew what

---

terseness. This happened in Arabic as well: even today, a *ḥuṭba*-like style is used to elevate discourse above ordinary prose: see A. F. L. Beeston's example from a modern scholarly article in his "Parallelism in Arabic Prose," *Journal of Arabic Literature* 5 (1974): 141–42.

84. This might be associated with his other stylistic concerns aimed at "biblicizing" Hebrew poetry (on which see M. Zulay, האסקולה הפייטנית של רס'ג [Jerusalem, 1968] pp. 14–40). This "neo-classical" impulse is a major force from Sa'adya on, and, as far as parallelism is concerned, is clear not only in Menahem b. Saruq's opposition to Arabic meters (and his concomitant quasi-biblical style) but in Yehuda ha-Levi's "repenting" of his use of meter (as reported by Parḥon); on both see chapter 5.

85. Allony believes this fragment is part of the אגרון; see his edition of it (Jerusalem, 1968), pp. 386–87. But this view is not universally shared; cf., among others, E. Fleischer, עיונים בדברי השקילה של שירת הקודש הקדומה, in הספרות 8 (1977): 72, ns. 18 and 19. That these words are not Sa'adya's seems supported by the fact that in the Arabic introduction of the אגרון (Allony ed., p. 154, line 69), Yose b. Yose is described as one of the "first poets," while in this fragment he is specifically excluded from the poets. Moreover, this fragment cites Job 12:11 (on which see below) as if it were a self-contained verse, while Sa'adya's own translation of the verse takes both halves as comparisons to the verse that follows (see J. Kafih, איוב עם תרגום רס'ג [Jerusalem, 1972], p. 86). Nevertheless (and apart from its

parallelism was, indeed used it and recognized it in other writers, seems to have found it less than poetry. It was more like the style of elegant prose in Arabic. As has been argued above, this view is basically right; Sa'adya's attitude will avoid the difficulties that have arisen from identifying the presence of parallelism with poetry. Yet in another way, his attitude (which is basically the rabbinic attitude) leads inevitably to parallelism's being overlooked. Once there was poetry, parallelism became "mere" prose, and even the attempted distinction between "levels" of prose[86] was not sufficiently striking or clear-cut to be maintained.

Thus, as Jews ceased to write parallelistic songs and prayers, it was to replace this loose, hard-to-define eloquence with a more consistent and mechanical piece of structure, rhyme. Later developments in Hebrew poetry, and notably the introduction of Arabic meters and rules for rhyming, only helped to obscure the role of parallelism in the Bible: the absence of these outward signs made everything equally "prose." It is interesting to note how Sa'adya's ideas (seen above) were transmuted in a book clearly influenced by them, Moses ibn Ezra's *Kitāb al-Muḥāḍara waʾal-Muḏākara*,[87] written about a century later:

> We have found nothing in [the Bible] that goes beyond the realm of prose, save for these three books: Psalms, Job and Proverbs.[88] And

---

common points with M. ibn Ezra's views, on which see below), the fragment is most important, not only because of its apparent view of parallelism as a subpoetic feature of style, but because of its remark on "the poetry which is called *piyyut*." *Piyyut*— unlike *ḫuṭba*, *rajaz*, and *sajʿ*—is both rhymed and regular in its meter, yet different from Arabic-style poetry in that it has no precise arrangement of quantities, but "its test is in its taste, just as it says [in Job 12:11], 'Does not the ear test words, and the palate taste food?'" This seems to indicate the belief that its rhythm is arranged, as Bede and later Latin writers were to express it, *ad iudicium aurium* (as opposed to the strict numbers of quantitative meters in classical Latin and Greek). The fragment continues: "The meaning of this is the connectedness of the ideas of the lines so that they will not be split up, for if they are split the line will be skewed and thus ruined." This somewhat troubling wording (see Allony's interpretation, pp. 388–89, and Fleischer's, p. 78) seems to indicate that each line must be end-stopped and that no full stop occur before the end. For the fragment apparently understands Job to refer to the *ear's* testing of words as opposed to strict numbers' testing of them, hence to its hearing units of thought ("the *ideas* of the lines") rather than sequences of metrical feet. Cf. Sa'adya's ספר הגלוי (ed. A. Harkaby, Petersburg, 1891), p. 156, lines 6–8.

86. האגרון, pp. 80–81.

87. M. ibn Ezra, *Kitāb al-Muḥāḍara waʾal-Muḏākara*, ed. A. S. Halkin (Jerusalem, 1975), pp. 46–47.

88. That is, those with the distinctive *ṭeʿamim*.

as you will see, these books had recourse to neither meter nor rhyme, in the way of the Arabs, but are only like *rajaz* compositions.[89] Sometimes by chance some of them may indeed be found to follow the method of *rajaz* [i.e., rhyme], such as these: [Job 28:16, 33:17, 21:4] and the like. Some of the songs [שירות] in the Bible depart from prose, such as the Song of the Sea, *Ha'azinu* (Deut. 32), David's Song and Deborah's Song. Now I have said only some of the songs because some of what is called שירה is [actually] in prose, such as the Song of Songs and the Song of the Well (Num. 21:17) and so forth, as I have explained.[90] The halakhists [compilers of the treatise שירתא] set the number of Biblical songs at nine, but most of them are prose.[91] The Bible attests that Solomon

89. An irregular meter, basically symmetrical but of variable length. See R. A. Nicholson, *A Literary History of the Arabs* (London, 1930), pp. 74–75. Ibn Ezra probably makes this comparison because he wants to assert that these books are poetic, yet metrically irregular. But his comparison then leads him to deal with the question of rhyme in these books because *rajaz* compositions are, of course, rhymed. Note that the fragment attributed to Sa'adya's אגרון (Allony, p. 386) to which ibn Ezra's words here bear some resemblance, describes as *rajaz* "that which is found to rhyme in the Bible, but it is not poetry." It then cites as examples Job 28:16, 21:4, and Isa. 49:1. M. Ibn Ezra used the first two but not the third, perhaps because it did not come from a "poetic" book.

90. Ibn Ezra had begun his treatise with a discussion of *ḥuṭba*, the rhetorical, somewhat parallelistic sermon style mentioned above; he characterized as *ḥuṭba* various biblical farewell speeches (כ'טבה אלוודאע), such as those beginning at Deut. 29:9, Josh. 23:1 and 24:1, 1 Kings 2:1 and 8:5 (all "prose" by modern standards), plus certain prayers and songs of a more overtly parallelistic character, including the Prayer of Hannah (1 Sam. 2:1), which all modern critics treat as "poetry." In this same passage he notes that some of the compositions called song (שיר) are actually prose, "such as the Song of Songs, and 'I will sing to my beloved' (Isa. 5:1) and the like." See Halkin ed., pp. 20–21.

91. See J. Z. Lauterbach, *Mekilta de R. Ishmael* 2 (Philadelphia, 1935), p., 2; also H. Horowitz and I. Rabin, מכילתא (Jerusalem, 1970), p. 116 and notes. The tradition that Ten Songs mark ten decisive points in Israel's history is obviously an ancient one, and, as with the Ten Trials of Abraham and other such traditions, there are competing lists of the ten items involved. To date there is no satisfactory treatment of the tradition in its entirety. A useful article on some Jewish sources is A. Epstein, "שירת אברהם אבינו," in ממזרח וממערב 1 (1894): 85–89. Note also the references cited in L. Ginzberg, *Legends of the Jews* 6 (Philadelphia, 1928), pp. 11–12. The tradition of Ten Songs presented in the opening section of the exegetical targum of Song of Songs is discussed by R. Loewe, "The Apologetic Motifs in the Targum to Song of Songs," in A. Altmann, *Biblical Motifs* (Cambridge, 1966), pp. 169–70. Origen, in his homily on the Song of Songs, lists seven songs (Num. 21:17–18, שירת הבאר, though not cited, is alluded to in the words "ad puteum quem foderunt reges"). Now there are five songs specifically referred to in the Bible by the feminine form *šîrâ* (as opposed to the more common form *šîr*): Exod. 15, Num. 21:17–18,

wrote both verse and prose, which are the proverbs, "And Solomon spoke three thousand *māšāl*"—this is the prose—"and his song was one thousand and five"—this is the poetry.[92] There are sages who hold them to be *qaṣīda*.[93] But of the nature of these poetic compositions, and even of their existence, I know nothing, for not the slightest trace of them has come down to us.

Deut. 32, 2 Sam. 22, and Isa. 5. All five figure in Origen's list of seven; he adds Judg. 5 (not called *šîrâ* in the text, but frequently so designated in later writings, perhaps because of the targum of Judg. 5:1 or its tradition of stichography) and the Song of Songs. Though of course Origen's remarks make nothing of the form *šîrâ*, his list seems to derive from a tradition quite separate from that of the Ten Songs, namely, the rabbinic enumeration of five songs called by the form *šîrâ*. It is the conflation of these two traditions that one finds in the targum of Song of Songs, *Mekilta*, and elsewhere. All of Origen's songs except Isa. 5 appear in the Song of Songs targum, which adds (to make ten) Psalm 92, Josh. 10:12, 1 Sam. 2, and Isa. 30:29. The *Mekilta* lists Ten Songs but also preserves the remark, "All the *šîrôt* are called by the feminine name," etc., which could only have applied to a list ot the five *šîrôt* plus some eschatological *šîr* such as Isa. 30:29, 42:10, or the like. Note also that Origen's *commentary* on the Song of Songs, preserved in the translation of Rufinus, also lists seven songs, but substitutes for Isa. 5 the Song of Asaph (1 Chron. 16:8), thus preserving the apparent chronological order. Origen adds: "If anyone think that the song of Isaiah should be included with the others—though it does not seem proper that the song of Isaiah be placed before the Song of Songs, since Isaiah wrote much later—if, nevertheless, anyone is of the opinion that the prophetic utterances are to be judged by their content rather than their date, he will add that song (Isa. 5) as well, and will say that this song that Solomon sang is indeed the 'song of songs' not only in relation to those that were sung before it, but also to those that came after it as well." Note also that early Christian liturgy contained various "odes" or "canticles" from the Hebrew Bible and the New Testament, overlapping with some lists of the Ten: see *SB*, pp. 139–40; Schirmann, "Hebrew Liturgical Poetry," pp. 160–61; and H. Leeb, *Die Psalmodie bei Ambrosius* (Vienna, 1967), pp. 27–28; and cf. b. *Pes.* 117a. J. Goldin has attempted to explain the origin of the tradition of Ten Songs (in his "This Song," in S. Lieberman, *Salo Baron Jubilee Volume* 1 [Jerusalem, 1974], pp. 539–54), but ingenuity outstrips credibility. Finally, it is to be noted that the Aramaic equivalent of *šîr* is שבח ("praise") and is used for the verb "sing" in many passages (cf. above, n. 82). Similarly תושבחתא translates *haššîrâ*, e.g., Deut. 31:20, 2 Sam. 22:1. In biblical texts not specifically labeled as *šîrâ*, the fact that the targum reads שבח may have fostered their association with the *šîrôt*. Thus, Josh. 10:12 is rendered בכן שבח יהושע קדם ה' וג', the same formula as is found in Num. 21:17, Exod. 15, etc.

92. Cf. Song of Songs Rabba 1:10.

93. "Odes"—another very old Arabic verse form and one viewed as the archetype of poetry; see Nicholson, *Literary History*, p. 76. Ibn Ezra's repudiation of the idea that the biblical compositions ascribed to Solomon constitute "poetry" may be based on the talmudic discussion of the canonicity of Solomon's *mĕšālim*: see b. *Meg.* 7a.

FOUR

BIBLICAL POETRY AND
THE CHURCH

1

Philo, the first person known to have described Hebrew writing in the terminology of Greek meters, was also a consistent allegorizer of the biblical text, and these are not unrelated facts.

Allegorizing of the Bible is, of course, older than Philo: it is found even in the Greek translation of the Bible, which in the course of translating also sought to harmonize biblical teachings with Greek doctrines.[1] Aristobulus of Paneas (second century B.C.) and the Letter of Aristeas (ca. 100 B.C.) present allegorical interpretations of the Bible, as of course the New Testament does. Before all these come purely Greek instances of allegorizing, for example, the Stoics' harmonizing of stories of the gods with their own ideas, or allegorical interpretations of Homer going back to Theagenes of Rhegium (sixth century B.C.).[2] The impulse to allegorize, in all these cases, comes at least in part from a perceived contradiction or inconsistency within a text, or between the text and something outside it (one's senses, ideology, knowledge of history, etc.). By looking for an *allegoria*, an "other speaking," or *hyponoia*[3] (Philo's usual term) the difficulty can be resolved:

1. See H. A. Wolfson, *Philo* (Cambridge, 1947), p. 94.
2. H. I. Marrou, *St. Augustin et la fin de la culture antique* (Paris, 1938), p. 495. See also S. Lieberman, *Hellenism in Jewish Palestine* (New York, 1950), p. 64. Theagenes of Rhegium was apparently not the first allegorist of Homer, but the first *defensive* allegorist (nothing of his allegorical work survives). According to J. Tate, "On the History of Allegorism" (*Classical Quarterly* [1934]: 105–14) the first use of allegory was "positive" or "exigetical," an attempt by later readers to find in Homer or Hesiod hints of doctrines which they felt the poets surely knew. (This article is also valuable in its discussion of the Greek view of poetic inspiration.)
3. The same term used earlier in allegorizations of Homer. See Lieberman, *Hellenism*, p. 64, on Stesimbrotus (fifth century B.C.).

If taken literally, this point presents, I feel, great difficulty. The penalty inflicted by law on those whose offenses are identical is unequal. . . . Let us then have recourse to the scientific mode of interpretation which looks for the hidden meaning (*hyponoia*) of the literal words. . . . We say then that the High Priest is not a man, but a Divine Word. . . . Moreover, his head has been annointed with oil, and by this I understand that [the Word's] ruling faculty is illumined with a brilliant light. . . . Now the garments which the Supreme Word of Him that is puts on are the world.[4]

A second, related motive for allegorizing is to lift the discourse from the specific to the general, and (in the case of the Bible) to turn what is historical and particular into something universal and (hence) potentially personal.

This is why [Abraham] is said to emigrate first from the land of Chaldea to that of Haran. Now Haran translated into Greek means "holes," a symbol for the seats of our senses.[5]

Beyond the harmonizing and generalizing accomplished by allegory, there is another, typically Greek appeal to it: it makes apparently straightforward utterances into gnomic ones. The text becomes a surface, concealing essences of universal dimension beneath it. Now to the Greeks, the very idea that the Bible, like an oracle, spoke in riddles, was a confirmation of its Divine character; and the fact that it did not seek to say, but only, through its histories and odes, pointed to truths that lie beyond the capacity of speech—well, here was a sign that it was a truly worthy text, one meriting the careful analysis that the Jews were said to lavish upon it.[6]

It will be instructive, then, to consider briefly the difference between allegorical exegesis of the Bible and its (more Semitic) competitor, midrash. Both are systems which can be used for smoothing over "irregularities of surface" in a passage: apparent contradictions, irrelevancies, anthropomorphisms, etc. And both accomplish this smoothing over by making reference to something

4. Philo, *On Flight and Finding* xxi, F. H. Colson, tr. (Cambridge, 1968), pp. 67–69.

5. Philo, On Abraham xvi (Colson, p. 41).

6. The notion that the plain truth must be "represented" to humans to be understood is fundamental. Thus the Latin Father Cassiodorus notes: "In terris nobis pro captu ingeni, parabolis et propositionibus sumptis, coelestis veritas intimatur" ("But for us on earth, so that our own intellect may comprehend it, Heavenly truth is represented in figures and propositions.") See *PL* 70:1131. This idea is much older, however, and is the theme of Book 5 of Clement's *Miscellanies*.

outside the passage. For this reason, the two have been described as essentially the same process.[7]

But there is an important difference. In midrash the governing supposition is that the text of the Bible is a single whole, its Divine character the stuff of which all its several separable units are made. On this basis alone we should be justified in explaining a verse in Deuteronomy in terms of a verse from Isaiah, for the same God is speaking to us through two different prophets. (However, it is probably more accurate to think of this as a later stage in development of a process whose first steps would be more simple-minded: understanding a now-obscure phrase via a clearer use in another biblical book; the comparison of two texts that present similar versions of the same law or narrative [as we have seen in the case of the גזרה שוה]; understanding A in terms of B.)

The "something else" in terms of which the text is read, then, is always another biblical text. So it is with what has been cited as a typical piece of rabbinic allegorizing, the interpretation of Exodus 15:22 "They found no water" adduced in the *Mekilta*.[8] Here the "allegorizers" (דורשי רשומות)[9] understood "water" to mean Torah. Now on the face of it, this does resemble Greek allegorizing. What makes it midrash instead is the proof text which is immediately brought in support of this reading: "Ho every one that thirsteth, come ye for water!" (Isa. 55:1). The midrashist is saying: "Many times—as here in Isaiah—the word 'water' is used where it obviously means not water but something like Torah or Divine learning." (He could have cited other instances: Isa. 49:10; Jer. 2:13, 17:13; Ezek. 47:1; Zech. 14:8, etc., and, of course, numerous rabbinic parables.) "We must, therefore, be careful to consider this other meaning of 'water' wherever it appears in Scripture; even here, where actual water seems to fit the text, perhaps we ought to understand 'Torah.'" This is the method not so much of the allegorist as of the philologist, or perhaps the cryptographer. It is not on the basis of one's fancy or mere

---

7. See Wolfson, *Philo*, pp. 134–35; also *The Philosophy of the Church Fathers* on the allegorical method, pp. 24–72. These discussions are useful in breaking down the "literalistic vs. allegorical" polarity that characterizes other discussions of the subject, but Wolfson fails to make the point about midrash that it proceeds via other parts of the Bible (see below). This is the important difference between the two: see also R. J. Loewe, "Apologetic Motifs in the Aramaic Targums to the Song of Songs," in A. Altmann, ed., *Biblical Motifs* (Cambridge, 1966), pp. 158–59. On תורה מתוך תורה see j. *Megilla* Ib, b. *BQ* 2b; also Lieberman, *Hellenism*, p. 49.

8. J. Z. Lauterbach, ed., *Mekilta de R. Ishmael* (Philadelphia, 1935), p. 89.

9. See Wolfson, *Church Fathers*, p. 25.

impressions that a midrashic reading may be put forward, but on the basis of some adduced text. Even in the most allegorical of rabbinic exegeses, those of the Song of Songs, the focus never shifts from the words of the text; if it is even proper to speak here of "literal" and "figurative" meanings at all, these words should be used in a way quite distinct from their normal application, "for the letter is not, as in Christian exegesis, the potentially jealous stepmother of allegory, but rather her willing handmaid or research assistant."[10]

This difference in method reflects a still more profound difference. For the rabbinic mind, the holiness of the Bible resides in its details: "Turn it over and over, for everything is in it."[11] The fact that it comes of Divine source means that it is perfect. We have seen that the rabbinic idea of the Bible's omnisignificance meant that the slightest details of its manner of speaking are to be considered both significant and intelligible. Furthermore, no words are wasted, and by this we must also understand that nothing is repeated or said for emphasis or purposes of rhetoric. This is of course true for parallel verse-halves, but it is evidenced elsewhere as well. For the imperative perceived by the midrashist in the Bible's holiness is to understand it as fully as possible by sifting every word and comparing it to every other part of the text. The text's Divinity is thus both the guarantee that such searching will be fruitful (for nothing is said in vain, for emphasis, and so forth) and the key to how to search (elsewhere in the same Divinely inspired text).

Not so the allegorist. For him the essence of the text's sanctity is the fact of its allegorizing: what vouchsafes its Divinity is that, in seeming to present history, it alludes allegorically to what is eternal and perhaps ineffable.[12] As a consequence, the allegorist will not be concerned with harmonizing two apparently contradictory laws, since they are in any case mere allusions (on the contrary, an apparent contradiction will only tend to confirm him in this reading). But his attention will especially focus on the little details which, although at

10. R. J. Loewe, "Apologetic Motifs," 159.
11. M. *Abot*, 5:25.
12. This attitude developed slowly and unsystematically. Origen and his successors had to walk what they considered a middle path between the extreme allegories of sects that refused literal meaning (and, in the New Testament, the historicity of Jesus!), and on the other hand the rejection of allegorical reading whatsoever (see Wolfson, *Church Fathers*, pp. 73–96). Still, the insistence in this early period on the "perfection" of Scripture (pp. 91–92) is not the same as the midrashist's; it is perfect in that apparently irrelevant details have an allegorical dimension, hence "nothing is said in vain."

home in a narrative, are too particular for his notion of a holy text. "Whatever in the text has nothing to do with right conduct or questions of faith," said St. Augustine, "must be understood figuratively."[13]

Ironically, Christian exegesis is, from our perspective, sometimes more "Jewish" than Philo. For its reading of the "Old Testament" as prefiguring the New is connected both to Greek allegorizing and to the midrashic idea of the essential unity of all parts of a divinely inspired text.[14] Here the precise wording of laws, tales, and the like is scrutinized for possible allusions to subsequent history, viz., the events surrounding the life of Jesus as set forth in the Gospels. This search for foreshadowing, if not quite the philologist's type of operation recognizable in midrash, is not purely Philo's either; it moves from one historical frame to another. (A similar notion of large-scale correspondence is observable in such Jewish practices as the *haftarah*, wherein a section from the Prophets is selected as a matching text to the weekly reading from the Pentateuch.)[15] Of course, this is not all there is to Christian interpreting. In St. Paul one finds an allegory reminiscent of Philo's (Gal. 4:21–31), as well as typology (Gal. 3:14, 16 etc.), as in later Christian exegesis. Soon these were to become systematic.[16]

The rabbinic exegete, as we have seen, is "blind" to parallelism by conviction and temperament. The text's holiness both allows and requires him to search out the highest possible reading of a verse. Repetition, rhetoric, emphasis—these are traits best not attributed to the word of God, all the more so because "searching" a verse through its canonized surroundings will yield so much richer a meaning. But for the allegorist, the text's holiness resides in its multiplicity, in the fact that it can be read on two, three, or four different levels. Of these,

13. *De Doctrina Christiana* 3.10.14. See Marrou, *St. Augustin*, p. 478. This is an extension of the earlier doctrine, "whatever *contradicts* right conduct . . . ."

14. On the latter, see 2 Tim. 3:16, where Paul specifically states that every part of the divinely inspired Bible is useful to the Christian. Now Judaism also has Messianic readings, as well as other species of what Wolfson calls "historical predicative" texts; see *Church Fathers*, p. 27.

15. See J. Mann, *The Bible as Read and Preached in the Synagogue* (Cincinnati, 1940, reissued New York, 1971) and the "Prolegomenon" of B. Z. Wacholder.

16. On this whole question consult H. de Lubac's exhaustive *Exégèse médiévale: les quatre sens de l'Ecriture* (Paris, 1959). For his distinguishing of Christian from pagan allegory, see esp. vol. 1, pp. 373–96; note also his connection of Christian allegory with phenomena such as the historicization of Israelite agricultural holidays in Exodus, and with "infra-biblical" midrash, 1, pp. 312–16. Cf. N. R. M. deLange, *Origen and the Jews* (Cambridge, 1976), pp. 103–21.

its surface meaning is the least important—often even incidental. Therefore, there is no blasphemy, or lèse majesté, in reading that surface as if it were a human text. To say that it is composed in meter, or follows the laws of Greek rhetoric; to see tropes and figures in it, or to read it in a way not essentially different from the way one reads other books—these do not touch the sanctity of the text, *because that is not where the sanctity lies.* And this is why Christian exegesis of the Hebrew Bible, though often hampered by incomplete mastery (if not total ignorance) of the Hebrew text, is far more attentive to real and imaginary nuances of style as such than the Rabbis—why in our specific area of concern, the Church Fathers here and there discoursed on parallelism *per se* while talmudic exegesis never did so. And, curiously, it is also why, in the end, Christian exegesis failed to understand the essence of parallelism, and began a process of misreading that, as we have seen, continues to this day.[17]

2

Philo, as we have seen in *The Contemplative Life,* attributed hexameters, trimeters, and other Greek meters to Hebrew poetry. It may be that a reference here to the "poets of an earlier age" (*Contemplative Life* 10) implies biblical authors, or he may have had in mind the immediate ancestors of his Therapeutai, the authors of compositions probably comparable to the "Thanksgiving hymns" discovered at Qumran. The same ambiguity surrounds his statement (*Contemplative Life* 3) that the Therapeutai "sing hymns and psalms to God composed of many meters and melodies (*pantoion metron kai melon*)." Are these biblical psalms and canticles, or postbiblical compositions? About Moses, Philo says that he learned "the study of rhythm, harmony and meters" from the Egyptians (*Life of Moses* 1, 23); however, though he describes the antiphonal structure of the Song of the Sea in several places (*Contemplative Life* 11; *Life of Moses* 1, 32; 2, 46) he does not attribute a specific meter to it. Neither does he say anything about the meter of Balaam's oracles, for example.

    Josephus, that other chief purveyor of the metrical hypothesis in Hebrew poetry to the Greek-speaking world, was somewhat more specific about the Bible: in three separate instances in the *Jewish Antiquities* he names the meter of biblical compositions:

17. On the history of Christian ideas about biblical poetry, in this and in subsequent periods, consult L. Alonso-Schökel's valuable guide, *Estudios de Poetica Hebrea* (*EPH*).

Moses also composed a song to God [Exod. 15] containing his praises and thanksgiving for his kindness, in hexameter verses. [*Jewish Antiquities* 2, 16:4]

After this he read them a song [Deut. 32] composed in hexameter, and left it to them in the sacred Scriptures. [4, 8:44]

And now David, free from wars and danger and enjoying the prospect of peace, composed songs and hymns to God of several sorts of meter; some of these he made with trimeter, some pentameters; he also made musical instruments and taught the Levites to sing hymns to God. [7, 12:3]

These include, of course, some of the "songs par excellence" of Jewish tradition, those calle *šîrâ* and (as was seen earlier) frequently singled out by special stichography. Yet of Deborah's Song (Judg. 5) Josephus is curiously silent (5, 5), and about Solomon he observes only, "He also composed books of odes and songs, one thousand and five, and of parables and figures three thousand [an allusion to 1 Kings 5:12]," without saying anything of their form.

This is the somewhat spare basement of that imposing structure, the patristic and medieval notion that the Psalms, Job, and other biblical books are "metrical." Nearly two thousand years of scanning, syllable-counting, and the like have failed to yield a consistent metrical structure in them—certainly nothing to which the terms "hexameter," "pentameter," or "trimeter" might be meaningfully applied. What possible motive, then, can be attributed to Philo and Josephus in these statements? It is of course possible that the designations actually corresponded to rough rhythmical schemes in their minds, schemes that were known in Hebrew under generic names (קינה, "lament," etc.) for which "hexameter," "trimeter" and like terms were selected as rough equivalents, "translations."[18] One modern critic has suggested that the Greek quantitative terms used in regard to biblical poetry actually suggested a corresponding number of stress accents.[19] But in view of modern failures to substantiate this, or indeed any metrical hypothesis, this approach seems hardly worthwhile. A second alternative is that the terms were not used as rhythmical designations at all, but to indicate the character of the composition. For (as we have seen in Philo) meters were associated with certain subjects and life-settings; by "hexameter" Josephus may

18. See Joh. Döller, *Rhythmus, Metrik und Strophik* (Paderborn, 1899), p. 20.
19. G. Castellino, "Il Ritmo ebraico nel pensiero degli antichi," in *Biblica* 15 (1934): 508.

mean a heroic song, an epic speech such as those found in Homer; by "trimeter" or "pentameter" he may mean a lyric comparable to those composed in these meters.

Beyond these possibilities, it may simply be that the terms were used because, for a Greek readership, some account or mention of the meter of a poem or song was only to be expected. "No meter" was hardly credible. For their part, Hellenic Jews (and even one so intimately connected to the Temple service as Josephus) must have been puzzled about the laws governing the structure of psalms and other Hebrew songs they heard. Surely, some meter stood behind the very evident musical regularity, determining even the occasional lapses in that regularity. Furthermore, the Greek association of music and meter with mathematics encouraged Jews to seek this branch of wisdom in their own Divine service; failing to find it there, they were more likely to blame their own inabilities (who knew the rules? which syllables were long and which short?) than the text. And in this there was a matter of prestige as well: something so fine as meter they were not willing to concede to the Greeks' exclusive domain. This last point has been nicely summarized:

> The Hellenistic Jews, once they had come in contact with Greek culture, sought to integrate themselves amongst the Greeks by countering philosophy with philosophy, history with history, literature with literature, divesting all their thought of its specifically Semitic character and attempting to present it in keeping with the language of the Greek cultural milieu in which they found themselves.[20]

The truth of the matter is probably that neither Josephus nor Philo had any real notion of the "meter" of biblical songs, but they never doubted that it existed. Their use of metrical terms was probably chiefly intended to communicate that belief, and also perhaps, as noted, to "translate" the character of the compositions into Greek analogues.

3

Certain elements of the Early Church maintained a hostile attitude toward "pagan" (i.e., non-Christian Greek and Latin) literature, and were consequently reluctant to speak of Moses or David as "poets." But this was not uniformly true of the early Greek Fathers: some had a

---

20. Castellino, "Ritmo ebraico," p. 505.

high opinion of poetry in spite of its excesses, and this opinion survived amid their Christianity. So, for example, Athenagoras, Clement of Alexandria and others frequently cite verse from Homer to support their theological arguments, and of course Sybilline verse, the oracles of a Hebrew "prophetess."[21]

Connected to this phenomenon is the firm belief of the period that Greek poetry, philosophy, and other learning had originated with the Hebrews.[22] The roots of this notion are pre-Christian: it was a Jewish bulwark against the inroads of Hellenization, but one that at the same time helped Jews to accept Greek learning without conceding it priority or even originality. Thus, Aristobulus of Paneas reports that even before the Septuagint Jewish wisdom had been translated and spread among the Greeks:

> For others before Demetrius Phalereus, and prior to the supremacy of Alexander and the Persians, have translated both the narrative of the exodus of the Hebrews our fellow countrymen from Egypt, and the fame of all that happened to them, and the conquest of the land, and the exposition of the whole Law; so that it is manifest that many things have been borrowed by the aforesaid Philosopher [Plato] for

21. *PG* 8:177, 187. The Hebraic Sibyl, located exactly halfway between poetry and prophecy, remained throughout a most important figure to Christianity. See on this Theophilus, "To Autolycus" (written c. 181 A.D.) Book 2, 36. (The Sibyls later flanked the Hebrew prophets in Michelangelo's Sistine ceiling.) But before this, Sibylline oracles were for the Jewish community of Egypt an attempt "to establish common ground between the Jewish and gentile worlds. . . . This was attempted on the basis of the structural similarity of Hellenistic political oracles and Biblical prophecy, and by the functional equation of an expected Ptolemaic ruler with the Jewish messiah" (John J. Collins, *Sibylline Oracles of Egyptian Judaism* [Missoula, Mont., 1972], p. 118). See also R. Marcus, "Hellenistic Literature," in L. Finkelstein, *The Jews* 2 (New York, 1949), pp. 62–63.

22. On this theme consult M. Hengel, *Judaism and Hellenism* (Philadelphia, 1974), pp. 83–106. Clement (*Stromateis* 6, 11) argues that Greek music (hence meter) came from David. Cf. Justin Martyr, 1 *Apologies*, 44; Theophilus, *To Autolycus* 3:16; Augustine, *De Doctrina* 2.28.43 and *City of God* 8, 11. Note the discussion in G. L. Ellspermann, *The Attitude of the Early Christian Latin Writers toward Pagan Literature and Learning* (Washington, D.C., 1949), pp. 9–13, and the passages cited in L. Ginsberg, *Legends of the Jews* 6 (Philadelphia, 1968), pp. 282–83. Origen, noting the three branches of learning in Greek science—ethics, physics, and enoptics—observes: "It seems to me that all the sages of the Greeks borrowed these ideas from Solomon, who had learnt them from the Spirit of God at an age and time long before their own, and that they then put them forward as their own invention" (prologue to his Commentary on the Song of Songs). On the persistence of these ideas, see E. de Bruyne, *Etudes d'esthétique médiévale* 1 (Brugge, 1946), pp. 210–11.

he is very learned; as also Pythagoras transferred many of our precepts and inserted them in his own system of doctrines.[23]

Similarly, the Letter of Aristeas (written ca. 100 B.C.) is devoted to demonstrating the superiority of Jewish wisdom (i.e., the Torah and its allegorical interpretation) to Greek philosophy. Josephus repeats and elaborates this theme in *Against Apion*. Among other proofs he reports an account from Clearchus, a pupil of Aristotle, that his master had discoursed at length with a Jew "and since he [the Jew] had lived with many learned men, he communicated to us [i.e., Aristotle] more information than he received from us."[24]

Clement of Alexandria was familiar with Aristobulus, and attempts[25] to document the idea that Greek wisdom was "stolen" from the Hebrews by adducing examples of infra-Greek plagiarisms (to show their thieving ways!). The same theme was sounded by other writers: one such "plagiarism," the borrowing of the story of Gideon and the fleece (Judg. 6:37–40) for the Argonaut legend (!) is reported by Eusebius and carries through to Dante.[26] In fact, Eusebius's *Preparation for the Gospel* presents a whole compendium of arguments in support of the Hebrew origin of all wisdom: Aristobulus, Josephus, Tatian, Diodorus, and others are cited at great length. Artapanus, in a passage preserved in Eusebius (*Preparation*, Book 9),

---

23. Cited in Eusebius, *Preparation for the Gospel* 13, chapter 12, p. 664a–b. Cf. Ginsberg, *Legends* 6, pp. 282–83.

24. Josephus, *Against Apion* 1, 22. See also E. J. Bickerman, "The Historical Foundations of Post-Biblical Judaism" in L. Finkelstein, *The Jews* 1, p. 75; he says this account is "a fiction, but not one which is improbable." Cf. Hans Lewy, "Aristotle and the Jewish Sage According to Clearchus," *HTR* 31 (1938): 205–35. Additional evidence of this kind of thinking is to be found in Tatian's *Address to the Greeks* (*PG* 6:803). Tatian (born 120) believed all worthwhile Greek learning and institutions derived from the "Barbarians" (chiefly the Hebrews), to which the Greeks added "nothing save their own errors." Related is the idea that "natural reason" was given to the Greeks as a preparation for accepting Christianity. This theme, perhaps hinted at in Rom. 2:14, is taken up by Clement and, of course, Eusebius in his *Preparation*. See on this E. Gilson, *History of Christian Philosophy in the Middle Ages* (New York, 1955), pp. 32–33. Later, Theodoret (c. 386–458) wrote a tract entitled "Cure for Greek Maladies, or the Discovery of the Evangelical Truth Beginning from Greek Philosophy": see Gilson, *Christian Philosophy*, pp. 596–97.

25. *Miscellanies* 6: 2, 4. Cf. de Bruyne, *Etudes* 1, pp. 214–15.

26. See G-R. Sarolli, *Prolegomena alla Divina Commedia* (Florence, 1971), p. 400. Cf. the equation of Enoch and Atlas, Hamor and Hermes, etc.; see Hengel, *Judaism and Hellenism*, p. 89.

maintained that Moses was the teacher of Orpheus and the founder of philosophy.[27]

The result of the tendency was to allow poetry and other "pagan learning" a small place within Christianity. It might not have happened without it. For it was precisely because he believed all wisdom came from the Hebrews that Clement (and others) felt free to look for learning also in its somewhat corrupted Greek form: Aratus, Hesiod and others had taught "fragments of the true theology."[28]

Allegorical interpretations also saved a great deal, and not just by the "smoothing over" already discussed. Thus Clement, who learned from Philo the practice of allegorical interpretation of the Bible (and in turn passed it on to Origen), in the fifth book of his *Miscellanies* defends the doctrine of "concealment"—that wisdom must be passed on in a form not comprehensible immediately, or to all. But this doctrine reflected quite favorably on Greek literature as well, and specifically on its form. For, Clement says, Greek poets are comparable to Hebrew prophets in their allegorizing, and he cites Psalm 78:1-2, "I shall open my mouth with figures" (*māšāl* here is translated in the Sepuagint as *parabole*) to show that the manner of hidden meaning in biblical writings is comparable to that of Homer and Hesiod in their (by then well-established) allegorical interpretation.[29]

Beside these procedures, poetry and other Greek achievements could be countenanced within early Christianity by attributing to them some sort of supernatural source short of Divine inspiration. This is evidently Athenogoras's aim when he writes (in *A Plea for Christians*, A.D. 176):

> Poets and philosophers have proceeded by conjecture. They were driven each by his own soul and through a sympathy with the Divine Spirit to see if it were possible to comprehend the truth. They were able indeed to get some notion of reality, but not to find it, since they did not deign to learn about God from God, but each one from himself. For this reason they taught conflicting things about God, matter, forms and the world. We, on the contrary, have as witnesses for what we maintain and believe the Prophets, who

27. See Marcus, "Hellenistic Literature," p. 48; Hengel, *Judaism and Hellenism*, p. 91.

28. R. B. Tollington, *Clement of Alexandria* 1 (London, 1914), p. 217.

29. See *PG* 9:44, 9:80. This continues well into the Middle Ages: de Bruyne, *Etudes* 2, p. 328.

have spoken through the divine spirit itself about God and theology.[30]

Similarly, Origen:

There is a particular energy or power who is the inspirer of poetry, another of geometry, and in the same way . . . of every such art and subject of instruction. Finally, many Greeks have been of the opinion that the art of poetry cannot exist apart from madness, and accordingly in their histories it is recorded that those whom they call seers were suddenly filled with the spirit of a kind of madness. And what is to be said also of those persons whom they call divine, who through the control of the demons that are over them utter responses in verses formed according to the rules of the poetic art?[31]

In both these passages there is an obvious dissonance, the clash of the authors' admiration for Greek poetry and philosophy with the exclusive nature of Divine inspiration as presented in the Bible and Christian doctrine. For Origen, especially, it was a difficult problem.[32] But by these and similar efforts to strike a compromise, the door between biblical and secular literature was left open: it was possible to dwell in the biblical chamber without sealing oneself off from the secular. Now inevitably, movement through this door was not unidirectional. (Supposedly) historical and analogical connections between the writings of the Greeks and the Hebrews[33] left many early Christians favorably disposed to the notion that the Prophets (including, of course, David) were *at least poets*, poets-and-something-more; that their Divine inspiration was comparable (though, of course, superior) to poetic inspiration or the madness from which pagan auguries had come; and that, finally, the songs and poems of the Old Testament were, as any self-respecting poem would be, written in meter. In short, their undaunted feelings for Greek literature helped to prepare the ground for the metrical hypothesis of biblical poetry. The testimony of Philo and Josephus—Jews, and hence authoritative on matters of Hebrew culture—was welcomed as definitive, and repeated.

---

30. Translated in C. R. Richardson, *Early Christian Fathers* (Philadelphia, 1953), pp. 306–07. Cf. Clement, *Miscellanies* 6: 5.

31. G. W. Butterworth, tr., *Origen on First Principles* (based on Koetschau's text) (Gloucester, Mass., 1973), book 3, chapter 3, p. 226.

32. About the priestess of the Delphic oracle, see *Contra Celsum* 3, 25; 7, 3.

33. Fueled everywhere by the syncretisms of Philo, who at one point even ventures to identify Terah with Socrates (*On Dreams* 1: 10, 58).

4

Origen discussed the meter of the Psalms in a now-famous[34] scholion to Psalm 118 (119). After citing the first verse in its Septuagint version, he notes:

> This how the verse is written. But the verses that the Hebrews possess, as has been pointed out already, are set in meter; the ode in Deuteronomy [32] is in hexameter, the Psalms are trimeter and tetrameter. Therefore, the verse the Hebrews have are different from the Greek. If we wanted to preserve them [i.e., their form] we would make these verses a single one, "Happy are those who are pure in their path, who follow the law of the Lord" [v. 1] and in the same way begin the second line "Happy . . . " and so forth. It must be understood that the Greek translators made two verses from a single Hebrew verse, just as whoever made this copy started a new line at the end of the clause. They [the translators] took for a second verse what was only the continuation of the first part. And so is it in every line.

The passage thus asserts Hebrew verse to be metrical. The unnamed source of the claim might be Josephus, since the works singled out as metrical were among those cited by him. But why, then, no mention of Exodus 15? And why are the Psalms "trimeter and tetrameter," where Josephus has "pentameter and tetrameter"? No other source has been found for the assertion. The main thrust of the passage has to do not with meter, however, but with what constitutes a line; this is naturally important in an alphabetical psalm. Origen's concern was that stichography not obscure the true number of verses (by seeming to double them) or the alphabetic nature of the psalm. Indeed, the whole reason he makes this metrical assertion is to introduce to his readers the idea that the Hebrew line indeed *has a caesura*, and that the translators mistook the caesura for a new line. He is otherwise not interested in meter here, still less with parallelism.

Eusebius also speaks of meter, in his *Preparation* 11, 5, a passage of (as usual) furious preferring of Hebrew to Greek wisdom:

> If anyone were also to study the language [of the Bible] itself with critical taste, he would see that the Barbarian writers are excellent

---

34. The passage was not known for long in the Church. We owe its frequent mention in modern discussions of Hebrew poetry to Cardinal Pitra, who resurrected it in his *Analecta Sacra* (2, p. 341) from a Vatican manuscript (Codex Vat. 11); and to Ernest Preuschen, who reprinted it in *ZAW* 11 (1891): 316.

dialecticians, not at all inferior to sophists and orators in his own language. He would also find among them poems in meter, like the great Song of Moses [Deut. 32] and David's 118th Psalm, composed in what the Greeks call heroic meter. At least it is said that these are hexameters, consisting of sixteen syllables; also their other composititons in verse are said to consist of trimeter and tetrameter lines, according to the sound of their own language.

While such is the relation of their diction to its logical sense, the thoughts must not be brought into comparison with those of men. For they comprise the oracles of God and of absolute truth to which they have given utterance, prophecies, predictions, and religious lessons, and doctrines relating to the knowledge of the unverse.[35]

Origen's scholion (or possibly some unknown source, perhaps one common to both) is the source for Eusebius's ideas about meter. But he seems skeptical: instead of all the Psalms he limits himself to Psalm 119, and insists that these opinions are only what he has heard. The last two sentences cited are a wonderful expression of the dualism that allowed Christian commentators to make observations about meter, tropes, etc. without endangering the sacred status of the text. The letter ("diction") may be compared to human works, but not the "thoughts."

In connection with the idea of biblical poetry, the names of two of the earliest Christian poets in Latin ought to be cited, Hilary of Poitiers (d. 367) and Ambrose of Milan (340–397). They introduced hymn composition to the Latin Church (Ambrose's iambic dimeter and four-line stanzas became the octosyllabic rhyming lines of later Church hymnaries). It is not surprising, then, that they showed some interest in the Psalter and its makeup.

Hilary asserts that the Psalms have a musical structure, but translation "caeterum modi musici disciplinam conservare . . . non potuit."[36] He was interested in the significance of *diapsalma* (Hebrew "*selă*") in this structure.[37] Beyond this, he was a defender of the classics in Christian education, and, of course, of the notion of Christian poetry.[38] Ambrose wrote a long and influential Psalm

---

35. *Preparation . . .* 11, 5, p. 514b and c.
36. *PL* 9:245.
37. See also Jerome's Epistles 28 and 138 on this.
38. See M. Roger, *L'Enseignement des lettres classiques d'Ausone à Alcuin* (Paris, 1905), pp. 150–51. For Jerome's appreciation of Hilary the poet, see *PL* 26:355; also J. Fontaine, "Hilaire et l'esthétique du style," in *Hilaire et son temps* (Paris, 1969), pp. 287–305.

commentary (he believed that psalm singing effected remission from sin).[39] The commentary follows Origen closely. In discussing Psalm 118 (119) he notes[40] that Psalms 111 and 112 are also alphabetical (as Origen had said,[41] which explains why they have twenty-two verses, and "unde et per metra asserunter esse descriptos"). Elsewhere, he speaks of the "rhythms" of the Psalms,[42] but it is primarily the question of musicality that interests him. He describes the blessings of Jacob as "songs," as if sensing their similarity to true songs, but clearly this is meant figuratively: they are prose that is sweeter than singing.[43] He speaks in similar terms of David, Job and other biblical singers.[44] Throughout there reigns the notion that the Divine Word is ipso facto musical, characterized by *suavitas*—in short, poetic. This higher notion of poetry makes him less interested in formal questions, and on the other hand, it supported the overlapping of poetic and prosaic modes in his own writing.

Their contemporary, Jerome, was far more interested in the specific question of meter; it is to him that one must turn for the source of all later metrical speculation.

5

Jerome had an obvious love for the masters of Latin poetry and prose, and his own style in his letters and introductions betrays an attention to elegant expression wholly in keeping with his classical education. His writings are full of citations from the poetry of "pagans," and, far from recanting later, he defended this practice against his accusers by showing that earlier Fathers had done

39. See his *Preface, PL* 14:963–70.
40. *PL* 15:1199.
41. *PG* 12:1585.
42. See Döller, *Rhythmus*, p. 32.
43. See *Fathers of the Church* 65, p. 171.
44. In his Psalms Commentary preface (*PL* 14:965–66), Ambrose distinguishes various canticles (*cantica*) that constitute the songs intermixed with "flat prose" in the Old Testament. Here too, songs are by their essence and function different from prose. The songs listed—Moses's in Exod. 15, Miriam's (Exod. 15:20), Moses's in Deut. 32, Deborah's (Judg. 5), Isaiah's (perhaps Isa. 12 or 26; probably not Isa. 5, since it is to "soften the hearts of the readers"); the apocryphal Prayer of the Three Men (Dan. 3:52), Hab. 3; and the Song of Songs. See also the article of J. Fontaine, "Prose et poésie: l'interférence des genres . . ." in G. Lazzati, *Ambrosius Episcopus* 1 (Milan, 1976): 124–70, and Ellspermann, *Attitude of the Early Christian Latin Writers*, pp. 101–25.

likewise; and, in fact, Paul.[45] One of his aims in retranslating the Hebrew Bible was to prevent the then-common experience of revulsion at the style of the Old Latin, its lack of classical elegance.[46] At the same time, of course, Jerome had inherited certain strictures against the Classics from his forebears. Tertullian (c. 150–240) had condemned all profane literature.[47] In *De Idolatria*[48] he ruled that Christian children could go to pagan schools—even in the time of Jerome and Augustine, the only schools available to Christian children were the state schools—where, presumably, they would be exposed to classical literature; but the children should be protected against being misled by the texts, and, of course, no adult Christian ought to seek employment as a teacher in such a school.[49] The Fathers, even the early Greek Fathers, had condemned classical literature for its polytheism, its erotic scenes and depictions of forbidden things, and for the "prideful" classical philosophy. Jerome echoed these sentiments.[50] In a famous letter (Number 22, to Eustochium) he recounts how, even after he began his ascetic way of life, he retained his books of pagan literature; but, stricken with fever and near death, he had a vision of being summoned before the seat of Heavenly Judgment, where he was reproached for having clung to these classical ways: "Ciceronianus es, sed non Christianus!" Upon his recovery, he reports, he devoted himself entirely to Christian

45. In his Epistle to Titus, Paul inserts verses of Menander and Epimenides; see M. Roger, *L'enseignement des lettres classiques*, p. 140.

46. Like others, Jerome's first impression of the Hebrew Bible was that it was a *sermo incultus*. On this, see below.

47. In *De Spectaculis, PL* 1:724–25.

48. *PL* 1:663–695.

49. See Roger, *L'enseignement des lettres classiques*, pp. 133–36. To be fair, much of this program of separation from the pagan world was never carried out. Tertullian's ideas were never enacted; even after Christianity ceased to be a minority religion the classics stayed. A more realistic statement of policy is Basil's "On the Reading of Profane Authors," where he suggests that pagan writings are acceptable reading if they are examined in the light of the Gospels and with judicious selection of texts. Nevertheless, in Jerome's day the outcome was far from certain—indeed, his was the age in which the classics were in greatest disrepute. (On this whole question, see Marrou, *St. Augustin*, p. 321; also Ellspermann, *Attitude of the Early Christian Latin Writers*, pp. 23–42.)

50. See *PL* 26:439, 449, 537. In Jerome's Letter 21, he interprets the pods eaten by the Prodigal Son as "the songs of poets, the wisdom of the world, showy displays of rhetoric." He adds: "Nowadays we see even bishops abandoning the Gospels and the Prophets to read comedies, hum the erotic words of pastoral poems, and rehearse Vergil, thus voluntarily making themselves guilty of what schoolboys do under compulsion." Later, his attitude became more liberal: see Letter 70.

reading. In the same letter, he cautions Eustochium against any mixing of two wholly separate ways of being:

> Do not wish to appear eloquent or go about performing merry little lyrics set to meter. Be not overly fastidious, imitating the slobbering lisp[51] of those married ladies who alternately slacken and snap their lips as their chattering tongue pursues its inane speech—for they think that anything that is left natural is boorish and unrefined. Adultery, including the verbal kind, pleases them immensely. "What do light and darkness have in common? On what can Christ and Belial agree?" [2 Cor. 6:14] Then what has Horace to do with the Psalter? Vergil with the Gospels? Cicero with the Apostle?

This passage does reveal a great deal of Jerome's attitude toward the Bible, for his question to Eustochium is not quite Tertullian's "Quid Athenae Hierosolymis?", what has one entire way of thinking to do with the other, but only: Where there is a Psalter, what need is there also for Horace? Implicit in this is some sort of equivalence of function, and, indeed, note: Horace with the Psalter (read: lyric with lyric), Vergil with the Gospels (epic with epic), Cicero with Paul (rhetorician with rhetorician). His attitude is really no different from that of the anonymous *Didascalia Apostolorum* (third century) which, forbidding the reading of pagan literature, proposed, "If you wish to read histories, take those of the Book of Kings: if you want poetry and wisdom, take the Prophets . . . if you desire songs, you have the Psalter."[52]

In both the *Didascalia* and Jerome is the quite definite notion that these holy books are somehow a literature, and are to be used as such. Apollinaris of Laodicea and his father had set about rewriting the Pentateuch as an epic, and other books as dramas, Pindaric odes, etc. (among these all that has survived is a Psalms paraphrase in hexameters).[53] Jerome's Vulgate did not go so far, but he had no doubt

---

51. In Jerome's day, lisping was a sign of culture. Martial satirizes this affectation in his *Epigrams*.

52. R. H. Connolly, ed., *Didascalia Apostolorum* 1 (Oxford, 1929), chapter 2, pp. 12 and 13. On this, see H. I. Marrou, *History of Education in Antiquity* (London, 1956), p. 320. Cf. Tertullian: "If the literature of the stage delight you, we have literature in abundance of our own—plenty of verses, sentences, songs, proverbs; and these are not fabulous, but true, not tricks of art, but plain realities" (cited in Ellspermann, *Attitude of Early Christian Latin Writers*, p. 38).

53. They did so in order to create a purely Christian course of study that nevertheless would provide classical learning (i.e., metrics, rhetoric); the program was not successful. See Marrou, *St. Augustin*, p. 324, and J. Quasten, *Patrology* (Utrecht-Antwerp, 1960) 3, p. 380.

that in Hebrew the Psalms were mellifluous lyrics comparable to the best of Greek and Latin literature. It was only translation that made them "dure sonantes":

> What is more musical than the Psalter? which, in the manner of our Flaccus or of the Greek Pindar, now flows in iambs, now rings with Alcaics,[54] swells to a Sapphic measure or moves along with a half-foot? What is fairer than the hymns of Deuteronomy or Isaiah? What is more solemn than Solomon, what more polished than Job? All of which books, as Josephus and Origen write, flow in the original in hexameter and pentameter verses.[55]

And so we have the proper context for Jerome's remarks about Hebrew meter. The rather haphazard observations of Josephus and Origen became for him confirmation of this notion of the Bible as a "holy literature" parallel to the secular; the Psalms were metrical because Horace was, and the Psalms were to replace Horace. One of the results of this particular view of things was that henceforth metrical speculation was to center on Psalms and other Hagiographa (though note that the *Didascalia* had said "If you want poetry . . . take the Prophets"), leaving the Prophets alone. Jerome was quite specific:

> Let no one, when he sees the prophets written down in verses,[56] think that they are read metrically in Hebrew or have something in common with the Psalms or the works of Solomon; but, following the practice that is often found in the works of Demosthenes and Cicero (who both write in prose, not verse) that they are written down in keeping with periodic style (*ut per cola scribantur et commata*) so I as well, out of regard for the reader's convenience,

54. A four-line stanza named after the Greek poet Alkaios (late seventh-sixth century B.C.). Jerome apparently did not mean the whole stanza pattern, but single lines with the characteristic choriamb (i.e., a combination of of trochee and iamb). The choriamb is also characteristic of Sapphic verse, which Jerome mentions next. These two are the favorite meters of, significantly, Horace. But he most intends to convey a mixing of meters, that is, to assert metricality without pinning things down to a consistent meter. In this connection the name of Pindar is especially important, for he was known as a metrical "wild man." See below and, on his Renaissance reputation, chapter 6.

55. "Preface to Eusebius," *PL* 27:36.

56. Jerome thus set off each verse "poetically." All the latter Prophets are done in this fashion, as are, of course, the "poetic books" of Psalms, Proverbs, Job, Lamentations, Song of Songs, Ecclesiastes; Daniel also appears this way. Despite what he says here, Jerome had some perception of the Prophets as speaking in "poetic language," and may have arranged them stichographically for that reason; it is also possible he had seen stichographically written texts in Hebrew. See E. Arns, *La technique du livre d'après S. Jérome* (Paris, 1953), pp. 114–15.

have distinguished my new translation with a new manner of writing.[57]

The question asked earlier of Philo and Josephus might now be asked in regard to Jerome: did he have any real notion of the metrical structure of the passages so described?

He had, of course, studied Hebrew, and from the year 386 on he lived in Bethlehem, where he worked at translating. Part of what was to become the Vulgate he had begun translating directly from the Hebrew text. Certainly his knowledge of Hebrew and feel for the Bible were impressive. But the study of Hebrew was not an easy thing in his day; there was no dictionary to consult; vocalization, and even pronunciation of the consonants, was not standardized;[58] grammar was uncertain. In the specific question of meter Jerome was not noticeably confident, or consistent. He must have tried to perform some kind of scansion in Hebrew, but never reports or duplicates it. The passage from his preface to Eusebius (above) has often been cited without being understood: the point is that the very profusion of metrical types put forth by Jerome translates his own insecurity with any one meter. The choice of Pindar is particularly significant. In any ode, though strophe and antistrophe are metrically matched, the epode is quite independent, thus creating a certain impression of irregularity. In Pindar, moreover, the pattern of lines and overall length varies widely from one ode to the next, so that from earliest times he was regarded as an unpredictable, even random, versifier. Lastly, in Jerome's metrical catalogue there is one phrase that sticks in the throat, that most anticlimactic "et nunc semipede ingreditur." This "half-foot" seems an escape clause of sorts, an admission that, try as he did, he could not get the Psalms to conform consistently to any of the previously cited meters.

Another passage that gives evidence of Jerome's actual attempts to resolve the metrical question is his preface to Job:[59]

---

57. *PL* 28:771. Jerome would exclude from this characterization the canticles that appear within the Prophets, such as Isa. 5 and 26 or the Canticle of Habakkuk (Hab. 3); about the latter he notes that it is "lyrico more compositum" (*PL* 25:1307).

58. In Epistle 54, Jerome says that the name Asher is translated either as "happiness" or "wealth" ("'Aser' vel in beatitudinem vel in divitas vertitur"); obviously he has conflated two separate roots, אשר and עשר in keeping with the tendency of later Hebrew not to distinguish between ɔ*aleph* and ʿ*ayin*. In the same letter he interprets Naomi to mean "consoled," confusing נעם with נחם. In some regions ḥet and ʿ*ayin* were pronounced similarly; see j. *Berakhot* 4d, b. *Moʿed Qattan* 16b. Cf. E. Burstein, "La compétence de Jérôme en hébreu," *Revue des Etudes augustiniennes* 21 (1975), 3–12.

59. *PL* 28:1081–82.

From the beginning of the book to the words of Job, the Hebrew version is in prose. But from the words of Job where he says, "May the day perish . . ." [Job 3:3] to the place before the end of the book where it says ". . . dust and ashes," there are hexameter verses made of dactyls and spondees, and, owing to the special character of the language, frequently containing as well other [sorts of] feet, which have not the same number of syllables, but the same quantities. Sometimes also a sweet and pleasing rhythm is obtained by the lines being set free from the laws of meter [*numeris lege metri solutis*][60] about which a master of metrics will know more than the ordinary reader. From the aforesaid verse to the end of the book the small remaining section is prose. And if it seems incredible to anyone that the Hebrews really have meters in the same manner as our Flaccus, and the Greek Pindar, and Alcaeus and Sappho—whether the Psalms, or the Lamentations of Jeremiah or almost all the songs of the Scripture are to be considered—let him read Philo, Josephus, Origen, Eusebius of Caesarea, and with their testimony he will find for sure that I speak the truth.

Here there are familiar elements: the "special character" echoes Eusebius's phrase in the *Preparation* 11:5, and the same catalogue of Greek and Latin poets has already been seen in Jerome's preface to Eusebius cited earlier. The singling out of these same authors again might lead one to suppose they had a special significance for Jerome, a metrical significance—as indeed they had.

If Jerome looked at the opening line of the "poetic part" of Job he singled out,

יאבד יום אולד בו והלילה אמר הרה גבר

he would (with current vocalization) have seen a line of seventeen syllables (sixteen if the third word was read as bisyllabic). This is easily rationalized into a hexameter line of five dactylls and a spondee (5 × 3 syllables and 1 × 2 syllables)—and behold:

Yobad yom/ iwwaled / bo weha- / laila a-/ mar hora / gaber

The trouble with this is that whatever notions of syllable quantity or stress one assigns, the division into feet becomes somewhat arbitrary. Still, the basic regularity of the line length was a powerful argument for metrical structure; how natural for Jerome to think that the Hebrews simply had feet not known to the Greeks and Romans. And

---

60. An allusion to Horace's *Odes* 4, 2. This is an ode about *Pindar*, see n. 54 and chapter 6.

for the lines that are just too long or too short he also sees a design: the patterns are periodically varied "numeris lege metri solutis," a sort of "law for the lawless."

Jerome did not always stick to his sources. Josephus, had said Deuteronomy 32 was written in hexameter; Jerome in a remark on Psalm 118 (119) says that both this Psalm and Deuteronomy 32 are said by Josephus to be in the same meter, elegiacs (a hexameter line followed by a pentameter),[61] "because the earlier verse consists of six feet and the lower verse ends in a pentameter, less by one [foot]." In another passage, however, he contradicts even this opinion. It comes in a didactic letter to Paula (Number 30) in which he explains the alphabetical poems in various books:

> In the former Psalms [111 and 112], the individual versicles, which are written in iambic trimeter, are joined together by a single alphabet [i.e., each clause begins with a successive letter], while those of the latter Psalms [119 and 145] are in iambic tetrameter, just as the song of Deuteronomy [32] is written. In Psalm 118 [119] eight verses follow the individual letters [of the alphabet]. In Psalm 144 [145] individual verses are set off by each letter. There are those who think other Psalms as well follow this arrangement. But they are wrong.
>
> You also have in Jeremiah's book of Lamentations four alphabetical compositions, of which the first two are written in a sort of Sapphic meter, since he ends with a "*comma*" of Heroic verse three versicles which are connected together and begin from one letter [in the alphabetical sequence]. The third alphabetical section is written in trimeter and in triplets of letters, but [i.e., unlike the groups of three verses in Lam. 1 and 2] the three verses begin each with the same letter.
>
> The fourth alphabetical section is similar to the first two. A final alphabetical section closes the Proverbs of Solomon, which is set off in tetrameter starting from the place in which it says, "A woman of valor who shall find?" [Prov. 31:10]

Here, then, Deuteronomy 32 is written in iambic tetrameter, the same structure as Psalms 111 and 112. He does not specify the meter of Psalms 119 or 145. The first two alphabets of Lamentation are in a "sort of Sapphic meter" because three metrically similar verses (unspecified) are followed by a "comma" of shorter duration. Lamentations 3

61. See also *PL* 26:1187.

is in "trimeter," and Proverbs 31:10–31 is in tetrameter.

What is one to make of this array? One critic[62] has attempted to rationalize these various remarks into a realistic description of "meters," substituting stress accents for quantity, but this seems most unconvincing. Besides, Jerome felt—if he thought in such precise terms—that Hebrew poetry was, like Greek, a quantitative system; in his Job preface he specifically notes that Hebrew has other feet "non earumdem syllabarum, sed eorumdem temporum." Throughout his critical writing he remained convinced of a basic premise: Hebrew songs are metrical. On this he had the agreement of four predecessors, plus his own observations—the obviously roughly equivalent line lengths in Psalms, Job, etc., and the evidence of something like stanzaic structure in Job. The only missing information was what the meters were. This was a difficult area, since vowel quantities were not defined. The fact that he contradicts himself, and his predecessors, only indicates that Jerome was probably proceeding by trial scansions, dissatisfied with earlier results but convinced that the metrical "answer" was out there somewhere. (It is a situation that should not seem unfamiliar to the metrical school of modern-day biblical criticism.) Jerome was probably never entirely satisfied that he had found the key to Hebrew poetry—how could he be?—and significantly, he never gives details about how the words of the text actually fit the meters he names. In the Job preface he comes close to confessing that his nomenclature is an approximation (in the sense that Hebrew had its own rules of substitution); but meter was in any case a question of mathematics, a question that goes beyond the "special character" of the language. And Hebrew *had* meter.[63]

6

The result of Jerome's writings about Hebrew meter was that the question of the structure of the Psalms and other parts of the Bible was answered before it had been properly asked. The metrical thesis remained unchallenged in Christian circles until the Renaissance. It need not have been so, for the fact of parallelism was perfectly obvious to many of the Church Fathers. All they lacked was the proper framework for understanding what they saw.

As noted earlier, Theodore of Mopsuestia (ca. 350–428) may be

---

62. Castellino, "Ritmo Hebraico."

63. Cf. other remarks by Jerome about poetry in the Epistle to Paulinus (*PL* 22:547); Commentary to Ezechiel (*PL* 25:295); and preface to Jeremiah (*PL* 28:848).

counted among the first[64] to consider some of the workings of Hebrew parallelism. About Hosea 5:9 he writes:

> Now here a single idea is being expressed in common by *diaeresis* ["dividing in two": it was a figure of rhetoric called in Latin *distributio*] just as is found here and there in the writings of blessed David, as when he says "By day I called, and at night I am before you" [Ps. 88:2] he does not mean he called during the day and at night spoke to God face to face, but rather "All day and night have I called out before you." So here when he says Benjamin will be wasted and Ephraim put in desolation, it is as if both are to be included in the same expression: they were wasted and put in desolation.[65]

About Hosea 5:12:

> He does not say one thing here about Ephraim and the next about Judah, but both are contained in the same exhortation and warning, as we have seen above.

And about Habakkuk 3:4:

> For also in this place he says something common to both by *diaeresis,* which manner of expression we have shown to be not unusual in the sacred Scripture.[66]

What Theodore noticed was that A and B make a single whole, and that their parallelism is significant. Even if distribution is somewhat reductive, it at least recognizes parallelism, and recognizes it as device, as artful speech. His remarks here and elsewhere might have had some greater notice were it not for the fact that his works were condemned by the Council of Constantinople—a ban that was followed much more strictly than a similar interdiction on Origen's works[67] and that caused his works to remain in obscurity for some time. But there were others who made similar observations. Paulinus Diaconus (fourth and fifth centuries) says about Genesis 49:11:

> The manner of Hebrew speech [lit. "sermo," which is sometimes

---

64. Diodorus (d. 391) speaks of "parallels" in regard 'o four psalms; on this see *EPH*, p. 197.

65. *PG* 66:156.

66. These passages from Theodore, as well as Paulinus and Gennadius, I owe to *EPH*, p. 198; Alonso-Schökel credits A. Vaccari with having pointed them out.

67. See Beryl Smalley, *The Study of the Bible in the Middle Ages* (Notre Dame, Ind., 1964), p. 15.

used specifically for "prose"] is such that it repeats one and the same thing in different expressions, as here. For what is wine if not "the blood of the grape"?

Far from prizing this insight, however, he continues:

But just as much as the surface of the letter is without importance (for no one will even wash his cape or mantle in wine!) so much the more pleasing does the inner meaning commend itself. For the Savior washed his cape in wine and his mantle in the blood of the grape since while hanging on the cross he had his holy flesh, which was his mantle, drenched in his own blood.[68]

Paulinus's words are telling: the coupling of valuable remarks about style with an immediate denigration of the literal is a curious leitmotiv. It was this attitude that prevented—just as surely as the rabbinic attitude did—a systematic approach to the structure of these passages. So Paulinus understood Genesis 49:7 ("I will divide them in Jacob, I will scatter them in Israel") as: (1) a single literal statement describing the dispersion of the Levites throughout the land; and (2) figuratively, as referring to two aspects of the Church.[69]

Adrian (sometimes "Hadrian"), a fifth-century Greek monk, wrote a brief biblical introduction ("Isagoge")[70] which, among other things, lists and catalogues figures of speech in the Old and New Testaments. He describes parallelism as a kind of

repetition [of ideas] in different words used everywhere, thus: "Behold I am conceived in iniquity and in sin my mother conceived me" (Psalm 51:7); "I have slept and am asleep" (Psalm 3:6); "Born of the earth and sons of men" (Psalm 49:3); "Who made his angels spirit, and his ministers a flame of fire" (Psalm 104:4); "The Lord is become my refuge, and my God the help of my hope" (Ps. 94:22); "God spoke and He called the earth" (50:1); "They spoke and said" (Psalm 78:19); "Hear my words, understand my expression" (Psalm 5:2).

He says Isaiah and Jeremiah are written in prose, while the Psalms of David and the songs of Moses in Exodus and Deuteronomy are songs—indeed, the presence of meter indicates they are not prophecy; the same is true of other songs, "such as the books of Job and Solomon."[71]

68. *PL* 20:718–19.
69. *PL* 20:718–20.
70. *PG* 98:1274–1312.
71. *PG* 98:1312.

Finally, Gennadius, a fifth-century presbyter of the Constantinople Church, remarks on another passage from the blessings of Jacob (Gen. 49:9):

> This phrase, "as a lion and as a lion's cub" consists of parallels (*paralleloi*) [expressing] the same idea [in different words]. It is like "What is man, that Thou shouldst remember him or the son of man, that Thou shouldst take notice of him?" (Ps. 144:3)[72]

It is noteworthy that in all these writers, as indeed in later Jewish exegetes, it is the phenomenon of apparent repetition that draws their attention to parallelism. Clauses that do not restate or otherwise clearly complement each other will pass unnoticed; hence, the greater role of "seconding" in shaping sentences eluded them. In effect (and quite explicitly in Theodore), parallelism presented itself as a rhetorical figure, an embellishment used now and again to beautify speech. This is not totally wrong, but it errs in considering only semantic parallelism, excluding other forms of "seconding." Moreover, any Greek or Roman knew there was nothing even quasi-structural about rhetorical figures. They were there to beautify, and part of their beauty depended on their intermittence, and indeed, their alternation with other devices. Thus, parallelism was already destined to be read as belonging to the Greco-Roman arsenal of literary figures. This is how Augustine read parallelism, and largely because of his great influence the "figurative" reading of parallelism became an institution of the medieval Church.

7

One of the major obstacles faced by early Christian proselytizers was—how difficult for us to imagine nowadays!—the perceived crudeness and lack of elegance in the biblical style. Jerome remarked on this, as we have seen, and indeed, the Vulgate is in some sense his attempt to rectify the situation. Augustine remembers a similar revulsion in his *Confessions* (Book 3 chapter 5):

> So I made up my mind to examine the holy Scriptures and see what kind of books they were. I discovered something that was at once beyond the understanding of the proud and hidden from the eyes of children. Its gait was humble, but the heights it reached were sublime. It was enfolded in mysteries, and I was not the kind of man to enter into it or bow my head to follow where it led. But these were

72. *PG* 85:1657.

not the feelings I had when I first looked into the Scriptures. To me they seemed quite unworthy of comparison with the stately prose of Cicero, because I had too much conceit to accept their simplicity and not enough insight to penetrate their depths.

Against similar revulsion in potential converts Augustine devised a twofold defense. The first half, elaborated throughout his critical writings, is to dismiss all matters of elegance and style as superficial, in every way secondary to the meaning in the author's heart. (Indeed, hints of this can be seen in the *Confessions* passage cited: its gait is "humble," but it reaches sublime heights; "I had too much conceit . . . and not enough insight.") Meaning saved the rudeness. Indeed, Augustine went beyond this idea: for him, it was specifically the *way* that Scripture means—that is, darkly and through ever-shifting allegories—that accounts for its apparent superficial bareness. Were the Bible written with the oratorical flourish of Cicero, our eyes might not even see its mysteries; they must be laid out plainly, so our minds will be spurred on to find the meaning.[73] If you wish to cure cultivated men of their repulsion at Scripture's style, Augustine wrote in *De Catachizandis rudibus,* "introduce them to the manner of its allegories."[74]

In fact, this aesthetic extended beyond the Scriptures. Augustine had a place in his universe for the Christian poet, for example; his job was not to delight the ear, but to instruct the mind. The classical heritage of poetry, he argues in *De Doctrina Christiana*, is seen as part of the gold and silver that the Israelites brought with them out of Egypt (i.e., the learning that Christians inherited from the pagan Greeks and Romans); it was valuable, but nothing in comparison to the riches that lay ahead in Jerusalem and the temple of Solomon. So a Christian poet ought not to be overly swayed by the superficial pleasures of poetry; for the real delight of the mind comes in finding hidden truth, Scripture's "salubris obscuritas" in Augustine's words,[75] and this aesthetic spilled over into poetry.[76] Isidore of Seville, echoing

73. See Marrou, *St. Augustin*, pp. 473–537, 551. Cf. Clement of Alexandria: "The divine Scripture and institutions of wisdom form the short road to salvation. *Devoid of embellishment, of outward beauty of diction*, they raise up humanity strangled by wickedness" (in "Exhortation to the Heathen" 1, 8).

74. Marrou, *St. Augustin*, p. 492.

75. See *De Doctrina* 4.8.22.

76. See F. Huppé, *Doctrine and Poetry* (New York, 1959), pp. 1–30; Marrou, *St. Augustin*, p. 489; both of these remark on the tremendous significance of this doctrine for later secular literature. Cf. de Bruyne, *Etudes* 1, pp. 47–48, 60.

Augustine, counsels the Christian poet to write "obliquely, figuratively, with a certain beauty."[77]

The second half of the defense quite contradicts the first: it is to demonstrate everywhere possible in the Bible poetic and rhetorical flourishes worthy of the greatest classical authors. This argument finds its definitive form in the *De Doctrina Christiana*; begun in 397, revised and completed circa 426, it represents Augustine's most considered statement on biblical style. The order of the four books of that work represents a definite hierarchy in the author's own mind. The first is concerned with the three Christian virtues of faith, hope, and love. These are the end of all Christian learning, Augustine asserts, and a Christian who possesses them perfectly has no need of the Scriptures whatsoever, unless it be to teach another. The middle two books are concerned with Scripture, its essence and its interpretation; the fourth book has as its subject rhetoric and eloquence. About the latter, Augustine shows the ambivalence of his day. His whole rhetoric is based on Cicero—"orator noster," he call him—yet his is mistrustful of the institutions of oratory, since they can be used to plead the case of falsehood as well as truth.[78] He was especially critical of the sophistic ideals that dominated contemporary oratory; in this sense his Ciceronianism is a yearning back to an earlier simplicity.[79]

The fourth book of *De Doctrina* contains several extended citations adduced to prove the rhetorical mastery of the Bible. Most of these come from the New Testament (from Paul), but Augustine also cites Amos 6:1–6. He is at pains to point out that the author of these words was a shepherd, hence unlettered; it is an eloquence arrived at without the benefit of tutoring. But here, as so often, Augustine seems to have little sense that he is dealing with a translated text whose original may be quite different in the very particulars he is defending.[80] Afterward he notes that the words of the Bible are not "composed by human industry, but poured forth by the Divine mind both wisely and eloquently, with a wisdom that is not bent on eloquence, but an eloquence that does not depart from wisdom" ("non intenta in eloquentiam sapientia, sed a sapientia non recendente eloquentia").[81] *Purus* became, through Augustine, a code word for the Bible's

77. Huppé, *Doctrine and Poetry*, p. 31.

78. *De Doctrina* 4.2.

79. See Thérèse Sullivan, *De Doctrina Christiana* (Washington, 1930), p. 8.

80. Cf. Augustine's remarks on Psalm 118 (119), where he wonders what it can be like to "desire a desire" (*PL* 37:1521–22).

81. *De Doctrina* 4.7.21.

stylistic simplicity; about Jeremiah 5:30–31 he exclaims, "O eloquence so much the more terrible for its being pure; and for its being restrained, so much the more vehement!"[82]

Now the study of tropes and figures, Augustine says, is important for a Christian to aid him in reading the Bible:

> Those who know these tropes recognize them in the Holy Scripture, and the knowledge of them is a considerable aid in understanding the Scripture. . . . In the Holy Books there are seen not only examples of these tropes, just as of all the figures, but even the names of some of them: for example "allegory,"[83] "enigma,"[84] and "parable."[85]

While his examples of tropes and figures make no allowance for differences between the Latin and the Hebrew, he does note that rhythmical closures (a feature of Roman eloquence) are lacking in the Latin Bible; but this is not to be counted a fault, for the careful reader "will find many types of expression of great beauty—which even in our tongue, but especially in the Bible's own, are beautiful; of which none are to be found in those works about which [our grammarians and rhetoricians] are so puffed up with pride."[86] By this he seems to mean the Bible has a rhetoric of its own, with its own tropes and figures—but he does not elaborate.

Specific instances of parallelism Augustine treats under the rubric of various figures, most often *repetitio*.[87] There is never any question about the Bible's having its own poetic system: Hebrew poetry is metrical.

> For that branch of music wherein rhythm [*numerus*] is taught most fully [i.e., poetry] is so far from lacking in our prophets[88] that that most learned man Jerome mentions the meters of some of them, but he left them only in the Hebrew and did not translate them, the better to preserve the truth that lies in the words.[89]

82. *De Doctrina* 4.4.30.
83. He is probably thinking of its use in 1 Corinthians (already cited).
84. In the OT, the translation of Heb. *ḥîddâ*.
85. Inter alia, the translation of *māšāl*. This passage is in *De Doctrina* 3.29.40.
86. *De Doctrina* 4.20.41.
87. See, e.g., *PL* 36:903; also *EPH*, pp. 197–98.
88. It is important to remember that for Christians at this time David is a prophet, too.
89. *De Doctrina* 4.20.41.

In a letter (Epistle 101 ad Memorium) Augustine confesses his own ignorance with regard to meter:

> I have not written in precisely which meters the verses of David are composed because I do not know. Nor can a person translating from the Hebrew language (which I do not know) capture the meter, lest he be thought to stray, because of the exigencies of the meter, farther from faithful translation than the meaning of the words permits. But that they do consist of meters I fully trust those who are experienced in that language [Hebrew].

The way was thus prepared for what was to become the Church's stand on the "poetry" of the Hebrew Bible. That it was written in meter was uncontestable: those who (one might suppose) knew the Hebrew language best—the Jews Josephus and Philo, Origen of the Hexapla, and Jerome, champion of the *Hebraica veritas*—all said it was metrical. Who could contradict them? At the same time, Augustine's *De Doctrina Christiana* had provided the theoretical basis for viewing parallelism, wherever it had been, or was to be, noticed, as a color of rhetoric: for though the Scriptures walked with a "humble gait," yet they were full of figures and tropes, so much so that the study of rhetoric was important to a Christian if only to help him penetrate the Bible's meaning. (Rhetoric was also important for effecting conversions.) As noted, in his Psalm commentaries Augustine identified parallelism primarily as *repetitio,* but soon the range of possible figures was widened.

Henceforth, the twofold approach to parallelism—metrical speculation for appropriately "poetic" genres, tropes and figures for poetry *and* prose—would continue unabated until Lowth's time. Now the fact of this twin standard is itself most revealing. The situation of these commentators is comparable to that of the blind men and the elephant. To one schooled in the ways of classical poetry and rhetoric, the approximate regularity of the lines of Job or certain psalms could have only one explanation, meter; at the same time, the various interrelationships of juxtaposed clauses, and the precise ordering of the words themselves (in Hebrew or indeed Latin), often bespoke those elevating *schemata* which characterized lofty discourse of any kind, poetry or prose.[90] And so this basic trait of Hebrew style ceased

---

90. In this and other respects, poetry and lofty prose had much in common. Meter per se existed in prose, i.e., in the metrical clausulae of the rhetoricians; at the same time, some songs—Church hymns, or the songs of the common folk in vernacular tongues—were not *metrical* in the classical, quantitative system, but nevertheless

to be a single animal: it became two, or rather, two sets of animals. Part of the work of biblical scholarship would henceforth be the faithful transmission (and later, scientific investigation) of the meters used by biblical poets, and the recognition in both biblical "prose" and "verse" of those devices which elevated the Divine Word to the heights of eloquence.

8

The contribution of Cassiodorus (ca. 487–580) to our question came primarily in two books, his *De institutionibus* and his commentary on the Psalter. In both he acknowledges as his masters in exegesis Hilary, Ambrose, Jerome, and especially Augustine. He repeats the Augustinian idea that training in rhetoric and the liberal arts is necessary to an understanding of Scripture.[91] But unlike his contemporaries, who were content for Christianity to exist within the old Roman system of education, he wanted to create an entirely new system, wherein a Christian rhetoric would be taught—"unde et anima susciperet aeternam salutem, et casto atque purissimo eloquio fidelium lingua comeretur." (He did not succeed.)[92]

In *De institutionibus divinarum litterarum* he explains that Scripture uses images and figures to set forth abstract ideas: "manus lavere significat non esse participem."[93] Sometimes figures are used to make comprehensible to humans the truth of Divine meanings, a truth that exists in each and every word of the Bible: "Everywhere in them truth reigns, and everywhere the Heavenly power shines

---

were characterized by some system of arrangement. J. Fontaine's study of the overlapping of prose and poetry in Ambrose ("Prose et poésie . . .") is relevant here. Even in classical times, the poet and the orator were straitly allied (see de Bruyne's examples from Cicero and Ovid; *Etudes* 1, p. 46); by the fourth century, the existence of Christian "prose hymns" (Fontaine, "Prose et poésie," p. 153) on the one hand, and, on the other, the language of ornaments and elevated diction common to prose and verse, had moved these two worlds of discourse close together. After Bede's famous distinction between *rythmus* and *metrum* (see below) one often finds three types of discourse distinguished by medieval writers: "prosaic," "metrical," and "rhythmical." See de Bruyne, *Etudes* 1, p. 94, and below, chapter 6, n. 74. Rhymed prose is found in early medieval works, and Bede admired the rhymed prose of Gregory the Great; this style was reborn in the eleventh century and reached its apogee in the twelfth (de Bruyne, *Etudes* 2, p. 9).

91. *PL* 70:1140; see also Roger, *L'enseignement des lettres classiques*, p. 176.
92. Roger, p. 176.
93. *PL* 70:1127.

through; everywhere things to come are explained to mankind."[94] Of all the biblical books discussed in *De Institutionibus,* the only one he specifically connects with poetry here is Job; he cites Jerome, "Prosa incipit, versu labitur, pedestri sermone finitur."[95] He praises the existence of rhetorical figures in that book, and asks, in view of its art and eloquence, "Who is there who will claim that the art of rhetoric does not begin with the Holy Scriptures?"

This is an idea that he developed in greater length in his preface to his Psalm Commentary.[96] He begins his discussion by citing Paul (Heb. 4:12):

> For the word of God is alive and active. It cuts more keenly than any two-edged sword, piercing as far as the place where life and spirit, joints and marrow, divide. It sifts the purposes and thoughts of the heart.

Paul meant to include in this (Cassiodorus says) the Bible's very style—"per commata procedens ad depromendum sensum." He identifies the presence of stylistic ornaments, "but these [ornaments] do not exist to beautify Scripture—on the contrary, they themselves are glorified by having Scripture's own dignity conferred on them."[97] The ornaments, which first appeared in the Bible, were later taken over by the Gentiles for their own purposes (the old Aristobulus theme) and reappear in Greek disputational and rhetorical art. He then cites Augustine, *De Doctrina Christiana* 3, 29, to support his claim, and adds the Augustinian notion that the Bible has its own colors of rhetoric which are impossible in Latin ("alios autem proprios in divinis eloquiis esse declaravit, quos grammatici sive rhetores nullatenus attigerunt").[98]

His Psalter commentary itself is filled with references to Greek tropes and figures. There are so many that J. Garet, in his edition of Cassiodorus, drew up a table of the figures with their Greek and Latin names and a list of references to them in Cassiodorus's commentary.[99] In the commentary itself, what we would recognize as parallelism is variously identified as *emphasis* (i.e., *exaggeratio*), *epanados* ("repetitio rerum quae junctim dictae sunt"), *epexegesis, epimone,*

---

94. *PL* 70:1131.
95. *PL* 70:1118. This is cited from Jerome, Letter 53 (to Paulinus).
96. *PL* 70:19–26.
97. *PL* 70:20.
98. *PL* 70:21.
99. The table was reprinted in Migne's edition, *PL* 70:1271–80.

exetasmos, hirmos, hypozeuxis, ison, metabole, periphrasis, schesis onomaton, etc. Thus, about Psalm 5:2 ("Hear my words, O Lord, understand what I say") Cassiodorus writes:

> This device is called metabole, that is, the repetition of a single idea in a variety of words: for here, one and the same thing is signified in a three-fold repetition. For he said "Take my words to your ears, O Lord" [i.e., the Latin translation of *ha'ăzînâ*]; thence "understand my cry"; thirdly, "hearken to the sound of my speech"—all of which goes to stating a single request. It is as if he had said "listen to my speech."[100]

About Psalm 24:10 he writes:

> "Who is the King of Glory? The Lord of Hosts, He is the King of Glory." This as well is a most lovely device which is called in Greek *anadiplosis,* and in Latin *congeminatio dictionis,* which can be done either in a whole verse, or in repetition of individual words.[101]

While such repetitions as these are laudable, they are to be distinguished from mere pleonasm. Cassiodorus has Augustinian difficulties with "set on fire" in Psalm 73:7:

> "Incenderunt igni sanctuarium tuum. . . . " Now its saying "they ignited with fire" is a device which in secular literature is called *pleonasmos,* where something superfluous is interposed. But in the Sacred Scriptures (so it seems to me) it is not fit to speak of this figure, for therein everything is useful, everything is necessary, and everything is perfect.[102]

The same notion of tropes is found in Isidore of Seville (d. 636), who passed it on to the Venerable Bede (672–735). In fact, Bede wrote a treatise on the subject, *De schematibus.*[103] He was familiar, of course, with Cassiodorus,[104] and probably also with Donatus.[105] He repeats the idea (stated also in Isidore) that the Greek rhetorical devices came originally from the Hebrew, and asserts that the Bible is superior to other books "not only because of its Source, which is

100. *PL* 70:54.
101. *PL* 70:175.
102. *PL* 70:528.
103. *PL* 90:175.
104. See Roger, *L'enseignement des lettres classiques,* p. 31.
105. Huppé, *Doctrine and Poetry,* p. 31.

divine, or by reason of its use, inasmuch as it leads to eternal life, but also by its antiquity and its manner of expression."[106] Bede then catalogues various devices, explaining them and giving examples from Latin literature and, *apud nos,* from the text of the Bible. Bede also went so far as to catalogue books of the Bible according to their poetic structure. Of the three classical types of poems, *dramaticon, exegematicon,* and *coenon,* the Song of Songs is an example of the first because it consists of two "voices," the Savior and the Church; Proverbs, Ecclesiastes and Psalter are in the second class (as are the first three books of Vergil's *Georgics* and part of the fourth) because in them "poeta ipse loquitur sine ullius interpositione personae": and the *Iliad,* the *Aeneid,* and Job are in the third class (the poet speaking both for himself and through his characters)—though he notes, following Jerome, that not all of Job is written in verse.[107] Finally, it should be noted that this classification is repeated almost word for word in another great medieval cyclopedia, the *De Universo* of Rabanus Maurus (784–856).[108]

Meanwhile, the metrical thesis was not lagging behind. Drepanius wrote in a verse epistle:[109]

Job prius heröo sua carmine bella retexit
  Divina David personat ipse lyra
Quid loquar insigni tumidum Solomona cothurno
  Qui thalamos Christi psallit et Ecclesiae

Similarly, Arator (sixth century) in another verse letter[110]

Metrica vis sacris non est incognita libris
  Psalterium lyrici composuere pedes
Hexametris constare sonis in origine linguae
  Cantica Hieremiae Job quoque dicta ferunt

It is no accident that these claims find themselves in the middle of poems, for the metrical thesis helped to guarantee poetry a place in the Christian world; indeed, attributing meters to the Bible made metrics, like rhetoric, an essential field of study.[111]

---

106. Cited in Roger, *L'enseignement des lettres classiques*, p. 308.

107. Bede, *De Arte Metrica*, in *PL* 90:174.

108. Book 15, under "De Poetis," *PL* 111:419–20.

109. *PL* 61:1089; cf. *EPH*, p. 198.

110. *PL* 68:80.

111. Roger, *L'enseignement des lettres classiques*, p. 140. Of course, it was part of the discipline of music, hence mathematics. Augustine's *De Musica* deals at length with the question of meter.

Junilius Africanus (sixth century) mentioned the question of meter in his catechismic "De Partibus Divinae Legis":

Student: How many are the types of discourse in the Scriptures?
Teacher: Two; for they are either written in the Hebrew meters in that language, or in prose.
S: What things are written in meter?
T: The Psalms, the story of Job, Ecclesiastes, and some parts of the Prophets.
S: What parts are written in prose?
T: All the rest.
S: Why are they not written in those meters in our (Latin) version?
T: Because no utterance is able to keep the meter in another language, unless it change the force of the words or their order.[112]

While all three of the foregoing writers agree that the Psalms and Job are metrical, each advances a different third example of verse: Drepanius singles out the Song of Songs, Arator Lamentations, and Junilius Ecclesiastes (along with, so it seems, the Prophetic Canticles).

Isidore's *Etymologies* repeated in great detail Jerome's claims about Hebrew meters, with occasional variation:

All the Psalms are composed in the Hebrew in metrical poetry. For in the manner of the Roman Flaccus and of the Greek Pindar, now some flow with the iamb, then resound with Alcaics, now shine with a Sapphic [measure], proceeding with tetrameter or trimeter.[113]

Of Job, he repeats the Jerome delimitations of poetry and prose, and says Proverbs, the Song of Songs, and Ecclesiastes are written in hexameter and pentameter verses. Isaiah, "evangelista potius quam propheta" (the formula is Jerome's), writes in "rhetorical prose," except, of course, for his Canticle, which consists of hexameters and pentameters.[114] He also repeats Jerome's description of Lamentations.[115]

Beyond this, Isidore presents the idea that the Hebrews invented the meters later adopted by the Greeks! This is an obvious parallel to what Augustine had said about tropes and figures:

Moses was the first to have sung [metrically] in the canticle of Deuteronomy, long before Pherecydes and Homer: thus it is apparent that the study of poetry is of greater antiquity among the

112. *PL* 68:20.
113. *PL* 82:231.
114. *PL* 82:232.
115. *PL* 82:232.

Hebrews than the Gentiles. Likewise Job, which goes back to the time of Moses,[116] flows in hexameter verse of dactyl and spondee.[117]

Similarly, Isidore (following Origen) attributes the first epithalamion to Solomon (Song of Songs) and the first lament to Jeremiah (Lamentations). To Gentile sources he ascribes the origin of elegiac and bucolic verses.

After Isidore, Aldhelm (seventh century) and Bede both repeated the metrical thesis as they had the attribution of tropes and figures to the Bible.[118] Again, it is to be noted that both were poets. Indeed, as a poet, Aldhelm was a thorough-going syncretist. What has survived of his poetry includes Latin verses in which "Olympus" is used to signify Heaven, "Tartarus" Hell, and the Deity is called "the King of Olympus"![119] He even seems to attribute some validity to pagan inspiration:

> I do not seek the rustic Muses for my verses and periods, nor for my metrical songs the Castalian nymphs. . . . But rather I strive to move the Thunderer [his poetic appelation for God] with my prayers, Who grants to use the oracles of peaceful word; I seek the word from the Word, whom the Psalmist sang.[120]

Bede, as we have seen, wrote a treatise on meter; in it he discussed the differences between meter and rhythm (rhythm can exist without meter, but not vice versa; meter is "ratio cum modulatione," rhythm "modulatio sine ratione").[121] He repeated Jerome's description of the meter of Job, and added that Proverbs and Ecclesiastes, like, indeed, the whole Psalter, are also written in meter "in their own language."[122]

Rabanus Maurus, the last great encyclopedist of this early period, discusses the question of meter in *De Universo,* Book 5.[123] Here, he repeats what he had gleaned from previous *auctores,* principally Jerome and Isidore. It is a summary of medieval knowledge on the

116. Here Isidore does not take sides in the dispute over whether Moses himself was the author of Job.

117. *PL* 82:119–20.

118. *PL* 89:171, 90:174.

119. For Aldhelm and tropes, see *PL* 89:171; he speaks of *allegoria* (*PL* 89:114, 165), *metaphor* (165), *climax* (169), etc. See Roger, *L'enseignement des lettres classiques*, p. 385, also de Bruyne, *Etudes* 1, pp. 145–46.

120. Huppé, *Doctrine and Poetry*, p. 69.

121. *PL* 90:174. See on this passage de Bruyne, *Etudes* 1, pp. 151–59, and below, chapter 6, n. 74.

122. *PL* 90:174.

123. *PL* 111:107.

question of meter, stating the view that would pass basically
unchanged until the Renaissance. It is the fruit of much of what we
have seen about meter and figures in the writings of the Fathers:

> The beginning and the end of the book of Job are composed of
> prose speech in the Hebrew: its middle parts, however, from the
> place in which he says "*Pereat dies . . .*" up until the place in which
> it says "*Idcirco . . .*" is all written in heroic meter. . . .
> All the Psalms are composed in Hebrew in metrical poetry. For
> in the manner of the Roman Flaccus and the Greek Pindar they run
> now with an iambic foot, now with an alcaic, now with a Sapphic
> they sound, moving along in trimeter or tetrameter. . . .

> The first of [the books of Solomon] is Masloth [*sic*] which the
> Greeks call *Parabolae* and the Latins Proverbs; in which book he
> shows, by comparisons and similitudes, figures of words and
> images of the truth, which truth however he leaves to be found out
> by the readers. . . .
> The songs of these three books [Proverbs, the Song of Songs, and
> Ecclesiastes] are said to be written in hexameter and pentameter
> verses, as Josephus and Jerome both write. Isaiah, more an
> evangelist than a Prophet, produced his book, all of which proceeds
> by rhetorical prose; however, the canticle is in hexameter and
> pentameter verse. . . . Jeremiah similarly wrote his book of
> Lamentations . . . in which he composed a four-fold alphabet in
> diverse meter; the first two parts of it are written in a Sapphic-like
> meter.

We have passed quickly over the wealth of material written in this
formative period of Christian ideas about the poetry of the Bible. No
doubt further inquiry would yield an even richer hoard of opinions
concerning the differences between poetry and prose in the Bible, and
the form and function of parallelism. But by the tenth century, indeed
well before it, the main lines of approach for future Christian exegetes
had been drawn. Like Greek or Latin literature, the Hebrew Bible was
written in poetry and prose, its poetry characterized by meter
comparable to those known from classical models, and its prose
studded with tropes and figures as befits any elegant discourse. This
basic set of assumptions did not change until the Renaissance—and
then, as will be seen, only gradually and incompletely. Somewhere
behind it lies a fleeting perception of the elusive truth about biblical
style. But the metrical–poetry/ornamented-prose view of things was
just accurate enough, and more than sufficiently appealing, to survive
questioning for some time to come.

FIVE

THE METER OF BIBLICAL SONGS

1

The exegetical path we have been tracing has thus split in two. The notion of parallelism with which we began conceived of it basically as an emphatic, elevating feature, "seconding." Sometimes what B added to A was significantly different, a definite going-beyond in force or specificity; sometimes A and B were related in a manner best expressed by some subordination in English ("when," if," "just as"); sometimes B's "what's more" was a reassertion of A via the most conventional pairs. At the fork in this road, rabbinic exegesis veers off to the "sharp" side. It takes the "what's more" inherent in B and (especially through the cross-referencing that is so great a part of midrash) insists that every B is significantly different from A, indeed, often a reference to some utterly separate matter. This reading masks the fact of parallelism itself, masks even the insistent seconding structure of line after line of the Psalter or Job, and, along with the other factors cited, dimmed Jewish awareness of this rhetorical feature in their own Scripture. Moreover, the concentration of parallelism and other heightening features in this or that passage was of no consequence. Scripture was of one piece, sacred, incomparable to human texts, and certainly not divided into "poetry" and "prose."

Christian exegetes also veered off, but in the Greco-Roman direction seen: following Philo-Josephus, they accepted as (metrical) poetry those songs, psalms, and the like in the Bible which, had they been written in Greek, would naturally, by reason of subject and genre, have been poetry. This identification was not, however, tied to parallelism, and the very obvious parallelism of, for example, prophetic discourse never moved these commentators to suggest that Isaiah or Jeremiah were metrical. On the contrary, these and other parts of the Bible were assimilated to another tradition, that of Greek rhetoric, and such parallelism as was present was perceived as periodic style, a form of (nay, the ancestor of) classical tropes and figures.

These Greco-Roman suppositions have been perpetuated by modern critics to an extent that most would find surprising. The idea of biblical poetry has survived, and all the erroneous scansions and metrical systems are the child of this view of things. In a more subtle way, so are the misleading categories of Lowth et al. About *De Sacra Poesi* it might be justly said, "it told us what we wanted to hear"; that Hebrew poetry had a *system*, one that was comparable to European poetry's various structural features. Lowth's great contribution was to extend the category of "poetry" to include prophetic writings (and to this extent his work was an important milestone on the way to English Romanticism). Since Lowth, new refinements have been introduced, but critics have always continued to demand of biblical texts that they by systematic, that they be *poetry*, even amending the text to suit their own notions of rhythm or parallelism of meaning.

This history, if it does not quite have a happy ending, has at least a happy middle. For there came a time when the Jewish part of the "fork" doubled back toward the Christian and, in trying to reconcile different traditions and perceptions, stated a view of parallelism more reasonable—less misleading—than what had preceded in either, and, sadly, what was to follow. The best-known figure from this exegetical swerve is Azariah dei Rossi, whose insights into parallelism are contained in his massive compendium מאור עינים (Light of the Eyes) (1575), which Lowth cites among his sources. But Azariah himself had sources; his remarks about the structure of biblical songs were made in the context of a definite exegetical tradition, that of the Jewish Middle Ages.

2

Medieval Hebrew exegesis began as the child of the Talmud and midrash. Of course, there is enormous variety in the method and focus of exegesis in this most fruitful and productive period: exponents of Kabbalah, philosophy, rationalism, and so forth, all used biblical commentary as a means of setting forth their ideas; commentaries were systematic or hodgepodges, literary, philological, mystical, scientific.[1] But they were all heir to the notion of exegesis embodied in rabbinic writings, and indeed, frequently had recourse to this body of work in order to buttress their own ideas. Among the presuppositions adopted by early medieval Jewish exegetes was the "sharp" rabbinic

---

1. See in general M. Segal, פרשנות המקרא (Tel Aviv, 1952), and E. Z. Melamed, מפרשי המקרא (Jerusalem, 1975).

approach to parallelism, and as a consequence, one finds very little of the stylistic explanations seen among the Fathers of the Church in their writings about the Bible.

Thus, Rashi (1040–1105) is, in general, scrupulous in reading B as a distinction over and against A. For example, on Numbers 23:7, "Come, curse Jacob for me, come condemn Israel" he remarks: "Balak had told him to curse them using both the names of the Israelites, lest one alone not be precise enough." Similarly, on Deuteronomy 32:7 "Ask your father and he will tell you, your elders and they will say to you," he (following Sifre) adduces the verse of 2 Kings 2:12 to show that "your father" refers to the Prophets of Israel, and then explains "your elders" as a reference to the talmudic sages. However, he is occasionally forced to confront a purely rhetorical feature, such as the parallelistic use of repetition. On Exodus 15:1 he writes about the phrase כי גאה גאה (He has triumphantly triumphed):

> The form is repeated here to show that He did what it is impossible for flesh-and-blood to do, for when a man fights with his fellow and conquers him, he throws him from his horse, but here "horse and rider He cast in the sea. . . ." And likewise you will find repetition throughout the Song: "My strength and power . . ." (15:2), "The Lord is a warrior, the Lord is His name," and so forth.

Rashi feels the necessity, just as the Rabbis had, to explain any form of repetition or other apparently superfluous usages—and to explain them not as a feature of rhetoric, but as *signifying* something. So, in quite talmudic fashion, he advances the idea that repeating—not only doubled verbs, but any repetition—is peculiar to this song to distinguish God's actions from human ones. He sticks to the same explanation in his handling of verse 6, but then adds something:

> "Thy right hand, O Lord, is glorious in power"—to save Israel; and the second "thy right hand" crushes the enemy, and so it seems to me that that same right hand [that saves Israel] also crushes the enemy, which is something a man cannot accomplish, two deeds with one hand. But the simple meaning of the verse is: "Thy right hand, O Lord, which is glorious in power—what does it do? Thy right hand, O Lord, crushes the enemy." And there are many such verses in the Bible, such as "For behold thy enemies, O Lord, for behold thy enemies will perish" [Psalms 92:10], and the others like it.

This verse presents another instance of repetition, and Rashi offers the same explanation for it: "right hand" is repeated to emphasize the difference between human deeds and Divine. But his addition about the "simple meaning" of the verse shows he was perfectly aware that the repetition in B was simply that, a repetition and continuation of A's thought. He even cites another example of this "repetitive parallelism," Psalm 92:10.[2]

The notion was dealt with in more explicit terms by Rashi's grandson, R. Samuel b. Meir (=Rashbam) in his commentary on the same passage.

> "Thy right hand . . ." etc. This passage is like "The waters have lifted up, O Lord, the waters have lifted up their voice "[Psalm 93:3], "How long shall the wicked, Lord, how long shall the wicked exult" [Psalm 94:3]. "For behold thine enemies, O Lord, for behold thine enemies perish" [Psalm 92:10]. In all these the first half does not finish its idea until the last half comes and repeats it and then completes its idea. In the first half it [only] mentions who or what it is talking about.[3]

It is clear from here that Rashbam understood the structure of the verses mentioned, that is, understood "repetitive parallelism" as a specific stylistic construction that divided the verses.

Equally perceptive are various remarks about parallelism in the commentary of Rashbam's contemporary, Abraham ibn Ezra (1089–1164). He frequently remarks on the repetition of meaning in sections identified as songs and the like. For example, about Balaam's verse in Numbers 23:7 he observes: "The idea is repeated according to the practice by which one idea is spoken twice in different words. They repeat for the sake of emphasis." He makes similar remarks about the "Song of the Well" (Numbers 21:17) and the Song of the *mōšĕlîm* (Numbers 21:27); about Deuteronomy 32:7 he observes, "The idea is repeated for this is a form of elegant speech (כי כן דרך צחות)."[4] One of his most interesting explanations is of Genesis 49:6:

---

2. Some editions of Rashi contain other examples, but this may simply be a back-formation from his grandson's commentary: see below.

3. Cf. his remarks on Gen. 49:22, where he adduces a similar list.

4. The notion of צחות has its own complicated history in Jewish writings. It is used in the Bible (Isa. 32:4) in a manner that might indicate "elegant speech," "rhetoric," and so it is used by some later writers. At the same time it was seen as the Hebrew equivalent of Arabic *faṣāḥa*, which came to denote purity or clarity of speech and specifically clear Arabic uncorrupted by later borrowings. As the concern for *faṣāḥa* among Arabs was transmuted into medieval Jewry's interest in pure biblical speech, the word צחות was also used to designate such purity; but here ibn Ezra seems to use it not in this specific sense but in the more general meaning of eloquent expression.

R. Moses ha-Kohen [ibn Gikatilia] said that "my glory" is like "my soul," and that there are many in the Psalms like this. It is a fine explanation, for the meaning is repeated as is the practice in prophecy: "Ask your father..." [Deut. 32:7], "How shall I curse..." [Num. 23:8]. Similarly here "in their company" is like "in their group," "go" is like "be united," "my soul" is like "my glory."

Another interesting comment on parallelism comes on Exodus 24:10, where he attempts to understand the meaning of the word ספיר (sapphire?) in the expression כמעשה לבנת הספיר by looking at another instance in which the word is parallelistically apposed:

> Sa'adya Ga'on has said that a ספיר is white, and (his proof) is this text, כמעשה לבנת הספיר. But on the contrary, a ספיר is red; this proven by the fact that it is the practice of Hebrew to repeat an idea in different words, so that where it says (Lam. 4:7), "Her princes were purer than snow, whiter than milk," the idea is being repeated. So when the verse continues, "Their bodies were ruddier than red coral, their form was a ספיר," ספיר ought to be compared to red coral."

Not only had ibn Ezra used parallelism of meaning as an exegetical tool, he also identified it (correctly in our view) as a "habit of the language" and דרך צחות, the "rhetorical" style, rather than associating it specifically with songs and poetry. This notwithstanding, it is noteworthy that in his שפה ברורה (*Clear Speech*) he discusses the same question of apparently needless repetition:

> If someone should cite as an example the verse "and the earth and the land were unformed" (Psalm 90:2) I would answer that the first word ארץ is a general name for the inhabited and uninhabited parts, while the second word תבל means specifically the inhabited part. But if one objected that there is then no need to specify the assertion for a part if that part is included in the whole, I would answer that *this is the way the divinely inspired speak* (ככה מנהג אנשי הקודש לדבר). For does it not also say, "Both the sons of Adam and the sons of men..." (Ps. 49:3)[5]

(See also below on Sa'adya's characterization of Isaiah's "style"). On Sa'adya's precise notion of clarity see E. Goldenberg, ... עיונים באגרון, in לשוננו 37 (1973): 121–25, and in general I. Twersky, *Introduction to the Code of Maimonides* (New Haven, 1980), pp. 347–48.

5. שפה ברורה (Fuerth, 1839) page 9a.

Here he avoids claiming the text repeats, preferring the "lesser charge" of stating a particular unnecessarily since the general has already been held to be true.[6]

Both ibn Ezra and Rashbam use the phrase כפל לשון ("repetition of an expression") and the like. The origin of this phase is apparently rabbinic: כפל is used in the general sense of "repeat" as well as the more common meaning of "to double," and one finds such usages as לשון כפול (*Song of Songs Rabba* 1:66) and נחמות כפולות (*Lev. Rabba* 10:12). There, however, actual repetition is meant. Similarly, when Rashi used this word (above) he meant actual repetition of a word or phrase. But in ibn Ezra and Rashbam, what is meant is not necessarily repetition but any form of reiteration or restatement.[7] Thus, on Exodus 15:2 Rashbam writes: "The repetition of the verse's ending (כפל סוף הפסוק) proves that נוא means to praise"; similarly, on Numbers 23:7, " 'From the eastern mountains' is a repetitive expression (כפל לשון) for the text has already said 'From Aram.' This is to emphasize the great trouble [it took to come] from a distant land." Although this looks like rabbinic language, it is broader in that it understands reiteration (like actual repetition) as emphatic.

Now ibn Ezra and Rashbam were, as noted, contemporaries, and it is certainly possible that the appearance of this expression in both is the result of direct influence (rather than a similar adaptation in both of an existing usage). But if so, who influenced whom? Ibn Ezra resorts to this explanation more often than Rashbam and more explicitly, "he repeated the same idea *in different words*," etc. But perhaps they have a common ancestor among earlier commentators. The celebrated dictionary of Menahem b. Jacob ibn Saruq (tenth century) shows some awareness of parallelism, and in at least one place uses phrases similar to those seen, thus: "The beginning of the verse and the end are a single matter, and one would have been enough"; "Here too he repeated the idea twice (הכפיל הענין פעמים)"; "And here are ideas which are spoken in an expansive manner,

---

6. Cf. Sa'adya Ga'on's explanation of the same phenomenon in 2 Samuel 22:2, Psalm 29:8, etc. (cited by Samuel b. Isaac ha-Sefardi in his Samuel commentary and reprinted in J. Kafih, פירושי רס׳ג על התורה (Jerusalem, 1963), p. 175. Of course it is unnecessary to explain a specification of a part *followed* by the whole, since what is said second is not included in the first. Thus, in solving this difficulty Sa'adya and ibn Ezra were separating off the only problematic usage of parallelism.

7. Rashbam uses the phrase כפל לשון for (1) repetition of the same word or root; (2) restatement in different words; and (3) "repetitive parallelism." For a brief list of usages, see Melamed, מפרשי המקרא, 1, p. 466.

restated in their words and repeated (הנכפלים) in their substance."[8] It is noteworthy, however, that none of the cited phrases describes a parallelistic line: all refer to repetitions of a single word, logical pleonasms, or aberrant morphologies ("extra" syllables and the like).

Mention ought to be made as well of the commentator David Kimḥi (c. 1160–c. 1235), since he has been cited, along with ibn Ezra, as describing parallelism *avant la lettre*.[9] On Hosea 12:5 he says, "He repeated the idea for emphasis since it was a great wonder for a man to fight an angel." About Habakkuk 3:8: "He repeated the idea for emphasis." On the other hand he does not discuss parallelism in either Exodus 15 or Deuteronomy 32, nor for that matter in those other songs of the Torah, Numbers 21:17 and 21:27. He uses the same phrase, כפל הפסוק לחזק העניין to describe an actual repetition (Psalm 118:8–9); like Rashbam and others, he does not distinguish between paralleling and repeating. Furthermore, like ibn Ezra, he speaks of "repetition" in the same way when it is individual words, rather than verse-halves, that are involved; for example, on Judges 5:27:

> "Between her feet he bowed he fell": such is the habit of Hebrew to repeat things in order to reinforce the meaning, for he bowed down to the ground so as never to rise again. [Hence the justification for emphasis.] That is why it says next, "where he bowed, there he fell stricken."

Similarly, Deborah's cry, "Arise, arise" is described as an emphatic "doubling."

Joseph ibn Kaspi (1279–1340) is another commentator who touches on the issue of parallelism. In general he is ready to admit the poetic character of parts of the Bible,[10] but for him this is a statement about the figurative quality of the language, not one with formal

---

8. H. Filipowski, ספר מחברת מנחם (London, 1854), pp. 70–71. In regard to Menahem's use of parallelistic apposition as an exegetical tool, cf. his explanation of the word גל in Song of Songs 4:12—מעין חתום יורה על גל נעול שהוא גולה (p. 51).

9. Kimḥi was so credited in L. Dukes, *Zur Kenntnis der neuhebräische Poesie* (Frankfurt, 1842), p. 125; in a reply, Schmiedl adduced ibn Ezra's comment on Gen. 49:6 (see *MGWJ* [1861], p. 157). For a fuller treatment of Kimḥi's ideas on biblical style, see F. E. Talmage, *David Kimhi* (Cambridge, Mass., 1975), pp. 102–08.

10. Thus, the virtuous woman section of Prov. 31 is written in the manner of "poetic embellishment" (מליצת שירים) in that the author "exaggerated in his list of particulars concerning this virtuous woman, just as he exaggerated earlier in recounting the particulars of the adulterous woman (Prov. 7)." Joseph ibn Kaspi, עשרה כלי כסף (ed. Isaac Last) (Pressburg, 1904), p. 130. Similarly, Job's cursing the day of his birth (Job 3:3) is a form of "poetic embellishment, for who can reverse what has already transpired?" (p. 153). Such statements show that for ibn Kaspi (and

implications. Among his biblical commentaries are two on Proverbs (a work in which the play of parallelism is particularly apparent). Like many of his predecessors, Kaspi interpreted in the "sharp" manner where possible, and in his first commentary even went to Lowthian lengths to catalogue the different sorts of ways in which the second verse-half relates back to the first.[11] But his concern is with the *logical* relation of the verse-halves: citing Boethius, "Logic is the silver key which opens the chamber in which Philosophy lies on a golden couch," he proceeds to examine different classes of assertions via logical categories. The fact of their binariness does not interest him as such.

Lastly, allusion must be made to Tanḥum Yerušalmi, a thirteenth-century commentator who lived first in Palestine, then in Egypt.[12] His surviving commentaries are remarkable for their freedom from convention and, occasionally, their striking insight. Tanḥum frequently resorts to Arabic literary terminology for describing biblical style: in his Habakkuk commentary he commonly labels expressions as "metaphor," "eloquence" (*balāġa*, connected in Arabic rhetoric to *faṣāḥa*, "purity"), "simile," etc., and at chapter 3 compares the style of the prophet to that of Deborah in Judges 5, Isaiah 38:9, and certain psalms for its "concision, obscurity, and use of metaphors." Now apparently in his commentary on Psalm 91:1 Tanḥum had explained at some length about repetition of meaning, for he refers to it not only in the Habakkuk commentary but (on the subject of

---

others) the quality of being "poetic" lay in הפלגה ("exaggeration"), the frequent Hebrew equivalent of *balāġa*. This in turn goes back to various Arabic restatements of Plato's *Republic* and Aristotle's *Poetics*; see below, ns. 37 and 38.

11. See עשרה כלי כסף, pp. 27–29. Kaspi asserts that most of the proverbs starting from chapter 10 "consist of two clauses, with the subject and predicate of the one opposed to the subject and predicate of the other." Therefore, in order to interpret them, aright, "there is no need to look closely at the words in this book's oppositions, but at the idea alone. . . . In a proverb of the first type, you will find that each simple clause of the two has an opposite in the overall statement, and each of them illuminates its fellow." He also remarks on other types of proverbs, in which the beginning of the second clause picks up the end of the first, and others characterized by apparent repetition, "with only a slight change from what was said previously"; in these, "whether [the change] be the addition of a word or words or whether it be omissions, that very addition or omission will now be the true subject which he wished to raise."

12. His work was well known among Oriental Jews, but was only rediscovered in the West in the nineteenth century. See I. Goldziher, *Studien über Tanhum Jeruschalmi* (Leipzig, 1870); also B. Toledano in *Sinai* 42 (1961): 339 (a general review) and Hadassah Shai, "Almurshid alkafī" in *Leshonenu* 33 (1969): 196.

repetition of meaning) in his commentary on the Song of Songs as well. Unfortunately, the passage has not yet turned up among the existing Tanḥum fragments.

This brief sketch should capture some of the flavor of medieval Jewish exegesis. In all these commentaries there is a quite obvious movement beyond the midrashic approach to parallelism. To some extent, this is a reflection of the precise nature of biblical commentary—whose task is, after all, to comment on all that is unclear, troublesome, or otherwise in need of explanation—as opposed to midrash, which has less of a commitment to completeness. Thus, as we have suggested, where midrashic exegesis did not have a "sharp" reading to propose, it proposed none at all; Rashi could not allow himself the same silences. But this in turn reflects a difference in orientation. There is something more open-minded, even scientific, about the undertaking of such biblical commentary per se. The commentaries seen probably represent not so much a new understanding as a new willingness to approach the Bible's manner of expression—its style, as it were—phenomenologically. Just as these commentators were at first handicapped by a rabbinic tradition committed theologically and temperamentally to the reading of B as significantly different from A, so they had a compensating advantage: as ibn Ezra, Rashbam, et al. evolved their increasingly phenomenological approach, they were somewhat freer than Christian exegetes from the canons of rhetorical orthodoxy. As a consequence (as we have seen) they were, like today's biblical form-critics, intent on deriving the Bible's rhetoric from itself: ibn Ezra's "This is the way the divinely inspired speak" is witness to this tendency.

Yet there is something quite wrong-headed in describing any of these commentators as "understanding" parallelism, for even in ibn Ezra it is a most passive act of comprehension. They embraced parallelism only in its most obvious form, and only to the extent that it aided them in their main task, explaining the meaning of the words. Where it was possible to read verse-halves as differentiated by nuances of meaning, they usually did so; only when the text literally repeated itself, or in an unmistakable way restated a single idea, did they speak of "doubling," repetition, and so forth. And "elegant style," "the manner or prophecies," and "the habit of Hebrew" all explain what, to these commentators, ought really not to exist, mere repetition or restatement. This was a lingering orthodoxy. Repetition still ran counter to their notion of the text's perfection, and likewise violated the rules of style set even for ordinary men.

On this last point, the testimony of Moses ibn Ezra, the author of a

lengthy treatise on poetry,[13] is most instructive. It is in his eighth
chapter that he takes notice in general of the phenomenon of repetition
and restatement of the Bible, observing that "in our language, the
repetition of an idea is permitted so long as the words are different; on
the contrary, in the opinion of one of the masters of the study of
rhetoric [Jonah ibn Janāḥ][14] this is a form of pure and elegant style
(faṣāḥa wabalāġa)." He then cites Isaiah 41:4, 43:7, 41:20,
Deuteronomy 25:18, Genesis 25:8, Leviticus 17:5, Exodus 25:23,
and others—some entire verse-halves, but most of them individual
pairs of words. (For him, as for the other commentators, there was no
difference. They posed the same problem, seemingly needless
repetition of ideas, and they received the same solution, the label
"rhetorical style.")

These examples notwithstanding, he cautions Hebrew poets against
imitating biblical practice: "In poetry, brevity is the correct thing."
He cites many verses that *seem* repetitive, interpreting their repetition
as adding in each case a significant nuance. (Psalm 115:12 is a
"general statement followed by a specification.") Then he adduces a
few examples of parallelism which he reads in the "distribution"
manner. Thus Leviticus 25:37,

> Do not lend your money out at discount / and your food do not give out at
> interest //

he reads, "Your money and your food do not lend out at interest or
discount." For parallelism itself he shows little feeling. His remarks
here, like those of the commentators, have a defensive quality—he
wishes to show it is *not bad style* to repeat in Hebrew, even though in
the values of Arabic rhetoric, which he had embraced as his own, it is.

These efforts were "passive" and defensive because their aim was
not to strike out on a mission of discovery, but only to explain away
something in the text which (they were willing to admit) contradicted
the midrashic assumption of the text's signifying even in its minutest
details—and, in the view of Moses ibn Ezra and others, violated the
canons of Arabic rhetoric as well. There is no doubt that thanks to ibn
Janāḥ, Abraham ibn Ezra and Rashbam, the emphatic function of
restatement and repetition came to be accepted as a fact of biblical
style. But that this explanation was not particularly comforting is
apparent from the other explanations these same commentators

---

13. *Kitāb al-Muḥāḍara waᵓal-muḏākara*, ed. A. S. Halkin (Jerusalem, 1975).
14. In *Kitāb al-lumaᶜ* (Hebrew translation ספר הרקמה, Wilensky edition [Berlin,
1931], p. 303).

adduce on occasion. Moreover, they were unable to see beyond repetition and restatement to grasp the *essential* of this style, B's subjunction to A (of which repetition and restatement are but a manifestation). Yet awareness of this last fact, and of its quasi-structural role in certain parts of the Bible, was not entirely lost on Jewish writers in the late Middle Ages. It owes its existence to one extremely significant development: the introduction of Arabic-style meters into Hebrew poetry, which began in Spain in the tenth century.

3

The story of medieval Hebrew poetry has been told elsewhere.[15] What is important to us here is not the poetry itself, but the effect of its existence on Jewish perceptions of the Bible. For poetry came, in a short period of time, to dominate utterly Jewish consciousness (as it already had the Arabs') in a way without analogue in modern societies. It was used for everything—praise of patrons, shaming of enemies; love songs, wine songs, occasional verse of all kinds; religious songs incorporated into the synagogue service; learned treatises and polemics; all these found the new poetry their natural medium. "If you wish to make some matter well known," said Yeda'ya ha-Penini, "put it in a poem. If you put it in a book, never on your life will it spread abroad."[16] An astonishing quantity of poetry was known by heart, for it was the medium of all memorizing:

> Since I saw rhyme superior to all else, and its use
>   so highly approved,
> I have metered my treatise and set it in rhyme, so that
>   it will aid the memory[17]

---

15. A brief summary is available in English in S. Spiegel's article "Medieval Hebrew Poetry," in L. Finkelstein, *The Jews* (New York, 1965), 2, p. 82.

16. See L. Dukes, נחל קדומים (reprinted Tel Aviv, 1970), p. 22. Dukes's excerpt is the eighth chapter of Yeda'ya's ספר הפרדס, which appeared fully in אוצר הספרות 3 (1889–90), pp. 1–18. The entire eighth chapter is most illuminating on the position of the poet in society, and on the oral transmission of verse (note above Yeda'ya's opposition of putting something *in verse* as against putting it *in a book*). He further notes: "The poet's advantage is that he can stay in his own place and wreak vengeance on his enemies across the seas."

17. S. ibn Gabirol, in שירי חול, ed. H. Brody and J. Schirmann (Jerusalem, 1975), p. 170. Cf. Joseph Kimhi's explanation of his title שקל הקודש (ed. Gollancz, London, 1919): "I have written [my book] in meter so that it will be easy to grasp and to copy correctly—therefore I have entitled it The Holy Shekel ('weight' but also 'meter')."

Jews learned poetic compilations of halakha by heart, and in the detailed course of study outlined by Joseph ibn Aqnin (contained in "The Healing of Souls") poetry plays a significant role. Moreover, secular and occasional poetry was well known. A wealthy man required his own house poet at least as a defensive weapon, to counter the withering epigrams aimed at him by the poets in his rivals' employ—for these passed among the people and spread fame and shame to every quarter. Similarly, he expected that if a song in praise of him was well wrought, it would survive long after his death. Poems passed from mouth to mouth; ibn Janāḥ recounts how he heard a line of his master, Isaac b. Mar Saul, misquoted many times in public, until he finally heard the correct line from his teacher's mouth.[18] Likewise, Moses ibn Ezra says of ibn Ghayat "His poems were recited and passed on from one person to the next."[19]

Qalonymos b. Qalonymos's fictional poet[20] is—or at least thinks himself—the superior of mere talmudic scholars. Indeed, though Qalonymos's aim is obviously satirical, it was certainly true that the poet's position was exalted—admired, feared, quasi-Divine in that "he builds a whole world" in his words—no wonder his immortality seemed assured: "He thinks his name will live on, perhaps its merits increase, 'Let his name be great in the world created at his will.' " (This last line is the familiar refrain of the Kaddish, where it of course is spoken of God.) Poets were compared to prophets: even the stern Shem-tob b. Joseph Falaqera (c. 1225–95), who had much to criticize in poets, speaks of "the prophets of song," and poetic inspiration was sometimes identified with רוח הקודש, divine inspiration:

> He whom the Creator has blessed with his own inspiration (רוח מאתו) to speak his words in poetic meters is considered to be among those who speak with the Holy Spirit.[21]

18. See B. Klar, מחקרים ועיונים (Tel Aviv, 1954), p. 102.
19. Ibid.
20. In אבן בחן found in J. Schirmann, ed., השירה העברית בספרד ובפרובאנס (Tel Aviv, 1959), 2, p. 514.
21. David b. Yom Tob Bilia (Villa?) (first half of the fourteenth century), דרך לעשות חרוזים, ed. N. Allony in *Kobez 'al Yad*, 16, p. 234. On poets as prophets cf. D. Yellin, תורת השירה הספרדית (Jerusalem, 1946), p. 3 n. Joshua b. Israel Benveniste (1595–1676) in פרק בשיר קונטרס cites an "ancient" anonymous treatise in which the equation of poet and prophet leads its author to apply to poets the same strictures and requirements imposed by the Talmud on prophets. Yeda'ya ha-Penini wrote: "The spirit of the poet pouring forth perfect song we would call 'the spirit of God.' " (ספר הפרדס, p. 12; missing in Dukes). Similarly, he says, "When a poet is wise, they call him a prophet" (or perhaps the Hebrew means, "When a poet is adept, call him a prophet" p. 12).

All this could not but keep the attention of Hebrew poets focused squarely on their biblical "homologues." Whatever of their own craft could be connected with the Bible, no matter how fancifully, was. Thus, the author of אמרי שפר ("Beauteous Words") [22] claimed the number of possible meters in medieval Hebrew was fifteen because "fifteen types of songs were sung in the Temple."[23] In a similar vein, by juggling a single letter the exhortation of Deuteronomy 22:10, "Do not plow with an ox and an ass together," was converted into an admonition to poets:

לא תחרז בשור ובחמר יחדו

i.e., do not rhyme šôr (ox) with ḥamōr (ass), for though the last vowel and consonant are the same, the penultimate consonants differ; hence, the rhyme is unfit.[24]

In the whole matter of Jewish awareness of the Bible as a *composed* and, as it were, literary text, Sa'adya Ga'on is again a figure of crucial importance. As M. Zulay argued forcefully,[25] it was Sa'adya's concern with biblicizing Hebrew style and usage that determined the direction taken by Hebrew poetry in the Golden Age of Spain; but this concern in turn sprang from Sa'adya's larger view of the Bible itself, his careful balancing of a willingness to countenance stylistic judgments of biblical language with a somewhat contrary tendency to assert the role of divine inspiration in the *meaning* of each verse.[26] It is likely his אגרון ("Poet's Dictionary") was in part the model for Moses ibn Ezra's stylistic reading of the Bible in *Kitāb al-muḥāḍara*,[27] but Sa'adya's overall influence was far greater—and again, it was his conception of the interplay between Divine

---

22. Attributed by E. Carmoli to Abshalom Mizrahi; but see A. Neubauer, מלאכת השיר (Frankfurt, 1865), p. iv. The name אמרי שפר also comes from Carmoli's edition.

23. In Neubauer, מלאכת השיר, p. 25. Cf. M. Sukka, 5:4.

24. For a discussion of this see Allony's introduction to Sa'adya's האגרון (Jerusalem, 1969), p. 114 and D. Pagis, חידוש ומסורת (Jerusalem, 1976), p. 125.

25. M. Zulay, האסקולה הפייטנית של ר' סעדיה (Jerusalem, 1964), pp. 19–31; see also Sa'adya's הגלוי (ed. Harkaby, St. Petersburg, 1891), pp. 155–57.

26. See especially his preface to his Psalms translation, where he refutes even the notion that the Psalter's prayers and exhortations imply words addressed to God and hence not given by God: "When it says [Psalm 39:132] 'Hear my prayer' [it means] 'I am [a God] who hears the prayers of my servant'; 'Keep me, God, for I rely on you' [Psalm 16:1] means 'I keep my servant because he relies on me.' " J. Kafih, ed., תהלים עם תרגום רס'ג (Jerusalem, 1966), p. 24.

27. See Allony, ספר האגרון, pp. 112–14.

inspiration and human composition that was the key. As Abraham ibn Ezra remarked:

> The Ga'on said that Isaiah's language was "clear and pleasant." [Dunash b. Labrat] said this was an error, since all the words of the Bible are the Almighty's own—but the error is that of [Dunash], for the meanings of the words are straight-forward and figurative together . . . and the prophet puts together the meanings with such power as he received from the Almighty.[28]

On the precise matter of parallelism neither Sa'adya nor (as we have seen briefly) Moses ibn Ezra was particularly influential, but this was perhaps, more than anything else, because the *Zeitgeist* was against them. To see the Psalms, Job, and other books as more than prose but less than poetry, to compare parts of Deuteronomy, Isaiah, Hannah's Prayer, and other passages to Arabic *ḫuṭba*,[29] is to understand a great deal about biblical style. But it seems that, having opened the door to biblical "poetry," Sa'adya (and later M. ibn Ezra) only encouraged further speculation about that poetry's meter or system.

The phenomenon of judgments of biblical style among writers like

---

28. See the work by ibn Ezra published under the title (apparently a mistake) שפת יתר ed. G. H. Lippmann (Frankfurt, 1843), p. 23 b, or the D. Torsh edition (repr. Jerusalem, 1960), p. 32. (On שפת יתר itself cf. N. Allony in *Leshonenu* 13 [1944–45]: 218–19.) The text here is apparently erroneous, and unfortunately I have been unable to consult manuscript copies. The remark attributed to Dunash comes in the "Book of Replies to Sa'adya"—whose connection with Dunash has sometimes been questioned—at the end of a passage on apparently aberrant forms. Dunash argues that regardless of who speaks the words in a scriptural passage, they must be correct, for "they are all the words of the Lord, Blessed be He, who ordered his Prophets to write it in their books which are called by their names [i.e., Book of Isaiah, etc.] but they are the books of our God, blessed and exalted be His name. And I am amazed at one who claims that Isaiah's language is clear *and so Amos*, for this [would mean he wrote] what he himself wished. And this is an error, for the words of the Bible are all the Holy One's, Blessed be He, and those that are not His [actual] words in it He had already approved and delighted in; and through it [the Bible] He made His covenant with us, as it is written, 'As for Me, this is My covenant with them, saith the Lord' (Isa. 59:21)." (ספר תשובות דונש בן לברט על רס"ג) ed. R. Schröter [Breslau, 1866], p. 29.) The "and so Amos" is apparently also unclear; perhaps ibn Ezra's ונעים is to be preferred. The significance of the Isaiah citation seems to lie in its continuation, "My spirit which is upon you, and My words which I have put in your mouth, shall not depart." Dunash seems to understand "spirit" as referring to words spoken through Divine inspiration (as in the Hagiographa), and "words" to the actual Divine word transmitted through prophecy. Cf. b. *Bab. Mez.* 85a. On this question Maimonides' view is articulated in his *Guide*, introduction and Part II, chaps. 43–45 and in his *Mishneh Torah*, "Principles of the Torah," 7:3–5.

29. See above, end of chapter 3 and especially notes 85 and 90.

Sa'adya and Moses ibn Ezra must also be considered in its Arabic context, specifically the Qur'an's reputation for stylistic excellence, which eventually engendered a host of learned discussions aimed at demonstrating that excellence in minute detail. Here, of course, things evolved slowly. Muḥammad himself had had to combat the accusation that he was a mere šāʿir (poet), and the excellence of Qur'anic style was at first not stressed, indeed, its style was compared to that of ordinary human writings; but gradually there developed the notion of the Qur'an's ʾiʿjāz, its "miraculous inimitability," which lay in its manner of expression, its succinctness, its metaphors, its eloquence (balāġa).[30] Jews did not regularly advance the same claims for the Bible, but no doubt such Moslem claims increased their willingness to talk about the Bible's manner of expression. Now the Qur'an is not written in verse—indeed, this fact led apologists to exalt the "freedom" of prose over metrical compositions, a theme that later resurfaced in some Jewish defences of the biblical poetry's lack of fixed meter. At the same time, the fact that the Bible did have compositions labeled "song" was most inviting: was it not in these songs most of all that one ought to look for the Bible's stylistic excellencies, for something approximating its own ʾiʿjāz?

The Hebrew translation of Arabic šiʿr (poetry) was the similar-sounding (but unrelated) Hebrew word šîr (song). Gradually but surely, šîr came to mean poetry in the minds of Sephardic Jewry, and it therefore became natural to examine those parts of the Bible specifically labeled šîr (or the variant šîrâ) to discover what was "poetic" about them. Though Sa'adya had felt that the category of poetry was inappropriate in the Bible, this hardly satisfied all parties, and it became an increasingly pressing concern to explain the presence of šîr-šîrâ in the incipits of Psalms and songs like Exodus 15 or Deuteronomy 32.

An obvious answer might be: some things in the Bible are called "šîr" because they were sung—the name refers to the manner of performance. But in the Middle Ages, singing, musical accompaniment, and the like all implied the presence of meter—an important point for the modern reader to grasp—and consequently biblical references to music and song, talmudic descriptions of the Levite choirs and their training, and midrashic discussions of the "Ten Songs,"[31] the meaning of the title "Song of Songs," etc., all

---

30. See on this G. E. von Grunebaum, *A Tenth-Century Document of Arabic Literary History and Criticism* (Chicago, 1950), esp. pp. xv–xxii.

31. See chapter 3, n. 91.

implied to Spanish Jewry a poetic art in ancient Israel that was in some basic way comparable to their own. Abraham ibn Ezra, in his commentary on Ecclesiastes 12:9, had interpreted the verb אזן ("balanced"?) as referring to the composition of songs, presumably metrical poems, perhaps those attributed to Solomon (= Koheleth) in 1 Kings 5:12.[32] Shem-tob b. Joseph Falaqera had defended poetry in his "Book of the Seeker":

> For in poetry are said the praises of God
> Which men have composed since Moses and the Israelites
>   [i.e., Exod. 15]
> And the Song of Moses [Deut. 32] which contains all
>   the Torah's principles
> Is written entirely in the manner of poetry
> And amongst poets have been righteous and upright men
> Who spoke in the Holy Spirit
> The Book of Psalms is written in the Holy Spirit and it
>   is entirely songs
> And our Sages called Song of Songs the Holy of Holies.[33]

They knew their own meters had been adapted from Arabic ones, but it seemed plausible to some that these, like the Arabic language itself, ultimately came from Hebrew. Would not an analysis of the Song of the Sea (Exod. 15) and others yield up the evidence necessary to prove Israel's precedence in every aspect of poetry and musical arts?

Other factors also pointed to a "poetic structure" in the Bible. As described in chapter 3, certain parallelistic parts of the Bible were written stichographically, that is, with some sort of break separating

---

32. See on this M. ibn Ezra, *Kitāb al-muḥāḍara*, pp. 46–47; for Sa'adya and ibn Ezra on Job 12:11 see האגרון (ed. N. Allony), pp. 112, 389.

33. In Schirmann, השירה העברית, 2, p. 338. In this passage, as indeed at the end of the poet episode in the ספר המבקש, it seems clear that Falaqera includes under the rubric "poetry" only those biblical passages labeled *šîr*, *šîrâ*, etc. or distinguished by special stichography or accents. Yet what is one to make of the Seeker's question of the Poet, "Why were the Prophets' reproaches (תוכחות) and prayers in poetic language?" It would be nice to imagine that Falaqera wishes here to compare the form of prophetic speech to that of the Psalms, the Song of Songs, and so forth. But it seems more likely that the question is a set-up for the Poet's Farabian answer, namely that poetry is "constructed on comparison, and the ordinary people in their ideas are swayed by comparison." What is "poetic" about prophetic speech is its use of images and ornamentation. However, the association of certain prophetic speech (including Deut. 32) with actual song (and hence some kind of metrical ordering) we have seen above, esp. chapter 3, n. 91, and, in keeping with the equation of שבח with song, cf. j. *Ber.* 5 (beginning), "And so we have found among the earlier prophets that they used to close their speeches with words of praise (דברי שבח)."

the verse-halves. The same convention existed in most Arabic poetry, and naturally led Jews to wonder if the formal resemblance did not stop there. Furthermore, special *ṭe'amim* of the books of Psalms, Proverbs, and Job, which from earliest times had suggested that these texts had some special connection with song, now were understood to mean that these books were, via the *šiᶜr-šîr* connection, the "poetry" par excellence of the Bible.[34] Even for those otherwise skeptical of the notion of a biblical poetry, the argument of the stichography and/or special accents was convincing. The question they were left with— indeed, the one that confronted medieval poets generally, as well as grammarians and other scholars—was: In what precisely does the poetic quality of biblical *šîrîm* lie?

To this question there emerged a whole range of possible answers: they date from the earliest days of metrical poetry in Hebrew until Azariah dei Rossi, and beyond. Some writers, searching for biblical "meters," attributed a structural role to the fairly regular binariness of biblical songs; others, rejecting the notion of meter, hit on another piece of the truth, viz., the lack of exact equivalence of line length, syllables, accents, and so forth in biblical verse-halves. The theories proposed were not necessarily mutually exclusive, and later commentators therefore often maintained that *šîr* consisted of two or more different subcategories of compositions, and then went on to incorporate several "answers" into their definitions. Sometimes these multiple definitions ware based on distinctions in Aristotle's *Poetics* or the various Arabic commentaries on Aristotle.[35]

Among the various approaches to this topic one may distinguish four basic "families" of answers:

1. *By poetry is meant figurative, indirect or hidden forms of expression.* Arabic and Jewish commentators were acquainted with the (Aristotelean) distinction between poetic form and poetic content, and could account for the appellation "song" in various parts of the Bible by demonstrating that the writing was "figurative" without

---

34. M. ibn Ezra identifies these three as the only poetic books of the Bible; Moses ibn Tibbon does likewise (see following); Judah al-Harizi (1170–1235) wrote in his *Tahkemoni*: "For whilst our forefathers were still dwelling in the Holy City / They were not acquainted with metered poetry in the Holy Tongue / Still, the books, of Job, Proverbs and Psalms / Have verses which are short and simple (פסוקים קצרים וקלים) / And they seem like poetic lines but they have no rhyme and are not metered." (Contained in Schirmann, השירה העברית, 2, p. 133); for al-Haziri's use of חרוז to mean "line of poetry" cf. Abravanel's commentary in Exod. 15, also דרך לעשות חרוזים, p. 235, n. 17.

35. See Aristotle's *Poetics* 1447a and b, and n. 48 below.

entering into meter or other questions of poetic structure. This was common practice in the case of the Song of Songs from talmudic times.[36] Joseph ibn Kaspi and Samuel ibn Tibbon both advance the argument that Solomon wrote three books (Ecclesiastes, the Song of Songs, and Proverbs) to illustrate three different sorts of writing, respectively: the wholly literal (or "revealed"), the wholly figurative (or "hidden") and the partially literal and partially figurative. But this tack held great dangers, for Arabs and Jews were also in possession of a pseudo-Aristotelean tradition that "the best part of poetry is its falsehood" (מיטב השיר כזבו).[37] Arguing that what constitutes the "poeticity" of biblical songs is their content was the equivalent of saying that they were full of lies, or at best, exaggeration and overstatement.[38] Under these circumstances, a formal or structural

36. See R. J. Loewe, "Apologetic Motifs," p. 161.
37. Cf. L. Dukes, נחל קדומים, p. 54; Schirmann, השירה העברית, 1, intro. p. xxxvii; and D. Pagis ... שירת החול ותורת השיר (Jerusalem, 1970), pp. 42–50. Cf. al-Fārābī's eightfold classification of logic or fivefold classification of types of statements, in which poetry is described as "wholly false." See A. J. Arberry, "Farabi's Canons of Poetry" in *Rivista degli Studi Orientali* 17 (1938): 274 and note. These classifications are widely repeated among Jewish writers. The *locus classicus* of poetry's falsehood, from which the Arabic tradition in part derives, is book 10 of Plato's *Republic*.
38. These two, via Arabic *balāġa*, were closely associated with all poetry and rhetoric. Caught in this predicament, the author of אמרי שפר notes: "Therefore, while the songs of David and Solomon, Asaph, Heman and Jeduthun are all truthful utterances, those of our day are either completely or largely falsehood and lying" (in Neubauer, מלאכת השיר, p. 25). The Renaissance Italian writer Messer Leon notes that "the word *šîr* sometimes applies to something hidden, false according to its exterior (נגלה) sense, in keeping with 'the best of poetry is its falsehood'; and sometimes it refers to something spoken according to musical notes, although its literal meaning is true and revealed. An example of the first is the Song of Songs, and of the second, 'And Miriam sang . . .' (Exod. 15:21)." See his נפת צופים (Vienna, 1863), p. 60. At the same time, the falsehood of poetry might serve good purposes. Thus Averroes wrote: "Aristotle came to the opinion that this art was highly useful, because by means of it the souls of the multitude could be moved to believe in a certain thing, and towards doing or abandoning a certain thing" (Short Commentary on the Poetics of Aristotle, in C. E. Butterworth, *Averroes' Three Short Commentaries* [Albany, 1977], p. 84). In a similar vein, Yeda'ya ha-Penini notes: "Were it not for the pleasing metaphors of poetry, religions would not survive, for it is the nature of every poem to strengthen a man's religion, and to increase his faith through the sweetness of rhetoric and the pleasure of metaphor, which can draw the soul towards them, so that minds will be moved in their direction and the listeners will adopt them, since the meaning [of the ideas, not the words] is true." He adds: "Rhetoricians [מליצים] established faith in the Creator through their *piyyutim*, poets through their poems, and wisemen through their homilies." See his ספר הפרדס (Luzzato edition), p. 12.

explanation for the use of the word *šîr, šîrâ*, etc. was usually to be preferred.

Furthermore, ornaments and devices such as are found in poetry could be found in parts of the Bible clearly not labeled as poetry, but prophecy.[39] Moses ibn Ezra's eighth chapter contains a catalogue of poetic devices used in Arabic and Hebrew, and for many he finds precedents and examples in the Prophets—yet he felt the only *poetic* books of the Bible were Psalms, Proverbs, and Job.[40] It is also significant about the "devices" approach to biblical style that it tends to obscure rather than illuminate the structure of parallelism: this is as true of ibn Ezra, ibn Kaspi, and their contemporaries as it was of Augustine, Isidore of Seville, et al. earlier. For in his search for different devices, the commentator mistakes for ornaments those features of surface (repetitions, restatements, chiastic balancing) which are specific manifestations of the overall seconding. Perhaps the most egregious of the Hebrew practitioners of this particular reading is the Renaissance commentator Judah b. Yehiel (Messer Leon) whose צופים נפת (written after 1454) viewed the Prophets as "masters of rhetoric" and set out to catalogue their various devices according to classical models, chiefly Cicero and Quintillian. Leon says nothing of the overall parallelism of biblical songs, but he defines צחות as the style in which "one idea will be said in different ways, and this sort of thing is found a great deal in Isaiah."[41]

2. *Original Hebrew meter—or meter's substitute—is now lost.* This view assumes a poetic craft going back perhaps even to the time of Abraham—an Ur-poetik, as it were—that has been forgotten by Jews during their long exile. We have already seen this implied by A. ibn Ezra, Falaqera, and others. Even earlier, in opposing the introduction of Arabic-style meters into Hebrew, the followers of Menahem b. Saruq (tenth century) had argued that grammatical distinctions crucial to Hebrew were swallowed up in the new style, and it was therefore irreconcilable with the "rhythmic structure"

---

39. Crucial here is the threefold division of the canon, for poetry, in the common view, was to be limited to parts of the *Ketubim* (Hagiographa), plus those parts of the Torah and Prophets specifically labeled as "song." In his commentary on Isa. 5:1, Abravanel specifically asserts that this "song" of Isaiah by its nature excludes divine inspiration.

40. M. ibn Ezra, *Kitāb al-muḥāḍara*, pp. 46–47. Even these were not "verse," but simply different from "prose." See chapter 3.

41. M. Leon, צופים נופת (Vienna, 1863), p. 184. Cf. about Psalm 44:7, כפל הענין על צד ההרחבה (p. 63).

(משקולת) of Hebrew; perhaps Hebrew had had some sort of meter of its own, but it was now irretrievably lost:

> And if we had not been exiled from our land but on the contrary possessed the entirety of our language as in days of old when we dwelt securely in our pleasant habitations, then we would know all the details of our language and the different types of structures produced in it and we would know its measure (משקל) and would keep within it. For the language of each and every people has its own rhythmic structure (משקולת) and grammar, but ours was lost to us because of our many sins and hidden from us for our great transgressions ever since we were exiled; what had been of such breadth was now diminished and hidden and became lost. Indeed, had not the God who works wonders looked on his people's suffering, even the small part that remains would have been closed off and lost as well.

The poet Yehuda ha-Levi (c. 1075–1141) similarly believed metrical poetry was natural to every language, and presumably could have existed in biblical times. However, his position was somewhat different:

3. *"Song" in the Bible means only something sung and does not imply meter.* Ha-Levi's position[42] was that biblical authors had purposely foregone the superficial beauties of meter for the sake of comprehension (*Kuzari* 2.72), for the rhythm and choice of words imposed by strict meter might impede understanding. For this reason the system of *ṭe'amim* was devised, so that the shades of meaning transmitted by phrasing and pitch in face-to-face conversation might also be carried in the written word: with the *ṭe'amim* "a hundred people reading the same text will all pause and continue in exactly the same places" (*Kuzari* 2.76).

What then of the appellation "song" in the Bible? Ha-Levi brilliantly perceived what has since been reforgotten, namely, "melodies do not necessarily require metrical texts" (*Kuzari* 2.70). In a refrain composition such as Psalm 136, he noted, the structure implies that a line like "To the worker of great wonders alone" is to be sung to exactly the same notes as "Praise the Lord greatly"—yet the latter is manifestly much shorter than the former, and could not possibly be its metrical equivalent. In other words, he succeeded in rejecting the idea of biblical meters while at the same time asserting that, far from being a defect, this aspect of the Bible makes it

---

42. It has been discussed at length in Allony, מתורת הלשון והשירה, pp. 1–17.

praiseworthy above the most elaborate of Arabic rhythms. Nor should one see in this an apologist's expedient: ha-Levi was apparently so persuaded by his own argument that at the end of his life he repented of ever having written in the Arabic meters of which he was such a master.[43]

So far as parallelism is concerned, Yehuda ha-Levi's stance eliminates the necessity of finding any structure in Hebrew songs (other then the *ṭe'amim*, which follow the "meaning").[44] Many later commentators repeated his arguments to show there was nothing resembling a formal structure in the Bible's songs. Thus, his student Solomon b. Abraham ibn Parḥon writes in his מחברת הערוך:

> If *piyyut* and rhyme and meter were good, then the sons of Korah would have produced them, and David the King of Israel, and Solomon, who were poets, for they made the songs and the melodies. . . . In the Temple there were outstanding poets, and why should they not have made their songs with rhymes and metered poems like the Arabs? For if we with our modest gifts and in our own age can make metered and rhymed poems, could not they do likewise? But surely it was after our exile that we saw the Arabs making rhymes and metered poems and we began to do like them and caused our Holy Tongue to go astray and enter into a place where it ought not to go.[45]

Among the many descendents of the *Kuzari*'s arguments, one of the most influential was Samuel ibn Tibbon's (c. 1160–c.1230) discussion of poetry in his Ecclesiastes commentary:

> The craft of poetry has requirements which are either common to all [literatures] or specific to each nation; Aristotle listed them in his book on poetry, and so he noted there that in the poetry of some nations no attempt is made to make the last letters [of the line] the same, but only to make them equal in the time of their reading. Likewise he mentions that the poetry of a few nations does not require that there be a uniform meter based on vocalization, that is, that the long vowels and shewas be of like number and placement in each line, but only that whatever is lacking be compensated for in the melody; though doubtless there was some [general] ordering in this, for they cannot compensate for *any* discrepancy [in line length].

43. See Solomon b. Abraham Parḥon, מחברת הערוך (Pressburg, 1844), p. 5a.
44. But, as seen earlier, often obscure the parallelism.
45. Parḥon, מחברת הערוך, pp. 4b–5a.

I have written this for you because it seems to me that at the time
of David and Solomon their songs were of this sort, for these will
not be found to contain either meter or rhyme. It might well be said
that in this their songs had an advantage over those that are brought
out nowadays, for their path was not so narrow, and they could put
into poetry exactly the idea that they wished to put in, and to place
it as they wished in its complete form. But nowadays [poets] have
accepted upon themselves many preconditions, things they must do
or must avoid doing, and have thus greatly narrowed the path before
them, so that they have not the slightest leeway, and this causes
them to concentrate and abbreviate and leave out, or to permit to
themselves the outrageous, all of which causes them to sacrifice the
ideas, or at least to make them difficult to understand.[46]

In these lines one finds a view of biblical poetry that is well argued and
full of insight. Ibn Tibbon flatly asserts that rhyme and meter are not
to be found in biblical songs, but since (as his pseudo-Aristotelean
auctor states) neither rhyme nor meter is a universal sine qua non in
poetry, their absence in Hebrew is not to be wondered at—indeed, he
repeats the *Kuzari* claim that this aspect of biblical song is an
advantage, not a defect. That advantage consists not, as in the *Kuzari*,
in the substitution of the *ṭe'amim* for metrical arrangements, but
simply in the greater freedom allowed the poet in framing his ideas.
Like the *Kuzari*, he argues that melody can make up for the lack of
exact equivalence in long and short vowels or total line length;[47]

46. The only part of this commentary to have been published is the passage cited,
which I have taken from Judah Moscato's commentary on the *Kuzari*, קול יהודה
(Venice, 1594 and subsequently), section 2, 70. Similar sentiments are found in
Yeda'ya ha-Penini's ספר הפרדס: "When the poet is moved to metrical poetry, a
throng of words fills him, and many comparisons requiring extended treatment; but,
he, by reason of the meter, clings to brevity, and swallows most of the extended
explanations and elaborations that have come to him. He is comparable to the
horseman riding on a high mountain, the path narrows and the horse whinnies and
takes fright, then the rider holds his rein and silences him. And he who writes
elevated language (מליצה) with rhymes but without keeping any meter, the path
before him is wider, yet he still needs restraint and pause. He is like the light-footed
deer, who in his course always looks in front of him, for if they have dug pits before
him he will fall into them; likewise he looks behind him. But those who write elevated
language without rhyme are like the bird who has escaped the hunter's net: he shall
not cease from flight until he gains his nest" (p. 13). Cf. also al-Baqillani in
Grunebaum, *Tenth-Century Document*, pp. 56–57 and notes.
47. This idea he passed on to his son, Moses ibn Tibbon (see his commentary to
the Song of Songs, Lyck, 1874, p. 7), who repeated it in the same formulation; thence
it was passed on to Abravanel in his comentaries to Exod. 15 and Isa. 5, to M. ibn

however, ibn Tibbon adds that there must be a general ordering to the poem, for melody's compensatory powers are not limitless.

Another discussion influenced by the *Kuzari*'s arguments was Isaac Abravanel's (1437–1508) treatment of biblical songs in his commentaries on Exodus 15 and Isaiah 5. Here he presents a three-fold classification of poetry;[48] his second class, biblical songs, are called songs not because they have meter or rhyme, but because they are actually sung. This is essentially what ha-Levi had said, but Abravanel goes on to assert that the fact that they are to be sung imposes upon their authors the necessity of composing them in a certain arrangement:[49]

> By "arrangement" is meant the arrangement of a structure which determines the order in which [a song's words] are read and its musical accompaniment. And this is what our Sages intended by saying, "large brick over small brick, small over large; small brick over small brick, large over large." The meaning of this is that those who founded [the rules of] ancient songs required that the number of letters be fixed according to the music to which they had determined to sing them, and that the arrangement of their placement in meter be the arrangement of their syllables; in this metrical arrangement they attached them to the music.

Habib in דרכי נעם, and ultimately to Azariah dei Rossi. (On all of these see following.)

48. This threefold division is found as well in Moses ibn Tibbon and elsewhere; see below, note 54. The threefold division seems to go back to Aristotle himself. His *Poetics* begins by classifying the three means of imitation used in poetry, namely rhythm, language (*logos*), and harmony, or, in another formulation, rhythm, melody, and verse (see Aristotle's *Poetics* 1447a 21 and 1447b 24). These passed into the Arabic-language reformulations of various Islamic Aristotelians, and in their now somewhat modified form (see F. Gabrieli, "Estetica e poesia araba nell' interpretazione della Poetica aristotelica presso Avicenna e Averroe," in *Rivista degli Studi Orientali* 12 [1929–30]: 305–06) passed into Hebrew learning. Todros Todrosi, in his Hebrew translation of Averroes's Middle Commentary on the *Poetics*, renders the three means of imitation as הנעימות המסכימות ("agreeing tunes," a cognate translation from Averroes), המשקל ("meter"), and הרמוי עצמו ("comparison [or "imitation"] itself"). F. Lasinio, *Il Commento Medio di Averroe alla Poetica di Aristotele* (Pisa, 1872), Hebrew section, p. 2 (Todros's Hebrew translation has been dated 1337). The affiliation between this Aristotelian tradition and the three categories of Abravanel or Moses ibn Tibbon is clear. See also V. Cantarino, "Averroes on Poetry," in G. L. Tikku, *Islam and its Cultural Divergence* (von Grunebaum Festschrift, Urbana, Ill., 1971), pp. 23–26.

49. Cf. also ibn Danaan in Neubauer, מלאכת השיר, p. 5, where he describes the fitting of words to "musical structures."

> For there is music arranged in such a way that the first part will correspond to the third and the second to the fourth, equal in the duration of the music's length or brevity; the musical arrangement of long duration they called "large brick" and that of short duration "small brick," since the latter is half the large brick's size. That meter which is set up so that the first part corresponds to the third and the second to the fourth they called "small brick over small brick, large over large," and in this fashion are composed the song *Ha'azinu* (Deut. 32), and the dialogues of Job, and Proverbs.

In other words, Abravanel has attached to the practice of stichography a new significance; it indicates a musical pattern of long and short phrases. Of the second sort of these patterns, "large brick over small brick" is the Song of the Sea (Exod. 15), and Abravanel then procedes to distinguish eight "musical structures" in its pattern of phrases. The classification is complicated and (so one must conclude after repeated attempts at making it consistent) somewhat arbitrary, but it was sufficient to qualify biblical poetry as *systematic*[50] for Abravanel, a significant departure from ha-Levi's position. (It is also remarkable that he does not disguise his preference for Arabic-style meters over the biblical "system.")

Finally, one of the most interesting reincarnations of ha-Levi's arguments is found in the Renaissance Hebrew tract ערוגת הבשם (*Bed of Spices*), by Samuel Archivolti (1515–1611). After repeating the *Kuzari*'s argument against strict meter (and adding some of his own from talmudic sources) he notes that there are two general categories of song:

> The first is melody which is built to fit the words in consideration of their ideas. For by melodic changes it is able to distinguish between pause and continuation, a hurrying tempo and a slow one, between joy and sadness, astonishment and fear, and so forth. And this is the most excellent type of melody in music, for not only does it consider the ear's pleasure, but also strives to give spirit and soul to the words that are sung. This type of song was used by the Levites [in the Temple], for it is the only way they could have arranged their music, and it is the type fit to be written for songs in our sacred language.

---

50. At the same time, by tying the "system" to melodies which Abravanel goes on to assert are forever lost, he in effect adopts the position numbered (2) above. Note that the modern printed editions of Abravanel's "scansion" of Exod. 15 are in error in several details.

The second type is the popular sort of tune in which the words are written to fit *it* [the music], and its only concern is for what the ear hears, so that a single popular melody will be applied to many songs whose subjects are from each other "as far as the west is from the east" (Psalm 103:12) [but will fit] so long as they are all written in one meter and with one rhyme scheme.[51]

Here we have a reversal that surely would have astounded Abravanel: the fact that there are a limited number of meters to which poems must conform is, far from a virtue, indication of their inferiority. For while biblical music was tailored to the words, here it is created to be sold, as it were, "off the racks" to poems of any subject and theme; their meter vouchsafes a proper fit, but of course the music will not be able to apply its resources to match the particularities of any one poem's words.

4. *Biblical songs do have meter.* In the earlier period of medieval Hebrew poetry this idea is frequently rejected quite specifically. Metrical poetry is an Arabic pursuit, and its appearance in Hebrew is relatively recent, the result of assimilation.[52] Even in the fifteenth century, Sa'adya ibn Danaan remarked:

> We know not when our countrymen first began to busy themselves with the practice of this craft, but it seems to me that it is not the product of our own ancestors, but to its case as well as others applies the verse "and they mingled amongst the nations and learned their ways" (Psalm 106:35). I have looked and searched a great deal and have concluded that before the poems of R. Eleazar Kallir nothing at all of verse (חרוזים) was known to our people.[53]

However, the opposite is also maintained. The already-mentioned introduction of Moses ibn Tibbon to his Song of Songs commentary assimilated to the category of metrical poetry the biblical books of Proverbs, Job, and "most of the Psalms,"

---

51. ערוגת הבשם (Amsterdam, 1730), pp. 100a and b. Cf. Martin Bucer's observation (in Libr. Iudicum ... [1554], p. 487): "In veterum musica, primum locum habiterunt sacra verba & secundum locum concentus verbis applicati, ad maiores affectus movendos. Non ut nostra ista musica, ubi tantum concentus ratio habetur, nulla verborum, acsi bruta essemus; & tantum ad demulcendos animos non ad erudiendos est accomodata."

52. See on this H. Yalon, שקל הקודש (Jerusalem, 1965), p. 52, n. 4; in regard to A. ibn Ezra's phrase "wisdom of the Arabs," in his ספר צחות (Fuerth, 1827), p. 11 b, see Yalon, p. 75.

53. In Neubauer, מלאכת השיר, p. 6; cf. note 34 above.

because they are verses that are divided up like [Arabic-style] poetic lines, even though the units are not equal in long and short syllables. This is why they are written "short brick over short brick, long over long," like poetic lines.[54]

This is a remarkable observation as far as parallelism is concerned, for it recognizes the essence of biblical "poems" as the *binariness of their lines,* the fact that a pause separates two corresponding halves. In this binariness they resemble Arabic-style poems, even though the two halves do not correspond in long and short syllables: the fact that they break into rough equal halves is enough for ibn Tibbon to classify them in the same category as Arabic poems, viz., metrical poetry.

Some writers even went so far as to suggest that the modern meters were themselves derived from biblical "meters." The anonymous thirteenth-century author of "Handbook of the Grammar of the Hebrew Tongue" claimed that all the resources of poetry are "indicated" or "implied" in the biblical text, including alphabetical verses, acrostic spellings, rhymes, notarikon, gematria, and, lastly, meter.[55] (His argument is more chauvinistic than his examples convincing, however.)

The author of שקל הקדש (*The Holy Shekel*)[56] invoked the popular

---

54. M. ibn Tibbon, שיר השירים, p. 7. The source of this threefold division seems to be that found in Aristotle's *Poetics* (see above, n. 48); Aristotle's *means* of imitation have been transmuted into *reasons* for a composition's being classified as poetry, hence types of poetry. M. ibn Tibbon's comments are repeated almost word for word in the Song of Songs commentary of his near-contemporary Immanuel of Rome (see the edition of Frankfurt, 1908, p. 5), who introduces this catalogue with: "It is well-known to every learned man that the classes of song are three in number," apparently an allusion to the Aristotelian classes in their Arabic formulation. There are, however, other threefold categorizations. M. ibn Habib's דרכי נעם (1486) distinguishes three classes of Hebrew songs corresponding to three purposes and effects of poetry: (1) תקון השכל (improvement of the rational faculty), (2) the correction of "accidents of the soul" (מקרים נפשיים) that threaten to overcome it (such as anger, pride, aggressivity, violence) and their redirection toward the good, and (3) elevation of the soul from "lesser accidents" such as pain, cowardice, and the like. His source for this classification is a passage in al-Fārābī's *Fuṣūl al-madanī* (ed. D. M. Dunlop [Cambridge, 1961], pp. 135–36). Note also that Falaqera's poet gives a (quite different) threefold classification in the *Book of the Seeker.*

55. See קונטרס בדקדוק שפת עבר, ed. S. Poznan'ski (Berlin, 1894). Note that liturgical poetry in Spain and elsewhere was sometimes written in simpler systems, "pure syllabic" or even free rhythms, to which biblical verses could be fitted—and compared! This was clearly significant for ibn Habib (below), who wrote such poems. See Fleischer, שירת הקודש pp. 350–61; Pagis, חידוש ומסורת 290–303.

56. Felt by H. Yalon to be Samuel Almoli; see his edition of the book (Jerusalem, 1965) for a summary of the argument.

argument that much, perhaps most, of the Hebrew language had been lost with the Exile[57] to argue that Arabic meter was in fact copied from Hebrew:

About this craft [of metrical poetry] we have not seen or heard of a single one of our sages who discussed it and did not attribute its roots to the Ishmaelites for [they say] from them did we take it, and [the proof is] they are most adept at it. But I myself have no doubt that on the contrary everything that the Ishmaelites know of this craft they took from the sages of our nation, just as they took their confused language from our Holy Tongue. For it has happened in this matter of poetry just as it befell us in the study of grammar as a whole; [for though our language and its grammar are far older than Arabic, and were certainly understood in biblical times, nevertheless it was forgotten and] from their language's grammar our own study of grammar has been derived.[58]

In a similar vein, Moses ibn Habib's דרכי נעם (*Paths of Pleasantness*) (completed 1486) records its author's being shown an ancient tombstone in Murviedro on which was written metrical verse. "Then I truly believed that this sort of metered poetry has existed and been with our people since the days in which our forefathers were dwelling in their own land."[59] Unlike שקל הקדש however, Habib's book goes

57. An argument already seen above in the students of Menahem ibn Saruq. Menahem himself made precisely the same point: "Surely the totality of the language is not to be found in our Scripture. Now if we indeed possessed the entire language, all those words which are deficient would be present and grasped fully." See H. Filipowski, ספר מחברת מנחם (London, 1854), p. 12. After Menahem it appears frequently: see, inter alia, S. ibn Gabirol, הענק, in שירי חול, p. 169; J. ibn Janāḥ, הרקמה (ed. Wilensky), 1, p. 3; Yeda'ya ha-Penini in Dukes, נחל קדומים, p. 23; Yehudah ha-Levi, *Kuzari* 2, 68; Abraham ibn Ezra in שפה ברורה, p. 46, and in his Song of Songs Commentary re. 8:11; Maimonides, *Guide* 1, 61, 67; J. ibn Tibbon's preface to his translation of Bahya ibn Pakuda's חובות הלבבות; P. Duran, מעשה אפד (Vienna, 1865), pp. 39–43. See also Moses b. Isaac b. Hanesia, ספר השהם ed. B. Klar (Jerusalem, 1945), p. 5. The question is also discussed in passing in A. S. Halkin, "The Medieval Jewish Attitude Toward Hebrew" in A. Altmann, *Biblical and Other Studies* (Cambridge, 1963), pp. 233–48.

58. Yalon, ed., שקל הקדש, pp. 52–53.

59. On the inscription see F. Cantera and J. M. Millas, *Las Inscripciones hebraicas de España* (Madrid, 1956), pp. 394–403. Cantera and Millas here reproduce the text of ibn Habib's remarks (from the Venice, 1546, edition, folio 7) and then cite further the reports of later historians and travelers who were shown the supposed inscription. Cantera and Millas associate ibn Habib's story with an actual extant stone (of later origin, however; the word read as Amaziah they correct to ᵓamaṣim, or, perhaps, "(V)alencia") and explain the townspeople's attribution of the

on to justify the claim of biblical meters with a (Tibbonide) threefold classification of poetry:

The first is poetry metered insofar as the number of syllables in its two lines[60] is concerned, save that the first agrees with the second neither in any part of its various parts nor in its ending [rhyme], unless this happens by chance, without having been intended.

The second is like the first, save that sometimes the first line will not agree with the second even in the number of syllables, but they will compensate for what is lacking by means of the melody or movements of the throat or they will swallow what is extra with notes of the voice. Of these two categories are the books of Psalms and Proverbs and Job. Examples may be found of the first type in Psalms:

קראתיך הושיעני ואשמרה עדתיך
[Psalm 119:14]

יתום ואלמנה יעודד ודרך רשעים יעות
[Psalm 146:9]

and many others like these, in which the first half of the verse agrees with the second solely in the number of syllables. Similarly in Proverbs:

שמע בני מוסר אביך ואל תטש תורת אמך
[Prov. 1:8]

אגר בקיץ בן משכיל נרדם בקציר בן מביש
[Prov. 10:5]

Likewise in Job:

ברעב פדך ממות ובמלחמה מידי חרב
[Job 5:20]

and many more in addition to these. But as for the second type, most of the verses are such, that is to say the number of [syllables in] the first half-verse does not agree with its fellow: and of this second type is the song of the Red Sea and the song of Moses and

_____

stone to biblical times as local legend-making, woven around the phrase שר גדול (great chief); cf. the "Adoniram inscription" discussed in *Inscripciones*, p. 313. I have discussed Habib's book in greater detail in "The Influence of Moses ibn Habib's '*Darkei No'am*'" in I. Twersky, *Jewish Thought in the Sixteenth Century* (forthcoming). See also below, chapter 6.

60. That is, verse-halves; in what follows he uses טור to mean an individual verse-half. D. Pagis has pointed out Habib's innovation here in counting the *shewa* as a full syllable; see "Development of the Hebrew Iamb," in הספרות 4 (1973): 686.

the song of David and the song of Deborah:[61] for whatever is missing or extra [and so destroys the syllabic symmetry] between the verse and its fellow will be stretched out or swallowed through the melody as we have explained. . . .

The third type is metered poetry in which lines agree in all respects, in the number of vowels and the correspondence of the two lines each with his fellow in an equal rhyme. Not only that, but even in the matter of long and short syllables poets are quite careful and will put a short syllable only under a short and a long only under a long; and these [are arranged] in various ways, as we shall show, with the help of the Almighty.

In this [third type] the Hebrew tongue has a degree and honor above all other nations, for among them it is impossible to meet this one requirement [meter] and also another connected to it, the practice of poets bringing Biblical verses into their poems,[62] either in their literal sense or via a homonymous meaning or metaphorical sense, and there is no other language that can attain this merit.[63] Any poem not metered in regard to its long and short syllables "shall surely be put to shame" [Song of Songs 8:7] amongst poets, and embarrassment and pain and injury will they cause to its author.

Ibn Habib views meter in the same way Renaissance poets in Europe viewed numerical symbolism: once the concept is accepted, there is no place where it can *not* exist. The notion of a poem without meter is for him a contradiction in terms. However, he has borrowed the idea (from the *Kuzari*, and from Moses ibn Tibbon's introduction to the Song of Songs) that melody can equalize unequal verse-halves by swallowing syllables or drawing them out, in order to assert that the traditional biblical songs are also (approximately) metrical. (His first and second classes of poetry might easily have been combined into a single class, since in either case the source is the Bible, and none of the biblical songs will be seen to fit all of its lines into Class One; perhaps he acted as he did in order to stay within the tradition of three classes.)

Thus it was that the problem of biblical "meters" led ibn Tibbon, ibn Habib, and others to set down what perhaps many others had

---

61. That is, those four songs named in מסכת סופרים.

62. On this practice, שיבוץ, see Yellin, תורת השירה, pp. 119–38; Pagis, חידוש ומסורת, pp. 70–76.

63. This idea comes from Duran, מעשה אפד, p. 43. Habib was an admirer of Duran and his influence is felt elsewhere in this work.

grasped without consciously formulating their ideas: that biblical verses often divide into rough halves, and that this structure can work in a way comparable to meter—it can shape the utterance and give it a regularity, line after line. This is not all there is to be said about biblical parallelism—it says nothing of the ways in which the relationship between the two clauses is established—but it is the proper beginning.

4

Azariah dei Rossi (c. 1511–c. 1578) was a true Renaissance scholar who brought to the Jewish world knowledge of texts previously known only to Christians. In his discussion of biblical poetry he cites the opinions of Philo, Josephus, Eusebius, and Jerome; among his Jewish authorities are Yehuda ha-Levi, Abravanel, and ibn Habib (though he does not cite the passage translated above). "According to these sages," Azariah writes, "our holy tongue, by its nature and by its usage from earliest times, does not exclude poems with measure and meter—not only by virtue of [the equalizing accomplished by] the melody to which the songs are sung, as Don Isaac [Abravanel] says above, but from the standpoint of the words themselves. Indeed, some of these songs may be found in the Bible." Azariah then relates how he arrived at his own solution to the metrical crux:

And "as my cares welled up within me" [Psalm 94:19] to resolve these opinions and discover at least part of what I wanted, my heart said to me: there exist without doubt poetic measures and structures to the Biblical songs mentioned, but they are not dependent on the number of complete or incomplete syllabic feet as in the poems written nowadays—since these are, as the Kuzari says, practices of the poems of Arabic (which is but our language somewhat confused)[64]—but their structure and measures are in the number of ideas and their parts, subject and predicate and whatever is connected to them, in every sentence or clause that is written. There are cases in which the clause will have two feet, and with the second part that is attached to it there will be four; others will have three, and with the second will have six perfect feet. For example, "Thy right hand, O Lord" which is a clause unto itself with two units, or if you will, two "feet": "wondrous in might" is quite the same and connected to it, and together they make four. Similarly, the second "Thy right hand, O Lord" has again two feet; "crushes

64. Cf. ibn Danaan in Neubauer, נחל קדומים, p. 52.

the enemy" two more, making again four. In the same manner are "The enemy said," "I shall pursue and get" "I shall divide and spoil" "I shall be sated," "I shall bare my sword" . . . [etc.] Unlike this is the song of Deut. 32, which is three-three, making six, to wit: "Listen O heavens, and I will speak," "and hear, O earth, my words," "Let my lesson flow as rain," "and my words drop as dew."

Sometimes in a single verse (and even more so in a whole song) these two types of measures will exist together, i.e. two-two and three-three, however the spirit may have rested on the prophet (and also because such variations befit the meaning). An example of this would be "And with the breath of thy nostrils the waters were piled up," which is two-two: "They stood up like heaps of water, the billows froze in mid-sea" three-three. . . .

Now in some of the utterances the learned reader must recognize a few words which for one reason or another do not count in the metrical arrangement, as in Deut. 32: "And he said, 'I will hide My Face from them' " the word "And he said" is a separate entity, thus [leaving] "I will hide My Face from them," three feet, and "I will see what becomes of them," another three. . . .

You must not count the syllables nor yet the words themselves, but the ideas (ענינים). And as regards this it often happens that a little word will be joined to whatever is next to it, so that verses from the Psalms will be seen to observe the order we have described: "Favor me, O God, with your love," "And with your abundant mercy erase my sin" [Psalm 51:3].

It does not escape my attention that there are many verses which I am unable to fit into the above systems: perhaps even the exceptions are more numerous than those that obey the rules. May the learned readers, following the lines of my presentation, be enlightened and so go forward to find out what I have been unable to find. Ought we not in any case to believe that all the songs found in the Bible—the Song of the Sea and of the Well, and Moses' Song, and Deborah's, and the Song of David, and the books of Job, Proverbs and Psalms—all of them without doubt have an arrangement and structure, this one in one manner and this in another, or one song alone possessing different measures? For we sense when we read them aloud some marvelous special quality, even if we do not completely grasp their structure.[65]

---

65. D. Cassel, ed., מאור עינים (1866), pp. 208–09.

Azariah's account of the genesis of his discovery is perhaps misleading in one respect: what his "heart" told him was not terribly different from what ibn Habib had told him (and even more so Moses ibn Tibbon, if he had read him): that Hebrew lines divide into roughly equal halves. The nuance added in Azariah's presentation rests on his insistence that one "must not count the syllables, *nor yet the words themselves,* but the ideas." As he shows, "little words," introductory phrases, exclamations, and so forth may be eliminated from this "count," for in distinguishing the ideas from the mere words themselves he has freed the question of the verse-halves' correspondence from the tyranny of syllable- and word-counting (this is why he need not invoke the Tibbon-Habib-Abravanel argument that imbalance of the verse-halves is covered over by the melody). By hinging the correspondence on the question of meaning, he had taken a great step forward in the understanding of parallelism. It is true, of course, that Azariah still thinks in terms of a quasi-metrical regularity, and consequently fails to perceive that the relationship of B to A was not a matter of meter, but emphasis, seconding. At least, however, he turned the search for regularity away from counting syllables or words and connected it to the meaning of the words.

Lowth, needless to say, perceived more; he saw the semantic-syntactic parallelism of A and B. Yet the interpretation he—and more than Lowth himself, his followers—imposed on this fact has proven more misleading than helpful: *parallelismus membrorum* became (what it really is not) a kind of conscious tinkering to symmetrize A and B, and this misunderstanding was then exaggerated into being a metrical substitute, the "system" of Hebrew "poetry."

The structure of biblical songs was one of those questions whose answer is far too simple to satisfy the questioner. The chief virtue of Azariah's answer may therefore lie in the fact that it made no grandiose claims. Like his predecessors, he felt that verse-halves should be numerical equals, for poetry was a matter of numbers; but his "equal" was flexible enough to accept extra syllables, constructs, particles, and so forth without disturbance. In counting up the number of ideas he came close to bringing together two matters before and since strictly segregated, line length and meaning: but the essence of biblical parallelism is that they are not separate.

In a spirit similar to Azariah's are later remarks on the subject of biblical poetry, notably those of Yehuda b. Yosef Moscato[66] and

---

66. See his commentary on *Kuzari* 2, sections 68–72; also נפוצות יהודה (Lwow, 1859), pp. 1 a–5 b, a remarkable synthesis of Jewish and Christian writings on music.

Abraham b. David Portaleone.[67] Noteworthy also is the statement of Immanuel Frances (1618–1710) that the first "poem" in the Bible appears to be Lamekh's war boast (Gen. 4:23–24) מכפל הלשון במלים שונות[68]: ibn Ezra's phrase is now actively applied to equate parallelism of meaning with the presence of poetry. Frances also classifies biblical writing as either narrative, rhetorical, or poetic, listing in the last category Exodus 15, Deuteronomy 32, Psalms, etc.:

> However I have not found these songs to have either rhyme or meter, save for the fact that in each and every line there is a pause (הפסק). Perhaps they were sung to a melody no longer known.[69]

Clear thinking such as this might not have satisfied those (particularly English and German Protestants) of Frances's contemporaries bent on finding the "secret" of Hebrew poetics, but had it been accepted, Lowth's "discovery" might have been properly tempered. Amid the confessions of ignorance or incomplete knowledge of Azariah, Portaleone, or Frances lies more wisdom than in the certainties advanced by other critics in the centuries that were to follow.

An examination of Jewish ideas about biblical songs is perhaps most interesting in what it shows about the nature of the problem. All the facts had long since been laid out for inspection: the only difficulty lay in freeing oneself from dogmatic ideas of what constituted good and bad style, of the requirements of poetry, and of what Divine inspiration implies about the nature of the text. The increasing willingness of biblical commentators to countenance repetition and restatement as such, and to view them as essentially emphatic forms of expressions, was an important step; the attention focused by various writers on the basically binary nature of biblical songs, and their acceptance of this binariness as *all the regularity there is,* was certainly another. What remained was only a somewhat greater exercise in abstraction, a questioning of the question itself, *What is the structure of Biblical poetry?*—and a rephrasing of it in such a way as to combine what was already known into an overall theory of biblical style.

---

67. A. Portaleone, שלטי הגברים (Mantua, 1612), p. 3b. See also below, chapter 6.
68. I. Frances, מתק שפתים, ed. H. Brody (Cracow, 1892), p. 30.
69. מתק שפתים, p. 30. The last idea is also stated in Abravanel's commentary on Exod. 15:1.

SIX

"WHAT IS THE SYSTEM OF HEBREW POETRY?"

As often happens with a bold and original piece of work, Robert Lowth's *De Sacra Poesi Hebraeorum Praelectiones* has gradually been stripped of its original context. That the work was but one entry in a centuries-old discussion of Hebrew poetics—that it was, in fact, a polemic aimed at destroying certain metrical theories and an argument in a still older debate, the relationship between poetry and prophecy[1]—has been largely forgotten by present-day criticism. For us Lowth is the "discoverer of biblical parallelism." Yet just as an examination of the true nature of biblical style suggests that the present notion of parallelism itself is overstated and misleading, so a look at Lowth in his historical setting will reveal his intentions, and his true originality, to have been somewhat different from those often supposed.

1

Renaissance ideas about the poetry of the Bible first derive from the sources already seen: Jerome, Augustine, Cassiodorus, Bede; and certain medieval Jewish commentators, especially Rashi, Rashbam, Abraham ibn Ezra, and later writers.[2] In both these Christian and Jewish traditions, there had been a tension implicit in the whole undertaking of the "literary"

---

1. Sharply distinguished, as we have seen, in Jerome (preface to Isa.), as well as in the last sentence of Adrian's *Isagoge* (fifth century)—see *PG* 98:1312, where Adrian claims that "metrical" compositions such as the writings of Job and Solomon cannot be prophecy.

2. It is well known that the *Postillae* of Nicholas de Lyre were the principal means by which Rashi's biblical commentaries entered the Christian orbit (see in general H. Hailperin, *Rashi and the Christian Scholars* [Pittsburgh, 1963]), but Nicholas was not alone. On knowledge of Jewish commentaries among Christians see B. Smalley, *The Study of the Bible in the Middle Ages* (Notre Dame, 1964), especially pp. 361–62. Still, on the question of biblical poetry, medieval Jewish sources did not begin to play an important role in Christian thought until the Renaissance.

appreciation of the Bible.[3] On the one hand, the aesthetic sensibilities of critics had been shaped and were still governed by the conventions of their native traditions: judgments of biblical style, whether in Augustine or Moses ibn Ezra, were based on real or imaginary evidence of artful composition as defined in the rules of Latin or Arabic. At the same time, this act of imposition was sometimes resisted, and by the same critics. The repetition of the same idea in different words, as Moses ibn Ezra and others had said,[4] was to be avoided nowadays, but in biblical style it was, far from a defect, "how the divinely inspired speak." Now it is interesting that, among both Jews and Christians, biblical style is approached precisely through this polarity of Divine and human speech. What was recognizably rhetorical or poetic was attributed to the fact that human beings were the utterers of the Divine Word, or that (as R. Ishmael and Augustine both argued) the Divine Word was framed for human understanding. But all that seemed awkward, unrhetorical, and even incomprehensible was explained by the text's divinity. It was a lawless text, framed by the Lord of all—and "Who shall say to Him, 'Do not act so!' " (Job 9:12). Thus, Cassiodorus warned Latin readers of the Bible:

Do not correct the prosaic beginning and ending of a heroic verse; do not venture to reject five long syllables and as many short ones; let a laudable neglect hide a triple trochee. Pay no attention at all to the mispronunciation of a final *m* elided before a vowel and to the hiatus of vowels, since matters which teachers of the liberal arts are known to observe regularly cannot have any place here. The avoidance of these faults is proper in human words; in divine communications, however, such stylistic arrangements are found by no means blameworthy. May a phrase which is known to have pleased God remain uncorrupted wherever it occurs, so that it may shine with its own splendor and not be

---

3. About this phrase one ought to note, in passing, the extraordinary lack of historical perspective in the whole modern reading of the Bible "as literature." Of course, as has been seen, reading the Bible in accordance with the stylistic norms of secular texts is a practice with ancient roots; in this sense the Bible "as literature" is not a modern approach at all. But this is only a small part of the modern school's misapprehension of its own activities. For the point is that the Bible itself has been the most important generative force in the development of literature in the West. And just as it itself has, in this sense, *created* the literature of Christian Europe (on which see H. Schneidau, *Sacred Discontent*, [Berkeley, 1977]), so its exegesis has shaped the practices of criticism that are now turned back upon it by exponents of the "literary" approach. See, e.g., the introduction of Kenneth R. Gros-Louis to his *Literary Interpretations of Biblical Narratives* (Nashville, 1974); also Leland Ryken in ibid., pp. 24–40.

4. See chapter 5.

subject to the enfeebling influence of human desire. For it instructs the untutored pleasantly, and in becoming fashion it delights the learned in proportion to their reverence.[5]

These contradictory tendencies coexist—thrive on each other—in antiquity: Jerome, Augustine, Cassiodorus find such human institutions as meter, tropes, and figures in "Divine letters," yet at the same time attribute the Bible's very obvious breaking of the rules to its Divine character: *far from a defect*, as we have heard Augustine assert, it is this stylistic lawlessness which vouchsafes the Bible's Divine character and leads the reader to look more deeply for its hidden significance. Thus, the "literary" position meant reading the Bible as if it were a human text, subject to the familiar rules of human composition; the only alternative was that it was a Divine text wholly untrammeled by human convention. But another approach is possible. It begins with the conviction that the world of the Bible's composition, "oriental" and "ancient," was governed by rules and conventions different from our own. Divinely inspired human beings wrote the words of our text, and whatever the implications of that inspiration might be, the texts are, from a stylistic standpoint, human creations that will differ from our own compositions principally because they were written in another land centuries ago. Now this attitude is hardly new either—it has been see above in Sa'adya, and, in the narrow matter of biblical "meter," it underlies the conclusions of Moses ibn Habib, Azariah, and others. Certainly Thomas Aquinas believed that the prophets themselves were responsible for the precise form of their prophecies, and had chosen their own words.[6] But as a force in the history of exegesis, this approach is a product of the overall humanism associated with the Renaissance. It came to be applied to many questions touching on the Bible, and one of the first was that of biblical poetry.

One of the factors contributing to the Renaissance's fascination with the whole question of biblical poetry was the growth of knowledge of Hebrew among Christian scholars, represented in the school of "Christian Hebraists" trained by Johannes Reuchlin (1455–1522) and his followers. The study of Hebrew among Christians certainly did not begin with the Renaissance. But in the medieval period, with *auctoritas* so strong a force and the chief Hebraist no less imposing a figure than Jerome, those scholars who did gain mastery of Hebrew were scarcely in a position to challenge current doctrine on the meter of biblical songs. Even when, in the twelfth century, Jerome's *Hebraica veritas* became the rallying cry of

5. Cassiodorus Senator, *An Introduction to Divine and Human Readings*, trans. L. W. Jones (New York, 1946), p. 107.
6. See Smalley, *Study*, p. 293.

those who sought to reexamine the Vulgate in the light of the Hebrew text and later Hebrew commentaries, Jerome's authority in other matters, and specifically on our question of biblical poetry, survived intact. It is symptomatic that one of the pioneers of Hebrew's rebirth in Christian learning, Hugh of St. Victor (1078–1141)—whose writing in other respects shines with insights newly acquired from Jewish writers, especially Rashi and Rashbam—on the question of biblical poetry does no more than repeat Jerome's traditional formulae.[7] Similarly, Nicholas de Lyre, not only a scholar of biblical Hebrew but a transmitter of medieval Jewish knowledge as well,[8] was not impelled to look into the structure of biblical songs.[9] Thus, if non-Hebraists were interested in the structure of biblical songs, they had little more than Jerome's dicta to read: Jewish ideas were not yet translated, and those who could read them in the original either repeated Jerome's orthodoxies or said nothing.

All this changed in the Renaissance. Christian interest in, and mastery of, Hebrew increased dramatically. Grammars of Hebrew by C. Pellicanus (1506), Reuchlin (1508), and others, written in Latin, brought knowledge of the language within the grasp of all interested scholars.[10] The invention of the printing press not only spread these books abroad, but helped to diffuse the Hebrew text of the Bible and works of medieval and Renaissance Jewish learning. Among others, those who wished to convert the Jews now sought to master their sacred tongue. The growth of classical studies in the Renaissance, and the constant counterpointing of Greek to Hebraic language, wisdom and science, certainly encouraged a new comparative approach to the Bible, as well as the application of classicists' scholarly standards (in translation and consequently in textual accuracy) to the Bible. Finally,

7. See Jerome Taylor, trans., *The Didascalion of Hugh of St. Victor* (New York, 1961), pp. 108–09. Hugh was at pains to separate the reading of the Bible from mere literature; see E. de Bruyne, *Etudes*, (Brugge, 1946) 2, pp. 205–06; 313.

8. See again Hailperin, *Rashi*.

9. His whole claim that David's inspiration was of a higher order than that of Moses (see the introduction to his *Postillae in Psalterium*) pitted him against the notion that David was a poet at all. (When he speaks of "versification" in this commentary, e.g., in reference to Psalm 118 [119], he means the alphabetical arrangement of verses.)

10. A Hebrew grammar, "the first of any consequence written by a Christian scholar," was published by Aldo Manuzio around 1500, according to Cecil Roth (*The Jews in the Renaissance*, [Philadelphia, 1959], p. 142n). Before this Peter Nigri had prepared a brief glossary in Germany in 1475 and 1477; see G. Weil, *Elie Lévita* (Leiden, 1963), pp. 249–52. On grammars in general, see Roth, p. 142.

the whole movement of Church reform and revolt against papal
authority, culminating in the Reformation but starting far earlier,
pushed the Church's critics to view all aspects of current religious
practice as tainted by centuries of external influences; time and again,
their reform was to adopt the posture of a *retour aux sources*, and this
more than anything whetted the appetite for Hebrew learning. With it,
the notion of Hebrew language and culture as rather different from the
Church forces that "corrupted" it—as, specifically, "ancient" and
"oriental"—took hold.

For advice about the nature of Hebrew poetry, it was now possible to
turn first to that remnant of this ancient and oriental people. Various
Christian Hebraists paraphrased or translated late medieval and
Renaissance Jewish writings on the subject, and, as we shall see, some
added their own ideas. Of course, Jerome's ideas were not readily
abandoned for the uncertainties pronounced by medieval Jewry.
Eloquent in this respect is the writing of Gilbert Genebrardus (1537–
97), bishop of Aix and a translator of, inter alia, part of the treatise
שקל הקודש—surely a man well acquainted with the difficulties in
Jerome's writings: yet how conservative he is in the brief treatment of
the subject presented in his popular *Chronographia*:

> Moses outshone all poets. For the story of Job he represented in
> spondaic verses, and composed the canticles, such as that of
> Deuteronomy 32, in elegiac song, so that they consist alternately of
> hexameter and pentameter lines. (Euseb. lib. 11 praep. cap. 3
> Hieron. ex Iosepho) Of this fashion are the three canticles of Isaiah,
> namely, that of the vineyard, of the city of Zion, and Hezekiah.
> (Isidor.) Emulating this, the ancient Greeks composed their songs
> and odes in hexameter . . . .
>
> Odes, hymns, psalms and canticles of every type did he [David]
> compose in varied meter; some were trimeters, others pentameters,
> tetrameters, hexameters etc. fitted for ten types of musical instru-
> ments (Kimhi e Talmudicis in Ps. 4) From him, therefore, and from
> Moses comes the origin of poetry . . . .
>
> Julian the Apostate, in his hatred of religion, is the only one to
> have denied, in Book VII of Cyril against the same, that the Hebrews
> had poetry. However, it is true that its system of scansion has been
> forgotten since those days, just as the scansion of a large part of
> Pindar and those like him is today unknown. This notwithstanding,
> almost all of these six books are metrically written: Job, Psalms,
> Proverbs, Ecclesiastes, Song of Songs, and Lamentations, plus
> countless canticles and verses which are inserted in the rest of the

Sacred Scriptures, such as Exodus 15, Deut. 32, Judges 5 and 6, Isaiah 5 and 38, and Hab. 3.[11]

This is an extraordinary hodgepodge of new and old learning. Genebrardus retains as much as possible the old doctrines of Josephus, Eusebius, and Jerome about biblical "meter." However, because of a comment in the writings of his contemporary Mercerus (see below), Genebrardus qualifies Job as "spondaic"; to Jerome's ascription of meters to the Psalms he adds, as if by way of confirmation, the citation of David Kimhi's musicology; and he appends a reference to Cyril of Alexandria's *Contra Iulianum*, which preserved the latter's allegation that Hebrew in fact had no metrical poetry.[12] Of the books listed as metrical, all had been directly or indirectly classified as "poetry" by Jerome: yet in the inclusion of the (often neglected) Proverbs, as well as that of the songs of Exodus 15 and Judges 5, one ought to see some Jewish influence, for the special *ṭe'amim* of the first, and the title *šîrâ* and prescribed stichography of the latter two, had given them a special poetic status among medieval Jewry, a tradition Genebrardus knew well.

A bit later, Genebrardus deals with the specific question of the metrical *system*, and here his knowledge of Jewish sources figures more prominently:

Josephus, Eusebius in book 11 of the Preparation, Jerome, Isidore, and others tried to name the system and dimensions of measure or meter in David and Solomon. On this question the Hebrews are silent—they say they do not know the method of scansion. This one thing they say in the Tractate Sopherim, or Scribes, that not a few verses of the biblical songs and canticles have been restored by the scribes in their proper arrangement according to the system of the measure, where before they had been written by copyists in a careless and confused manner.

As far as I know, only R. Moses Habib deals with this matter: The sacred songs of the ancients [he says], such as those in Psalms, Job, and Proverbs, are distichs. Some of these are measured by a specific number of syllables, so that the first verse will now be longer than the second, now shorter, as the genius of the author moved him. Others

11. G. Genebrardus, *Chronographiae libri vi* (Paris, 1600), pp. 81–82, 109–10.

12. Julian's original remark, contained in his "Against the Galileans" (written circa 363), has been lost; apparently he contested Eusebius's attribution of hexameter to the Hebrews—see *PG* 76:837. The work itself was popular in the educated resistance to Christianity, hence the lengthy refutation by Cyril in the following century. See A. Kerrigan, *St. Cyril of Alexandria* (Rome, 1952), p. 2.

consist of equal measure, except that occasionally the first verse will differ from the second in the exact number of syllables, but not in their time. But this difference is compensated through having them sound the same to the ear and through the motions of the throat, or else the melody and allurements of the voice will absorb the inequality (as, in Latin or Greek, a tribrachus is used in place of an iamb, a dactyl or an anapest in place of a spondee, and for a dactyl, a proceleumaticus, etc.) These afterwards he illustrates with examples from Psalms 119, 146, Proverbs and Job 6.[13]

By such efforts were Jewish ideas transmitted. Certainly one of the most important Christian Hebraists in this regard was Johannes Buxtorf II (1599–1664), who appended to his translation of Yehudah ha-Levi's *Kuzari* (itself, as we have seen, an important resource on the subject of biblical poetry) five other texts on the subject: Abravanel's commentary on Exodus 15, Azariah dei Rossi's remarks in the sixtieth chapter of מאור עינים, chapter 31 of Samuel Archivolti's ערוגת הבשם, the brief excerpt from Samuel ibn Tibbon's Ecclesiastes commentary which Judah Moscato had printed in his commentary on the *Kuzari*, and a section of Abraham b. David Portaleone's שלטי הגברים. This storehouse of Jewish learning was in Lowth's hands as he prepared his *Lectures*. Meanwhile, Jewish interest in the question of biblical poetry continued. The same Judah Moscato wrote at length about poetry and music in the Temple,[14] as did others of Italian Jewry. That some of the ongoing Jewish speculation spilled into Christian circles is clear, and no doubt it spurred Christian scholars to attack the problem on their own, armed with a knowledge of various metrical systems and a new willingness to question established dogma.

2

There had been a force at work from the start of the Renaissance pushing our question to the fore, one of such energy and dimension that no brief treatment of it can do justice.[15] Literature was "reborn"—in a sense it would be more proper to say it was *born* plain and simple, for this peculiar notion "literature" had never existed before—in fourteenth-century Italy; then it was boosted and shoved by relentless argument from its old haunts on the outskirts of

---

13. Genebrardus, *Chronographia*, pp. 109–10.
14. See his נפוצות יהודה (Lwow, 1859), pp. 1a to 5b.
15. See in general Joel Spingarn, *Literary Criticism in the Renaissance* (New York, 1899, reprinted 1963).

respectability to the very center of Renaissance culture, to be read and pondered with an adoration that had previously been reserved for one book alone. None of this was attained without opposition. Literature's promotion was a tremendously vigorous and widespread activity—it was the beginning of modern literary criticism—and in the end it jarred many of the institutions of the medieval world, including the *sacra pagina*.

"The first problem of Renaissance criticism was the justification of imaginative literature." So begins Joel Spingarn's treatment of this period, and for this justification Renaissance criticism turned to the Bible. For poetry, in the fourteenth century, was a matter of allegory; the essence of the poet's craft was the cloaking of eternal verities in the garb of poetic diction and narrative. Now, surely in allegory lay the most obvious legitimating connection between literature and Scripture, for what else was the *sensus spiritualis* of the Old Testament? And indeed, as Augustine had urged in *De Doctrina,* it was the Bible's very "manner of allegorizing" that constituted its true beauty (which was the true beauty of all poetry) and compensated for its superficial lack of elegance. Was it not therefore possible to argue that the whole Bible was by its nature *poetic* (especially the parables of Jesus or the Song of Songs or Isaiah's Canticles); or indeed (as Pico della Mirandola had said) that theology and poetry bore a somewhat reciprocal relationship, with Christian thought existing in latency in the pagan classics? Was not theology itself a kind of Divine poetry?[16] Of course allegorical interpretation predates Christianity, and was used in the reading of Homer long before it was applied to biblical exegesis; so similarly, Christianity adopted typology, in part to preserve a place for the Old Testament in the Christian scheme of things.[17] But these were seen as typically biblical modes; moreover, once accepted as a principle, the *sensus spiritualis* had undergone its own complicated development and quickly became more than the

16. On Pico, see P. O. Kristeller, "Moral Thought of Renaissance Humanism," in his *Renaissance Thought II* (New York, 1965), p. 39. Among others, Boccaccio described theology as "the poetry of God," in his *Genealogy of the Gods*, chapter 12 (see following). Tasso said the same; cf. W. K. Wimsatt and C. Brooks, *Literary Criticism: A Short History* (New York, 1957), p. 152.

17. The roots of Christain typology may be traced to elements within earlier Palestinian Judaism, as well as to Philo. See R. P. C. Hanson, *Allegory and Event* (Richmond, 1959) pp. 14-35; G. von Rad, "Typological Interpretation of the Old Testament," in C. Westermann, ed., *Old Testament Hermeneutics* (Atlanta, 1963), p. 34. A brief treatment of the early *sensus spiritualis* may be found in Kerrigan, *St. Cyril of Alexandria*, pp. 24–65; in more detail, Hanson.

assertion of deeper meaning. There was thus no small audacity in the comparing of the ways of biblical polysignificance with the method of ancient heathen poets, or even modern Christian poets. When Dante arrogated for his *Commedia* the fourfold "allegory of the theologian,"[18] he performed an audacious act of equation, treating what was modern and human as if it were ancient and Divine. Indeed, his whole stance as a Nathan-like prophet and *scriba Dei* was of a nature to exalt poetry to heights unknown in Christian history, unprecedented in Western verse save perhaps for the Sibylline oracles in Greece and the (later) oracular use of Homer and Vergil.

Poets of the Renaissance had a second route to the Bible—the argument that poetry itself had sprung up as the natural accompaniment of religious ceremony, and that, indeed, the place of its origin was in the East, where man himself, Adam, had first dwelt. In his "Genealogy of the Gods," one of the earliest Renaissance defenses of poetry, Boccaccio argues:

> If, my king, you should ask under what quadrant, in what century, and by whose efforts it [poetry] first appeared on earth, I should scarcely be able to give you a sure answer. But there are some who think that it had its origin with the holy rites of the ancients, and that it therefore arose among the Hebrews, because the Sacred Scriptures affirm that it was they who first made sacred offering to God, in what it relates about how Cain and Abel, brothers and the first men born in the world, had sacrificed to God. Likewise by Noah, when the waves of the cataclysm subsided and he had left the ark, was an offering prepared for the Almighty; and similarly by

18. See on this G-R. Sarolli, *Prolegomena alla Divina Commedia* (Florence, 1971), pp. 40–51. Aquinas had said in his *Quaestiones Quodlibetales* (7 q. 6 a. 16) that the mere use of figures and comparisons does not qualify a text as having a "sensus spiritualis"; this can only be found in texts authored not by humans, but by the Holy Spirit: "Significare autem aliquid per verba vel per similitudines fictas ad significandum tantum ordinatas, non ficit nisi sensum litteralem, ut ex dictis patet. Unde in nulla scientia, humana industria inventa, proprie loquendo, potest inveniri nisi litteralis sensus, sed solum in ista Scriptura, cuius Spiritus sanctus est auctor, homo vero instrumentum." However, before Thomas and after him, there were nevertheless frequent assertions of multiple significance in secular authors. Thus, Alain de Lille specifically attributes a threefold significance to his *Anticlaudianus* (the passage is cited in de Bruyne, *Etudes*, 2, p. 287); troubadour poets celebrate the polysignificance of their own hermetic works (ibid., 2, pp. 332–33). While some theologians sought, like Thomas, to distinguish Scripture from other writings on the basis of its *sensus spiritualis*, others argued that Scripture's preeminence resided in the fact that its literal sense was *always true*, whereas poetry was literally false. See H. de Lubac, *Exégèse médiévale* (Paris, 1959) 1, pp. 483–87.

Abraham, with his adversaries overcome, when he brought wine and bread to Melchisedek the priest.

Once created, poetry became the hallmark of Israel's heroes, the "heavenly harpist" David, who "soothed the wrath of Saul with the sweetness of his song . . . and you, Job, who sang your labors and your suffering in heroic meter,"[19] this last an allusion to Jerome's qualification of that book as consisting of hexameters.

Of critical importance at this juncture was the figure of the great Italian poet Petrarch. It was in part his standing as a scholar, the devoted student of Augustine and of Christian doctrine, that allowed him to take on the difficult question of "the Bible as literature" with authority. As Hebrew poets had done before, and as both Jews and Christians were to do on his example afterward, he evoked "David the shepherd poet" in luxuriant pastoral to bring together the world of secular and sacred texts:

> *Monicus.* O! iterum breve si mecum traducere tempus / contingat sileatque fragor rerumque tumultus, / dulcius hic quanto media sub nocte videbis / psallere pastorem! Reliquorum oblivia sensim / ingeret ille tibi; non carmen inane negabis, / quod modo sollicitat, quod te suspendit hiantem.
>
> *Silvius.* Quis, quaeso, aut quonam genitus sub sidere pastor / hoc quaeat? Audivi pastorum carmina mille, / mille modos; quemquam nostris equare caveto.
>
> *Monicus.* Audisti quo monte duo fons unicus edit / flumina? Sive ubinam geminis ex fontibus unum / flumen aquas sacrumque caput cum nomine sumit?
>
> [*Bucolicum carmen* 1. 53–64]

Commenting on this passage in a letter, Petrarch explained:

The shepherd whose singing Monicus prefers to Homer and Vergil is none other than David. The expression "singing to psaltery" is particularly appropriate because of the psalms, which are his creation. The "two rivers from a single source," as Monicus puts it by mistake, are the Tigris and the Euphrates. . . . The "single river from a double source" is the Jordan. . . . [Later on] the "hoarse voice" and "never-ceasing tears" and "oft-repeated name of Jerusalem" are intended as a reference to David, because of his style, which at first seems rough and full of lamentation.[20]

19. G. Boccaccio, *Opere*, ed. G. Ricci (Milan, 1965), pp. 946–48, 1010. The association of the birth of poetry with religious ceremony is found in the sources cited by Isidore in his *Etymologies*; see E. de Bruyne, *Etudes* 1, pp. 97–98.

20. *Epistolae de rebus familaris* 10:4.

Some time later, in a reference to the same passage, Petrarch wrote:

> You remember that years ago, in the first eclogue of my *Bucolicum carmen,* I contrasted [David] with Homer and Vergil, and I left the victory among them undecided. But now, in spite of my old deep-rooted habit, experience and the shining revelation of truth leave me in no doubt as to the victor. But although I put the Christian [i.e., biblical] writers first, I do not reject the others. Jerome said he did so, but it seems to me from the imitative style of his writing that he actually approved them.[21]

In his attitude toward "the Bible as literature," Petrarch was not far from Augustine, contrasting secular and sacred writings as "those I prefer for style and those I prefer for substance."[22] David's style seems "rough" but his subject elevates him above more secular masters. The difference was that Petrarch could fully accommodate secular literature within a Christian context; nay, he saw the making of "literature"—in his own day as in biblical times—as the highest of activities. Most significantly, that gulf that separated the divinely inspired "poems" of biblical authors and the poems of himself and his contemporaries was collapsed: Petrarch himself wrote Latin imitations of the Psalms (therein creating a model for all Renaissance poets), and, in a well-known letter to his brother,[23] lays claim to the new status poetry was to acquire first in Italy, then all over Europe.

> The fact is, poetry is very far from being opposed to theology. Does that surprise you? One may almost say that theology actually is poetry, poetry concerning God. To call Christ now a lion, now a lamb, now a worm, what pray is that if not poetical? And you will find thousands of such things in the Scriptures, so very many that I cannot attempt to enumerate them. What indeed are the parables of our Saviour, in the Gospels, but words whose sound is foreign to their sense, or allegories, to use the technical term? But allegory is the very warp and woof of all poetry. Of course, though, the subject matter in the two cases is very different. That everyone will admit. In the one case it is God and things pertaining to him that are treated, in the other mere gods and mortal men.
> Now we can see how Aristotle came to say that the first theologians and the first poets were one and the same. The very

21. Ibid., 22:10.
22. Ibid.
23. Ibid., 10:4.

name of poet is proof that he was right. Inquiries have been made into the origin of that word; and, although the theories have varied somewhat, the most reasonable view on the whole is this: that in early days, when men were rude and unformed, but full of a burning desire—which is part of our very nature—to know the truth, and especially to learn about God, they began to feel sure that there really is some higher power that controls our destinies, and to deem it fitting that homage should be paid to this power, with all manner of reverence beyond that which is ever shown to men, and also with an august ceremonial. Therefore, just as they planned for grand abodes, which they called temples, and for consecrated servants, to whom they gave the name of priests, and for magnificent statues, and vessels of gold, and marble tables, and purple vestments, they also determined, in order that this feeling of homage might not remain unexpressed, to strive to win the favour of the deity by lofty words, subjecting the powers above to the softening influences of songs of praise, sacred hymns remote from all the forms of speech that pertain to common usage and to the affairs of state, and embellished moreover by numbers, which add a charm and drive tedium away. It behooved of course that this be done not in every-day fashion, but in a manner artful and carefully elaborated and a little strange. Now speech which was thus heightened was called in Greek poetices; so, very naturally, those who used it came to be called poets.

Who, you will ask, is my authority for this? . . . The first of these is Marcus Varro, the greatest scholar that Rome ever produced, and the next is Tranquillus, an investigator whose work is characterised always by the utmost caution. Then I can add a third name, which will probably be better known to you, Isidore. He too mentions these matters, in the eighth book of his Etymologies, although briefly and merely on the authority of Tranquillus.

But you will object, and say, "I certainly can believe the saint, if not the other learned men; and yet the fact remains that the sweetness of your poetry is inconsistent with the severity of my life." Ah! but you are mistaken, my brother. Why, even the Old Testament fathers made use of poetry, both heroic song and other kinds. Moses, for example, and Job, and David, and Solomon, and Jeremiah. Even the psalms, which you are always singing, day and night, are in metre, in the Hebrew; so that I should be guilty of no inaccuracy or impropriety if I ventured to style their author the Christian's poet. Indeed the plain facts of the case inevitably suggest some such designation. Let me remind you, moreover, since

you are not inclined to take anything that I say to-day without
authority, that even Jerome took this view of the matter. Of course
these sacred poems, these psalms, which sing of the blessed man,
Christ,—of his birth, his death, his descent into hell, his resurrection, his ascent into heaven, his return to judge the earth,—never
have been, and never could have been, translated into another
language without some sacrifice of either the metre or the sense. So,
as the choice had to be made it has been the sense that has been
considered. And yet some vestige of metrical law still survives, and
the separate fragments we still call verses, very properly, for verses
they are.[24]

Here are the seeds of later Renaissance defenses of poetry: the Divine
origin of all poetry, springing from primitive man's desire to praise
God; the poetic nature of the Bible as a whole, as evidenced by its use
of allegory and figurative language; and finally, the metrical
construction of the Psalter and other books and sections, which
supports both points and which (because in translation is lost the very
sweetness poetic form had been devised to confer on such Divine
praises) legitimates the creation of a new Divine poetry in the
vernacular, in Psalter paraphrases such as those undertaken by
Petrarch and many later Renaissance authors, or in bold new acts of
interpretation and justification such as crowned English literature at
the end of this period.

    Even those who opposed literature's rise did not often go so far as to
deny that the Bible itself contained poetry, for to do so was to fly in the
face of Church doctrine;[25] they could only argue that the poetry of
David and Job was incomparably higher than modern works or (with
Savanarola and, indeed, Falaqera)[26] that the abuses to which poetry
had been subjected since the days of the Bible required that it now be
approached with caution and not encouraged among the masses. But
the Divine service which poetry had once rendered was an irresistible

    24. Translated in J. H. Robinson, *Petrarch, The First Modern Scholar* (New
York, 1907), pp. 261–64.
    25. Note, however, F.Berni's *Dialogo contra i Poeti* (1526): "Anzi per farsi da
buon capo ad impugnare la fede nostra, e levarle l'autorita, quelli che furno il
principio di essa, cioè li Profeti e buoni autori della Scrittura Sacra e del Testamento
Vecchio, dicono che furno poeti e che feciono versi." See his *Opere* (Milan, 1864),
pp. 8–9.
    26. See Spingarn, *Literary Criticism*, p. 10. On Falaqera see chapter 5; cf. the
extremely restrictive view of poetry voiced by Abraham b. Nathan Hayyarhi (of
Lunel) (c. 1155–1215) in his commentary on מסכת כלה רבתי (Tiberias, 1906), pp.
20–21.

example for the poets of the Renaissance, and the argument was repeated again and again. Politian, in his *Sylvae,* composed a treatise on the poet in which he argued the Divine origin of poetry and sang the praises of Vergil and Homer. How natural, amidst all this, to apostrophize the great poets of the Old Testament:

An memorem solymos, praelustria nomina, vates;
Psallentemque Deo regem, qui turbine fundae
Icta philistaeo secuit puer ora giganti;
Teque palestini laqueantem culmina templi,
Mentis opumque potens, Salomon nec odora tacentem
Oscula solicito languentis amore puellae?
Pars hymnos fudere Deo; sic maximus ille
Nondum clara sacris radiatus tempora Moses
Ignibus, ut rubras sicco pede transiit undas,
Demerso insignem cecinit Pharaone triumphum;
Tuque puer, modo dicte mihi, Jessaee, vicissim
Dulcia terribili mutans psalteria bello,
Voce deum placas: ut quo, Babylone rebelli
Lambit in horrisonis non noxia flamma caminis;
Quosque alios, veteris gens servantissima ritus,
Retrorsum Judaea legit.[27]

A. S. Minturno, in an influential prose treatise *De Poeta* (1559), also declared the Divine origin of all poetry, and argued:

And so it is that this manner of expression [poetry] may be seen to have been employed not only to imitate life and men's customs, and as an image of the truth and a likeness of all private and public affairs, but likewise every sort of learning, all the arts, and all manner of writing are richly accommodated within it. This being the case, and poetry's delight being so great, there is no nation or race of men to be found that has not gladly welcomed it with fond embrace. For shall we omit mention of the Hebrews, who, that men the world over might receive the true knowledge of God, framed His praises in verse in so marvellous a system?[28]

In such argument one must see more than a mere reference to the doctrines of Jerome and Augustine, for in them breathes as well that new—"humanistic" is the Renaissance cliché—feeling for the Bible as the work of divinely inspired *men,* and the awareness alluded to above that the Scriptures were the product of an ancient and Eastern

27. A. A. Poliziano, "Nutricia," in *Prose volgare e poesie latine e greche* (Florence, 1867), p. 384.
28. A. S. Minturno, *De Poeta* (Venice, 1559), p. 9.

people. This people had poets of its own just as the ancient Greeks had, and if we read in Minturno's qualification of Hebrew's poetic system as "marvellous" some of a growing feeling that biblical meter was not so simple as Jerome had suggested—was this not simply because, Eastern and ancient, Hebrew poetry obeyed a different set of rules?

3

The gulf between the Bible and human works was shrinking. Since the early Church, Christianity had understood the sacredness of the Bible as expressed in the fact of its multiple significance. But increasingly, especially since the thirteenth century, that tenet's strength had been eroded. Thomas Aquinas held that the Bible's Divine inspiration made it unique among all documents, and that that uniqueness was embodied in the combination of literal and spiritual senses;[29] but in a famous passage[30] he argued that the letter itself could contain multiple senses, thus be-clouding the issue of polysignificance. He also suggested that the spiritual aspect of certain historical passages might be only that they conveyed, in addition to the intentions of the human author of the text, those of the Author of history as well.[31] The revival of interest in the literal sense in that century,[32] if it did not lead to a reexamination of doctrine in the matter of Hebrew meter, in any case focused attention on precisely the sort of interpretation *all* texts have in common. Moreover, the insistence of such thirteenth-century Hebraists as Roger Bacon (who himself composed a Hebrew grammar)[33] that the Scriptures be studied in Hebrew, and on the inability of translation to convey the text's nuances, further weakened the position of many spiritual expositors. Meanwhile, as we have noted, the similarity between poets' allegorizing and the Bible's was stressed by critics and writers. Thus, if the Bible's uniqueness resided in its spiritual sense, this uniqueness was under double attack,

29. Smalley, *Study*, p. 300.

30. *Summa Theolog.*, part 1 Ques. 1, art. 10.

31. The letter, for Thomas, was the foundation of all spiritual meaning: "Holy Scripture sets up no confusion, since all meanings are based on one, namely, the literal sense." See briefly Karlfried Froehlich, ' "Always Keep to the Literal Sense . . . ' " in E. Miner, ed., *Literary Uses of Typology* (Princeton, 1977), p. 34, where he also notes: "Thomas' authority was not widely accepted outside his own order. It is also true that his hermeneutic theory in its components said nothing new but rather systematized and slightly modified elements from various sources, especially Augustine." See also Smalley, *Study*, p. 299.

32. Smalley, *Study*, p. 281.

33. Smalley, *Study*, p. 330.

increasingly neglected and undermined by Hebraizing commentators, and in the meantime encroached upon at the other side by poets of secular and (still worse!) Divine intention.

The Reformation only brought these tendencies into greater relief. When Luther read the Psalter, it was no longer as a book important to Christians primarily for its prefiguring of the Crucifixion; it was a universal compendium of human emotion, David as Everyman:

> Fear and worry over what is to come, sorrow and sadness over present evil, hope and pride of future happiness, assurance and joy of things presently enjoyed—such are the winds that blow and teach the tongue to speak and open the heart to pour out its contents. In the Psalms the chief thing is such a speaking in all manner of stormy winds. Where does one find a finer word of gladness than the psalms of praise and thanksgiving?
>
> There you look into the heart of all the saints as into lovely blessed gardens. . . . And so also where they speak of fear and hope they use such words that no artist could paint the fear and hope, and no Cicero or other orator form them in such a way. . . .
>
> Hence it comes about that the Psalter is the booklet of all saints, and everybody in whatsoever situation he may be, finds Psalms and sayings in it that rhyme with his affairs, and seem to him as though they were formulated thus just for his sake.[34]

34. Cited in E. G. Kraeling, *The Old Testament Since the Reformation* (New York, 1955), p. 18. Note the striking contrast between Luther's views and those of John Calvin: "What wonderful confirmation [of the Bible's superiority to all other books] ensues when, with keener study we ponder the economy of the divine wisdom, so well ordered and disposed; the completely heavenly character of its doctrine, savoring of nothing earthly; the beautiful agreement of all the parts with one another [shades of Lowth!]—as well as such other qualities as can gain majesty for the writings. But our hearts are more firmly grounded when we reflect that we are capitivated with admiration for Scripture more by grandeur of subjects than by grace of language. For it was also not without God's extraordinary providence that the sublime mysteries of the Kingdom of Heaven came to be expressed largely in mean and lowly words, lest, if they had been adorned with more shining eloquence, the impious would scoffingly have claimed that its power is in the realm of eloquence alone. Now since such uncultivated and almost rude simplicity inspires greater reverence for itself than any eloquence, what ought one to conclude except that the force of the Truth of the Sacred Scriptures is manifestly too powerful to need the art of words? . . . Read Demosthenes, or Cicero; read Plato, Aristotle, and others of that tribe. They will, I admit, allure you, delight you, move you, enrapture you in wonderful measure. But betake yourself from them to this sacred reading. Then, in spite of yourself, so deeply will it affect you, so penetrate your heart, so fix itself in your very marrow, that, compared with its deep impression, such vigor as the orators and philosophers have will nearly vanish" (from *The Institutes of the Christian*

If such was the Psalter's importance, or Job's, or Lamentations's, then their preeminence no longer rested on their being the *verbum Domini.* It had to be won on distinctly literary grounds, as the expression of the promptings of every heart in language "no Cicero or other orator" could rival—this and the fact that they are words addressed directly to God, for, as Luther also states, "when one merely speaks to men of such things, it does not come out of the heart so deeply." But men can speak to God at any moment, and if no Cicero could rival David's words, there was certainly no harm in a Christian poet trying, or at least giving expression, in the most exalted language and style of his day, to the deepest longings of his own soul. Herein lies the whole calling of Renaissance religious poetry.

These ideas about the Bible and biblical style quickly spread elsewhere in Europe—and especially to England. It is to be recalled that the British concern with "the Bible as literature" goes back at least to Aldhelm and Bede, and the latter's catalogue of tropes and figures in the Bible, while no match for Cassiodorus's, is an important milestone in this (Augustinian) area of rhetorical criticism. In the Renaissance, interest in classical rhetoric was revived,[35] and, perhaps to make the revival more consonant with Christian values, the Bedean recourse to the scriptural illustration of *schemata* was reinstituted with a vengeance: In the sixteenth and seventeenth centuries English schoolboys learned the figures of rhetoric from textbooks by Richard Sherry (1555), Dudley Fenner (1584), John Barton (1634), Thomas Hall (1654), John Smith (1657), and John Prideaux (1659), all of whom relied on biblical examples to illustrate their lessons.[36] But harmonizing Christianity and the classics was only part of the story: equally important was the new feeling for the Bible as a human document.

Now for reasons that are probably not altogether knowable, England has long had a fascination with Israel,[37] and in the

Religion, [1559], vol. 1, chapter 8, contained in Calvin, *Selections . . . ,* ed. J. Dillenberger [Missoula, Mont., 1973], p. 361.) This is pure Augustine.

35. See Sister Miriam Joseph, *Rhetoric in Shakespeare's Time* (New York, 1962), pp. 18–20.

36. "It is no mere coincidence that the early leaders of the Renaissance in various countries were school-masters and authors of school texts which were used internationally." (Sister Miriam Joseph, *Rhetoric,* p. 12). Of those she treats, a crucial figure is Phillip Melancthon, a Hebraist and student of classical rhetoric, the author of an *Institutiones rhetoricae* (1521). For a discussion of the English rhetoric books see I. Baroway, "The Bible in the English Renaissance," *Journal of English and German Philology* 32 (1933): 470; the article as a whole is a valuable treatment of our subject.

37. For the Middle Ages, see Smalley, *Study,* p. 369.

Renaissance it blossomed. Quite apart from the extremes of what has been called British Israelitism—the belief that the English people are a remnant of the Ten Lost Tribes, occasionally bolstered by the folk etymology *Brit-ish* i.e., pertaining to the Covenant[38]—it was increasingly the Englishman's pleasure to name his children with Old Testament names, see the affairs of his day in terms of the politics of Samuel or Kings, and in other ways to think of himself and his countrymen as *the true Jews.* (One writer, remarking on this phenomenon, suggests that the absence of any "other" Jews from her shores since 1291 could not but stimulate British imaginings in this regard.)[39] "Nowhere in the Christian world did the Old Testament receive such a warm reception or penetrate so deeply into the lives of men as in England."[40] There should be nothing surprising, then, if the poets of such a nation should see themselves as psalmists and prophets, and rely, for critical support for their activities, on many of the arguments seen above.

George Puttenham (1532–90) basically followed the line of argument seen above in Petrarch for his *Arte of English Poesie.* Religion was the natural creation of all peoples, and poetry was its first product:

> Hymns to the gods was [*sic*] the first form of Poesie and the highest and the stateliest, and that were song by the Poets as priests, and by the people or whole congregation, as we sing in our Churches the Psalmes of David, but they did it commonly in some shadie groves of tall tymber trees.[41]

It was therefore natural that "King David also and Solomon his sonne and many other of the holy Prophets wrate in meeters, and used to sing them to the harpe, although to many of us, ignorant of the Hebrue language and phrase, and not observing it, the same seeme but a prose."[42]

---

38. See in general s.v. "British Israelites" in *EJ* 4:1381, which further adduces the connection of Saxons to "Isaac's sons" and the tribe of Dan with such names as Denmark and Danube. Menasseh b. Israel argued for the legalized reentry of Jews to England on Messianic grounds, connecting the biblical מקצה הארץ ("end" or "corner" of the earth) with England (= Angle-terre), an association going back at least to the time of ibn Ezra. See C. Roth, *A Life of Menasseh b. Israel* (Philadelphia, 1934), p. 207.

39. Kraeling, *OT Since the Reformation*, p. 42.

40. Ibid., p. 41.

41. In O. B. Hardison, ed., *English Literary Criticism: The Renaissance* (New York, 1963), p. 161.

42. Ibid., p. 153.

Not only did Puttenham use the existence of biblical poetry to defend poetry in general, he even relied upon it to exalt English poetic convention above that of Greek and Latin:

And the Greek and Latine Poesie was by verse numerous and metricall, running upon pleasant feete, sometimes swift, sometime slow (their words very aptly serving that purpose) but without any rime or tunable concord in th'end of their verses, as we and all other nations now use. But the Hebrues and Chaldees, who were more ancient than the Greekes, did not only use a metricall Poesie, but also with the same manner of rime, as hath bene of late observed by learned men.[43] Whereby it appeareth that our vulgar running Poesie was common to all nations of the world besides, whom the Latines and Greekes in speciall called barbarous.[44]

Similarly, Thomas Lodge defended poetry on biblical grounds:

Among the precise Jewes, you shall find Poetes, and for more majestic Sibilla will prophesie in verse. Beroaldus can witness with me, that David was a poet, and that his vayne was in imitating (as S. Jerom witnesseth) Horace Flaccus, and Pindarus, sometimes his verse runneth in an Iambus foote, anone he hath recourse to a Saphier vaine, and aliquando, semipede ingreditur. Ask Josephus, and he will tell you that Esay, Job and Salomon voutsafed poetical practices, for (if Origen and he fault not) theyre verse was Hexameter, and Pentameter. Enquire of Cassiodorus, he will say that all the beginning of Poetrye proceded from the Scripture.[45]

Perhaps the best known of these Renaissance defenses, Sir Philip Sidney's, invoked the same argument:

And may I not presume a little farther to show the reasonableness of this word *vates*, and say that the holy David's Psalms are a divine poem? If I do, I shall not do it without the testimony of great learned men, both ancient and modern. But even the name Psalms will speak for me, which, being interpreted, is nothing but "Songs"; then, that it is fully written in metre, as all learned Hebricians agree, although the rules be not yet fully found. Lastly and principally, his handling his prophecy, which is merely poetical.[46]

---

43. On rhyme in the Bible, see below.
44. Hardison, *English Literary Criticism*, p. 154.
45. Thomas Lodge, *A Defense of Poetry* . . . (London, 1853), p. 12.
46. In J. W. Hebel, et al., *Tudor Poetry and Prose* (New York, 1953), p. 806.

Connected to this phenomenon is the whole matter of Bible translation. Even before the Reformation proper, translating the Bible had often been an act of political significance.[47] The religious reformer John Wyclif's translation (ca. 1380) was regarded as tainted not only because of his own heretical beliefs, but because his supporters were among those involved in the Peasants' Revolt of 1381. (He was condemned by the Church and, nearly half a century after his death, his remains were exhumed and burned.) Meanwhile, any unauthorized use of an English translation of the Bible was condemned in England in 1408. With the Reformation, retranslation of the Bible became a tangible declaration of independence from Popishness; such was Luther's New Testament translation (1522), and Tyndale's, which was later published in 1536 with the approval of Henry VIII, as part of the "Thomas Matthew Bible."[48] Many of these new translations, anxious to distinguish themselves through the new knowledge of Hebrew and so return to the long-obscured *true* sense of Scripture, embodied some of the notions about the Bible "as literature" already seen, including late medieval Jewry's theories of biblical poetry. The Latin Bible that was to become the "Vulgate of Protestantism" was the work of an Italian Jewish convert, Emmanuel Tremellius, and Francis Junius. First published in 1575–79 and subsequently in many editions, it was translated directly from "the Hebrew and the Syriac" and copiously footnoted. Five books— Psalms, Proverbs, Job, the Song of Songs, and Ecclesiastes—were distinguished as poetic, "for these are rhythmical, not written in prose as are all the other books (save that even in them are interspersed the **elegant canticles belonging to Moses, Deborah, David, Isaiah, Ezekiel, [49] Jeremiah and Habakkuk), but confined to numbers for ease of memory and for singing.**"[50]

That the Psalms and other books were poetry was so obviously true

47. Thus the Waldensians of southern France (twelth century); see A. C. Partridge, *English Biblical Translation* (London, 1973), pp. 21–22.

48. This Bible, though it bore Matthews's name, was actually Tyndale's Pentateuch and New Testament with the translation of Coverdale's Bible (1535) for the remaining sections. A mere ten years earlier Tyndale's work had had to be smuggled into England from Germany. See Ibid., pp. 69–70, and on the earlier Wyclif translation, pp. 22–24.

49. This is apparently a misprint for Hezekiah, whose prayer in Isa. 38 was one of the Church's Canticles. Cf. Genebrardus's reference to Hezekiah's prayer in the passage translated above. The other "canticles" mentioned by Tremellius-Junius here are: Deut. 32; Judg. 5; 2 Sam. 22; Isa. 5 and 26 (again, cf. Genebrardus); Lam. (attributed to Jeremiah), and Hab. 3.

50. E. Tremellius and F. Junius, *Biblia Sacra* (Hanover, 1603), pp. 105–06.

that it seemed to some only proper to translate them into verse.[51]
Moreover, the new Churches had need of vernacular Psalms that
could be introduced into the liturgy. Between 1532 and 1543, the poet
Clément Marot translated fifty psalms into French. Like several of his
English counterparts, Marot was a court poet, and probably never
imagined his versified psalms would be put to congregational use,[52]
but they were, and soon the entire Psalter was in French verse.
(Théodore de Bèze, Calvin's disciple, completed Marot's start in
1562.) Meanwhile, Sir Thomas Wyatt had translated seven penitential
psalms into verse (they were published in 1549), on the model of
Italian verse translations such as those of Petrarch and, more
particularly, Pietro Aretino (1492–1557). Other verse paraphrases
were undertaken by his friend Henry Howard, Earl of Surrey, and
somewhat later by George Gascoigne, Sir Philip Sidney and his wife,
the Countess of Pembroke, and many others. These translations were,
as noted, initially inspired by the artful Italian model,[53] but the
practice later converged with the congregational use of metrical
paraphrase. For congregational singing of the Psalms had been taken
up by the English exiles in Geneva in the 1550s, and spread back to
England by 1560;[54] in 1556 the Anglo-Genevan Psalter had
appeared, fifty-one psalms rendered into English by Sternhold,
Hopkins, and Whittingham, and in 1562 their *Whole Book of Psalms*
appeared. Shackled to the monotonous "Poulter's measure" or
"fourteener" (for easy adaption to standard tunes) and of undistin-
guished language, the collection nevertheless became an all-time hit,

51. It is to be recalled that Jerome had only refrained from so doing because it was
impossible to maintain both meter and sense, and Augustine repeated this
explanation; see chapter 4. This point was often stressed in the Renaissance. Thus
Comentarii Io. Pomerani in Librum Psalmorum (Basle, 1524): "In psalmis neque
modos neque tempora verborum exacte servare possunt interpretes. Intelligentia
tamen certa est, modo tropum noveris Scripturae" (unpaged introduction). In
England a metrical Psalter had been made in the late thirteenth century, and
individual psalms were often translated or paraphrased in verse as a pious exercise.
See J. R. Kreuzer, "Thomas Brampton's Metrical Paraphrase," in *Traditio* 7 (1947–
48): 359–403.

52. J. C. A. Rathmell, *The Psalms of Sir Philip Sidney and the Countess of
Pembroke* (New York, 1963), p. xvii.

53. Note the remark of a later English commentator: "Four famous French poets,
Mich. Hospitalis, Adr. Turnebus, Joh. Auratus, Th. Beza; six Italians, A. Sannazi,
H. Fracastorius, A. Flamminius, H. Vidas, A. Nangerius, P. Bembus; and one
Scotchman, G. Buchanan, have exercised their poetical abilities in Rendering
Davids Psalms in verse" (Edward Leigh, *Annotations on Five Poetical Books of the
Old Testament* [London, 1657], unpaged).

54. Rathmell, *Psalms of . . . Sidney*, p. xiii.

going through more than six hundred printings by 1828 (it was, however, officially supplanted by Tate and Bradley's "New Version" in 1696). Those who had at first derided vernacular psalm-singing as the "Geneva Jig" and "Beza's Ballets" (ballads) were drowned out by a thousand choirs.[55]

And verse translations of the Psalms, either for private piety or intended for public singing, continued to be reproduced: Campion, Bacon, Crashaw, Carew, and many others set themselves to this task, and two of the seventeenth century's greatest poets, John Donne and John Milton, distinguished themselves as translators of biblical poetry. In so translating, they added their own not inconsiderable energies to the identification of the Psalms and other books with poetry, and indeed to the growing conviction that some meter or meterlike system lay beneath the order of their words. As Milton had argued in "The Reason of Church Government," "Those frequent songs throughout the law and prophets . . . not in their divine argument alone, but in the very critical art of composition may be easily made appear over all the kinds of lyric poesy to be incomparable."[56] And in *Paradise Regain'd* he chastened the style of ancient Greek poetry:

Remove their swelling Epithetes thick laid
As varnish on a Harlots cheek, the rest,
Thin sown with aught of profit or delight

55. George Wyther mentions these disparaging names in *A Preparation to the Psalter* (London, 1619), p. 6.

56. D. M. Wolfe, ed., *Complete Prose Works of John Milton* (New Haven, 1953–66) 1, p. 816. Milton's words here seem to come from Francis Junius's "Oratio de Lingua Hebraica": "One book of the Psalter, a single prophecy of Isaiah, has more majesty, beauty, grace, pleasure and any other word by which my meaning might be expressed—than all the Homers and Vergils, than all the books of Demosthenes and Ciceros. *Not by their argument alone* (*non argumento solum*) (for who in good faith shall compare human tales and petty trifles with God's truth?) but by their very speech (*sed oratione ipsa*), which the Holy Spirit, author and originator of all grace, has tempered more judiciously for the advancement of their argument" (*Opera Theologica* 1 [Geneva, 1613], col. 10). Similarly, John Donne maintained that "David is a better poet than Virgil." (*Sermons of John Donne*, ed. G. R. Potter and E. M. Simpson [Berkeley, 1953] 4, p. 167). This claim, that biblical poetry is aesthetically superior to other poetry, is not to be confused with the (rather common) contention that the Bible's form of expression is superior to that of other texts, for this argument, whether in Augustine or Thomas, is aimed at the *sensus spiritualis*. Cf. Gregory, *Moralia* (20:1): "Holy Scripture by the manner of its speech transcends every science, because in one and the same sentence while it describes a fact, it reveals a mystery" (Cited in R. Grant, *A Short History of the Interpretation of the Bible* [New York, 1963], p. 123).

Will far be found unworthy to compare
with Sion's songs. . . .   4. 343–47

On this issue was Milton's stance as a Divine poet, a recipient of "the inspired gift of God, rarely bestowed, but yet to some (though most abuse) in every Nation"[57] partially predicated. His celebrated invocation of the "Heav'nly Muse" at the beginning of *Paradise Lost*, with its exaltation of Horeb/Sinai and Sion's hill above the mountain haunts of the Greek Muses, is but one instance of his rapprochement of Divine to poetic inspiration, and of the Bible to works of secular art. To sing Man's Fall was, for Milton, a "sad task, yet argument / Not less but more Heroic than the wrath / Of stern Achilles."[58] And could its representation in words have been any less "Heroic" the first time around, when the Heav'nly Muse whispered her promptings in Moses' ear?

4

Renaissance theories of biblical style begin, as noted, with the approaches inherited from the Middle Ages. Two dominant themes have been seen: the attempt to identify in the Bible tropes and figures such as existed in classical rhetoric; and the imputation of classical meters to those songs and books identified as biblical poetry. Behind the former stand the Latin works that were so seminal in the medieval period, Augustine, Cassiodorus, Isidore, and Bede, and some lesser-known works, such as the aforementioned Adrian's *Isagoge,* which catalogued a host of possible figures in the Bible, naming specifically metaphor, simile, syncrisis, synecdoche, hypodeigma, metonomy, antiphrasis, periphrasis, anacephalaoiosis or epanalepsis, apochresis, prosopoia, schematismos, allegory, hyperbole, epitothasm, irony, sarcasm, enigma, apeile, apophasis, aposiopesis, and parainesis.

The imputation of Greek-style tropes and figures continued after the early medieval period, stimulated in part by the medieval *arts poétiques*[59] and the revival of interest in the classics. The English

57. *Prose Works*, 1, p. 816.
58. *Paradise Lost*, 9, 13–15.
59. See E. Faral, *Les arts poétiques du 12ᵉ et du 13ᵉ siècle* (Paris, 1962). Two figures catalogued by Faral bear particular importance to our subject: the first is called *interpretatio*: "Interpretatio est quae non iterans idem redintegrat verbum, sed id cummutat quod positum est aliquo verbo, quod idem valeat, hoc modo: 'Republicam radicitus evertisti, civitatem funditus dejecisti.' " Similarly *expolitio* refers to the "polishing" or developing of an idea through proof, opposites, similitude, example, and conclusion. See pp. 63–64.

rhetoric books have already been mentioned. At the same time, the Renaissance began to spell out some of the implications of earlier remarks about the "special quality" of Hebrew style and the *proprietas*[60] of the language. As new grammars and lexicons were prepared, the differentness of Hebrew syntax and forms had to be approached head on, and this perception spilled over into analyses of Hebrew style. A significant contribution to the tropes-and-figures approach was the book *Institutiones Hebraicae*, by the distinguished Hebraist Sanctes (Xantes) Pagninus (1470–1536). Pagninus gives a standard justification for the cataloguing of figures: "Many figures are contained in sacred literature, some of which I shall include here, so that adepts of secular letters may be shown that all devices originated with the sacred."[61] There follows an extensive list of figures: anaphora, antiprosopon, antiptosis, apostrophe, and so on. At the same time, he carefully catalogued usages that had no exact Latin or Greek equivalent:

> There is also the use of the figure of apposition, with or without prepositions, especially when the latter part of the apposition is a proper noun and explains the former: "That they make an attack on the man, on Lot" (Gen. 19) and "Attend to the boy, to Absalom" (2 Kings 18). . . . Similar to these is anadiplosis, in which, for the sake of increased emphasis, strength, and significance, it repeats the same words, as "For behold thine enemies, Lord, behold thine enemies shall perish." (Psalm 92)

Similarly:

> A doubled substantive, spoken in the plural in the latter instance, signifies excellence in its class, and attributes the former noun the strength of a Latin superlative: thus, "holy of holies," that is, the most holy. . . .
>
> Two nouns placed together and having almost the same meaning, of which the latter is in the genitive, are used to connect the former as part of the latter's meaning, as "the earth of dust" in Dan 1:2, that is a portion of dust, or earth so minute that it is as dust.[62]

This section of his *Institutiones* did much toward approaching biblical

---

60. On this idea see Hailperin, *Rashi*, p. 261, where he traces its existence to the time of Roger Bacon, but perhaps a longer chain exists.

61. *Institutiones Hebraicae* 4 (Lugduni, 1575), p. 412. This edition was under the editorship of J. Mercerus, on whom see below.

62. Ibid.

style with fresh eyes; an abstract of it was reprinted with the text of the Bible, and on its model later authors wrote their own *institutiones.*

Surely one of the greatest of all students of biblical style, and a neglected commentator in our own day, is Matthias Flacius Illyricus (1520–75), the author of an immense compendium, *Clavis Scripturae Sacrae.* It is in extraordinary work: modern in its knowledge of Hebrew and its concern with the special qualities of the language, yet extremely conscious of past interpretation, especially of patristic writings; sensitive to the slightest nuances of style and yet positively Augustinian in its insistence on judging everything from the standards of Greco-Roman rhetoric; a champion of the *Hebraismus,* which nevertheless lumps Old and New Testament together in all matters of expression. It is, in sum, a work of great erudition, repetitive, rambling, and pungent, full of information but in some measure unusable because of its very bulk.

The work is divided into two parts. The first, and somewhat longer, section is an alphabetical glossary of biblical words and concepts (in the Basle edition of 1609 this glossary occupies more than six hundred oversize pages printed in two columns). For each entry Flacius presents a summary of biblical information and, where possible, his own gleanings from the rabbinic and patristic writings and later medieval and Renaissance scholarship. The second section begins with a lengthy essay, "De Ratione Cognoscendi Sacras Litteras," in which he discusses some of the difficulties confronting the modern reader of Scripture and outlines various remedies, general rules for the student of biblical style, and so forth. He expounds the question of multiple senses from a historical standpoint, from Origen to Melancthon, and legitimizes the validity of allegorical interpretation by showing the use of such interpretation in the New Testament itself. Then he goes on to discuss different classes and genres of biblical books.

Following this essay is a section of patristic exhortations about the study of Scripture, including a brief paraphrase of Junilius Africanus (sixth century), "De Partibus Sacrarum Litterarum," in which Flacius takes up the question of biblical poetry:

Junilius says that the Bible has poetic structure in that certain of its books are written with Hebraic meters in the original; others are mere prose. He says the metrical books are Job, Psalms, Ecclesiastes, and a few others in the Prophets: I am of the opinion that Lamentation might rightly be added to those, and perhaps Song of Songs as well. When these metrical books were translated into other languages for our use, they lost their meters, while retaining however certain traces and indications of the songs.[63]

But Flacius is not interested in the metrical debate. His book's special value lay in its appreciation of style, and especially of parallelism, restatement, and repetition as peculiarities of biblical Hebrew. These he approaches first via the usual Greek categories in his fourth section, "De Tropis et Schematibus Sacrarum Litterarum"—parallelism is discussed as anadiplosis, epizeuxis, epanados, etc. just as in Adrian and Cassiodorus. He describes the distribution of meaning over two clauses ("unicum sensum in duo membra . . .")[64] and then broaches the whole topic of repetition and restatement:

> While the Greek and Latin languages have their anadiploses, epanalepses, anaphoras, synonymia, expolitio, and other figures, by which means—and others—they repeat words and ideas, Hebrew, in this domain, surpasses them by far, both in the frequency and variety of iteration.
>
> There is, however, a two-fold deception to be feared in these reduplications: the one that, where one idea is repeated in various and sundry means, we think that it be not one but many; and the other that, on the contrary, when different matters are dealt with in separate clauses (*colis*), we not think them to be one and the same, or (to put it another way) that we not think repetition to exist where it does not, or not exist where it does.[65]

With this piece of imitative form as introduction, Flacius goes on to catalogue repetition and restatement in all its manifestations, in both Old Testament and New. Here are a few excerpts:

> The third type of Iteration, which above we called the Rhetorical sort, is likewise multi-faceted. Sometimes it is done for the sake of ornamenting, for it satisfies the ear by having the whole unit repeated, which otherwise the brevity native to Hebrew would not be able to satisfy. Furthermore, such repetitions in this style often contain pleasing allusions, and also homioptata and homoteleuta, all of which serve to create a poetically-ordered speech (*ad efficiendam orationem numerosam*) as in Psalm 2, "Let us throw off their chains, and cast their yoke from upon us"—but in Hebrew

---

63. M. Flacius, *Clavis Scripturae Sacrae* (Basle, 1609), 2, p. 205; this last sentence may refer to the *ṭe'amim* and/or psalm incipits.

64. Ibid., p. 390.

65. Ibid., p. 437.

the repetition, causing the two hemistichs to end in the same manner [-*emo*], makes for a pleasing effect. Similar examples are to be found in the same psalm. . . .

At other times the meaning is repeated rather for the purpose of polishing[66] and inculcating the idea more deeply; in which type the sense is repeated in the same form of speech, but with different words: thus Psalm 37: "And the Lord will help them and free them, free them from evil ones and guard them, for their trust is in Him." Psalm 6, "For the Lord has heard the sound of my cry, the Lord has heard my prayer, the Lord has accepted my supplication." Likewise in Romans 2, it refers twice to the castigation of good and evil men, verses 7, 8, 9, and 10. . . .

Frequently in the Scriptures the same idea is repeated in different words for the sake of emphasis, or explanation, or strengthening. "Let us cast off their chains" [etc.]. Psalm 8, "What is man, that you have memory of him, or the son of man, that have mind of him?" Psalm 33, "The counsel of the Lord stands for ever, and the thoughts of His heart from generation to generation." About which St. Augustine admonishes that it is not a useless tautology, but that repetition of this sort makes for emphasis and a definite strengthening. . . .

To Rhetorical repetitions pertains as well the usage whereby sometimes several half-verses, or whole lines or [biblical] verses, either begin with the same word, or the word with which the earlier unit ended the next begins, concerning which it was already explained in the section on tropes with regard to Psalm 67. . . . Such repetitions are also found in profane poetry to be both frequent and pleasing. . . .

Here one might mention as well emphatic anadiploses, made for the purpose of impressing some point, or also to make something specific. Psalm 92, "For behold thine enemies, Lord, behold thine enemies are borne away." The same word, enemies, is repeated for the sake of emphasis and, as it were, sticking in its stinger. Thus also Psalm 93: "In magnificence is clothed, is clothed the Lord," and Psalm 94, "How long shall the wicked, Lord, how long shall the wicked exult?" In just the same manner do grammarians and rhetoricians assert Homer repeated the name of Nereus in Book II of the Iliad. . . .

It is most common in Hebrew that when they want to express something most clearly, they say the thing briefly first, and then, repeating these, connect the things remaining to be said. Thus

66. *Expoliendae*, see note 59.

Psalm 145: "Close is the Lord to all who call upon him, to all who call upon him in truth."[67]

Here certainly is an impressive survey of biblical parallelism, an understanding of its essentially rhetorical and emphatic character, and perhaps an assimilation of syntactic parallelism (above, "the same *form* of speech") to the phenomenon of actual repetition and restatement. But our excerpting is in one way misleading, for these insights come amid examples of all sorts of repetition truly unrelated to our theme; and despite his observation that this characteristic is found much more in Hebrew than in Greek, Flacius does not pursue the point adequately, but on the contrary finds many of his examples from the Pauline Epistles.

Before leaving Flacius, mention ought to be made of the section of his book entitled "De Stylo Sacrarum Litterarum." It is a freeflowing essay on style and the manner in which larger biblical passages are put together; notable are his treatments of Amos 6:1 (discussed by Augustine in *De Doctrina*) and the opening chapter of Isaiah. He discusses different levels of style, and it is noteworthy that in this connection he separates the Bible into two main classes, the pedestrian speech of historical narrative and the elevated speech of the rest of the Bible:

> The Sacred Scripture, except for the historical books, consists of pure oratory [*conciones*—"sermons"]. For the Prophetic books are just such oratory, and likewise the Gospels, and to a certain extent the books of Moses are composed in this manner; furthermore the apostolic letters in large measure are oratorical in nature; nor do the Psalms, though they be poems, seem to be far from this sort of oratory.[68]

He discusses the terseness of biblical idiom and the "plenitudinous" style, sections strongly reminiscent of Lowth's later excursions on Hebrew's "sententious," "parabolic," and "sublime" ways of speaking. But, unlike Lowth, Flacius so often seems unable to come to the point, or even look over his shoulder. His oft-stated hope in writing was that his work "vindicabit Sacram Scripturam a contemptu istorum eruditulorum . . . qui solos Cicerones, Demosthenes, Homeros ac Marones mirantur"[69]—a problem in Antiquity that reappeared

---

67. Flacius, *Clavis*, pp. 442–45.
68. Ibid., pp. 449–50. Is not this like the biblical ḫuṭba described by Moses ibn Ezra?
69. Ibid., p. 450.

with the revival of the Classics in the Renaissance—for which aim an endless maze of examples and demonstrations was aptly suited. But perhaps this goal was what prevented him from taking on Hebrew style without reference to Greek authors or categories, and, as in the matter of repetition, failed to bring him to synthesize his perceptions and distinguish Hebraisms from classical style.

Stylistic criticism along the tropes-and-figures line, by Pagninus, Flacius, and others, was bound to imply a kinship between classical and biblical rhetoric. This seems, of course, a step in the wrong direction as far as Hebrew's true nature is concerned; but, especially thanks to the classical criticism of J. C. Scaliger, the classics were increasingly recognized as belonging to another age, one with norms of its own. What the Bible and Homer had in common was their antiquity, and this served to explain in the Bible curiosities that used to be explainable only by its Divine origin. Prominent among these were repetition and restatement. Indeed, somewhat later (1665) the French biblicist Claude Fleury invoked this argument—a double reverse!—to defend the style of Homer:

> Il emploit ses comparisons à la manière des Orientaux qui de tout temps ont esté diserts et ont pris plaisir à les expliquer avec beaucoup de circonstances quoiqu'il n'y ait qu'un certain point sur quoi elles tombent, tout le reste n'estant ajousté que pour la vraisemblance et pour la grace du langage. Cecy auroit besoin d'estre expliqué davantage mais il faudroit trop de discours; car cette remarque s'estand sur touttes les comparaisons du Cantique et des autres livres poétiques de l'écriture et sur les Paraboles de l'Evangile. Pour les épithètes il est certain qu'il y en a grand nombre dans Homère qui nous semblent inutiles parce que la chose s'entend fort bien par le seul nom substantif auquel elles sont appliquées. On doit croire néantmoins que ce ne sont pas des chevilles et que le style poétique des anciens consistoit principalement à dire les choses en plus de parolles et avec plus de circonstances et ces parolles n'estoient pas perdues pour cela, au contraire elles estoient fort utiles puisqu'elles servoient à faire paroistre les choses plus grandes et à faire que l'esprit s'y arrestast plus long temps. Ainsi nous voyons que dans plusieurs Pseaumes chaque verset ne contient qu'une pensée expliquée en deux manières différentes.[70]

70. From Noémi Hepp, *Deux Amis d'Homère au XVII siècle* (Paris, 1970), pp. 153–54. See also pp. 160–61.

The last sentence is, in addition, valuable evidence of the extent to which the tropes-and-figures approach came to focus on parallelism in the Psalter and other books.[71]

5

The metrical approach continued to be pursued, but here one encounters an important change: scholars began to believe that biblical poetry was organized not, as the Jerome tradition had it, in meters comparable to those of Latin and Greek poetry, but more loosely, like the vernacular poetries of Europe. To the general resemblance of Hebrew "metrics" to Italian or English verse we shall return presently. But first it will be useful to chart briefly one extreme in this school of thought, the belief that biblical poetry actually rhymed, just like Dante's and Petrarch's, and even that in *rhyme alone* lay the answer to that oft-posed question of the period, "Quae est carminum Hebraeorum ratio?" To begin properly, one ought to return to an already-cited passage in Jerome's description of Hebrew meter in his preface to Job:

> Hexametri versus sunt, dactylo spondeoque currentes, et propter linguae idioma crebro recipientes et alios pedes non earundem syllabarum, sed eorundem temporum. Interdum quoque rhythmus ipse dulcis et tinnulus fertur numeris lege metri solutis: quod metrici magis quam simplex lector intellegunt.

In Jerome's day, the general term for metrical arrangement was *numerus,* which meant "numbers" (as in Pope's claim that as a child he "lisp'd in numbers"), musical measure, time, rhythm, harmony, order, or arrangement, as well specifically meter or metrical line. (*Metrum* was of course also meter, but specifically the Greco-Roman quantitative system.) Another general term for poetic arrangement was *modus. Rhythmus* was used much more rarely. In Greek its

---

71. Cf. Fleury's own treatise, "Discours sur la poésie des Hebreux," reprinted in the posthumous *Histoire ecclésiastique* (Paris, 1763), pp. 253–54: "Mais d'un autre côte le style Poétique est plus long [que le style prosaïque], en ce que la plûpart des pensées sont répétées & exprimées deux fois en deux manières différentes. Mon Dieu, ayez pitié de moi par votre grande miséricorde, & effacez mon péché par la multitude de vos bontés. Et ainsi, dans presque tous les Pseaumes; soit qu'ils le fissent pour donner plus de tems a l'esprit de goûter la même pensée, soit parce que ces Cantiques se chantoient a deux choeurs. *Ces repetitions sont la marque la plus ordinaire du style Poétique.*" (Emphasis added.)

meaning was close to *numerus* or *modus* in Latin—it referred to regular, recurring motions, hence symmetry, harmony, rhythm, and (like *modus*) manner or form in general. *Rhythmizare* was coined later to mean to arrange or set in order.

In the passage cited, Jerome identifies Job's meter with that of Latin and Greek, hexameters made of dactyls and spondees, but he notes two levels of divergence; first—a principle underlying Greek metrics in general—substitution is permitted, so long as the substituted foot is of the same temporal quantity, just as indeed spondee (i.e., two long syllables) and dactyl (long short short) are temporally equivalent and hence alternative in most feet of the dactyllic hexameter line. Beyond this, a *rhythmus dulcis et tinnulus* is achieved when the "numbers are set free from metrical law." Here Jerome is citing (so it appears) a line from Horace's *Odes* (book 4, ode 2) that comes in a poem written in homage to Pindar. It begins:

> Pindarum quisquis studet aemulari,
> Iule, ceratis ope Daedelea
> Nititur pennis vitreo daturus
>   Nomina ponto.
>
> Monte decurrens velut amnis, imbres
> Quem super notas aluere ripas.
> Fervet immensusque ruit profundo
>   Pindarus ore,
>
> Laurea donandus Apollinari,
> Seu per audaces nova dithyrambos
> Verba devolvit *numerisque fertur*
>   *Lege solutis....*

In context, Horace clearly means by the phrase a reference to Pindar's apparently "free" metrical arrangements. One critic, recalling the usage "legibus solutus" (used in a legal sense for anyone exempted from the provisions of a law), says Horace's phrase is "a sort of oxymoron, 'verse which is as free of law as if it were not verse.' "[72] This would accord well with the *nova verba*—neologisms, poetic coinages—and both together describe the "poetic furor" and freedom that was Pindar's.

Now Jerome, in using this same phrase—whether or not he wished to allude to Pindar specifically, to whose "lawless meter" he had elsewhere compared Hebrew verse—intended something similar: not only do the Hebrews sometimes use the principle of substitution to

---

72. E. C. Wickham, *The Works of Horace* (Oxford, 1877), 1, p. 267.

insert feet "of the same times" but not the same number of syllables, but the *numeri* (poetic arrangements in the broadest sense) are occasionally set free from the laws of meter. *Rhythmus,* the Greek word that Latin *numerus* approximates, should be translated here "poetic" or even "rhythmical effect"; note that it is combined with *tinnulus,* a jingling or ringing, perhaps as a kind of hendiadys. Thus: "A pleasant rhythmical effect and a jingling is achieved with the poetic arrangement being set free from the laws of meter, about which students of metrics will understand more than the common reader."

Rhythmus did, however, have another sense which, whether or not Jerome was alluding to it here, later came to influence the interpretation of his words. *Rhythmus* was used not only (like the Latin *numerus*) as a general term for poetic arrangement, but specifically for arrangements that are not properly metrical according to the Greco-Latin system. Thus, Quintilian, *Institutes of Oratory* 9. 4, asserts: "*Rhythmus,* that is *numerus,* consists of lengths of time; meter, besides length, requires the time to be in a certain order."[73] Later on, *rhythmus* came specifically to describe the poetic structure of "vulgar" poems which, if they did not observe the rules of quantity and position in Latin verse, nevertheless had some sort of arrangement. Thus Bede, in the treatise on meter mentioned earlier, observed a sharp distinction between meter and *rhythmus*:

> *Rhythmus* will be seen to be similar to meter: it is an arrangement of words governed not by a metrical system, but weighted (*examinata,* perhaps "balanced") in the number of the syllables as determined by the ear's discernment, as are the songs of the vulgar poets. Thus, while *rhythmus* can exist without meter, meter without *rhythmus* cannot be. It might more sharply be distinguished as follows: meter is both a system and an arrangement, *rhythmus* an arrangement without a system.[74]

---

73. See on this I. Baroway, "The Hebrew Hexameter," in *English Literary History* 2 (1935): 83–84; and cf. Baroway's other articles, "The Bible in the English Renaissance" (cited above), "Tremellius, Sidney and Biblical Verse," *Modern Language Notes* 40 (1934): 149; "The Lyre of David," *ELH* 8 (1941): 119–42; and "The Accentual Theory of Hebrew Prosody," *ELH* 17 (1950): 115–35. Anyone perusing these articles will recognize our great debt to Baroway throughout. It ought to be noted, however, that he was somewhat off the mark in the last-cited article: there was no "accentual" theory in the works he cites. The word "accentus" in Buxtorf, Vossius, and other writers about Hebrew at this time refers to the Masoretic *ṭe'amim.* Moreover, poetry that does not observe vowel quantities but only counts the number of syllables per line is not therefore *accentual!* These are serious errors.

74. *PL* 90:174, cf. de Bruyne, *Etudes* 1, p. 152. The distinction between

With such an understanding of *rhythmus*, it was possible to read Jerome's sentence as asserting that biblical verse is (at least at times) not *metrical*, in the Latin sense, but arranged only according to the number of syllables without regard to their quantitative values. If so, biblical verse is more like the poetry written in the barbarian tongues of Europe than the classical verse of Greece and Rome.

Enter, in the Renaissance, various Hebrew writings about the poetry of the Bible, and specifically the idea found in Samuel ibn Tibbon, Moses ibn Habib, and others that biblical verse is *approximately metrical.* They had argued that while the תנועות and יתדות ("cords" and "pegs," quantitative values assigned by the Judeo-Arabic system) are not symmetrical between biblical verse-halves or consistently disposed in line after line, nevertheless many verses will be seen to be equal in the total number of syllables, and where a slight inequality in the syllable count exists, it may be compensated through "movements of the voice" and/or musically. This idea entered the Christian world through the Christian Hebraists. We have already seen Genebrardus's reference to ibn Habib; before him an Italian Hebraist, Augustinus Steuchus of Gubbio (1496–1549) stated the same conclusions as Habib's, as did others.

It will be recalled that ibn Habib at one point in his dissertation reported having visited an ancient gravestone, reputedly belonging to an army commandant of the biblical king Amaziah, on which was engraved a poetic epitaph:

---

rhythmus and *metrum* was established clearly here by Bede for future generations. Prior to this time there were varying opinions as to what constituted the distinction. Thus Marius Victorinus (fourth century) describes *rhythmus* as "what is called *numerus* in Latin"; it is different from *metrum* because (1) the latter term refers to a strictly verbal ordering, the former a musical one found also in dance ("metrum in verbis, rhythmus in modulatione ac motu corporis sit"); (2) because meter is an ordering of feet (i.e., longs and shorts) and *rhythmus* of times; and (3) because meter is defined by the fixed number of syllables or feet, while rhythm is *never* a matter of precise numbers ("et quod metrum certo numero syllabarum vel pedum finitum sit, rhythmus autem numquam numero circumscribatur"). See H. Keil, *Grammatici Latini* (Hildesheim, 1961), 6, pp. 41–42. Similarly, Diomed (fifth century) observed: "Distat enim metrum a rythmo, quod metrum certa qualitate ac numero syllabarum temporumque finitur certisque pedibus constat ac clauditur, rythmus autem temporum ac syllabarum pedumque congruentia infinitum multiplicatur ac profluit" (Keil, 1, p. 474; cf. p. 289). The concept of *rhythmus*—especially after Bede—allowed the notion that there were *three* modes of discourse instead of the simple prose-poetry polarity. Thus Alberic of Monte Cassino (d. 1180): "dictaminum autem alia sunt metrica, alia rithmica, alia prosaica" (cited in de Bruyne, 2, p. 10). See above, chapter 4, notes 90 and 121.

שאו קינה בקול מרה   לשר גדול לקחו י־ה

O sing lament in bitter voice   for the great prince whom the Lord hath taken

"We were unable to read more [than the first line]," ibn Habib wrote, "because the writing had been eroded, but the second line ended 'to Amaziah.' Then I truly believed that this metrical sort of poetry had existed since the days when our forefathers were dwelling in their own land."[75] For what ibn Habib thought he saw in this inscription was evidence that the "Judeo-Arabic" style meters went back to the days of Amaziah: the line falls into two symmetrical halves, each of which consists of two units both composed of one "peg" and two "cords." This is the meter known as המרנין, the same scheme as that of the celebrated hymn אדון עולם ("Eternal Lord"). Moreover, he adds that the last word of the second line was "Amaziah" to show that it rhymed with the first. (The internal rhyme qînāh-mārāh-yāh would not strike ibn Habib as "rhyme" because it was as such unacceptable according to Judaeo-Arabic rules; moreover, it was not necessary that half-verses rhyme, but only that each whole line rhyme with the next.)

But ibn Habib's Christian readers misunderstood what he was trying to say. Arabic-style meters did not look *metrical* to them (in that they did not consist of Greek-style feet),[76] and in any case if (as ibn Habib maintains in the same treatise) biblical songs consist only of equivalent numbers of syllables, Christian readers were perfectly content to see that same system at work in this supposedly ancient epitaph. And indeed, the number of syllables is equivalent. On the other hand, qînāh-mārāh-yāh they read as rhyme, and it is no doubt in part because of this passage that the idea of biblical rhyme caught on to the extent that it did in Christian scholarship.

Only in part, of course, for there were other contributing factors.

75. See chapter 5, n. 59.

76. Note, for example, this description of the medieval Hebrew poetic system written by Valentinus Schindler, *Institutionum Hebraicorum libri V* (Wittenberg, 1575), p. 320: "The [medieval] grammarians however write verses in imitation of the French and Germans, taking into consideration the numbers (*numeros*) or equality of the syllables, and also a rhyme at the ends of the verses." Note also that because other commentators "translated" the patterns of תנועות and יתדות into Greek terms— i.e., a יתד (peg) was a "short" plus a "long," hence an *iamb*; two consecutive תנועות (cords) were a spondee—even the regularity of the arrangements had a certain erratic quality to it because of the apparent jumble of types of feet. This act of "translation" (which continues to this day) is fundamentally misleading. See M. Hak, "How are we to read Sephardic Poetry?" (in Hebrew) in נתיבות החנוך (Tel Aviv, 1945): 112–21, esp. 114.

The idea of biblical "rhyme" goes back at least to Sa'adya's time, as seen in the putative fragment of his *Poet's Dictionary*; this list of rhymes was taken up by Moses ibn Ezra in *Kitāb al-muḥāḍara*, with slight modification.[77] An independent notion of rhyme underlies the assertion of the thirteenth-century grammar, קונטרס ברקדוק שפת עבר, that rhyme is "hinted at" in the Bible; its examples are 1 Kings 8:57 and Isaiah 63:17.

Somewhat later, the sixteenth-century poet and grammarian Samuel Archivolti's ערוגת הבשם ("Bed of Spices") (1602) had listed a new selection of rhymes, including Deuteronomy 32:6, Judges 14:18 (Samson's retort), Psalm 115:8, Proverbs 31:18 and 15:15, Psalm 2:3, "and many others."[78] Abraham b. David Portaleone (1524–1612) also wrote about rhyme. After having confessed his inability to find an exact metrical system in biblical songs, he adds:

> However, I am unable to hide from the fact that in certain ancient *mešalim* which resemble poems I have found rhymes at the end of the lines. But the number of their syllables is in general not equal, as in this case (Num. 21:27 ff.): *Bōʾû ḥešbôn*, four syllables with a rhyme-word at the end, *tibbāneh wĕtikkônen ʿîr sîḥôn*, which are ten syllables with a rhyme-word almost similar to the first; *kî ʾēš yāṣĕʾâ mēḥešbôn*, eight syllables with a true rhyme similar to that of the first line of four syllables, *lehābâ miqqiryat sîḥōn*, also eight syllables with a true rhyme similar to the rhyme word of the ten-syllable line; *ʾākĕlâ ʿār môʾāb*, six syllables without a rhyme. *Baʿălê bāmôt ʾarnōn* is likewise six syllables if the ʿayin of *baʿălê* is muted; this line also has a similar-looking rhyme, although I am aware the ʾarnōn is not a true rhyme with *siḥon*.[79]

He was apparently not bothered by the fact that all the "true rhymes" of this passage consisted of actual repetitions of the same word!

Beyond these (and perhaps other) specific assertions, the widespread notion among all Jews that rhyme was a truly wonderful invention, an aid to memory and indeed the essence of poetry—fed by the confusion (observed earlier) whereby חרוז was used to mean not only "rhyme" but also "poetry" and "line of metrical verse" in

---

77. Sa'adya's (or his student's) examples were Job 28:16, Job 21:4, and Isa. 49:1 (see N. Allony, ed., ספר האגרון 386–89). Moses ibn Ezra dropped the last verse from his list and added Job 33:17; see Halkin, *Kitāb al-Muḥāḍara*, pp. 46–47.

78. See ערוגת הבשם (Amsterdam, 1729), p. 102b.

79. A. Porteleone, שלטי הגברים (Mantua, 1612), p. 3b. Portaleone then goes on to scan שירת הבאר (Num. 21:17) which, with some juggling, he manages to find "with equal numbers of syllables," though "lacking rhyme."

Abravanel and others—certainly would have led Jews to prize any sort of rhyme they might hit upon in the Bible, and to foster the notion that, however sparingly, this feature might be found amongst the "poetic" books of their sacred Scriptures.[80]

A confusion parallel to the חרוז one existed in Renaissance Latin. For the word *rhythmus* was now increasingly used both to describe the nonmetrical (in the Greco-Latin sense) lines in which Italian, Provençal, German, French, English, and other poems were written, and also to denote the *rhymes* with which these lines regularly ended. Whatever the true etymology of rhyme, it was now supposed to be a corruption of *rhythmus* (a belief reflected in the current English spelling of rhyme, though the spelling *rythmus* was also common). Moreover, it was inevitable that these two meanings were not always segregated: *rhythmus* was understood to designate a particular sort of poetry, with rhymes and equal numbers of syllables in each line, but without the measuring of long and short quantities as in Greek or Latin.

With this background, we can now appreciate some of the Renaissance's elaborations on Jerome and their overall conception of the structure of biblical "poetry." In his preface to his Commentary on the Psalter, Augustinus Steuchus wrote:

> Hebrew poetry is not the same as that of the Greeks and Latins, just as Italian, or Etruscan, is not the same as Latin. And indeed, Hebrew has more in common with Italian than with Latin. For Latin, in imitation of Greek, takes into account the times of the syllables; Hebrew does not account times but at most the number (*numerus*) and the similarity of the ending syllables. Just as in Italian poetry there is no such thing as a spondee, or a trochee, or a dactyl, but only the counting of so many syllables and the taking care that they end in the same way, so similarly is it in Hebrew. Therefore, when Jerome writes that either Job or the Psalms contain dactyls and spondees, and when, in the Preface to Job, he says it "slips into verse," and when Augustine with others says these things concerning Hebrew poetry, you should recognize that not exactly the same sort of metrical feet nor indeed our type of poetry is meant by them but merely something similar. Therefore, neither does "heroic song" exist in Hebrew, nor iambic or the other

---

80. Note that Moses ibn Ezra excluded the earlier example from the Prophets and replaced it with one from Job. Did he not "correct" thereby any imputation of a poetic device to a book other than the three which he considered poetry, Psalms, Proverbs, and Job?

types, but something similar, and such things as the Barbarians sing in different ceremonies.[81]

The basic idea of this passage, and an important theme throughout this period, is that Hebrew poetry is a simpler system than Latin or Greek, based on *numerus* alone, rather than *metrum*. This idea does indeed reflect Jewish writings about biblical meter, specifically the ideas we have seen in Samuel and Moses ibn Tibbon, Moses ibn Habib, and other writers. And it is significant that the idea gains expression here in the writings of an Italian commentator; it is to be recalled that Moses ibn Tibbon's preface to the Song of Songs was (in its discussion of the classes of poetry) cited almost word by word by Immanuel of Rome in his Song of Songs commentary. Later on, the Spanish and Portuguese expulsions of the Jews brought many exiles to various Italian states, among them men who became theorists on the question, like Isaac Abravanel and Moses ibn Habib, as well as a great many teachers and scholars acquainted with current thought. (Still later, Italian Jews like Azariah, Samuel Archivolti, and Abraham Portaleone published their work in Italy.) It is reasonable to suppose that this notion, soon widespread, of Hebrew's "system" as *numerus* but not *metrum* was essentially an Italian synthesis based on earlier and contemporary Jewish writings plus the distinction, enunciated in Bede and elsewhere, between mere "numbers" and true "meter."

Now Steuchus, who stands at the beginning of this tradition, also invokes this curious notion of biblical rhyme. Here we may be right to see the influence of ibn Habib, but two other possible influences ought to be cited. First is the force of analogy between vernacular poetry, specifically Italian (which rhymed and counted syllables), and biblical verse. In this the ambiguity about *rhythmus* may have had a part (though it is noteworthy that Steuchus avoids the word); songs that merely counted the total number of syllables *needed* something more, something like rhyme.[82] A second possible influence is the fact that some Hebrew verse written by Italian Jews at this time had adopted the syllabic rhyming meters of Italian Christians. On this last point, it is noteworthy that Steuchus asserts that Hebrew does not take into account times (*tempora*); if he were acquainted with medieval

---

81. Augustinus Steuchus Eugubinus, *Ennarationum in Nonnullos Psalmos Praefatio* (Venice, 1590), unpaged.

82. On the association of rhyme with mere *numerus* or *rhythmus*, cf. Bede: "In rythmo ergo consideratur numerus syllabarum sine tempore, aliquando cum finis similitudine" (*PL* 90:174).

quantitative poetry, or had even glanced at the rest of ibn Habib's handbook on Hebrew meters, he might have wanted to qualify this statement a bit. If, on the other hand, he thought only that Hebrew poetry (of his day) was like the Italian poetry of his day, he might think it in the nature of the Hebrew language not to be able to observe vowel quantity.[83]

Similar sentiments were voiced by another Italian, Marianus Victorius of Rieti (d. 1572), who edited and annoted Jerome's Letters. In a scholion to Epistle 117, he fixed on a phrase in Jerome's distinguishing of prophetic from poetic style:

[Jerome says:] "Or hold anything similar to what is the case with Psalms or the works of Solomon": The Psalms [in Latin] contain those brief utterances (*sententiae*) which are the mark of verses in Hebrew, therefore they admit neither periods [i.e. periodic sentence structure] nor uninterrupted discourse [as, by inference, do the works of Isaiah et al. from which Jerome is distinguishing the Psalms]. Nor do they proceed by being confined to the rules of metrical feet, as is done in Greek or Latin, but go along in the same manner as, in Etruscan, as they now call [Italian], those songs which are called "loose."[84] Such is the case in the works of Solomon, especially the Song of Songs, in which you will find not only the ideas broken up in the manner of verse, but also the ends corresponding to the middle [of the verse], as in: 'apirion 'asa *lo* hammelek Selo*mo*,[85] "A litter did King Solomon make for himself." Of this manner are amongst us those songs which are called *leonine*,[86] such as those lines in the apse of Saint Peter's above his tomb in Rome, which read as follows: Summa Dei *sedes* haec est, sacra Principis *aedes*. Mater cuncat*arum* decus, & decor ecclesi*arum*."[87]

It seems that the force of analogy between "Etruscan" poetry and Hebrew was what suggested the presence of rhyme in the Bible to

83. On the development of the Italian prosodic system in Hebrew at this time see D. Pagis, "Hebrew Metrics in Italy and the Invention of the Hebrew Accentual Iambs," *Hassifrut* 4 (1973): 650–712.

84. Soluta: "*oratio soluta*" was the common expression for prose; these songs are *soluta* in the same way Jerome had used the word, set free from metrical constraints.

85. Song 3:9. The text here is written in Hebrew script in the Antwerp (1573) edition I have consulted; however, there are several mistakes in the Hebrew.

86. Leonine verses contained an internal rhyme, sometimes at the caesura. See below.

87. Marianus Victorius Reatinus, *Epistolae D. Hieronymi* (Antwerp, 1573), p. 620; emphasis added.

Victorius, though perhaps he was familiar with the other sources seen above. It is difficult to imagine how, having found one example in the Song of Songs, he could have failed also to notice that the overwhelming majority of verses do not fit the scheme he seems to describe as general; perhaps he is citing another writer's conclusions? It is worth noting as well how he had fixed upon the *breves sententiae* as a prime characteristic of Hebrew "poetry." This certainly is an important insight.

The early seventeenth-century Hebraist Johannes Buxtorf added a small treatise and his immense reputation to the idea of biblical rhyme. The treatise, "Tractatus Brevis de Prosodia Metrica," was appended to his *Thesaurus Grammaticus*[88] and widely circulated. Buxtorf's tract derives, as he notes, largely from Moses ibn Habib, but also from David Kimhi and the booklet שקל הקודש. One interesting facet of Buxtorf's approach is that he mingles everything together— medieval Hebrew terminology (דלת, סוגר, בית) is used to describe biblical lines, and medieval Hebrew meters are described in terms of Greek metrics (thus, אדון עולם consists of "an iamb and spondee alternately placed").

He begins by asserting that the Bible contains poetry—he cites specifically Psalms, Proverbs, Job, Exodus 15, Deuteronomy 32, the Song of Deborah, (but not David's Song [2 Sam. 22], perhaps because he includes it among the Psalms [i.e., Psalm 18]), then two of the Church's canticles, 1 Sam. 2 (Hannah's prayer) and the third chapter of Habakkuk. He notes that biblical poetry has long been discussed, and cites Jerome's preface to Job and Josephus's remarks about Exodus 15.

> But although the method and skillful organization of sacred meter began to be neglected shortly after the time of the Prophets, and thence, with the ancient wisdom of the Hebrews more and more on the decline, alas finally was cast into a shameful oblivion amongst them, nevertheless we shall have a few words to say of its general characteristics, and explain in greater detail the system of metrical speech in common use.[89]

He then defines poetic *numerus* as being either *metrum* or *rhythmus*. However, *metrum* according to Buxtorf means not only the Greco-Latin quantitative system, but any system that counts the total number of syllables as well. What then is *rhythmus*? To Buxtorf it

88. J. Buxtorf, *Thesaurus Grammaticus* (Basle, 1629).
89. Ibid., p. 627.

means rhyme, either an individual rhyme or rhyme as an organizing principle of poetry:

Meter [in the Bible] consists of a certain specific number of syllables, according to R. Mosche Schem Tobh [ibn Habib] and other Hebrews; the sacred poem is represented in the highest degree by the books of Job, Psalms and Proverbs, as well as several of the canticles of the sacred. Here, depending on the idea, a metrical line is completed with a single half-verse (*versus*), or by two hemistichs, or even three or four strung together so that one פסוק or verse will include a tristichon or tetrastichon.

Each hemistich has either an equal number of syllables, or else one or the other will go beyond the number. [He gives examples from Job 3:10, 5:27; Prov. 1:8 and 10:5, Psalm 119:146 and 146:6]. Of the exceeding meter, that is when one hemistich or the other has a greater number of syllables, there are infinite examples, and almost all the sacred songs are so defined, in which either the extra number is absorbed by a speeding up of the time-measuring, or the deficiency is filled out and made complete by a musical varying and drawing-out of the voice.

So far, this is a paraphrase of ibn Habib. But now he comes to the matter of rhymes and its different classes.

Rhyming verse (*rhythmus*) was not cultivated in a manner other than what might be produced spontaneously and happen quite by chance,[90] not that it seem to be summoned up by some belabored attention; yet not infrequently, especially in the case of David, we have noticed its occurrence, of whom we have previously heard Jerome saying that a certain *rhythmus* and jingling (*tinnulus*) may be heard [in the Psalms], as:

ואם מדוע לא תקצר רוחי	האנכי לאדם שיחי	Job 21:4
משל עמים ויפתחהו	שלח מלך ויתירהו	
ומשל בכל קנינו	שמו אדון לביתו	Psalm 105:20-21
לשמח בשמחת גויך	לראות בטובת בחיריך	
להתהלל עם נחלתך		Psalm 106:5
אל תקנא ברשעים	אל תתחר במרעים	Prov. 24:19

If in this poetry there was any other system of ordering, as perchance

---

90. This also comes from ibn Habib's words; Habib speaks of one verse "agreeing" with another by chance either in its "parts" ("cords" and "pegs") or its ending (rhyme).

the hidden arrangement of *te'amim*[91] would indicate, from hoary antiquity it lies buried in oblivion with the Hebrew sages. Thus was the, as it were, infancy of this sacred poetry bound solely by the number of the syllables, which popular practice then polished with the sweetness of rhyme and more exact arrangement. So may it be observed in other peoples, that early poetry was delimited solely by *rhythmus*, without any measuring of longs or shorts.

Somewhat later, Buxtorf recounts ibn Habib's tale of the rhyming tombstone:

Rhyming verse (*rhythmus*) is a poetic arrangement (*numerus*) containing a fixed number of syllables and ending with fixed concluding parts; this is called *ḥerez* or *ḥiruz*[92] and thence *śir ḥaruzi*, rhyming poetry. . . . R. Mosche Schem Tobh, from the celebrated Chabhibh family, which flourished at one time in Spain, wrote in the pamphlet מרפא לשון that he had seen, during his long wanderings, on a certain high mountain the tombstone of Amaziah the king of the Jews, on which he was able to read these words incised, the rest having been obliterated by age:

שאו קינה בקול מרה לשר גדול לקחו י־ה
לאמציה

He understood from the similar ending of these words, that rhyming verse was then in use at the time when the Israelites still dwelt in their own land.[93]

In these passages a host of possible misprisions seem to come into play. Jerome's "rhythmus" is taken here to mean "rhyming verse." Of the illustrations that follow, the first is one of ibn Ezra's rhymes (a coincidence?), and the last would also fit the medieval Hebrew notion of rhyme; but the citing of Psalm 105:21 and the last third of Psalm 106:5 are probably Buxtorf's own contribution, hardly suitable by the Judeo-Arabic standard. Then, in the gravestone story (it was not Amaziah's grave in Habib's version, but that of his general) the line is apparently split into four and misread as a quatrain with the rhyme scheme: *a a b a*. (Evidently the *le'amaṣiyah* is understood as the identifying name on the stone, perhaps not even part of the poem.) But no matter—rhyme was now in the ascendant.

George Wyther, who translated the Psalms into verse and wrote a

91. On the debate concerning the antiquity of the *ṭe'amim* and their precise function see below.

92. *Sic*; in vocalized Hebrew characters.

93. Buxtorf, *Thesaurus*, p. 636.

Preparation to the Psalter (1619), was not much of a Hebraist, but he had a keen sense of biblical style and little timidity in the question of biblical poetry: "Even with that glympse, which I have had of the Hebrew, and the poesy thereof, I doubt not but I may ghesse as neere the manner of their Verse, as those who have fought for it by the Greeke or Latin rules." His idea about Hebrew poetry's structure—and an important theme for seventeenth-century England—was that it had far more in common with English than with the meters of classical literature:

I think it not unlikely that the ancient Jewes had both such kinde of Verses, as some of ours are, and the same freedome in the Composures that we use: Yea, that they varyed the Staffe at their pleasures, making it now longer, now shorter, as they listed, or best fitted the matter, for so you see it appears by their Verses.[94]

As with the Italians fixed on the same vernacular analogy, Wyther accepted the existence of biblical rhyme:

The Hebrews are full of variety in their Numbers, and take great liberty in their Verses. For as Marianus Victorius reports, they are not alwaies measured out by the same Number or quality of Syllables, as the Greeke or Latin verses are: but sometime lengthened and abbreviated in the pronountiation by accents of time, according to the manner of the Italian Measures, and the liberty which it seemeth our English used in their Poems, about foure hundred yeeres agoe; for to us now (though I am perswaded, they are as they were at first intended to bee) there appeares sometime to be a want, and sometime an Overplus, in the Syllables of many of their Verses. For example, to shew you what an Affinity the Ancient Hebrew Verses have with those, both in the nature of the Verse, and in the manner of the Ryme: See here a Verse or two; for by reason the Characters are difficult, I will not trouble you with many:

כל־היום חרפוני אויבי מהוללי בי נשבעו
כי־אפר כלחם אכלתי ושקוי בבכי מסכתי

Psalm 102:8–9

Col-hayom cherephuni oyebai
Meholalai bi nishbau
Chi epher callehhem acalthi
Veshikkuvai bi bhchi masachthi

The first two of these are unequall Numbers, according to our

94. George Wyther, *A Preparation to the Psalter* (London, 1619), p. 61.

pronountiation; but it might be, that anciently in the reading, they could decently enough abbreviate the first, and lengthen the second; yea, and perhaps with some grace to that Tongue. Or if they did not, the Manner of verse is not so strange, but wee have had, in our Language, the same unequall Measures in use. For if I were to translate them according to the fashion of the Hebrew verse, it might be thus:

> All day, my foes revile me! And who were
>   mad at me, against me sweare.
> For, Ashes I, as bread, devour'd;
>   And teares, immingled with my drinke, I shed.[95]

Something of a new tack in the matter of biblical rhyme appeared with Johannes H. Alstedus's *Praecognita Theologica* (Hanover, 1623). Alstedus's book is a general introduction to, and defense of, Scripture, in outline and many details comparable to Flacius, including a treatise on biblical tropes and figures, biblical style—here again are Flacius's *plenitudo* and *brevitas*—as well as a paragraph on the "modus patheticus legendi Sacra Biblia" that foreshadows some of the "Bible as literature" insights of the following century. Alstedus was somewhat noncommittal on the organization of biblical poetry:

> For indeed numbers [i.e. poetry] aid the memory, insofar as they confine the words so that their precise form adheres more easily for long periods in the memory. Song works best by teaching the mind, delighting the spirit and moving to emotion, which three things we see come together in the books of the Psalter. Nevertheless, howevermuch this be the case, we ought not to inquire too deeply into the system of their poetical numbers. This much is certain, that Eusebius in his eleventh book of the Preparation for the Gospel, Chapter V, Jerome and Epiphanius, report in many places that some of the Psalms are written in hexameter verse, as Psalm 119, others in hexameter and pentameter, and still others which, as is the case with many odes and epodes, are put together with different types of verses, which sort of structure is called in Hebrew Sigaion.[96]

But having counseled his readers not to "rationem numerorum istorum laboriose quaerere," Alstedus doubtless felt some lingering dissatisfac-

---

95. Ibid., pp. 59–60. The word "devour'd" should apparently be "devoured."

96. Johannes H. Alstedus, *Praecognita Theologica* (Hannover, 1623), pp. 602–03. The word שגיון appears in the incipit of Psalm 7 and again (in the plural) at the beginning of Habakkuk's Song (Hab. 3:1). Alstedus's remark, whose ultimate source I do not know, seems to relate the word to the root שגה, "wander." A similar idea is found in Azariah's sixtieth chapter and was translated by Buxtorf the Younger.

tion, for while the threefold benefit of poetry was present in the Psalter, still it lacked those salient features of *numerus* which play on the memory most sharply; nor could the pedagogical benefits of musical setting (on which Alstedus has touched in his treatise on music, the *Templum Musicum*)[97] be enjoyed by the Hebrew Psalter as much as by, for example, its German translation, which was not only set to music but rhymed. And so he proposed to, as it were, *retranslate* the Psalter into Hebrew so as to fit the rhyme scheme and music of those "*rhythmi sacri* which the common-folk are wont to sing [in German] in Church." He offers a sample of ten such reworkings-in-Hebrew, Psalms 47, 130, 121, 128, 131, 133, 134, 100, 117, and 23, all with musical notes and, beneath the title, the opening of the German "original" to which his Hebrew was a contrafact. Thus, Psalm 121, "Mein Augen ich 'gen Berg aussricht":

אשא עיני אל ההרים
מאין עזרי בוא
כי האמנתי לו
עזרי מעם האלהים
אשר עשה שמים
וארץ וכל מים

אל יתן למוט רגליך
יראה בטובה
יציל מכל דבה
ואל ינום שומרך
לא ינום ולא יישן
שמר ישראל עולם

It is not recorded whether the project was ever put into practice. It was in any case an ingenious idea, and managed with some skill, although the rhyme of the last-cited couplet, *yišan-ʿolam*, could not but have caused the most sympathetic eyebrow to raise.

Surely the most scholarly treatment of biblical rhyme was that prepared by Jean Le Clerc (Johannes Clericus), a well-known biblical critic of the late seventeenth and early eighteenth century. It was published first in French in *La Bibliothèque universelle* in 1688,[98] and later translated into Latin and included in Le Clerc's *Veteris Testamenti Prophetae.*[99] The author begins by arguing that it is not in the nature of Semitic languages to create a truly metrical poetry (in

97. J. Alstedus, *Templum Musicum* (London, 1664), pp. 3–4.
98. *Bibliothèque universelle* 9 (Paris, 1688), p. 219.
99. J. Clericus, *Veteris Testamenti Prophetae* (Amsterdam, 1731), 2, pp. 621–32.

the Bedean sense),[100] because they are ill suited to distinguishing between long and short syllables. Moreover, Hebrew, because word order is fixed by such features as noun constructs, does not have the flexibility necessary for metrical compositions. Therefore, there is no sense in looking for a Greco-Latin-style metrical system.

On the other hand, rhyme is extraordinarily easy in Hebrew. Le Clerc points out that rhyme is favored in poetry of other Semites, and mentions the three classes of rhyme in medieval Hebrew.[101] It is only natural to conclude that it might then have had some place in biblical poetry as well. However, two factors have helped to obscure its existence. The first is that biblical poetry has no set number of syllables per line, because it is, after all, a very primitive stage of poetry:

> Rarely are the verses of equal length. Obviously, the Hebrews care little about this matter: where two verses of the same length spontaneously occurred, of course they did not refuse them but neither did they actively seek such an equivalence. This shows that their poetry was not of the most elegant.[102]

The second is that the Bible's concept of rhyme was somewhat freer than that of later poetry: thus, in Psalm 1 one finds *yehgeh* rhyming with *palgei,* and *mišpāṭ* with *ʿădat*.[103] No wonder that, as the conventions of rhyme tightened up and true *numerus*, the measuring of syllabic equivalence, entered world poetry, the more flexible and primitive system of the Bible was overlooked. It was ignorance of the Hebrew language, Le Clerc says, that led the Jews Josephus and Philo to attribute hexameter meters to biblical songs—ignorance and perhaps also a desire to please the Gentiles.[104]

Le Clerc gives various illustrations of biblical rhyme, including the "rhyming" section of Psalm 2 mentioned by earlier commentators (including Flacius):

---

100. An argument he borrows from Scaliger, see below.

101. On which see Pagis, חידוש ומסורת, pp. 125–7; also see E. Goldenberg in *Leshonenu* 38 (1974): 86–87.

102. Le Clerc, *VT Prophetae*, p. 624.

103. In connection with this last rhyme, it is to be noted that Le Clerc says the Jews consider it a license to rhyme in medieval poetry with two words that sound the same but end in different letters, such as *sukkah* and *ṣuqah*. Now this is the example seen above in Archivolti's ערוגת הבשם, p. 102b. It is interesting that Archivolti's second example, *massah–maṣṣah* is not cited—perhaps he did not know of the Italian pronunciation of *ṣadi*.

104. Le Clerc, *VT Prophetae*, p. 630.

Eth mosrotheMO
Venaschlica mimmennou abotheMO
Joscheb baschamajim jischAK
Adonai jilAG
LaMO
Az jedabber eleMO
Baappho oubacharono jebahaleMO

The fact that the unusual suffix "MO" replaces the more normal -*HEM* indicates, Le Clerc says, that rhyme was cultivated and not accidental (here he is apparently arguing against Buxtorf's treatise); the same is proven by the use of rare words and forms not found elsewhere in the biblical poetry corpus (Abravanel had advanced precisely the same argument to support his metrical theory in Exod. 15). He also cites Psalm 150 as a fine "brief" example of rhyme. Acknowledging Cappelus's misgivings about the accuracy of Masoretic vocalization,[105] Le Clerc says there may be many other rhymes whose existence is obscured by artificial differences in the vowel points; nevertheless, enough evidence exists to leave no doubt about the role of rhyme as the sole structural element in biblical poetry. Elsewhere, Le Clerc gave a still more impressive demonstration of biblical rhyme, dividing up Deuteronomy 32 according to its true units;[106] here is the beginning:

1.   Haazinu haššamaim vaadabbɛrah
                    vetišmaʕ
                haarez imrɛ pi
     2.   jaʕrop cammatar likḥi
              tizzal caṭṭal imrathi;
                   cisʕirim
     ʕalɛ deše, vecirbibim
ʕalɛ ʕɛseb.   3.   ci šem jahovoh
                ekra; habu
            godel l'elohenu.
        4.   hazzur tamim poʕalo,
     ci col deracau mišpat, ɛl
            emunah veɛn avel;
          zaddik vejašar hu.

(About lineation, at least, he had much to teach William Carlos Williams.) Le Clerc's theory did gain some admirers, but eventually it

---

105. See below.
106. This does not appear in the Latin version of this treatise; the version cited here is reprinted from F. Hare's *Psalmorum Liber* (London, 1736), 2, p. 834.

was noticed that *any* part of the Bible can be made to rhyme as well as
the Psalms or Deuteronomy 32. (It is interesting that this was a
sufficient proof of its falsity—that this observation led no one to
contend that the whole Bible was poetry.[107] For the notion that only
the so-called metrical books of Job, Proverbs, and Psalms, plus the
canticles and possibly other books of the hagiographia, *could* be
poetry, was an article of faith until Lowth's *Lectures*. Louis Cappel
used the same argument to refute Gomarus's metrical scheme; see
below.) Thus, T. Edwards's *Psalms* (1755) observed:

> If it be considered that, according to [Le Clerc's] hypothesis, the
> historical as well as poetical parts of the old testament may be
> reduced into rhyme, this most evidently shews it to be entirely
> visionary [i.e., illusory]: which would still farther appear, were the
> learned reader to consult a specimen of it, at the end of Bishop
> Hare's Psalms in which, (not to mention that some of the verses are
> so far from rhyming to each other, that there is not the least
> similitude of sound in the last syllables) he will soon, very soon be
> convinced, that the rhymes are not the inspired Poet's, but Le
> Clerc's.[108]

With that, the whole idea of rhyme in the Bible was dismissed as
"evidently fantastical," and rightly so. Yet, before leaving the subject,
it is well worth meditating on the similarity between the theory of
biblical rhyme and the overall notion that biblical "poetry" must have
some *system* comparable to those familiar to us from our own poetry.
Present-day metrical theory, less absurd than rhyme on the face of it,
shares this same premise and proceeds in the same manner, viz., by
looking at the conventions of our own poetry and seeking equivalents
in the Bible. And so it has always been. It is noteworthy that the idea
of biblical rhyme appeared among the Jews at a time when they used
rhyme in their own poems; Christian commentators took up this theme
when rhyme became established as a respectable feature of their
(vernacular) poetry. What rhyme *was* was always defined by the
conventions of the theorists' own poetry, conventions that, as we have
seen, changed from time to time and place to place. So too in metrical
hypotheses: those advanced by Josephus and the early Church
followed the metrical conventions of classical Greek and Latin.
When, with the Renaissance, other poetic systems began to be

107. As, for example, the metricist E. Sievers was to argue in the early part of this
century, and later, Arvid Bruno.
108. T. Edwards, *Psalms* (Cambridge, 1755), p. 4.

legitimated in Italian, French, and English poetry, the vernacular poets argued that it was not within the capacity of their tongues to distinguish between long and short syllables, and hence that there was no profit in trying to impose the classical system on their languages.[109] And soon, emboldened by the force of this analogy, biblical critics began to say the same thing about the meter of the Bible.

6

Two important figures in the movement away from Jerome's metrical pronouncements have already been seen, the Italians Steuchus and Marianus Victorius. Quite apart from what they said about rhyme, they were influential in suggesting that Hebrew poetry was *simpler* than Latin or Greek, and that like Italian it depended solely on the number of syllables per line without any measuring of long and short syllables. (Support for this view was later sought in what Jerome had said about substituting feet "not of the same syllables, but of the same times," and his attributing of *rhythmus* to Job).[110] For a time, biblical critics seemed to hesitate between these new notions and the old orthodoxy. Robert Bellarmino, in his brief *Institutiones Linguae Hebraeicae* (1580) simply says that biblical poetics are "unknown."[111] Similarly, the Tremellius-Junius Bible (1575–79), mentioned earlier, describes biblical songs as *rythmici,* that is, confined to "numbers" (*numerus*), but does not describe the system further. Jean Le Mercier (Mercerus; d. 1570), in his commentary on Job, observes:

109. There were nevertheless attempts, in the sixteenth century and even after, to write "quantitative" verse in Italian, French, and English, and (a concomitant of this) debates about the fitness of rhyme in these languages. See Wimsatt and Brooks, *Literary Criticism*, pp. 158–59.

110. Marianus Victorius, in a comment on Jerome's Epistle 113 (in his *Epistolae Hieronymi*, p. 620), seems to support Jerome's metrical claims with his own experience. In relation to Jerome's assertion that "they are hexameters," Victorius remarks: "If anyone were to experiment seriously and in keeping with Jerome's rules, he would find, *as I myself have found*, that what he says is really true, namely that there are in Job hexameter verses of Spondee, Dactyl, and other feet, such as the Trochee, Iamb, and Proceleumaticum. For the system contained in them is not one of syllables, but of times, so that two short syllables are put in place of one long one. Now that a Proceleumaticum, which is four shorts, may be put in place of a Dactyl, which consists of one long and two shorts, everyone knows; which is done with a Spondee in quite the same system in Job." Note, however, that Victorius, while seeming to restate and support Jerome, actually claims the *system* is different, i.e., that it is based on "times" and *not* syllables.

111. R. Bellarmino, *Institutiones Linguae Hebraicae* (Coloniae, 1580), p. 127.

According to Jerome, this book is written as poetry from the third chapter to the fifth verse of the last chapter, in (as he notes) hexameter verses which run with dactyl and spondee and which because of the particular character of the language, also occasionally accept other feet as well, not of the same number of syllables, but of other times [*sic*]. Meanwhile, a sweet *rythmus* and a jingling (he says) are carried with the numbers of the feet set free,[112] all of which metricists will understand more than the simple reader. . . . We have not yet been able to discover it. Certain it is that meters exist, although their system is unknown to us, as indeed to the Hebrews today, just as the system of the Psalms, the Lamentations of Jeremiah, Proverbs, and the other songs of Scripture are unknown. Surely the system of accents [*ṭe'amim*] of this book [Job] is different from that of the twenty-one [prose] books (along with the Psalter and Proverbs, which three books are represented in the symbol אמ"ת), except for the first two chapters, and from the sixth verse of the last chapter, which are written in prose.

On Job 3:1 he adds:

I have tried, according to Jerome's prescriptions, to rearrange many verses into feet, and measuring many I have found them to be hexameters, in which, however, there do occur here and there other feet in place of dactyl and spondee, according to the language's manner of speaking, as Jerome said; many are spondaic verses, as the first for example, which ends *hora gaber,* "a male is conceived." But this is often disturbed by the fact that rather frequently the metrical lines begin from the end of the verses as they are divided up by the Hebrews, by which fact it appears that they [the scribes] had not figured out the system of the songs, unless they had purposely followed the sense more than the metrical arrangement.

I have heard it said that D. Vatable[113] of blessed memory had figured out the system of the verses of Job and the Psalter, and had set down certain rules to facilitate an understanding of their system, to wit, that there are no rules of position[114] in Hebrew, and that a Schewa, even when doubled, is not to be counted for anything; and other things of this sort, which one day we hope will be brought out. Nor do I despair that, should someone diligently set himself to the

112. *Numeris pedum solutis.* This variant of "numeris lege metri solutis" had often been transmitted as Jerome's words before the edition of Marianus Victorius.
113. François Vatable (ca. 1490–1547), French biblical commentator.
114. I.e., lengthening a short vowel because of its position before a consonant cluster.

task, the system of these meters might be found. I myself shall try to look into this question if time permits. For here is a wonderful elegance and richness of expression. He curses the day of his birth, repeating *the same idea* with different words and remarkable poetic figures.[115]

In Le Mercier's words one can read the misgivings produced by the clash of two apparently authoritative traditions, Jerome on the one hand and the *ṭe'amim* and scribal traditions, plus the more recent writings of medieval and Renaissance Jewish scholars, on the other. But there is the new hesitant voice of science as well, the commentator trying to test the conclusions of authority by his own experience and unwilling to accept any scansion simply because others have asserted it to be true.

The same experimental spirit may be read in an attempt by Andreas Masius (1514–73) to make sense of Joshua 10:12, which he knew from the *Mekhilta* (via the Joshua commentary of R. David Kimhi) to be one of the Ten Songs[116] sung at different key points in Israel's history:

> Now, the very fact that Kimhi is so uncertain as to whether or not the words cited are those of the song shows in what ignorance of their own language the Jews of today are cast, and how they have

---

115. "Verbis commutatis & insignibus figuris Poeticis eandem sententiam iterans." Ioannis Merceri, *Comentarii in Iobum, et Salomonis Proverbia, Ecclesiastes, Canticum Canticorum* (Lugduni Batavorum, 1551), preface and p. 19. Emphasis added.

116. See chapter 3, n. 91. Radak, noting the targum "And so Joshua *praised* . . .," observes: "Perhaps after the prayer came the song, but the text did not cite the song; or else the song is: 'And the sun was still . . .' and the prayer was 'And he said in the presence of all Israel, Sun of Gibeon be still!' . . . This song is mentioned among the Ten Songs, and the expression 'And he spoke' implies song and not prayer, as in 'And David spoke to the Lord the words of this song' (2 Sam. 22:1)." The midrashic association of this passage with "song" is found in Midrash Tanhuma, פ' אחרי מות, par. 14 (Buber edition, repr. Jerusalem, 1964, p. 34b). The "peg" for this assertion is the word אז ("then"), which also introduces the Song of the Sea (Exod. 15). However, the fifth Oxford manuscript catalogued by Buber also adduces the connection of וידבר ("spoke") with 2 Sam. 22:1. Josh. 10:13 implies that more details are to be found in the mysterious ספר הישר. The midrashic compilation by that name contains a rousing hymn in the appropriate place, written in biblical style. For a discussion of that compilation and a hypothesis about its date, see Y. Dan, קרית ספר 49 (1973–74): 242–44, and Y. Dan, ספר הישר in לשאלת דפוס נאפולי של ספר הישר, and Y. Dan, ספר הישר מתי התחבר in ספר רב סרן (Jerusalem, 1977), pp. 105–10.

not the slightest discernment about it. For there can be no doubting or quibbling over the fact that these words are bound to numbers (*numeris*) and transcribed from the Book of the Just. These are the words I mean:

שמש בגבעון דום וירח בעמק אילון

And again these:

וידם השמש וירח עמד עד יקם גוי איביו
ויעמד השמש בחצי השמים ולא אץ לבוא כיום תמים

Now the very type of speech and the construction of the words immediately declares itself in the most apparent way. However, whether it pertains to the numbers of individual syllables, and measures, or times, I scarcely know if there is anyone today with sufficient knowledge of these matters in Hebrew to say: perhaps in the age of Saint Jerome the study of these matters and their art had not yet utterly disappeared. This appears not only from the writings of that most saintly man, but also from the Deuterosis [i.e., rabbinic writings]. For this type of Hebrew learning was also written down almost in the same period in which Jerome flourished, or indeed somewhat later. For in that tractate entitled *Masseket soferim* [it says that] the words of those songs which occur here and there in the sacred history are, not a few of them, restored in their right status according to a system of measurement (*mensurae ratione*), whereas previously they had been written down in a confused jumble by scribes, as they are to this day in our own books. I myself (for why should I not confess my own curiosity?) have devoted no small effort toward discovering this matter, but in vain. For without a guide I find myself unable to perceive anything sufficiently certain about the numbers of the Hebrew syllables, and hence about the measures and arrangements of the verses. But surely my own ability is not sufficiently sharp and incisive; why should others be frightened off by my example? Indeed, let me not hide such insight—but why should I call it insight? nay, such vague impression—as I have been able to gather concerning these three verses which I just cited. I seem to sense in them those numbers by which our own iambic tetrameter acatalectic, as we call it, is bound, if only in the first verse, we write *haššemeš* and *wĕhayyārēăḥ* and in the third *šemeš* and *šāmayîm* are placed with the letter *he* set aside, such as the many scribal errors which even the Hebrew Doctors in the aforementioned tractate remarked upon.

Now if in my hypothesis and conjecture I have strayed far from the truth, the reader ought rightly to forgive me; for I have not said these things arrogantly, nor do I hold them to be certain.[117]

Masius is still willing to credit Jerome's quantitative orientation, but the fact that Jerome never attributed a meter to this passage left him free to try his own hand (note that he is convinced by the "construction of the words" that this is poetry; that and the fact that it is listed among the Ten Songs). Here also we see what has never ceased to be the recourse of metrical theorists in the face of a recalcitrant text: proposed emendation.

Even in his rejection of Jewish learning, Masius's words are revealing, for it is Jewish tradition that has put him on his search for the system of this song in the first place. So in the other commentators seen, the gradual centering of the metrical search on the so-called *Libri Metrici* of Job, Proverbs, and the Psalter is telling. Valentinus Schindler noted, in his Hebrew grammar of this same period, "The ancient system of Hebrew songs, used in Psalms, Proverbs, and Job, is today unknown."[118]

Henricus Mollerus, in his commentary on the Psalter, suggested (as Abravanel had) that with the loss of the ancient Hebrew music also disappeared the system of Hebrew poetry. Having mentioned the former, he notes:

> Here the readers ought to be instructed about the sorts of poems in Hebrew, but as we noted earlier, nothing certain of this matter is to be found among suitable authors. . . . Josephus . . . mentions the hexameter which Moses used in his ode after the Exodus of the Israelites from Egypt and bears witness to Pharoah's downfall. But this type of meter in no way corresponds to the system which is in use in Greek and Latin.[119]

As if *par acquit de conscience* he goes on to cite Jerome and the other *auctores,* but concludes: "However, fixed laws by which these verses are to be read neither Jerome nor those who followed him were able to demonstrate, since they did not know the system of the music. Therefore let us abandon this obscure and unresolved subject in the middle."

The uncertainty of these sixteenth-century commentators turned

---

117. Andreas Masius, *Iosuae Imperatoris Historia* (Antwerp, 1574), pp. 185–86.

118. Schindler, *Institutionum Hebraicorum*, p. 320.

119. Henricus Mollerus, *Ennarationes Psalmorum Davidis* (Geneva, 1591), preface (unpaged).

into out-and-out denial with the publication of J. J. Scaliger's commentary on Eusebius's *Thesaurus Temporum*, which first appeared in 1606. Jerome's introduction, it will be recalled, had asked that famous question, "What is more poetic than the Psalter, which in the manner of our Flaccus and the Greek Pindar now runs with an iamb [etc.]." In response to which Scaliger wrote:

Perhaps those who never read Pindar, nor know what Iambic, Alcaic, or Sapphic meter is, shall believe that the poetry of Pindar runs with Iambic, Alcaic or Sapphic meter; and you may read the same thing [by Jerome] in the Preface to Job. I am more amazed by what he says about the Psalter, for neither in it nor in Lamentations is there any poetry confined by metrical laws, but it is pure prose, albeit animated by a poetic character. The speech of Isaiah and the other prophets is likewise sometimes figurative, in the manner of poetry, but it cannot properly be called poetry for all that. Only the Canticle of Moses at the end of Deuteronomy, the Proverbs of Solomon, and almost all the book of Job are bound by some requirement of *rythmus,* which *rythmus* is like two iambic dimeters and jingles [*tinnulus accidit*—Jerome's word in his Job preface] in the ears. But sometimes they are of fewer syllables and sometimes more, like the Greeks *stichoi katalektikoi, brachykatelektikoi, hypermetroi*—not that any compensation is made *kat' isochronion* [according to the same time, i.e., the principle of substitution], as is customary in Greek, for this cannot be expressed by the special character of Hebrew; but however the meaning dictates, the verse is now longer in numbers (*rythmis*), now shorter.

For *rythmus*, as the learned Bede had gathered from the writings of Marius Victorinus, Augustine, and others, is a "measured arrangement of words similar to metrical poetry, but ordered not by a metrical system but by the number of syllables as discerned by the ears"—such as, he says, are the songs of vernacular poets. And "while rhythm can exist without meter, meter without rhythm cannot be." . . .

Thus the book of Job, and the Proverbs of Solomon, are simply *rythmus* and not a metrical arrangement; in them, most of the verses are two iambic dimeters, sometimes three dipodies, sometimes indeed there is a marked inequality, so that they follow not even the rule of *rythmus*. For in Hebrew, Syriac, Arabic and Abyssinian no type of meter is conceivable, no one can produce it, for the nature of the language will not allow it. Therefore, his statement in the Preface to Job that "the verses of this book are hexameters . . . [etc.] also accepting other feet not of the same number of syllables but of the same times . . . " is without support. We deny such to be the case in this book: on the contrary, we say there are not even meters, but merely something like meter.[120]

Somewhat later, Scaliger fixes on the (by then well known) contradiction in Jerome's metrical ascriptions:

"All of which consist of Pentameters and Hexameters. . . " But in his Epistle to Paula Urbica he describes as Tetrameter what here he calls Hexameter. But, as we have already said, the verses of Job and of Solomon are dipodies, or like two dimeters, but sometimes cut short and sometimes lengthened, however the meaning dictates. For meaning is governed by meter, but *rythmus* is governed by meaning, and for this reason a metrical line will never exceed its rule, but *rythmus* does exceed when the meaning so dictates. Therefore, it is so far from being the case that a Hexameter or Pentameter line may be found in the holy Bible, that their lines are composed not even of [a constant] *rythmus*, but the *rythmus* is now lengthened or shortened to express the meaning.[121]

The Renaissance willingness to read Pindar as a completely untamed poet not only opened the way for Scaliger's attack on Jerome's authority but supplied the analogy to Hebrew. For like Pindar, the poet David did not use meter; if the Psalms are ornamented with figures such as are found in poetry, the same might be said of Isaiah and the other prophets, but no one maintains that those books are poetry! Scaliger also invokes the Bedean distinction between *rhythmus* and *metrum* to differentiate Hebrew and classical poetry. *Rhythmus,* although he allows that it does not consist in precise numbers, obviously implies some rough limits to Scaliger, for he twice asserts that biblical poetry sometimes does not even keep within a *rhythmus*.

It is difficult to know how much of all this is Scaliger's own innovation. Obviously he was familiar with Steuchus and Marianus Victorius (indeed, in a passage not cited Scaliger compares leonine verses with Jewish poetry). His inclusion of Proverbs within the poetic canon, and perhaps as well his exclusion of Lamentations, may be a reflection of the special *ṭe'amim*. Yet he denies that the Psalter is poetry! The supremacy of meaning over meter in the Bible was Samuel ibn Tibbon's theme, and the "now longer, now shorter" lines is a description that may ultimately come (via Genebrardus?) from ibn

---

120. J. J. Scaliger, "Animadversiones in Prologum Hieronymi," in *Thesaurus Temporum Eusebii* (Amsterdam, 1658), 2, pp. 607.
121. Ibid., p. 7.

Habib. But he seems to have no firsthand knowledge of medieval Hebrew poetry, seeming to claim that no Semitic language can have a quantitative meter. Elsewhere he asserts that the Jews nowadays write poems that are purely *rythmi*, plus "another type, in which the system depends not on the number of the syllables but on the similarity of the ending,"[122] an apparent allusion to *maqāma*.

The influence of this passage, doubtless due as much to the overall scholarly reputation of the *Scaligeri* as to its particular claim, was in any case enormous. Few other writers followed its estimation of the Psalms as "pure prose" (on Vossius see below); but the distinction between meter and rhythm so strongly drawn here became a touchstone for later scholars, and an important legitimation of the system of vernacular poetry.

Nevertheless, the quantitative approach was far from dead. In 1632 Francis Gomarus published a learned treatise, *Davidis Lyra,* which laid out in painstaking detail dozens of different sorts of feet and arrangements of feet that were possible in the Bible, a system whose extraordinary complexity was, far from a defect, evidence of its composers' genius.[123] Somewhat later (1699), Marc Meibomius advanced another quantitative system, whose reliance on frequent textual emendation, coupled with the author's insistence on the role of Divine inspiration in his own discovery, dampened the reception accorded him by his contemporaries.[124]

Gomarus's system, applauded at first, was resoundingly put down by the Hebraist Louis Cappel (Ludovigus Cappelus) in 1643. Actually Cappel had stated a strongly antiquantitative position even before Gomarus's book, in a work on Hebrew vowel-points called סור הנקור הנגלה, *hoc est Arcanum Punctationis Revelatum* (1624). Here he had entered what was then a raging debate among Christian scholars, the question of the antiquity of the vocalization and *ṭe'amim* of the Hebrew text. Following the position stated by Elijah Levita (Bahur) in his prose introduction to *Massoret hamassoret* (1538),[125]

---

122. Ibid.

123. See on this n. 73 above for article of I. Baroway, "Davidis Lyra."

124. See, e.g., *Le Journal des sçavans* (1699), p. 4161: "M. Meibomius prétend que depuis deux milles ans nul autre que lui n'a sçu la Poétique des Hébreus sur laquelle il appuie les corrections qu'il a faites au texte original de l'Ecriture: dans son Epître à tous les Princes Chrétiens de l'Europe il propose une nouvelle Traduction des Livres saints, dont il donne ici un essai . . . il se vante d'avoir découvert par une inspiration divine l'ancienne Poésie Hébraique."

125. An English translation may be found in C. D. Ginsburg, *Jacob ben Chajim ibn Adonijah's Introduction . . . and the Massoreth he-Massoreth* (1867; reprinted

Cappel argued that the vowel-points were a relatively recent invention, and did not exist in biblical times. What then, he asks, of Jerome's pronouncements concerning the quantitative measures of Hebrew poetry?

> I do not deny the Hebrews their poetry; the sacred canticles extant in the Scriptures argue its existence. But although they have their poems, it is not necessary that there be long and short syllables. For nowadays the French, Italians, Spaniards, English, Germans etc. have their own poetry, and that most elegant too, which however does not recognize the distinction between long and short syllables. Ought not the same system to be possible in Hebrew?[126]

He went on to cite the passage from Steuchus seen above. Yet in his estimate of Jerome's statements, Cappel was, given his own views, rather charitable:

> The fact that Jerome said that some of the Psalms of David and the canticles of Jeremiah, Moses and Solomon consist of iambic and Sapphic poetry ought to be properly understood and treated with generous interpretation. For even if someone torture himself almost to death with twisting and turning these verses around, he will never manage to get them into Iambics and Sapphics as regards the quantity of the syllables, if the latter is judged from the two-fold classification of longs and shorts whereby the longs are *kametz* etc. and the shorts *patah* etc. But in regard to the number of feet and syllables there were no true Iambs or Sapphics, for in these songs the poetic arrangement (*numerus*) was not the same as in Iambic and Sapphic poetry, unless this should happen quite by chance— which in our vernacular French, Italian, Spanish etc. poetry can also sometimes happen, yet no one would say that French and Italian poetry is, properly speaking, Iambic or Sapphic verse, or

---

New York, 1968), pp. 102–43. As Ginsburg points out in his introduction, the idea that the vowel-points and *ţe'amim* were not of ancient origin had been stated before Baḥur (se pp. 44–48), but never so clearly and with such authority. Publicized in the Latin translation of Sebastian Muenster, Baḥur's view touched off a major controversy among Christian and Jewish commentators. He was opposed by Azariah dei Rossi, whose views were largely taken over by Johannes Buxtorf I; it was then Cappel who sallied forth againt Buxtorf. On Levita and Cappelus see G. Weil, *Elie Lévita* (Leiden, 1963), p. 315; P. G. Schneidermann, *Die Controverse des Ludovicus Cappelus mit den Buxtorfen* (Leipzig, 1879).

126. L. Cappel, *Arcanum Punctationis Revelatum* (ed. Th. Erpenius; Lugduni Batavorum, 1624), p. 96.

that the French and Italians recognize in their poetry long and short syllables in the Greek or Latin manner.

Jerome called these verses Iambic and Sapphic because they bear the outward appearance and look of Iambic and Sapphic poetry, if we consider the number of the syllables and the anastrophes and the epanodos [i.e., inversions in the normal word order and repetition in different forms], both of which are conspicuous in the Horatian Odes, although (as I have said) they will not be found to correspond to true Iambics and Sapphics, as will be made apparent to anyone who tries. Therefore, Jerome did not say "truly Sapphic," but "quasi-Sapphic poetry," for he doubtless saw that it was not the same type of poetry.

And indeed, how could the poetry of the Hebrews correspond to that of the Latins and Greeks in numbers or the system of meter that pertains thereto, if (as the Grammarians have it) the Hebrews, in addition to long and short syllables, also recognize the very short or seized[127] vowels which Greek and Latin know not at all? Surely this type of syllable or vowel which is, according to the opinion of these same Grammarians, peculiar to Hebrew, makes it impossible for the same system of poetic meter to exist in Hebrew as in Latin and Greek.[128]

This last argument goes back to the days when Menahem b. Saruq and his students opposed the imposition of Arabic meters onto Hebrew on the grounds that a binary quantitative system failed to capture distinctions possible in the (ternary) Massoretic vocalization. But Cappel's reasoning here is rather all-inclusive; according to Steuchus, biblical poetry is not quantitative at all; and *even if it were,* the three classes of Hebrew vowels (long, short, and very short) show clearly that biblical meter could not possibly be the same as classical. So obviously is this the case that Jerome could not possibly have meant that biblical poetry was iambic, he was only focusing on a general surface resemblance between Horace's poetry and parts of the Psalter.

The vowel-points have nothing to do with the meter, Cappel further argued: one certainly could not say they were included in the text from biblical times so as to teach the people the proper reading of biblical poetry, for they are recorded "no less scrupulously and exactly" in the historical books, which are clearly prose.[129] Moreover, if they had

127. That is, *ḥaṭaf.*
128. Cappel, *Arcanum*, pp. 97–98.
129. Ibid., p. 100.

anything to do with meter, then the system of Hebrew poetry would have long ago been found:

> For when we know the quantity of the syllables of a given poem, when we have the beginning and the end of individual verses, it is impossible that we should be ignorant of the system, arrangement, artifice and structure of those verses. For wherein might the structure and artifice of a given song be observed, save in a set sequence and order and number of the long and short syllables? This sequence, this order and number cannot be unknown or ambiguous if the long and short syllables are marked, and the beginning and end of individual verses are apparent and sure. Yet with one voice all the Hebrew grammarians of today, Jews and Christians alike, say they do not know the system and structural arrangement of the sacred poetry contained in the Psalms, Canticles, and metrical books.[130]

Cappel went on to cite ibn Habib (via Buxtorf I) to the effect that only the number of syllables is important in biblical meter, and that while there are cases of numerical equivalence, there are many other lines in which one verse-half is markedly longer or shorter. Lest one argue that the beginnings and ends of verses in the Bible are unclear and not faithfully recorded by the tradition, he advances the case of the alphabetical psalms (he names only 111, 112, 119, and 145), the four first chapters of Lamentations and the end of Proverbs: here surely there can be no doubt about lineation, yet "the system and arrangement of these poems is no more marked than in the other metrical writings."[131]

Following the same line of reasoning, Cappel later argued that the *ṭe'amim* were also of recent origin—not in them was to be sought the organizing system of Hebrew songs, as for example ha-Levi had urged in the *Kuzari*. Thus, in the end, Cappel had no solution of his own to put forward; but his immense erudition in regard to the Masoretic punctuation, and later in his attack on Gomarus (*Animadversiones in novam Davidis Lyram,* 1643), were an important contribution to the discussion.

Cappel was opposed in almost every matter by Matthew Wasmuth (1625–88), who defended the antiquity of the vowel-points and the *ṭe'amim*. He showed that the special *ṭe'amim* of Job, Proverbs, and the Psalms parallel those of the "prose" system in their parsing

---

130. Ibid., p. 101.
131. Ibid., p. 101–02.

function. For this reason, he rejected the idea that the *ṭe'amim* were a musical notation invented by later Jews; for if so, he asked, why does the recitation of the Sephardim differ so markedly from that of the Ashkenazim, and why does one find precisely the same *ṭe'amim* (he compares those of Psalm 66:8 with those of Job 3:8) used for a jubilant exclamation and a droning dirge?[132] No, there is no historic connection between synagogue music and the accents: "Their singing is no more set up to the system of accents than once was the braying of Balaam's ass, which is assigned the very same accents."[133] On the contrary, the *ṭe'amim,* like the vowel-points, are of ancient provenance; but, as the word *ṭa'am* ("sense") itself argues, their original function had nothing to do with music, still less with meter—they were a system of parsing the Bible into sense units. Curiously, this brought him to state a position very close to Cappel's on the question of biblical poetry's structure:

> The Metrical Books, or אמת, which are תהלים Psalms, משלי שלמה the Proverbs of Solomon, & איוב Job ... are popularly called metrical, although they have no poetic meter (unless this occur by chance), nor do they have a specific musical system, but consist for the most part of brief *sententiae* and verses, for which reason the accents *(ṭe'amim)* are arranged in different ranking of function or dignity and which follows a system other than that of the prosaic books.[134]

The matter of the *ṭe'amim* illustrates how many different areas of study were affected by the question of biblical poetry's *ratio*, and why, as a consequence, scholars from many disciplines turned their attention to it. G. J. Vossius, in a treatise on poetry, *De Artis Poeticae Natura ac Constitutione* (1647) adopted a position similar to Scaliger's in order to argue that biblical poetry represented a primitive stage of poetic art, not a full quantitative meter, but only *rhythmus* "hoc est, syllabarum numerus, non quantitas, attenditur."[135] This in turn served his claim that poetry, like mankind itself, had originally come to Europe from the East. (He goes on to derive the names of

132. Matthias Wasmuth, *Vindiciae S. Habraeae Scripturae* (Rostochii, 1664), pp. 365–66.

133. Ibid., p. 368.

134. M. Wasmuth, *Institutio Methodica Accentuationis Hebraicae* (Lipsia, 1694), p. 14.

135. G. J. Vossius, *De Artis Poeticae Natura ac Constitutione* (Amsterdam, 1647), p. 77.

Linus, Musaeus, and Orpheus[136] from, respectively, Hebrew *helin,*
musar, and Arabic *'arifa,* and claims they were not the names of
ancient poets, but types of poetry.) Thus the idea that the Bible
counted syllables but not quantities was now fitted into an evolutionary view of poetic art, while at the same time—in Vossius, and in
others—the resemblance of the biblical "system" to that of European
languages reflected favorably on the latter and fueled, as we have
seen, the enterprise of devotional poetry.

An argument parallel to Vossius's was made a few years later, by a
Catholic writer, Athanasius Kircher,[137] who wished to show that
music too had originated among the Hebrews, who subsequently
taught it to the Greeks. He attributes to the *ṭe'amim* a musical
function[138] while conceding their parsing function, "so that you might
know where to suspend the breath, where to distinguish a verse, place
a comma, where you ought to put a pause, where a verse ends and
begins, what ought to be pronounced slower and what faster." About
meter (and rhyme) he repeated the current wisdom:

> Therefore I say that one ought not to think that the hexameter,
> trimeter, and sapphic verses of the Hebrews are of the same sort as
> our own poets' songs, or consist of the same quality or quantity or
> arrangement of feet, for the arrangement, location and order of the
> feet is different. Inasmuch as the poetry of the Hebrews is so old,
> often amid the dactyls and the spondees it accepts other feet as
> well, while at the same time the order of the places in which feet are
> normally put amongst us is likewise varied . . . [He then cites
> Jerome's *non earundem syllabarum*]. Moreover I should say that
> the Hebrews customarily placed, contrary to our own poets'
> practice, somewhat unusual rhythms [*rythmos*] in their songs, such
> as the ordinary reader is unable to understand, but only one highly
> skilled in metrical art. For surely not as amongst us do individual
> types of *rythmus* keep the same number of syllables and the same
> endings of the lines, as we showed in our Panglossia Musurgica.
> Nor indeed did the Hebrews employ this type of poetry without
> system (*sine ratione*): but in most marvellous fashion were they
> capable of exciting all kinds of emotions in the minds of men, as is
> obvious from the Psalms of David, who with his poems created
> wondrous and almost unbelievable effects.[139]

136. Reckoned at this time to be Greece's three most ancient poets. Sometimes
Musaeus is said to be the son of Linus.
137. Athanasius Kircherus, *Musurgia Universalis* (Rome, 1650).
138. Ibid., p. 63.
139. Ibid.

Thus, by the end of the seventeenth century, there was virtually no one willing to defend Jerome's metrical statements about the Bible without qualification. Some, like Cappel, gave Jerome's statements a broad and approximate validity; others, like Scaliger, denied he had even understood Pindar properly. Other quantitative systems had been advanced, most notably that of Gomarus, but by and large the notion of a more simple *numerus*, based solely on syllable count (and that only approximate, "according to the ear's judgment," and so forth) held the field. This was the much-cited opinion of ibn Habib, and was further bolstered by the analogy between vernacular poetry and the Bible, and by the evolutionary view of music and poetics just seen.

It was, above all, a question that no biblical scholar could rightly overlook, for in addition to its intrinsic interest, it was connected to the debate on the vowel-points and *ṭe'amim* (hence to the authenticity of the text), to Bible translation and vernacular psalm-singing, to the relation of biblical to classical literature, and to the whole issue of poetry in the Renaissance. Indeed, we have scarcely cited all the opinions advanced by critics in this period.[140] While some concluded that, since "among the learned they can scarcely agree on this matter, the reader ought not tire himself further with this hardly useful toil,"[141] the debate continued to be renewed.

It was no doubt frustration at finding a workable answer to the metrical crux that led to Le Clerc's fantastic exposition of biblical rhyme, and the same sort of frustration underlies the last major treatment of biblical poetry before Lowth, the metrical system of Francis Hare, bishop of Chichester.[142] Hare begins his eighty-three page dissertation by summarizing the difficulties in past critical approaches, and in an appendix he attacks at length the systems of Le Clerc and Marc Meibomius;[143] yet he seems to misapprehend the sense of the earlier distinction of the period between *metrum* and *rhythmus*, claiming that the Hebrew line "depends on the number of

---

140. Note these other treatises: Theodorus Herbert (Ebertus) (d. 1630), *De Poetica hebraica*; Samuel Bohlius (d. 1639), *Dissertatio de Accentibus*; Ludovicus de Dieu (1519–1652), *Animadversiones ad Vetus Testamentum*; Hugo Grotius (1583–1645), *Commentarium in Novum Testamentum* (re. Luke 1:46); Andre Rivet (Rivetus) (1573–1651), *Psalmi*; A. Calovius (1612–1686), *Prolegomenon in Genesin* and *Ad Lamentationes Praefatio*.

141. Matthew Poole, *Synopsis Criticorum . . .* (London, 1671), 2, p. 4.

142. Set forth in the preface of his *Psalmorum Liber in Versiculos Metrice Divisus* (London, 1736).

143. Hare, *Psalmorum Liber*, 2, pp. 831–34.

syllables, and is therefore a *metrical*, not a *rhythmical*, poetry as many have thought."[144] Hare recognized the problem of lineation as central to any metrical theory, and therefore began (as others had) by considering the metrical structure of the alphabetical Psalm 111. From it he deduced a series of rules for Hebrew scansion, which he then applied to the entire Psalter, dividing up each Psalm into half-verses which, by and large, corresponded to the old Masoretic division but, printed flush right, had the advantage of presenting the ancient Hebrew poetry in short, poem-like chunks instead of in long verses continuously printed.

The main curiosity of Hare's system is that it is predicated on a notion of stress accent in Hebrew through which quasi-metrical patterns, primarily iambic and trochaic, express themselves. In other words, it is something like the accentual-syllabic system of English poetry saddled to Hebrew, with, however, great flexibility in the assigning of accents, plus the possibility of collapsing the shewa into the next syllable or elevating it to an independent syllable, and finally no fixed number of syllables per line. The only real requirement of Hare's rules was that if the total number of syllables was even, the line be read as "iambic," with the first stress accent falling on the second syllable; if it was odd, the line was "trochaic," and had to begin with a stressed syllable. But since both syllabification and stress were subject to easy manipulation, this was no enduring obstacle.

Awareness of stress accent in poetry had been around for some time,[145] yet Hare's terminology was not always accepted by others. In a later addition to his "Confutation of Bishop Hare's Hebrew Metre," Lowth notes: "I will freely confess that I neither did understand, nor do I yet understand, what metre can exist without any distinction of long and short syllables, or what can be meant by Trochaic, Iambic, and Anacreontic feet and verses, where no regard is paid to the quantity of the syllables."[146] No doubt Hare's own lack of clarity was to blame. Clear or not, however, Hare's system was immediately welcomed, for it had all the markings of a solution to the metrical

144. Hare, 1, p. xxv. Cf. above, Buxtorf's use of *metrum* to include a system based solely on the number of syllables.

145. Sometimes the word *tonus* was used, but also *accentus*, causing some confusion. See, e.g., the use of *accentus* in Giovanni Pontano's *Dialoghi* (Florence, 1943), pp. 146–47. In relation to the Bible, *accentus* was used to translated the Massoretic *ṭe'amim*, adding to the confusion; but moreover their placement usually (but not always) indicates word stress. Hare was aware of this, but because it interfered with his own "scansion," rejected it out of hand. See his p. xxvi.

146. *SP*, p. 297.

impasse: it was flexible, it fit the analogy between Hebrew and vernacular poetry, it avoided the controversy over the authenticity of Hebrew vocalization, and, while it had virtually nothing in common with the metrical schemes of Greece and Rome, it allowed (because of the unspoken English example) the use of Greek metrical terms. In point of fact, the "trochees" and "iambs" were a sham. The essence of Hare's scansion is alternation (with, however, room for the inevitable exceptions); lines either start with a stressed syllable or they do not, then alternate (thanks to Hare's license) to the end of the line.

But no student of biblical "metrics" ought to be surprised by the welcome accorded the flimsiest of theories. And Hare was certainly a learned Hebraist. His system had, unlike Gomarus's, enough simplicity to be credible, and he applied it to the entire Psalter. Moreover, the "metrical" units now once again corresponded to the sense units, which made for a far more reasonable-looking lineation than that seen in Le Clerc and other theorists. All in all it seemed a manageable solution, albeit one that did not really "solve" much, and won enthusiastic support, especially among Englishmen on both sides of the Atlantic. T. Edwards, in the "Preliminary Dissertation" of his *Psalms* (1755), wrote a lengthy defense and summary of Hare's exposition, and a "Sketch of Hebrew Poetry" based on Hare was included in I. Lyons and R. Grey, *Hebrew Grammar,* the latter noting specifically the similarity between Hebrew and "that which we call in English, Blank Verse."[147] Hare was pronounced "the great Restorer of the Hebrew Poetry,"[148] and those who doubted the truth of his system were declared to "have either very unmusical ears, or are of tempers very hard to be convinced."[149]

7

Before passing on to Lowth's *Praelectiones,* one final treatise is to be considered. It is a remarkable pre-Lowthian discussion of biblical parallelism, "De Exergasia Sacra," a fifteen-page essay at the end of Christian Schoettgen's *Horae Hebraicae et Talmudicae* (1733). Now as we have seen, much of what Lowth was to say about parallelism had already been apprehended via the tropes-and-figures approach to

147. I. Lyons and R. Grey, *Hebrew Grammar*, 2nd. ed. (Cambridge, 1806), p. 76.
148. Ibid., p. 79.
149. T. Edwards, *Psalms*, p. 29.

Hebrew style; certainly Flacius had a grasp of repetition, emphasis, and restatement in the Bible. The same Meibomius whose metrical scansion was refuted by Hare and others had insisted on the basically binary character of biblical poetry and on its semantic implications:

> The distichs of the Psalms were recited or sung in the temple or at other ceremonies not by one priest or by one choir, but by two. . . . This observation is of great application in uncovering errors committed especially by recent translators, who interpret not, as they ought, each and every verse-half as a separate entity, but everything mixed together, throwing the words out of the order of the Hebrew scripture and treating them as if they were one continuous statement. But individual verse-halves express individual ideas.[150]

Quite apart from his ideas about meter, Meibomius was right to insist on this binarism, though the verse-halves are neither as consistently independent nor as consistently binary as he claims. Other writers, too, were sensitive to the basically binary sentence structure of Hebrew "poetry."[151] But certainly the most astute and penetrating remarks on the subject up until (and in some respects including) Lowth were those made in this brief study by Christian Schoettgen, which certainly marks the high point in the tropes-and-figures approach to biblical parallelism.[152]

Schoettgen's essay begins with a definition of terms: "All books of the Rhetoricians teach what *Exergasia* is, namely, the joining together of whole *sententiae* of the same significance. . . . It is also called *expolitio,* for it is a trope by which writing may be ornamented in a marvellous manner. . . . Others call it *isocolon,* since the clauses

150. Cited in Hare, *Psalmorum Liber*, p. v.
151. Hare himself says: "By far the greatest number of the sentences in the Psalms are two-membered, but not for the reason Meibomius states, that they were used in alternate recitation or singing, but from the nature of Hebrew poetry (*ex Poeseos Hebraeae indole*), since the same thing is found in Job and Proverbs a great deal, which books no sane person would ever dream were composed for use in the Temple or were sung by priests." *Liber Psalmorum*, p. v.
152. Schoettgen's anticipation of Lowth has been known since J. Jebb's *Sacred Literature* (London, 1820); see A. Baker, "Parallelism: England's Contribution to Biblical Studies," *CBQ* 35 (1973): 433. A contemporary of Schoettgen's, A. S. Mazzocchi, also approached parallelism via the tropes-and-figures method; he identified it as *epexegesis* (apposition), and felt it was one of the characteristics of Hebrew poetry. See U. Bonamartini, "L'Epesegesi nella S. Scrittura," *Biblica* 6 (1925): 439. But Mazzocchi's treatment is far inferior to Schoettgen's; he is Lowth's "predecessor" only in the sense that Flacius and so many others were. On Schoettgen, see also J. Lundbom, *Jeremiah* (Missoula, Mont., 1975), pp. 121–27.

or members of the sentence are equal." He also associates it with J. C. Scaliger's treatment of the poetic figures *repetitio, frequentatio,* and *acervatio,* but distinguishes it from the mere repetition of a single word in various forms (*synonymia*). Now, having adduced examples of these figures from classical rhetoricians and poets, Schoettgen notes this same figure was described by Jewish exegetes under the phrase הענין כפול במילים שונות, and cites examples. "It is remarkable that this figure, then, should be so completely neglected, or at least sparingly treated, by men learned and endowed with the greatest discernment such as have commented on the Scriptures in the Christian world."

With this preface he moves to the heart of his exposition:

> Before all other things, Reader, it should be pointed out that the Exergasia of which we are speaking occurs only in that sort of writing which goes beyond history and the ordinary manner of speech. For Hebrew style is indeed two-fold, the pedestrian or historical, and the rhetorical or poetic. Let it not seem strange to anyone, that I declare the rhetorical and poetical style to be the same, for anyone who investigates the matter correctly will apprehend it to be just so. The poetry of the Hebrews should not be forced into any numbers or rhythms: they labor in vain who would assign meters to the Psalms or prophetic texts. The Psalms and other texts were sung by the Hebrews in almost the same manner in which, amongst us, the hymn of Mary and other prose Psalms are sung publicly: that is, in such a way that individual verses are divided into twin members (*in bina cola dividantur*) which we easily measure out in some fashion in singing them to the familiar tune. It is as absurd to force the verses of the Psalms and other canticles to fit the laws of iambs and hexameters as it would be if we tried to have Greek and Latin verses measured by the French or German meters. The whole majesty of the Hebrew's poetry and oratory consists in this, that it rises above the historical style and abounds in images and verbal flourishes.
>
> Amongst these types of images Exergasia occupies no lowly place, indeed, I should say there is nothing more common amongst the Prophets and Hagiographic writers. From this it also follows that profane men cannot rightly reproach the Bible that it speaks in *tautologias* and *battologias*, for such is the genius of ancient tongues and times. If, therefore, we correctly observe this figure, we shall make swift work of many things in the sacred text which have presented difficulties to other learned interpreters. The things which I have considered in this part I shall now connect with others,

so that I may first set forth certain basic rules, and support each with three very clear examples. Thence I will adduce certain disputed texts, and apply these rules to them.

RULE I. Exergasia is perfect when individual members of the two clauses (*singula duorum commatum membra*) correspond to each other in such a way that there is nothing missing or extra.

Psalm 33:7[153]

| Congregans | sicut in utre | aquas maris: |
| Et ponens | in thesauris | abyssos. |

Num. 34:17

| Veniet | stella | ex Jacob |
| Et surget | sceptrum | ex Israel |

Luke 1:47

| Magnificat | anima mea | Dominum |
| Et exultavit | spiritus meus | in deo salutari meo. |

RULE II: Sometimes however the subject is not repeated in one part of the sentence but is omitted through ellipsis and understood from the context:

Isa. 1:18

| Si pecata vestra | erunt sicut dibaphum | sicut nix albescent: |
| et si--- | sicut coccus rubebunt | sicut lana erunt |

Prov. 7:19

| Quoniam vir | non est in domo sua |
| | profectus est viam longinquam |

Psalm 129:3

| Super tergo meo ararunt | aratores |
| Longum fecerunt sulcum suum. | |

RULE III. Sometimes also a *part* of the subject is missing:

Psalm 37:30

| Os justi | meditabitur | sapientiam |
| Lingua eius | loquetur | judicium |

Here only part of the subject is repeated, for the added *eius* is not truly the whole subject.

Psalm 102:29

| Filii servorum tuorum | habitabunt |
| Et semen ipsorum | ante faciem tuam firmum erit |

153. Here we shall retain the Latin text of his examples.

Isa. 53:5
Et ille   vulneratus est   propter transgressiones nostras
               contritus est   propter peccata nostra

RULE IV: There are many examples in which the predicate is omitted in the exergasic repetition:
Num. 24:5
Quam pulchra sunt tentoria tua   O Jacob
                   habitationes tuae O Israel
Psalm 33:12
Beata   gens ista   cuius Dominus Deus est
           populus ille   quem elegit in haereditatem sibi.
Psalm 123:6
Satura est sibi   anima nostra   irrisione insolentium
                                   despectu superborum.

RULE V: Sometimes part of the predicate is missing.
Psalm 57:11
Confitebor tibi   inter populos   Domine
Psallam tibi   inter gentes
Psalm 103:1
Benedic   anima mea   Domino
Et   omnia intestina mea nomini sanctitatis eius
Psalm 129:7
Ut nos impleat   manum suam   messor
Aut   pygillum suum manipulos faciens

RULE VI: Sometimes are added in one member things which are not present in the other:
Num. 33:18
Surge   Balak   & audi
                Fili Zippor   ausculta mihi
Psalm 102:29
Filii servorum tuorum   coram facie tua   habitabunt
Et semen ipsorum   stabit
Dan. 12:3
Et qui sapientes reddunt   fulgebunt sicut splendor firmamenti
Et qui justos reddunt   multos   sicut stellae

                                       . . . .

                                       in aeternum

RULE VII: Sometimes two statements dealing with different matters occur, but which, understood as a *merismus*, can and ought to be related to a single general statement:

Psalm 94:8

| Plantans | aurem | annon audiet? |
| Fingens | oculum | annon videbit? |

Psalm 128:3

| Uxor tua | sicut vitis fructifera | ad latera domus tuae |
| Filii tui | sicut plantationes olearum | circa mensam tuam |

Ecclus. 3:16

| Sicut blasphemus est | relinquens | patrem |
| Et maledictus a Domino | ad iram concitans | matrem |

Let no one think that we believe *eye* and *ear* or *father* and *mother* to be the same, and so forth; but these two same statements elaborate [*expoliunt*—cf. the figure *expolitio*] a single general one. Thus the general statement of the first example is: God is aware of all things; and of the second: He will be happy in marriage; and of the third: unhappy is he who despises his parents.

RULE VIII: There also exists an Exergasia in which the second statement maintains the opposite of the first:

Prov. 15:8

| Sacrificium | impiorum | abominatio est Domino |
| Et preces | rectorum | beneplacitum eius |

Prov. 14:1

| Sapientia mulierum | aedificat domum |
| Et stultitia in manibus eius | destruet illam |

Prov. 5:11

| Domus | impiorum | devastabitur |
| Et tentorium | rectorum | florebit. |

RULE IX: We also have examples of this sort of Exergasia wherein individual statements correspond to each other, but the same subject and predicate are not, as heretofore, the same.

Psalm 51:7

Ecce in iniquitate conceptus sum:
Et in peccatis concepit me mater mea

Psalm 119:168

Custodivi mandata tua & testimonia tua
Quoniam omnes viae meae coram te

Jerem. 8:22

An opobalsamum non est in Gilead, neque medicus est ibi?
Curr enim non pervenit ad sanitatem filia populi mei?

RULE X: There are also three-membered *Exergasiae*:
Psalm 1:1

Beatus vir	qui non ivit	in consilio	impiorum
Et	non stetit	in via	peccatorum
Et	non sedit	in cathedra	irrisorum

Psalm 130:5

Expectavi Dominum
Expectavit anima mea
Et in verbo eius speravi

Psalm 52:9

Ecce vir, qui non posuit Deum auxilium suum
Et . . . confisus est in multitudine divitiarum suarum
Et . . . rubustus erat in inanitate sua

This first part of Schoettgen's treatise is remarkable in many respects. His refusal of a separate category for biblical "poetry" as distinct from "rhetoric" is most insightful: it anticipates Lowth's assimilation of "poetry" and prophecy, and avoids entirely the notion of biblical poetry, which led Lowth to the edge of, and so many others into, the quagmire of biblical meter. His comparison of biblical singing to Church recitation is likewise most apt.[154] Essentially, what he is arguing is that there is no special system or arrangement in the Bible's "high style," that it is differentiated from the "historical" style only by its ornaments, chiefly "Exergasia." This is something of an oversimplification—the historical and oratorical styles will blend into each other even in the use of exergasia. But it is strikingly perceptive.

Schoettgen also presents the notion that exergasia, properly understood, will lead to the solution of many biblical cruces, a claim Lowth made for parallelism and, indeed, Meibomius seemed to have advanced (above) in arguing the binary nature of Hebrew song. In the second part of his essay, which we shall not cite, he uses exergasia to supply new meanings to certain difficult verses: thus יודע in Psalm 1:6

---

154. His "decantantur" ("sung, performed") might, with the force of its prefix, also imply singing that is not particularly precise or prepared, an "adjustable" rendition characteristic of plain-song.

he understands as to "cause to prosper," and he derives כפירים in Psalm 34:11 from כפר "deny," and translates as "*abnegatores.*"

But certainly Schoettgen's "Rules" and examples are the most interesting thing he has to say. It is noteworthy that he took his examples from a wide selection of books, not only the Prophets and traditionally "poetic" books, but from the highly parallelistic oracles of Balaam in Numbers, from Daniel, and even two bits of parallelism recognized in Greek, the examples from Ecclesiasticus (ben Sira) and Luke.[155] His different categories anticipated Lowth's "synonymous, antithetical and synthetic" parallelism, and his analysis of "synonymous" as either "perfect" or "imperfect" in its paralleling is both well executed and an uncanny foretaste of the discussion of parallelism earlier this century in G. B. Gray's treatise, *The Forms of Hebrew Poetry*. Finally, his recognition of *merismus* in the Bible and its role as a concomitant of parallelism has only recently been renewed.[156]

In sum, many of the insights we now credit to Robert Lowth had already been advanced in some form by those who came before him. No doubt this is the cruel lot of many a modern biblical critic! And yet it is important so to state in Lowth's case for what it reveals about the nature of our problem. By Lowth's time all the elements of the puzzle he was to deal with had been laid out. His task was primarily that of arrangement and synthesis—but this was no small matter. Lowth was fortunate, in addition to possessing all the gifts of a natural exegete and litterateur, to have been charged specifically with the preparation of a series of lectures on what might with justice be called "The Bible as Literature," and to have thus had both the imperative and the genius to prepare an overall approach to biblical style; one that, for all its revolutionary claims, would manage to preserve enough of the existing framework of critical thought and correspond sufficiently to his own day's feelings about the Bible and Christianity,[157] so as to make his ideas immediately understandable and acceptable. It is in such terms that his own achievement ought to be weighed against those of Schoettgen, Flacius, Cappel, and other predecessors.

155. Cf. Flacius in similar citing of Greek parallelisms in his *Clavis* (described in chapter 4).

156. See A. M. Honeyman, "Merismus in Biblical Literature," *JBL* 71 (1952): 11-18.

157. For in every period, changes in one's concept of the Bible's manner of expression reflect changes in theology; people apprehend God to act in the Scriptures as they apprehend God to act in the world.

8

Lowth began his lecture series by integrating the Bible into the same world of aesthetic standards occupied by the Greek and Roman classics. This basically apologetic posture goes back to the Greek Fathers, and had to be revived, as we have seen, with the Renaissance's renewed admiration for Greek and Latin. With Lowth, however, it is not mere apologizing. He had seized from the Renaissance defenses of poetry that spark that was to become Romanticism,[158] the alliance of poetry and "natural piety," and so he begins first by promoting poetry not only that it might "stand eminent among the other liberal arts" but indeed tower above them by reason of its "original office and destination,"[159] the service of religion. Hebrew poetry—and by this he means, to an extent his listeners could not have grasped in the first lecture, *most of the Bible*—is to be exalted for having remained faithful to that original office, and for having served the religion of the one God. Moreover, it is to be praised on the very grounds for which Homer is praised; its aesthetic worth must be explored. So Lowth must begin by justifying this act of comparison:

> It would not be easy, indeed, to assign a reason, why the writings of Homer, of Pindar, and of Horace, should engross our attention and monopolize our praise, while those of Moses, of David and Isaiah pass totally unregarded. Shall we supppose that the subject is not adapted to a seminary, in which sacred literature has ever maintained a precedence? Shall we say, that it is foreign to this assembly of promising youth, of whom the greater part have consecrated the best portion of their time and labour to the same department of learning? Or must we conclude, that the writings of those men, who have accomplished only as much as human genius and ability could accomplish, should be reduced to method and theory; but that those which boast a much higher origin, and are justly attributed to the inspiration of the Holy Spirit, may be considered as indeed illustrious by their native force and beauty, but not as conformable to the principles of science, nor to be circumscribed by any rules of art? It is indeed most true, that sacred poetry, if we contemplate its origin alone, is far superior to both

158. See Norman MacLean, "From Action to Image," in R. S. Crane, et al., *Critics and Criticism* (Chicago, 1952), pp. 408–60; M. Roston, *Prophet and Poet: The Bible and the Growth of Romanticism* (Evanston, Ill., 1965).
159. *SP*, p. 22.

nature and art; but if we would rightly estimate its excellencies, that is, if we wish to understand its power in exciting the human affections, we must have recourse to both: for we must consider what those affections are, and by what means they are to be excited.[160]

In order to exalt biblical *style*, however, Lowth well understood that it was necessary to judge it by its own standards and not those imposed by classical rhetoric. This is what led him to argue forcefully the idea of Israel as an ancient and Oriental people, and for Lowth (and others) this theme opened the door to a new stylistic criticism, derived as much as possible from the Bible itself. With any work, he said, "if the reader be accustomed to habits of life totally different from those of the author . . . many descriptions and sentiments, which were clearly illustrated and magnificently expressed by the one, will appear to the other mean and obscure." And while these difficulties will be present to some extent in contemplating any poet's writing,

> they must be still more numerous in such of the poets as are foreign and ancient; in the Orientals above all foreigners, they being the farthest removed from our customs and manners; and of all the Orientals most especially in the Hebrews, theirs being confessedly the most ancient compositions extant. . . . There is therefore great danger, lest viewing them from an improper situation, and rashly estimating all things by our own standard, we form an erroneous judgment.[161]

We have been concerned with two main currents in Renaissance criticism of the Bible, the tropes-and-figures approach to biblical style and the search for biblical meter. Each is, in its way, precisely the sort of retrojection that Lowth is arguing against here. It is significant, however, that he was able to free himself from only one: for the notion of biblical meter remained the cornerstone of Lowth's conception of biblical poetry. But at least so far as tropes and figures are concerned, Lowth showed a revolutionary scorn:

> I shall also venture to omit the almost innumerable forms of the Greek rhetoricians, who possessed the faculty of inventing names in the highest perfection; I shall neglect even their primary distinction between tropes and figures, and their subdivision of the figures themselves, denominating some figures of expression and

160. Ibid., p. 26.
161. Ibid., pp. 47–48.

some figures of sentiment. In disregarding these distinctions, I might in my own justification allege the authority of C. Artorius Proculus, who gave the name of figure to a trope, as Quintilian informs us; and indeed the example of Quintilian himself. I omit them, however, upon a different ground: for I do not pretend to say that in their proper place they are destitute either of reality or use; but our present concern is not to explain the sentiments of the Greek but of the Hebrew writers.[162]

With this brave credo Lowth sets forth. One of the first differences between classical and Hebrew poetics he fixes on is the brief proverb-like quality treated above under the name of "terseness." Lowth first adduces the didactic function of Hebrew poetry and suggests that the "sententious" form was ideally suited to inculcating wisdom; from this early use the stylistic terseness overflowed into other forms of poetry as well. But he further argues that it is a reflection of deeper differences between the nature of the Greek and Hebrew languages:

For the Greek, beyond every other language (and the Latin next to it), is copious, flowing and harmonious, possessed of a great variety of measures, of which the impression is so definite, the effects so striking, that if you should recite some lame and imperfect portion of a verse or even enunciate hastily several verses in a breath, the numbers would nevertheless be clearly discernible: so that in these every variety essential to poetry and verse may be provided for almost at pleasure, without the smallest injury to the different metres. But in the Hebrew language the whole economy is different. Its form is simple, above every other; the radical words are uniform, and resemble each other almost exactly; nor are the inflexions numerous, or materially different: whence we may readily understand, that its metres are neither complex, nor capable of much variety; but rather simple, grave, temperate; less adapted to fluency than dignity and force: so that possibly they found it necessary to distinguish the extent of the verse by the conclusion of the sentence, lest the lines by running into each other, should become altogether implicated and confused.[163]

This last sentence simply means that, unlike Greek and Latin, Hebrew poetic lines are end-stopped—for if they were not, listeners would perhaps be unable to determine line endings on the basis of meter alone. This ingenious argument breaks ground for what he will

162. Ibid., p. 46.
163. Ibid., p. 35.

assert next, that the presence of parallelism—which clearly marks the ends of lines, and so is a form of closure—demonstrates that Hebrew poetry is indeed metrical.

As we saw in chapter 1, Lowth thought that meter was an "essential" characteristic of poetry, and that writing that lacked meter could "scarcely deserve the name of poetry." Since he was not about to question the very existence of a biblical poetry, that settled matters. But toward the age-old metrical ghost he made a bold thrust. Following the Levita-Cappel line on Hebrew vocalization, he asserted that all attempts to discover the true scansion of Hebrew poetry were destined to fail, for "not so much as the number of syllables, of which each word consisted, could with any certainty be defined, much less the length or the quantity of the syllables."[164] How, then, could he be so sure that meter exists in Hebrew? Because of *parallelism*, that is, "a certain conformation of the sentences, the nature of which is that a complete sense is almost equally infused into every component part, and that every member constitutes an entire verse."[165] He is quick to assert that parallelism itself is not entirely consistent: "We find, if not a rule and principle, at least a characteristic of the sacred poetry";[166] but parallelism, as an indication of closure and hence a lineation, is consistent enough to convince him that underlying even parallelism's inconsistencies is a consistent meter. To which subject he—and we—shall return in greater detail presently.

In addition to meter and terseness, Lowth found other characteristics of poetic style. It was often figurative, "parabolic," and he names *mašal*, along with *mizmor*,[167] as one of the Hebrew terms for poetry. He attempts to derive the sources of figurative language's images in order to show the uniqueness of Hebrew figurative language and explain its peculiarities. The four sources he cites are nature, everyday life and its institutions, Hebrew law and religious institutions, and the sacred history of the Israelites. Of these, the last two sources are certainly responsible for some of the uniqueness of "ancient and Oriental" Israel's figures and their apparent strangeness from a modern vantage point. Likewise, in his subsequent discussion of allegory, he distinguishes a "mystical" class of allegory that "can

164. Ibid., p. 34.
165. Ibid.
166. Ibid., p. 35.
167. Following Cappel and other writers, Lowth derives *mizmor* from *zmr* "prune, cut" and suggests that the term refers to Hebrew poetry's being "cut or divided, in a peculiar manner, into short and equal sentences." Ibid., p. 38.

only be supplied with proper materials from the sacred rites of the Hebrews themselves."[168] This explains why it is to be found only in biblical poetry:

> Hence that truly Divine Spirit, which has not disdained to employ poetry as the interpreter of its sacred will, has also in a manner appropriated to its own, used this kind of allegory, as peculiarly adapted to the publication of future events, and to the typifying of the most sacred mysteries; so that should it, on any occasion, be applied to a profane and common subject, being diverted from its proper end, and forced as it were from its natural bias, it would inevitably want all its power and elegance.[169]

Typology, then, becomes assimilated to biblical *poetics*—it is a kind of allegory which, however, only the Holy Spirit employs (hence, a form of allegory found in the Bible, but not Homer).

The last general characteristic of Hebrew poetry Lowth deals with is the "sublime." Now sublimity in Lowth's England was in its heyday. The concept itself goes back to the treatise *Peri Hypsoys*, attributed to Cassius Longinus[170] (third century A.D.; probably, however, the treatise was written closer to the middle of the first century, the name of its true author unknown), which distinguished a loftiness or sublimity (*hypsos*) of writing in the greatest works of literature.[171] The sublime, the author holds, derives from the greatness of the writer's soul, and expresses itself indifferently in thoughts, feeling, figures, diction, and "arrangement."[172] Now although the early Renaissance resurrected many discussions of poetry and classical style, this particular treatise was neglected until the late sixteenth century, when it was finally published in Greek and

---

168. Ibid., p. 89.

169. Ibid.,

170. Longinus had no appreciable effect in England until the late seventeenth century, but then sublimity became a literary vogue, peaking indeed just before Lowth's time. See Wimsatt and Brooks, *Literary Criticism*, p. 412. Many writers have discussed Lowth and the sublime in England; see S. Monk, *The Sublime* (Ann Arbor, Mich., 1960), pp. 77–83; V. Freimarck, "The Bible and Neo-Classical Views of Style," *Journal of English and German Philology* 51 (1952): 507–28; also M. Price, *To the Palace of Wisdom* (Carbondale, Ill., 1964), p. 370; J. H. Lehmann, "The Vicar of Wakefield," *English Literary History* 46 (1979): 97–121.

171. One of Longinus's examples of sublimity was the sentence of a Barbarian author: "God said, 'Let there be light,' and there was light. 'Let there be land,' and there was land."

172. Lit. *synthesis*, "composition."

translated into Latin.[173] Thence it passed into European aesthetics, was embraced by French and English neoclassicism, and eventually, with its exaltation of the passions and the lawless dictates of the spirit, helped to usher in Romanticism.

Certainly Lowth's identification of *sublimitas* as a characteristic of biblical poetry was not an insignificant event in English literary history.[174] He begins by defining his terms:

> The word sublimity I wish in this place to be understood in its most extensive sense: I speak not merely of that sublimity, which exhibits great objects with a magnificent display of imagery and diction; but that force of composition, whatever it be, which strikes and overpowers the mind, which excites the passions, and which expresses ideas at once with perspicuity and elevation; not solicitous whether the language be plain or ornamented, refined or familiar: in this use of the word I copy Longinus, the most accomplished author on this subject, whether we consider his precepts or his example.[175]

The characteristics of the sublime style in Hebrew are, first of all, any features of surface that distinguish it from ordinary parlance: Lowth specifically mentions unusual syntax, ellipses, and shifts in grammatical person or tense. None of these observations was new with him—they had all been catalogued before by Reuchlin, Pagninus, Witzel, Bellarmino, Flacius, and other compilers of *Institutiones*. But Lowth unified these observations under one heading, *sublimitas*, and gave them a credible rationale: the lawlessness comes from, and is in turn capable of producing, the excitement of the "passions."[176]

> The language of reason is cool, temperate, rather humble than elevated, well arranged and perspicuous, with an evident care and anxiety lest any thing should escape which might appear perplexed or obscure. The language of the passions is totally different; the conceptions burst out in a turbid stream, expressive in a manner of the internal conflict; the more vehement break out in hasty

173. The first edition of the Renaissance was by Robortello (Basel, 1554); it was translated into English by John Hall in 1652.

174. See MacLean, "From Action to Image," pp. 416–18.

175. *SP*, pp. 112–13.

176. The figures (*schemata*) catalogued by Longinus tend to have to do with abnormalities of syntax and other peculiarities of structure—asyndeton, hyperbaton (inversion), changes of number, person, tense, periphrases, and so forth (see Wimsatt and Brooks, *Literary Criticism*, p. 103). Thus Lowth's conclusion follows quite naturally from Longinus.

confusion; they catch (without search or study) whatever is impetuous, vivid or energetic. In a word, reason speaks literally, the passions poetically.[177]

In *Peri Hypsoys* the sublime was capable of finding expression in a multitude of genres, it was a quality of greatness in many forms of imitation. In Lowth, too, it was to span biblical genres, yet the notion that the passions speak poetically is crucial. For the sublime—not only sublimity of sentiment (Lecture 16) but also these unusual forms and shifts in syntax—became, along with terseness, meter (as witnessed by parallelism), and the "parabolic" style, signs specifically of *poetry* in the Bible.

The heart of Lowth's argument is the third section of his book, which a modern critic might have entitled "The Genres of Hebrew Poetry." The first "genre" he discusses, prophecy, was the most difficult, controversial, and ultimately the most significant part of his argument. It will be recalled that the sharp distinction between the artful ways of biblical "poetry" and the divinely dictated utterances of the prophets goes back to Jerome, Adrian, and other early writers. Although this notion has rabbinic analogues,[178] the opposition of prophecy to poetry represents (as we have seen in Clement, Origen, and Jerome) an attempt to exalt Divine Inspiration over the merely poetic and refers specifically to the works of pagan literature. This notion, reinforced by the threefold canon, was remarkably tenacious even in the face of Renaissance sallies into Divine poesy of vulgar expression.

In taking it on, Lowth shows his characteristic concern for terminology. The root נבא (prophesy) sometimes means to make songs of praise (he adduces 1 Sam. 10:5–10, 19:20–24; 1 Chron. 25:1–3); similarly משא means "poem" in Proverbs 30:1 and 31:1. Moreover, both poetry and prophecy were accompanied by music. Do not these suggest a definite kinship between the two? Furthermore, the office of prophecy (albeit pagan) was performed metrically in the

---

177. *SP*, p. 113.

178. Thus Ecclesiastes's place in the canon was attacked on the grounds that the book was merely "Solomon's wisdom" (see b. *Meg.* 7a); the equally heretical Job, because it presented God speaking *in propria persona*, was never so questioned. See R. Gordis, *The Book of God and Man* (Chicago, 1965), p. 222. The ordering of biblical books in early Christian Bibles, which probably represents a Hellenistic Jewish prototype, clearly separates the "literary" books from the Prophets and the Divine Law and History. Thus, Codex Alexandrinus (fifth century) groups together Psalms, Job, Proverbs, Ecclesiastes, Song of Songs, Wisdom of Solomon, Ben Sira, and the Psalms of Solomon. Cf. Josephus, *Against Apion*, 1, 8.

Sibylline oracles, and reached the heights of sublimity in Vergil's fourth eclogue.[179] Yet while Lowth felt readers would readily concede the loftiness of prophetic diction, he anticipated some difficulties with the claim that it is actually poetry—"I mean verse, or metrical composition."[180] Jerome's objection (preface to Isaiah) and that of other early writers he sweeps aside—Jerome "imperfectly understood" the metrical question and was not even internally consistent; Philo, Josephus, Origen, and Eusebius "were no less ignorant of the nature of the Hebrew meters" than Jerome.[181] As for the distinction in the *ṭe'amim* used for Job, Proverbs, and the Psalter—which the Renaissance Hebraists referred to as the *libri metrici*, an appellation that implied that the other twenty-one books were prose—Lowth again invokes the lateness of the Masoretes. By the time these special accents were assigned, he says, Hebrew was a dead language, and knowledge of its true metrical system had long since been forgotten. (This is obvious, he says, from the fact that books "no less evidently metrical" such as Lamentations or the Song of Songs had been treated as "absolutely prosaic" by the Masoretes, that is, assigned the normal system of *ṭe'amim*.) Thus, neither Jewish nor Christian authority was to be trusted on the question.

What was to be trusted was the set of characteristics of poetry enumerated earlier, and in them—the "sententious" and "parabolic" style, sublimity, but most especially the *presence of meter* as evidenced by the parallelism—prophecy and poetry may be shown indistinguishable. In service of his metrical hypothesis for the prophetic books, Lowth now presented a fuller exposition of parallelism. It was in his nineteenth lecture that Lowth detailed his threefold classification of parallelism, "synonymous," "antithetical," and "synthetic," illustrating each with copious example. Certainly some of the effect of this classification[182] was to give the impression of a *system* at work, something with its own definite taxonomy which, once accepted, shows itself everywhere applicable. No doubt even Lowth was impressed by this feature. For though he begins his exposition with the assertion that parallelism itself is merely evidence of meter—"In order to prove that the predictions of the prophets are metrical, I must in part have recourse to the same arguments, by which I formerly endeavoured to evince that the Hebrew poetry in

179. *SP*, pp. 182–83.
180. Ibid., p. 146.
181. Ibid., p. 147.
182. Discussed in greater detail in chapter 1.

general consisted of a kind of metre"[183]—by the end he seems to imply that parallelism in itself was a form of meter, possibly even the only form that existed:

> In this peculiar conformation, or parallelism of the sentences, I apprehend a considerable part of the Hebrew metre to consist; though it is not improbable that some regard was also paid to the numbers and feet. But of this particular we have at present so little information, that it is utterly impossible to determine whether it were modulated by the ear alone, or according to any settled or definite rules of prosody. Since, however, this and other marks or vestiges, as it were, of the metrical art are alike extant in the writings of the prophets, and in the books which are commonly allowed to be poetical, I think there is sufficient reason to rank them in the same class.[184]

This paragraph opens the way for George Buchanan Gray and later critics in our century, who first took parallelism as a concomitant of meter (rather like rhyme), then saw in it the only sure *system* Hebrew "poetry" had.

Parallelism was hardly the subject of Lowth's series of lectures, or even a central point. If he had to fix on one aspect of his treatment that was new and important, no doubt he would have singled out the point his treatment of parallelism supported, that from a stylistic standpoint prophecy was a form of poetry, for the two had "one common name, one common origin, one common author, the Holy Spirit."[185] With this established, he was then free to analyze various prophetic books on their aesthetic merits. Isaiah is "the most perfect model" of a poetic prophet, "at once elegant and sublime, forcible and ornamented."[186] Jeremiah is second to Isaiah: his sentiments are not as lofty, "nor are his periods always neat and compact." Moreover, many of his writings are in fact prose, "so that I can scarcely pronounce above half the books of Jeremiah poetical."[187] Ezekiel is inferior to Jeremiah in elegance, yet he is "deep, vehement, tragical." These three prophets together "as far as relates to style, may be said to hold the same rank among the Hebrews, as Homer, Simonides, and Aeschylus among the Greeks."[188]

183. *SP*, pp. 147–48.
184. Ibid., pp. 150–51.
185. Ibid.
186. Ibid., p. 176.
187. Ibid., p. 178.
188. Ibid., p. 178–79.

9

But if parallelism per se was not the point of Lowth's exposition, it was fixed on by his contemporaries and those who came after him as an important "discovery."[189] Herder, in his well-known volume *The Spirit of Hebrew Poetry*, did much to popularize parallelism as the vigorous and spontaneous prototype of such occidental features as meter:

The meterical system of the Greeks, constructed with more art and refinement than that of any other language, depends entirely on proportion and harmony. The hexameter verse, in which their ancient poems were sung, is in regard to its sounds a continued, though ever-changing, parallelism. To give it greater precision, the pentameter was adopted, and especially in the elegy. This again in the structure of its two hemistichs exhibits parallelism. The finest and most natural species of the ode depends so much on parallelism as nearly to justify the remark that the more a less artificial

189. In modern Jewish exegesis, Lowth's view of things has been widely adopted, albeit with modification. Moses Mendelssohn was the first major Jewish luminary to endorse Lowth's reading (in a review of *De Sacra Poesi*, reprinted in his *Gesammelte Schriften* [Stuttgart, 1977], 4, p. 20). In an excursus on Exod. 15, Samuel David Luzzatto wrote: "SUCH IS MY GOD AND I WILL PRAISE HIM [etc.]: He repeated the idea in different words, and this is found a great deal in Biblical songs, that there utterances will be divided into two corresponding parts. This is what they call Parallelismus [in Roman characters], sometimes the two halves contain a likeness between two subjects, such a 'As a lily among the thorns, such is my love among women' (Song 2:2); sometimes the two halves contain matters opposed one to the other, such as 'A wise son makes his father glad, a foolish son is his mother's grief' (Prov. 10:1); 'Sons have I raised up and fostered but they have sinned against me' (Isaiah 1:3); sometimes the second is the explanation of the first, such as 'I will sing to the Lord how He has greatly triumphed, horse and rider He cast in the sea' (Ex. 15:2); sometimes the second is the continuation of the preceding, or a word or two of the preceding is repeated in it, such as 'With me from Lebanon, my bride, with me from Lebanon come' (Song 4:8); and sometimes the second is the continuation of the first without any repetition of the same words, but repeating the same ideas, such as 'Listen, O Heavens and let me speak, and hear, O Earth, my words' (Deut. 32:1); sometimes the second part is nothing but a repetition of the first but in different words, like 'Let my teaching drop as rain, let my speech fall as dew' (Deut. 32:2), and the case at hand as well. And all this seems to have been done so that the speech would be cut up into tiny parts, and would be deeper imprinted on the mind of the listener, and also that it would be fit to sing" (בית האוצר [Lemberg, 1847], p. 39b). Only the nineteenth-century commentator M. Malbim, in his *Introduction to the Prophetic Books* (Vilnius, 1923), pp. 2a–3a, rejected utterly the idea of parallelism. See chapter 7.

parallelism is heard in a strophe in conjunction with the musical attenuations of sound, the more pleasing it becomes. I need only adduce as examples the Sapphic or Choriambic verse. All these metrical forms are artificial circlets, finely woven garlands of words and sounds. In the East the two strands of pearls are not twisted into a garland, but simply hang one over against the other. We could not expect from a chorus of herdsmen a dance as intricate as the labyrinth of Daedalus or of Theseus. In their language, their shouts of joy, and the movements of the dance we find them answering one another in regular alternations and the most simple proportions. Even this simplicity seems to me to have its beauties.[190]

Indeed, even in Lowth's later days he himself seems to have made more of his find: in the "Preliminary Dissertation" to his translation of Isaiah he is no longer quite so definite about meter (there is "some sort of rhythm"), while parallelism occupies the center of his attention. In his nineteenth lecture, Lowth had cited Azariah dei Rossi briefly; here he gives Buxtorf's translation *in extenso*, and concludes:

I agree therefore with Azarias in his general principle of a rhythmus of things: but instead of considering terms, or phrases, or senses, in single lines, as measures; determining the nature and denomination of the verse, as dimeter, trimeter, or tetrameter; I consider only that relation and proportion of one verse to another, which arises from the correspondence of terms, and from the form of construction; from whence results a rhythmus of propositions, and a harmony of sentences.[191]

Lowth's original position on meter had been weak; but it is important to understand the undeniable appeal it presented. To the jumble of confusions left in the wake of *Davidis Lyra*, and to the internal contradictions in such systems as Bishop Hare's scansion, Lowth's argument that meter was simply irretrievable had a certain neatness. While not new—it is found in various forms throughout the Renaissance, and earlier (as we have seen) among the students of Menahem b. Saruq—it brought to the metrical debate an all-inclusive

190. J. G. Herder, *The Spirit of Hebrew Poetry*, tr. James Marsh (Burlington, Vt., 1833), pp. 39–40; see the whole passage, pp. 37–41, also 2, pp. 46, 50. On Lowth and Herder see also H. Frei, *The Eclipse of Biblical Narrative* (New Haven, 1974), pp. 103, 183–84.

191. R. Lowth, *Isaiah: A New Translation* (Cambridge, 1834), p. xi.

"solution" that was, however, saved from nihilism by the inference of *some* meter *parallelismi causa*. Now why the "conformation of the sentences" ought to be taken as evidence of meter, rather than simply evidence of itself, is a question that must have troubled Lowth too— hence his movement away from this position. But to those whose notion of biblical poetry dictated some meter yet whose critical sense rejected all hypotheses thus far presented, Lowth's original dogma, a kind of "There is no God and Mary is His Mother," remained a welcome haven.

What Lowth had to say about the phenomenon of parallelism was in obvious ways inferior to the treatment it had already received by Schoettgen. His threefold classification was deceptive for reasons explained earlier; Schoettgen's sense of the variety of parallelism, his anticipation of Gray's distinction between "complete" and "incomplete" paralleling, and above all his reading of parallelism as essentially an emphatic and elevating phenomenon, all represent a far more sophisticated understanding than Lowth's. But precisely this last item led Schoettgen into error. Understanding parallelism as a form of emphasis and heightening, he—like Flacius and others before him—could only conclude that it was a color of rhetoric, albeit the most "common" figure to be found in the Bible. Lowth, if he in good conscience could not give parallelism a truly structural role ("if not a rule and principle, at least a characteristic"), insisted that it was something more than a mere ornament. His threefold classification, like Schoettgen's generous definition of exergasia, served to bring under one roof phenomena that had earlier been viewed as three or four different figures, or indeed had not been noticed at all. But Lowth's scheme did not even make Schoettgen's perfunctory gesture toward the Greek notion of rhetorical colors.

The historical inability of poetic terminology to describe Hebrew style might be compared to modern physicists' difficulty in deciding between "wave" and "particle" theories of light. For centuries, what we recognize as parallelism had been assimilated to various *figurae*; Lowth read parallelism as no *figura* at all, but evidence of lineation, hence meter. After Lowth, the metrical thesis continued earnestly to be pursued, but in the meantime parallelism itself had been raised to quasi-metrical status. This is approximately correct: in Job, in much of the Psalter, in Isaiah, the high style of Hebrew—"sententious" and full of "what's more"—does attain a metrical regularity, two or three terse clauses strung together in sentence after sentence. But it is a meter of emphasis and syntax as well as length, nor is it inviolable. So it drops from "wave" back to "particle."

Moreover, Lowth's stance could not be won without sacrifice. In order to relieve himself of the mental discomfort of something that was only inconsistently consistent—sometimes parallelism was regular in binary line after line, sometimes only an emphatic turn ending most lines, sometimes less than that—he treated it as evidence of a neat but irretrievable system. Like a sheet thrown over a reportedly beautiful statue, parallelism's bulging and bunching now took on a most enticing allure: however irregular and ungainly an artifice it might seem on its own, did not its very irregularities now turn seductive in the suggestion of an infinitely rich and detailed harmony underneath?

In the end, the most significant long-term result of Lowth's presentation has been the equation of "parallelism" with poetry. Even today, critics are busy discovering "poetic fragments" in Genesis and other "prose" books.[192] This is right and it is wrong, for the whole notion of biblical poetry is both right and wrong. But before Lowth, in any case, the discovery of exergasia, or anadiplosis and epizeuxis, or repetitio, expolitio, and so forth, in a passage of Genesis did not therefore suggest its kinship with the Psalter, or a resemblance of both with Homer, Horace, and the Western tradition. Lowth's argument, as we have seen, was aimed largely at the Prophets; he wished to suggest that prophecy is a kind of "Divine poesy." Revolutionary enough: but he could not confine poesy to the books he named precisely because "parallelism" was not an either/or matter; and so "biblical poetry" has spilled over from the poetical Isaiah and the semipoetical Jeremiah to other books with their histories, genealogies, blessings, curses, speeches, and so on. In this way, more than any other, Robert Lowth changed the way we read the Bible.

---

192. See most recently J. S. Kselman, "The Recovery of Poetic Fragments from the Pentateuchal Priestly Source," *JBL* 97 (1978): 161–73; also chapter 2 above.

SEVEN

A METRICAL AFTERWORD

1

With Robert Lowth, "parallelism" took on its definitive form. The rhetorical approach to this stylistic feature, pursued so successfully by Schoettgen and earlier writers, was now dropped in favor of Lowth's newly discovered structural constant which, in one of its three forms, was infallibly present in biblical "poetry." In this apparent regularity lay its great appeal. Lowth's specific categories were subsequently supplemented and redefined—George Buchanan Gray even proposed doing away with them in favor of the Schoettgen-like distinction between "complete" and "incomplete" parallelism[1]—but Lowth's underlying notion has survived these tamperings, survived even the "linguistic" and "structuralist" approaches of the past decades.[2] Even the texts from Ugarit, whose "paralleling" is so often asymmetrical, and so obviously emphatic, have only been read as confirmation of Lowth's claims.[3] Boling's point, that in a given pair

---

1. See G. B. Gray, *The Forms of Hebrew Poetry* (reprinted New York, 1972), pp. 112–13.

2. One of the best such studies is A. J. Ehlen, "The Poetic Structure of a Hodayah from Qumran" (Harvard Ph.D. dissertation, 1970), which in turn is dependent on R. Jakobson, "Grammatical Parallelism and its Russian Facet," *Language* 42 (1966): 399–429. Ehlen painstakingly searches out correspondences in the Qumran hymn 1 QH 3:19–36 on all levels, auditory, grammatical, and semantic (his approach here also recalls that of L. Alonso Schökel's analysis of Isaiah in *Estudios de Poetica Hebrea*). Yet the results are strangely old-fashioned: "There are three basic modes of correspondence which can exist between the referents of two words: they may be identical . . . they may be in polar contrast with respect to some characteristic . . . even though they belong to the same order of being; or they may be associated in various ways, e.g., as separate aspects of a larger whole, or as contiguous, one leading to the other, coming next to mind, or the like" (p. 87). Is not this Lowth all over again?

3. Thus C. Gordon, *Ugaritic Handbook* (Rome, 1955), p. 108; John Gray, *Legacy of Canaan* (Leiden, 1965), pp. 292–302; *Psalms I*, p. xxxiii; etc. etc.

the B words were often rarer and more literary than the A words,[4] was
not seized upon as evidence of the basically "seconding" nature of
this feature; instead, the fixity of the order was taken as an instance of
formulaic language, hence evidence of spontaneous, oral composition.

One lone voice in the post-Lowth period might well have been
heeded. It belonged to an itinerant nineteenth-century rabbi and
preacher, Meir Loeb b. Yehiel Michael (1809–79), generally known
by his acronymous surname Malbim. His uncompromising stand on
parallelism we shall examine presently, but it is worth noting that
Malbim was uncompromising in nearly all things. He was an
opponent of the new Reform Judaism, and his disputes with Jewish
communal leaders led to his imprisonment by Rumanian authorities
and eventual banishment from Rumania. Thence he served as rabbi in
Leczyca, Kherson, and Mogilev "and was persecuted by the
assimilationists, the *maskilim*, and the Hasidim,"[5] certainly a well-
rounded selection of enemies. Somehow amidst all these travels and
controversies he managed to write an impressive collection of biblical
commentaries, halakhic works, sermons, and poems.

In his biblical exegesis Malbim was a careful yet colorful expositor.
He saw himself as a champion of the פשט, the literal or simple
meaning of Scripture: "Here you shall find no homily and no science,
no mysticism or allegory, just the simple פשט."[6] He felt that deviation
from the simple meaning had since the Middle Ages (with whose
expositors, incidentally, he shows a profound familiarity), led to
numerous abuses which he now indicted for the religious laxities of his
own day. The literary approach to the Inspired Word, that is, the
reading of it as if it obeyed the canons of human rhetoric, he rejected
utterly, and this brought him into conflict even with such medieval
expositors as Abraham ibn Ezra. His approach to the Bible is, in this
sense, profoundly retrograde, the product of a thoroughly talmudic
outlook.

About the nature of biblical style, and parallelism in particular, he
discourses at length in his introduction to the Book of Isaiah. He
begins by stating the three principles of his commentary's approach:

1. In prophetic discourse there is no such thing as "repetition of the
    same idea in different words" [ibn Ezra's phrase] no repetitions of

4. R. G. Boling, "Synonymous Parallelism in the Psalms," *JSS* 5 (1960): 221–
55. This fact had been noticed by previous writers, especially Moshe Held in his
unpublished Ph.D. dissertation, "Studies in Ugaritic Lexicography and Poetic
Style" (Johns Hopkins, Baltimore, 1957). He is cited by Boling, p. 223.
5. Y. Horowitz in *EJ* 11:822.
6. M. L. Malbim, נבאים וכתובים (Vilnius, 1923), 5, p. 2b.

speech, no rhetorical repetitions, no two sentences with one meaning, no two comparisons of the same meaning, and not even two words that are repeated.

2. Prophetic discourse and sayings, whether simple or doubled, contain no words which were set there haphazardly without some special purpose; so that all the nouns, verbs and other words out of which each utterance is composed not only must by necessity come in that particular utterance, but also it would have been impossible for the divine orator to substitute even one word for another, for every word in the divine speech is weighed upon the scales of wisdom and knowledge, and all are arranged, appointed, preserved and counted by the measuring standard of almighty wisdom, which alone is capable of speaking in this fashion.

3. Prophetic discourse has no husk without a kernel, no body without a soul, no garment without a wearer, no utterance void of lofty idea, no expression in which discernment does not dwell, for the words of the living God all have the Deity alive within them, the breath of life is in their nostrils, the awesome, noble, exalted, moving spirit.[7]

If the reader hears in this the ring of Jewish fundamentalism, he will not be mistaken. Malbim's notion of prophecy rejected utterly the approach to biblical style that had been adopted increasingly by Jews and Christians since the Renaissance. Although he was clearly aware of the binary structure and semantic pairing of parallelism (note in 2 above, "whether simple or doubled"), he frequently stated that repetition as such did not exist, that even when the same word appears twice in a single verse, its significance in the second appearance must by definition be different from its first use; moreover, apparent synonyms are never synonymous, and it is wrong to suppose that "the divine orator might have taken the words that appear in the first of a pair of clauses and put them in the second clause corresponding to it."[8]

"The fear of the Lord is the beginning of knowledge." It was precisely Malbim's unyielding ideology that eventually led him to argue the emphatic character of the B-clause, and to recognize wherever possible (and, in truth, sometimes elsewhere) B's "what's more" quality. For, he says, even in the few cases where the text appears to use absolute synonyms, some nuance in form or scope may

7. Ibid.
8. Ibid.

be salvaged;[9] however, the great bulk of restatements or apparent repetitions are not absolute synonymities, and it would be an error to treat the differences as insignificant. Malbim lists the three main sorts of distinctions he invokes in his commentary (many of them based on readings found in the Targum, in R. David Kimḥi, and Abravanel):

1. In some cases I have shown that each of the restated clauses contains some element which makes it different from the other, such as "I shall be comforted from mine enemies, and avenged of my foes" [Isa. 1:24], "Whom shall I send and who will go forth for us?"[10] [Isa. 6:8], "A shoot shall go forth from Jesse's stock, and a plant shall flower from his roots" [Isa. 11:1]. Similarly with two comparisons that seem to have the same import, I have shown that each referent is somewhat different, as "As a leaf falls from a vine, and a fruit from a fig-tree"[11] [Isa. 34:4], and "Like a garment they will grow worn, a moth shall eat them"[12] [Isa. 50:9].

2. Elsewhere we have shown that the repeated utterances are two matters that have come into existence one after the other or one beside the other, in two distinct times or locations, such as "Like a

---

9. To illustrate this, Malbim cites some of the verses already seen in Moses ibn Ezra's (and Jonah ibn Janāḥ's) discussion of synonymity and repetition. Thus Isa. 41:4, מי פעל ועשה, "who acted and did," Malbim reads as a distinction between the performing of an action and the bringing of an act to its conclusion; both ibn Ezra and ibn Janāḥ treat these as synonymous (see chapter 5). Similarly, Isa. 43:7 בראתיו יצרתיו אף עשיתיו, "I created, I shaped, yea I made him" Malbim takes as representing (1) creation ex nihilo, (2) formation, and (3) completion (reading the root עשה as in the previous מי פעל ועשה). David Kimhi (Radak) and earlier interpreters argue the same line on this verse in somewhat more specific terms: (1) insemination, (2) formation of the joints and limbs, and (3) creation of the outer skin. About this whole approach Moses ibn Ezra wrote: "This is the commentator's own hair-splitting, for the text's purpose is emphasis (al-taʾkīd)." (See Kitāb al-muḥāḍara, ed. A. S. Halkin [Jerusalem, 1975], p. 162). Pursuing such "hair-splitting," Malbim further argues the difference between "din" and "tumult" (i.e. המון vs. שאון) in Isa. 5:14 is the difference between the "usual" sound of the city and "unusual" tumult. Similarly, the difference between חלף and עבר in Isa. 8:8 is temporariness vs. permanence. Malbim, נבאים וכתובים, p. 36b.

10. Here it is not the "for us" that is the differentiating element, as one might imagine. For Malbim, the two questions reflect two conditions necessary for sending a messenger: Who is worthy to go? and Who is willing to go? See his comments in ibid., p. 30b.

11. Our translation reflects Malbim's [and Radak's] understanding: "The fruit of the fig-tree is [indicated by the feminine] nobelet, not the leaf, which would be masculine." Ibid., pp. 114a and b.

12. That is, worn out from use (conflict) as distinct from being consumed because of neglect; ibid., p. 169b.

harvest-booth in a vineyard, and as a shed in a field, like a city under siege"[13] [Isa. 1:8], "Raise up a standard and lift your voice, wave your hand"[14] [Isa. 13:2], "To take booty and seize spoils"[15] [Isa. 10:6].

3. Or I have shown that the second clause always adds something to the first clause paired with it, such as "Ah, sinning nation," (and more than this) "people heavy with transgression," (and more than this they are a) "family of evil-doers," (and more than this they are) "wicked children" (and more than this that they) "abandoned the Lord," and so forth [Isa. 1:4]. And similarly "if your sins be as crimson," (and more than this) "if they are redder than the dyeing worm [from which crimson dye is made]" [Isa. 1:18].

Eventually Malbim's stance leads where we cannot go, to finding significance in the slightest alternations[16] and (the talmudic corollary shown clearly in our history) so focusing on the distinguishing nuance as to lose sight of the obvious structuredness of the speech. But his approach is the proper beginning. If his espousal of omnisignificance leaves him easy prey to snipers, let it be noted that his distortion is no

---

13. Malbim explains in greater detail ibid., p. 9b: "The booth in the vineyard has within it only the guard of the vineyard; so similarly Jerusalem has no outsiders, only its inhabitants; the second time-frame comes when he compares it to a shed in a field, that is, a booth built in a gourd-field, whose guardian only stays there at night but during the day it is completely vacant (since the gourds are hard and need not be guarded during the day from birds, but only at night against thieves)—so the Jerusalemites used to secrete themselves in caves during the day and hide for fear of the enemy and were in the city only at night. And in the third period of time he turns to Jerusalem itself and its surroundings, which now was like a city besieged in a siege." (Cf. the Jonathan targum and Radak.)

14. The standard can be seen from afar, "and after they are closer to them they will 'lift up their voice,' for now they can hear, and they will follow it [the voice] closer and when they are still nearer 'they will wave hands' (to them), beckoning by hand for them to approach and enter the city." Malbim again elaborates on Radak; ibid., p. 52a.

15. The root שלל he takes as the undivided booty left in a city after its inhabitants have fallen in war; the root בז refers to the share of goods taken by each despoiler. See his proof-texts ad Isa. 8:1.

16. Indeed, Malbim later notes that his task as an exegete would have been easier if he had contented himself with finding for each pair only one nuance to separate them, as other commentators had done; instead, he insisted on distinguishing each and every word! "But I set down this rule inviolable, that no words came by chance into the council of the Lord," and consequently "in two clauses each composed of numerous words, I have been obliged to show that all the words that come in each clause must come only in that clause and not in the clause paralleling it," נבאים וכתובים, p. 4a.

greater than, indeed is the precise converse of, *parallelismus membrorum*. To say that there is no synonymity is just as much an approximation as to say that B *means the same thing* as A. Furthermore, the former is at least a positive and productive stand; it is rooted, as we have seen, in the very essence of parallelism, and is demonstrably the only reasonable reading of numerous "sharp" sayings and verses; and it is a reading that favors the text, allows it room to be precise and to slice sharp as a blade.

But Malbim's commentaries were unknown or ignored by the emerging movement of modern biblical criticism. It was Lowth's approach that prevailed and has continued to prevail, and the notion of poetic structure it supports has since his time generally complemented that other popular area of inquiry, the search for biblical meters. Lowth, as we have seen, thought Hebrew meter irretrievable, but his followers did not agree, and with the principle of parallelism basically unarguable, interest in Hebrew poetics since Lowth has largely centered on systems of scansion.

2

The always-difficult job of summarizing previous writers' researches is rendered still greater when one is not in sympathy with their approach or conclusions; and since, happily, other critics have recently shown great zeal in recounting the history of biblical metrics over the last two centuries, I will refer the curious reader to their compilations.[17] Let us here confine ourselves to the barest outline.

The modern period offers no radically new departures in Hebrew poetry: what it has been able to provide is more detailed development of themes already seen in the pre-Lowth period, and an integration of these with new evidence from archaeology and the study of cognate literatures. Investigations along the lines of classical prosody continued in the late eighteenth and early nineteenth centuries by E. J. Greve, C. G. Anton, and others.[18] J. Bellermann's *Versuch über die*

17. See *EPH*, pp. 119–93; *PsIW*, pp. 261–66; *OTI*, pp. 57–64; T. H. Robinson, "Basic Principles of Hebrew Poetic Form," *Festschrift A. Bertholet* (Tübingen, 1950), pp. 438–50; and many others, listed, inter alia, in the bibliography of D. N. Freedman's "Prolegomenon" to G. B. Gray's *Forms of Hebrew Poetry* (New York, 1972).

18. Anton published a *Conjectura de metro Hebraeorum* in 1770, and several other works, including a scansion of the Psalms (1780) after that. Greve, following Lowth's urging about the poetic nature of the Prophetic books, scanned Nahum, Habbakuk, and Isaiah.

Metrik der Hebräer (1813) analyzed syllables in terms of duration and deduced prosodic patterns from the syllabic distribution of *morae* (in Latin prosody, a *mora* was the amount of time required for the pronunciation of the simplest syllable). Meanwhile, the notion of word stress as a possible element in scansion was in the ascendant. Understandably, this line of inquiry was particularly popular among speakers of Germanic languages, and two of its strongest advocates in the nineteenth century were Julius Ley and K. Budde. Ley[19] postulated stress accent as the sole significant element in Hebrew prosody. Lines were determined according to parallelism, and, depending on the total number of stresses, were scanned as "hexameters," "pentameters," "octameters," and so forth. Budde's most important contribution was an analysis of the meter of Lamentations and other dirges,[20] in which he observed the tendency of A verses to be somewhat longer than their corresponding B's. Seeking to isolate the independent (*selbständige*) terms on each side of the "caesura" and assuming each such term received one stress in performance, Budde found that A usually had three stresses (but sometimes four), while B usually had two (though sometimes three). This would make for a truncated, "limping" gait (here the classical analogues are uncomfortably obvious) appropriate to a dirge; the *qinah* (lament) meter was born. (Budde remained admirably skeptical about all other metrical hypotheses that sprang up in the wake of his article.) It has since been pointed out that this 3:2 line, as it has been styled, can be "discovered" in many other Hebrew compositions that are not the least bit dirgelike.[21]

The ideas of Ley and Budde were passed on to Eduard Sievers. Sievers had started as a metricist interested in the special problems surrounding Old English and Germanic prosody; he wrote a classification for syllabic patterns first in *Beowulf*, then for Old Germanic poetry in general.[22] In these systems, which, in modified form, are still in use today, Sievers attributed primary and secondary stresses to important syllables in the line, as well as an unstressed notation to lesser syllables and even some small words—pronouns, prepositions, conjunctions, demonstratives, and articles. Through this approach he was able to isolate what he felt to be the five basic

19. See his *Grunzüge des Rhythmus, des Vers- und Strophenbaues in der hebräischen Poesie* (Halle, 1875).
20. "Das hebr. Klagelied," *ZAW* 2 (1882): 1–52.
21. See G. B. Gray, *Forms of Hebrew Poetry*, p. 116; T. H. Robinson, "Hebrew Poetic Form" in *SVT* 1 (1953): 134.
22. E. Sievers, *Altgermanische Metrik* (Leipzig, 1893).

patterns of stressed and unstressed syllables in the half-verses of *Beowulf*. In Hebrew, his approach was similar. Unlike the theories of Ley and Budde, his was not a "pure stress" one—he felt that the number and placement of unstressed syllables was significant, and argued that the Hebrew line was basically "anapestic," i.e., two unstressed syllables followed by a stress. (This foot could be varied, however, so that the end result was not markedly different from the Ley–Budde scheme.) Using this system, Sievers produced scansions not only of the (by now traditionally) "poetic" books, but of Genesis, Exodus, and other "prose" works. For he was honest enough to recognize that his scansion might fit such texts just as well, or badly, as it did the Psalter, and since, unlike Ley or Budde, he did not admit parallelism as the absolute determinant of lineation, there really was no reason to expect the historical books to be any less metrical than Job; all were "poetic." But this is symptomatic. His problem in Hebrew, no less than in Old English, was to demonstrate that there were certain syntactically possible distributions of stress that simply did not appear in "poetry," that is, to demonstrate that this system was more than the ability to scan and classify absolutely anything, like Gomarus's *Davidis Lyra*. There is no doubt that Sievers's own career—as a metricist who learned Hebrew in order to be able to solve its metrical crux—was responsible for the wide acceptance his theories won at the turn of the century.

Meanwhile, G. Bickell, drawing inspiration from the system of Syriac hymnody, had put forth a scansion of biblical poetry based on the syllabic alternation of stress.[23] He held that every line of Hebrew poetry was either trochaic or iambic, depending on whether its first syllable was stressed or not; thence stressed and nonstressed syllables alternated with perfect regularity. No doubt this system will remind the attentive reader of that advanced by Francis Hare; it was not, however, for a lack of originality that Bickell was criticized, but because, in order to make good the claim of alternation, he had to resort to an arbitrary and irrational system of assigning stresses. Syllables ending in aleph and heh were sometimes elided and sometimes not, and shewa was not handled consistently.

Despite criticism of Bickell, his ideas have survived somewhat in the writings of G. Hölscher and S. Mowinckel, whose distribution of stresses approximates an alternating, "iambic" meter (as opposed to

---

23. G. Bickell, *Carmina VT metrice* (Innsbruck, 1882), and *Dichtungen der Hebräer* (Innsbruck, 1882–83).

Sievers's "anapestic");[24] their advantage over Bickell consists in their flexibility—for example, permitting two stresses to occur side by side. Up until recently, the debate betwen this quasi-Syriac, alternating-stress approach and the Ley–Budde–Sievers line has occupied the center of attention. Certain writers since Lowth, notably H. Ewald, G. B. Gray, and T. H. Robinson, have urged parallelism as the central "structuring" element of biblical poetry and have allowed "meter" the widest latitude,[25] but their writing has not slowed the pace of metrical theories. An interesting compromise was put forward by S. Segert, who tried to establish three different periods of Hebrew poetry, each with its own system of scansion: "word-rhythm," pure stress, and alternating stress.[26]

With the availability of Ugaritic texts came various systems of Ugaritic scansion and attempts to correlate Ugaritic and Hebrew prosody.[27] One of the earliest, and best, was the already-cited study of G. D. Young, "Ugaritic Prosody."[28] Young began by arguing that the uncertainties of the Hebrew text tradition—possible errors, redactional changes, translations from other languages, or conflations—are not a problem with Ugaritic: if a meter is present, he said, we should have no trouble finding the form in which it manifests itself. He then tested various hypotheses based on the priciples of parallel stichoi, stress accent, syllabic arrangement, and so forth, and showed overwhelmingly that these hypotheses were not justified by the evidence. He concluded:

24. See G. Hölscher, "Elemente arabischer, syrischer, und hebräischer Metrik" in BZAW 34 (1920): 93; Mowinckel in *PsIW* 2, pp. 158–75, cf. his "Zur Problem der hebräischen Metrik" in *Festschrift A. Bertholet*, pp. 379–94.

25. Ewald's *Die Dichter des alten Bundes* (Göttingen, 1839) held that there was no precise line length in Hebrew, but that meter was "approximate" and followed the lineation of parallelism. See also J. Jebb, *Sacred Poetry* (London, 1820). G. B. Gray felt biblical poetry was governed by a stress-accent meter, but felt it was somehow connected to parallelism and sought to investigate the relationship (see *Forms of Hebrew Poetry*, pp. 112–13). For Robinson see the above-cited "Basic Principles" (n. 17); also *The Poetry of the Old Testament* (London, 1947).

26. "Problems of Hebrew Prosody," *SVT* 7 (1960): 283–91.

27. We have already seen W. F. Albright's attempt to classify biblical parallelism on the basis of Ugaritic in his *YGC* (see above, chapter 1). As to Ugaritic scansion and Hebrew, see recently B. Margalit, "Introduction to Ugaritic Prosody," *UF* 7 (1975): 289–313; various articles by O. Loretz in *UF* 3, 5, 6, and 7; S. B. Parker, "Parallelism and Prosody in Ugaritic Narrative Verse," *UF* 7 (1975): 283–94; D. K. Stuart, *Studies in Early Hebrew Meter* (Missoula, Mont., 1976).

28. G. D. Young, "Ugaritic Prosody," *JNES* 9 (1950): 124–33.

To Occidentals who associate poetry with meter, the illusion of
meter in the poetry of Ugarit is created by the accidents of Semitic
morphology and parallelism of thought. A poetry in which the
outstanding feature is parallelism of thought; a poetry written in a
language in which the majority of words are of one, two or three
syllables, and in a language in which almost any clause can be
couched in from two to four words; is a poetry which naturally lends
itself to the creation of the impression of lines of uniform metric
length.

Young's only shortcoming was a failure to state clearly what Lowth
and many others had, that this brevity of the clauses, their
"terseness," was particularly prized as a form of eloquence and
consequently, along with "seconding," was a fairly regular feature
of high style, hence the apparent distinction between "poetry" and
"prose" and the appearance of some metrical system in the former.
In any case, Young's article was clear and courageous, and should
have given metricists greater pause than it apparently did.[29]
    W. F. Albright followed the accentual-syllabic approach to
Hebrew prosody,[30] and indeed often invoked it in his analysis of
"poetic" passages. He passed on his interest in biblical poetry to his
students, several of whom, however, have been the leaders in a new
approach, which might with justice be described as the Syllable-
Counting Text-Rewriting school of biblical prosody. These critics
believe Hebrew meter is best approached by disregarding stress and
concentrating on the total of the syllables, whose number, ideally,
should be equivalent on both halves of the "caesura," though
equivalence in successive lines is not necessary. In order to achieve
syllabic equivalence in individual lines, it has often proven necessary
to emend the texts, omitting definite articles, conjunctions, and other
"prose" features, indeed sometimes whole words or phrases; hence
the descriptive title.
    It must be said that one schooled in metrics will be surprised to read

---

29. Albright labeled it "metric nihilism" that was "far beyond rational
discussion" (*HUCA* 23 [1950–51] Part I, p. 7 n.).
30. Albright's metrical ideas were neither clear, consistent, nor dogmatic. He felt
"Canaanite" poetry was "partly accentual and partly syllabic (i.e., it depended
partly on counting syllables), though the precise laws governing it are still obscure
and there was certainly a great deal of possible variation within still uncertain
boundaries" (*JBL* 61 [1942]: 117). His approach was thus like that of Sievers, but
no doubt the "syllabic" part, and especially his syllabic ideas about Ugaritic verse,
led to his students' theories for Hebrew: see below. Cf. his "The OT and Canaanite
Language and Literature," *CBQ* 7 (1945): 21.

some of these present-day writings. For however much one might have disagreed with earlier writers like Sievers, or for that matter J. J. Scaliger or Jerome, at least these men possessed a working knowledge of the metrical terms they employed and knew something about what meter in general involves. But how is one to judge a description of Hebrew metrics that does not even understand the significance of the word "foot"?[31] Or one that, for the purpose of analogizing to the "irregular meter" of Hebrew, adduces nothing less than a stanza of English "fourteeners," whose insistent thumping may be faulted on many counts, but surely not that of irregularity![32] Indeed, what does this concept of "irregular" or (still more diplomatically) "non-regular" meter mean when it cannot be distinguished from no meter at all? What can one say of a metrical theory that is purely visual, in which regularity is achieved by discounting a phrase in the middle of the line, or counting it twice, so as to make the "halves" equal?[33] What of metrical theories that mercilessly hack away at the text, here excising particles and words as "later prose accretions" but retaining them elsewhere in the same "poem" *metri causa*?! What of scholars who blind themselves to the bankruptcy of their own theories by branding all irregularities prose intervals, or "imperfect" meter, or by quite simply refusing to consider them?[34] When one begins to inquire into current metrical ideas and notices such inconsistencies and errors, he may hope that things will prove to be as Ecclesiastes describes (7:8), "Better is the latter part of a thing than the beginning,"—that some explanation for the lapses, or at least some compensatory new insight, will be put forward. But alas, the conclusion of his investigation into the modern metricist is likely only to bring to mind another verse from that same book, "The beginning of his discourse is foolishness, and the end a noxious stupidity" (10:13).

All metrical theories suffer from the same syndrome. It starts with the observation that "lines," or sentences, units of thought, major pauses, "periods" or whatever, are roughly equal in length in a given passage of "poetry." This rough equality surely is not coincidental (and it is not!), so some underlying rule or system must be found. This

31. *PsIW*, 2, p. 160; see also Stuart, *Early Hebrew Meter*, p. 1.
32. Ibid., p. 45, n. 50.
33. M. Dahood, "A New Metrical Pattern in Biblical Poetry," in *CBQ* 29 (1967): 574.
34. Here the transgressors are so numerous it would be unfair to single out individual works.

in turn proves frustrating, the meter is "elusive." The critic sighs wistfully, "If only we had a Ugaritic treatise on poetry!"[35] Out of this frustration are born other errors: textual emendation, the bracketing of "prose" that will not fit metrical schemes, the "survival" of "poetic fragments" in prose narratives, and so forth. Even with all these escape clauses, none of the "systems" seen above has credibly worked, because all of them basically misconstrue the nature of the "meter" involved: it is simply not a system.

What then may be said of the "descriptive" approach to Hebrew metrics, which seeks not to establish "strict numbers" but merely to pin down broad limits; or of the view (seen earlier) that Hebrew poetry is written in "free rhythms" whose basic regularity, if not systematic, is nonetheless apparent enough?[36] The argument of the present study has not only been that the approximate regularity of biblical songs does not correspond to any metrical system, but that this regularity cannot be properly understood apart from the fact of parallelism and its heightening devices. To speak of meter apart from parallelism is to misunderstand parallelism. Moreover, when considered in isolation, biblical "meter" will always prove rather half-hearted, suddenly dropping an established pattern of regularity without apparent purpose, as well as cultivating a semi-regular form which is neither quite "prose" nor yet of the same uniformity achieved in *very* regular sections. Still further, it has been shown above that the bulk of metrical theories tend to confine themselves to the most highly parallelistic passages of the Bible: once this implicit bond between metrical speculation and parallelism is broken (but of course while it is intact, meter and parallelism are still treated as merely coordinate features, rather than as aspects of one phenomenon)—once this bond is broken and meter as a truly independent feature is sought, there is scarcely a book of the Bible where, in the necessarily loose and "descriptive" approach this line of inquiry must follow, it cannot be found. For all these reasons, then, even the minimalist approach is basically wrong-headed, the chasing after a phantom. But there is yet another aspect of this approach, indeed of the metrical search as a whole, which, precisely because it is so obvious, is in danger of being overlooked.

35. See F. M. Cross, "Prose and Poetry in the Mythic and Epic Texts from Ugarit," *HTR* 67 (1974): 5.

36. See chapter 2, n. 21; also R. C. Culley, "Metrical Analysis of Classical Hebrew Poetry," in J. W. Wevers and D. B. Redford, *Essays on the Ancient Semitic World* (Toronto, 1970), p. 12.

The idea of biblical poetry, this study has maintained, is both right and wrong, enlightening and misleading at the same time. Like the old equation of *torah* and *nomos* (law), it is an approximation. But the search for biblical meter, however dismal its results, has not been without its effect on this idea. For while it is true that present-day concepts of prosody no longer require (as they did in Lowth's day) that all poetry be "confined to numbers," it is equally true that we never speak of meter and its attributes except in regard to poetry. Essays do not have meter, nor do doctors' prescriptions, business letters, book reviews, or inaugural addresses—and if they did, they would become *poetic* essays, doctors' prescriptions, and so forth. I daresay this is not because someone (especially a biblical metricist!) could not here and there isolate "strict numbers" in any of the above, or indeed lay them out on the page as "free verse." But to do so would be to make an absurd statement about their essence—indeed, it is on this absurdity that the 1960's phenomenon of Found Poetry played so strikingly.[37] The same principle, not absurdly but somewhat insidiously, has operated in regard to the so-called "free rhythms" of biblical poetry. For metrical statements, even at this harmless, "descriptive" level, are far more than an analytical tool: they are a statement about a composition's essence.

There is nothing illusory about the sentence regularity of the two most formally structured books of the Bible, Job and Proverbs. But so

37. Here, for the uninitiated, is one "found poem," by Ronald Gross (apparently "discovered" in an IRS circular):

Suppose, Instead

Whatever your father wills you
is not taxable to you
as income. It's a bequest,
a tax-free bounty.
Suppose, instead,
he's sick and wants you
to care for him.
In return, he agrees
in writing
to leave you
his property.
Then you've got a
transfer for a consideration—
all taxable income when
you receive your "bequest."

(from Ronald Gross and George Quasha, *Open Poetry: Four Anthologies of Expanded Poems* [New York, 1973], p. 476.)

much hangs on how one construes it! It *is* fairly accurate to say that Job is written in lines of six or seven stresses each, or that there are usually six major words per line, or six to ten syllables per hemistich. But so is it accurate to say that Job is written in the florid style of biblical rhetoric: highly parallelistic sentences, usually consisting of two clauses, each clause stripped to a minimum of three or four major words. It is this writer's conclusion, not arrived at without some reluctance, that of these two descriptions the latter is a better construction of the evidence. For we have seen how the former approach runs into trouble in the Psalter and other books; how it leads to the bifurcation of biblical style into poetry and prose; to the problem of apparently unmetrical poems and metrical or "semi-poetic" prose; and to the promotion of approximate regularity into metrical systems which in turn necessitate emendations of the most imaginative hue.

The second description not only does not create these problems, but partakes of a more far-reaching view of biblical style. This view begins by taking cognizance of the centrality of "seconding" as a trope of emphasis and ornamentation. It sees in the "pause sequence" an abstraction of that trope. Moreover, it argues that while the rules of American rhetoric, for example, push the speaker in the direction of *variety* in sentence forms and syntactic constructions, the Bible's "high style" prescribes rather the opposite: the sameness of terse, parallelistic clauses, usually meted out in pairs, making for sentences of approximately equal length. Of course to all this a biblical metricist might object, "But if it has four legs and whinnies, it's a horse!" Yet if sometimes its whinny is rather deep and raspy, and if, in addition to having four legs, it is distinguished by the hump on its back, perhaps this creature's horse-like-ness is not the important thing about it, indeed, perhaps one should not look to the barnyard to understand its way of life.

The heart of the metrical crux in Hebrew is now, and always has been, the assumptions of the metricists. Some writers, like G. B. Gray, have at least been moved to investigate the relationship between parallelism and line length, suspicious that the latter's apparent regularity might somehow be related to the former; but hampered by a faulty notion of parallelism, all that he and later writers have been able to come up with is the observation of "compensation," the apparent attempt of biblical authors to include some compensatory extra word or phrase in the B half to make up for an unparalleled term in A and so preserve the equality of clause length. This, instead of challenging their narrow idea of what

"parallelism" embraces, has only implied the inscrutable workings of
some metrical principle in addition to parallelism.

Surely an objective look at the origins and fruits of metrical
speculation should long ago have resulted in a rejection of the whole
idea. For, as we have seen, the Bible and rabbinic literature describe
musical instruments and singing arrangements, antiphony and cantillation; but there is nothing about meter. An elaborate system, nay three
systems, were developed to punctuate the biblical text, and these
reflected the slightest nuances of possible conjunction and disjunction
in public performance; but nothing in the systems has any sort of
regularity that might be associated with meter. Those who first
attributed meter to the Bible were Hellenized Jews, and later, Greek-
speaking Christians, whose desire to parallel the excellencies of
Greek poetry with their own sacred texts is all too easy to document.
The meters they attributed, hexameters and pentameters, are no
longer invoked; all that has been retained is their erroneous
assumption of metricality. Over the years, meter, rhyme, and other
trappings of poetry have all been "discovered" in the Bible, ever
defined according to traditions current in the writer's own tongue.
Meter has been quantitative in the Greco-Roman manner, with or
without rules of position and elision; quantitative in the Judeo-Arabic
manner; syllabic as in the vernacular poetries of Europe; accentual-
syllabic, as in English; pure accentual, as in English and German;
Wortrhythmus; *vers libre*; "irregular"; and so forth. All this should
have proven something long ago, but the metrical hypothesis has a
strange power which, as Budde himself noted in 1902, "during the last
centuries has again and again attracted amateurs and scholars."[38]

There is indeed an answer to this age-old riddle: no meter has been
found because none exists. Or, as others have urged, *parallelism is
the only meter of biblical poetry*—but even for this statement to be
correct, each of these terms must be understood in a nontraditional
manner. For by "parallelism" what we really mean is the subjoining,
"seconding" form of emphasis, abstracted and generalized to our
pause sequence; and by "meter" is meant only a loose and
approximate regularity, sometimes, to be sure, clearly cultivated, so
that sentence after epigrammatic sentence in Job or Isaiah rings true
with the click of a couplet. Finally, we must recall that the building-
block of this meter, the "seconding" clause, was not imported from
another planet, but grew organically out of ordinary speech and
remained an everyday trope of emphasis, so that its "irregular" use in

---

38. In J. Hastings, *Dictionary of the Bible* (New York, 1902), 4:5.

certain passages is not to be (and surely was not) read as a breakdown of the "meter," nor yet a residue or fragment of some more truly "metrical" subtext, but simply as a less intense, less consciously rhetorical, form of expression. "Prose" and "poetry" are a matter of degree.

3

At the risk of repetition, it may be worthwhile to stress what the foregoing pages have *not* said. It is not this study's contention that there is no difference between what has been called "biblical poetry" and "biblical prose," nor yet that the very idea of a "biblical poetry" is all one great mistake. Its argument is rather that the concepts of poetry and prose correspond to no precise distinction in the Bible, and that their sustained use has been somewhat misleading about the nature and form of different sections of the Bible, and about the phenomenon of parallelism. Of course there is some justification in speaking of the "poem of Job" and the like. But it should now be clear that there is also some distortion and risk. Though biblical poetry and its meters have an honored place in the history of scholarship, it might be wiser to restrict the use of these terms—to speak, in more neutral (and, alas, colorless) language, of biblical Hebrew's "high" or "rhetorical" style, and to call the Bible's songs simply songs, its prayers prayers, and its speeches speeches, without seeking to invoke "newfangled notions recently come, which your forefathers considered not" (Deut. 32:17).

4

The lessons of history may be hard, but they are not always hard to grasp; the metrical hypothesis in biblical poetry will not now be laid to rest, surely not by a statement that essentially says only what has been said a dozen times before by critics in the modern period, and indeed before them by others in the Renaissance, the Middle Ages, and late Antiquity. But there is, beyond this obvious point to our story, a less gloomy one.

It is, simply stated, that there is no such thing as an "objective" approach to biblical texts, no neutral set of literary tools that will take apart any book or passage and tell us what makes it work: the very sort of evidence one looks for, or overlooks, is more of a conclusion than the conclusions such evidence will be marshaled to support. This is clear in the case of parallelism. What was certainly a perfectly obvious feature of biblical style was not treated as such in rabbinic exegesis because this approach had no part in the Rabbis' view of what the Bible was and for what purpose it had been given to Israel. Translated into Greek or Latin, this natural, "pan-Semitic" form of emphasis was strange: why did not Moses more obviously employ anaphora, chiasmus, or zeugma to drive his points home? The answers given by the Church Fathers—(1) he in fact did, and here are examples; and (2) Divine rhetoric obeys its own rules and is not comparable to human style—were, in their way, quite correct and corresponded to the Fathers' view of the Bible's nature; but ours will find them unsatisfactory. Will we have found the *right* answer in stripping ourselves of all Indo-European and even Arabic rhetorical prejudices and deriving the conventions of biblical style only from the Bible itself? No doubt there is something "righter" in this, but it would be quite wrong to imagine it as some ultimate analysis. For "the conventions of biblical style" already says what we think is important about the Bible and what sorts of texts we think it is analogous to. To ask this question, and not another, is already a departure from neutrality; it validates a point of view.

So, in more general terms, with the whole notion of the "literary reading of the Bible." After all, one does not read the U.S. Constitution as literature, or *The Pageant of American History* as literature, or (to stick to an American context) Jonathan Edwards's sermons, *Poor Richard's Almanac*, or the Federal Reserve's *Monthly Bulletin* as literature. Respectively the legal, historical, sermonic, wisdom, and oracular genres surely account for the bulk of the twenty-four books of the Hebrew canon, and so one might well ask: what is literary about the Bible at all? Certainly it does not identify itself as literature, and often such self-definition as does occur seems clearly to place it elsewhere: "The word of the Lord came to me . . ." "Listen to my prayer . . ." "These are the generations . . ." "This is the regulation concerning . . ." "Hear, my son, your father's teaching"— all suppose a relationship between speaker and hearer which, we somehow feel, is double-crossed by being looked at *as* literature, as artful composition, as anything more than a faithful and naive recording. Of course we know better. Any text—that aforementioned U.S. Constitution, the warranty that comes with the clock-radio—can be opened and examined, its majestic or perhaps humble little strategies laid bare. Yet in this act the potential for inappropriateness, indeed absurdity, is high: in discovering alliteration here, or rhythmic patterns, we may truly find some of the unconscious or semiconscious "tinkerings of authorship," but we will seem to imply about the nature of the text and how it was written something that we actually believe to be untrue, or at least irrelevant. So with the Bible. We have shuddered to hear Joseph called "one of the most believable characters in Western literature," and not just because this statement puts the Bible on the wrong bookshelf. At such a remark one wants to object—on the model of the vaudevillian's "Who was that lady I saw you with last night?" "That ain't no lady, that's my wife"—and say that Joseph is no *character* at all, but someone far more intimately ours. And as true as this may be for us, how much truer must it have been when his story was first set down? That initial narrative act, "Come gather round and let me spin a tale," is not the starting point of biblical history. Its premise—"Let me tell you what happened to Joseph-our-ancestor, let me tell you how things came to be as you know them actually to be now"—is significantly different. Not to speak of "Let me tell you how God has saved us," "Let me tell you God's teachings."

One is reminded of the infinity of significance in kabbalistic exegesis, the Torah's "seventy faces," or Nahmanides' argument (in the preface to his Pentateuch commentary) that our division of the Torah into sentences and words is only one possible division (a strikingly modern argument!) of a text that is "entirely the Names of God"; or indeed the rabbinic principle that there are two *Torot*, and that the written Torah itself constitutes only part of the divinely communicated message. Surely there is an "Oral Law" that accompanies every reading of the Bible, one rooted in time and space, in the particulars of religion and theology and general culture, which will make a certain approach to the Bible right and wise and good and make all others wrong or irrelevant, superstitious or blasphemous. The history of biblical exegesis, to which the present volume is addressed, is thus of more than indifferent interest to those who seek to interpret the Bible by any standard, if not for the history's own sake then at least for what it has done to determine their task before they begin, whether they are moved to investigate the Bible's great themes and doctrines, or merely biblical parallelism.

APPENDIX A: THE PERSISTENCE
OF PARALLELISM

The following is a brief sampling of some of the parallelistic prayers and songs written in Hebrew during the rabbinic period and on into the Middle Ages. The full extent of parallelism's persistence is too ambitious a subject for the present format, for ultimately that issue must touch on the possible connection of parallelism to later phenomena: rhyme; binarism (including binary meters) in Hebrew and other verse; *maqāma*, "rhymed prose," *melitza*-style, and more. Rather than addressing these large issues, what follows is intended merely to illustrate what anyone acquainted with Jewish liturgy and early Hebrew poetry knows, namely, that biblical parallelism and its ways continued to characterize lofty style in Hebrew for many centuries after the close of the biblical period. How much this fact represents an actual continuity and development of biblical style in the postbiblical period, and how much it merely reflects the ongoing popularity of biblical pastiche and the general importance of the Bible as a stylistic model for later writers, will no doubt vary from composition to composition. Both factors seem undeniable influences in the persistence of parallelism.

In order to present even this brief sample, I have had to allow myself not to be concerned with the question of the "original" or "oldest" version of each text. Similarly, I have not shied away from obviously composite texts of different hands and perhaps periods. For neither precise dating nor textual precision is of prime concern here, but simply the continued use of the parallelistic style as a form of elevated speech long after the close of the biblical period.

1. From a Qumran *hodayah*

Many writers have remarked on the use of parallelism in Qumran writings, including the so-called "Thanksgiving hymns." The following brief excerpt is from the edition of J. Licht, מגילת ההודיות (Jerusalem, 1957), pp. 101–102:

1 כי אתה אלי סתרתני נגד בני אדם /
תורתך חבתה בי עד קץ הגלות ישעכה לי //
2 כי בצרת נפשי לא עזבתני / ושועתי שמעתה במרורי נפשי /
ודנת יגוני הכרתה באנחתי //
3 ותצל נפש עני במעון אריות / אשר שננו כחרב לשונם //
4 ואתה אלי סגרתה בעד שניהם / פן יטרפו נפש עני ורש //
5 ותוסף לשונם כחרב אל תערה / בלו[א כר]תה נפש עבדכה /
ולמען הגבירכה לנגד בני אדם //

1 For you my God have sheltered me against men / your Torah have you hidden in me till the end of your salvation's unfolding to me //
2 For in my soul's trouble you have not abandoned me / you have heard my crying in my soul's distress / and taken stock of my pains, recognized my suffering //
3 So that you saved a poor man's soul in the lions' den / whose tongues are as sharp as a sword //
4 But you my God shut up their teeth / lest they savage the soul of one poor and needy //
5 So you returned their tongues like a sword to its scabbard / leaving unharmed your servant's soul / and so as to show your power in the sight of men //

Typical of these compositions is the rather "unterse" style; especially striking are the articulated subordinations: פן, אשר, כי, למען, לבו[א]. At the same time, one ought to note the general omission of the definite article; its omission is a stylistic trait of the *hodayot* in general. Note also the differentiation affected through periphrasis (נפש עני line 3, נפש עבדכה line 5) and alternation in verbal forms, coupled with the repetition of whole phrases (נגד בני אדם lines 1 and 5; נפש עני lines 3 and 4).

2. עלינו לשבח

This liturgical piece, ascribed to the Babylonian sage Rab, has made its way from the New Year's service to the daily liturgy. It may belong to the third century, as some have argued, and share some traits with Merkabah hymns;[1] others attribute its origin to an earlier period, perhaps even to Second Temple times.[2] The text printed here is from

1. See G. Scholem, *Jewish Gnosticism, Merkabah Mysticism and Talmudic Tradition* (New York, 1960), pp. 27–28.
2. J. Heinemann, התפילה בתקופת התנאים (Jerusalem, 1964), pp. 172–75.

have remarked on the parallelism of the Mishnaic tractate *Abot* and on its connection with the parallelism of biblical wisdom.

6. נשמת כל חי

This ancient hymn, found in the Passover Haggadah and used in the Sabbath and holiday services, is in its present form apparently a composite of several independent texts, though the age of the sections and their division is in dispute.[7] Following are the opening lines as they appear in *Mahzor Vitry* (ed. S. Horowitz, Jerusalem, 1963), p. 153; remarkable are the multiple parallelism (within clauses, between clauses and whole lines) spread over what are essentially two long sentences:

1 נשמת כל חי תברך את שמך ה' אלהנו /
ורוח כל בשר תפאר ותרומם זכרך מלכנו תמיד //
2 מן העולם ועד העולם אתה אל /
ומבלעדיך אין לנו מלך גואל ומושיע //
3 פודה ומציל ומפרנס ומרחם /
בכל עת צרה וצוקה /
אין לנו מלך אלא אתה //

Let the breath of all beings bless your name, O Lord our God /
And the spirit of all flesh adore and exalt your mention, our king forever //
From eternity to eternity you are God /
And but for you we have no king, redeemer and savior //
Ransomer and rescuer, supporter and fosterer /
in any time of trouble and distress /
we have no king but you //

7. A Confession of Sin

The beginning of the following ודוי ("confession") is cited in b. *Yoma* is associated with the name of Rab, but may be earlier.[8] Text: the Babylonian order of prayer found in the Cairo Geniza and ed by N. Wieder in *Tarbiz* 37 (1968): 140–141.

1 אתה יודע רזי עולם / ותעלומות סתרי כל חי //

7. Goldschmidt, ההגדה של פסח ותולדותיה (Jerusalem, 1969) divides the text original fragments (pp. 107–08), but cf. J. Heinemann in *Tarbiz* 30

8. Mirsky above (n. 3), pp. 175–76, also I. Abrahams, "The Lost Confession *HUCA* 1 (1924): 376–85.

---

an Oxford manuscript of Maimonides' rite of prayer, reprinted in D. Goldschmidt, מחקרי תפילה ופיוט (Jerusalem, 1979), p. 206; cf. the wordy variant preserved in a northern Italian rite, Goldschmidt, 90–91.

1 עלינו לשבח לאדון הכל / לתת גדולה ליוצר בראשית //
2 שלא עשנו כגויי הארצות / ולא שמנו כמשפחות האדמה //
3 שלא שם חלקנו כהם / וגורלנו ככל המונם //
4 שהם משתחוים. להבל וריק / ומתפללים לאל לא יושיע //
5 ואנו משתחוים / [לפני] מלך מלכי המלכים ברוך הוא //
6 שהוא נוטה שמים / ויוסר ארץ //
7 ומושב יקרו בשמים ממעל / ושכינת עוזו בגבהי מרומים //
8 הוא אלהנו ואין עוד / אמת מלכנו ואין זולתו //

1 Let us now praise the Lord of All / give acknowledgement to the world's creator //
2 That he did not make us like the peoples of [other] lands / and did not set us as the families of the earth //
3 That he did not set our portion as theirs / [Nor] our lot like all their masses' //
4 In that they bow down to [or "in"] vanity and futility / and beseech a god unable to save //
5 While we bow down / before the kings-of-kings' King, blessed is he //
6 Who stretched out the heavens / and established the earth //
7 Whose place of glory is the heavens above / and his power's abode in the lofty heights //
8 This is our God, and there is no other / indeed our king, and there is none but him //

The parallelism, ellipsis, differentiation, and other biblical features are obvious. Note, however, the typically postbiblical use of elevating epithets and periphrasis.[3]

3. Rabbinic Benediction

The form and development of ברכות has been discussed by many writers, and see in general J. Heinemann, התפילה בתקופת התנאים (Jerusalem, 1964), pp. 52–66. Parallelism and its ways are evidenced in every rabbinic benediction. Even the shorter ברכות are in some measure parallelistic, for "seconding" is imposed by the appositional formulae, which provide a properly elevated idiom for these praises. In the longer ברכות, more obvious parallelism and other elevating features are found. The following example, part of the Musaf Service

3. On which see G. Scholem above (n. 1), also A. Mirsky, השירה העברית בתקופת התלמוד in ירושלים ב' (Jerusalem, 1966): 161–79.

recited at the beginning of the new month, exists in the same basic form in all rites, with, however, some variants (see below). This version is as it appears in the colletion of prayers made by R. Amram (ed. D. Goldschmidt, Jerusalem, 1971), pp. 88–89.

1 ראשי חדשים לעמך נתת / זמן כפרה לכל תולדותם //
2 בהיותם מקריבים לפניך זבחי רצון / שעירי חטאת לכפר בעדם //
3 זכרון לכלם יהיו / תשועת נפשם מיד שונא //
4 מזבח חדש בציון תכין / עולת ראש חדש נעלה עליו / שעירי עזים נעשה ברצון //
5 ובעבודת בית המקדש נשמח כלנו / ושירי דוד עבדך נשמע בעירך / האמורים לפני מזבחך //
6 אהבת עולם תביא להם / וברית אבות לבנים תזכור //

1 The beginnings of months you gave to your people / [as] a time of atonement for all their generations //
2 When they presented before you pleasing animal-sacrifices / goats for sin-offering to atone on their behalf //
3 These were a token for all / their own salvation from the enemy's power //
4 When you a new altar in Zion shall build / we will raise upon it the New Moon offering / and sacrifice he-goats in good favor //
5 And in the Temple service we shall all make rejoicing / and the songs of your servant David we shall hear in your city / spoken before your altar //
6 Eternal love you brought to them / and the Father's covenant visit upon the sons //[4]

4. A Personal Prayer

This is the version printed in standard editions of the Talmud, b. *Ber.* 60b.

1 יהי רצון מלפניך / ה' אלקי //
2 שתרגילני בתורתך / ודבקני במצותיך //
3 ואל תביאני לא לידי חטא / ולא לידי עון //

---

4. I do not know if the "missing link" to the problematic verbal forms in this prayer exists; in its present form it has disturbed many commentators, who have pointed out that by rights the last line should read either תביא לנו ("May you bring to us") or else הבאת להם ("You brought to them"). The order of prayers assembled by Sa'adya Ga'on (*Kitāb Jamiʿ al-ṣalawāt waʾal tasābīḥ*, ed. I. Davidson, S. Asaf and I. Joel [Jerusalem, 1970] contains the variant אהבת עמך תביא להם (p. 129) and the Benei Roma rite omits the entire middle part (see D. Goldschmidt, מחקרי תפילה ופיוט [Jerusalem, 1979], p. 165). Certainly the present version is problematic, but note the apparently past-continuative sense of the prefix form יהיו in line 3.

ולא לידי נסיון / ולא לידי בזיון //
כוף את יצרי / להשתעבד לך //
והקני מאדם רע / ומחבר רע //
ודבקני ביצר טוב / ובחבר טוב בעולמך //
ני היום ובכל יום / לחן ולחסד ולרחמים //
ניך / ובעיני כל רואי //
ולני חסדים טובים //
אתה ה' / גומל חסדים טובים לעמו ישראל //

1 May it be your will / O Lord my God //
2 That you make me familiar with your Torah / and make m[e] your commandments //
3 And do not lead me into the dominion of sin / nor that of tra[nsgression]
4 Nor that of trial[5] / nor that of shame //
5 But curb my thought / to be submissive to you //
6 And keep me from evil men / and from evil friends //
7 Let me cleave to good thoughts / and to good friends /
8 And make me find, today and every day / favor, love
9 In your eyes / and the eyes of all who see me //
10 And grant me acts of kindness //
[Closing:]
11 Blessed are you, Lord / granting acts of kindness to [...]

5. An Epigram

At the end of b. *Mo'ed Qat.* a number of lamen[ts] cited, including this brief epigram (p. 25b) on the who died on the very day on which a long-awaited to him:

ששון ויגון הדבקו //
ז חנינתו אבר חנינו //

Joy to sorrow is turned / rejoicing and lament
At the moment of joy he was stricken / at th[e]
"Hanin" passed away //[6]

The terse and elliptical style seems descen[ded]
Proverbs and "wisdom" literature in gener[al]
discussion see A. J. Baumgartner, *Poésie*
1896), and Mirsky, [...] ית בתקופת התלמוד

---

5. On the idea of "trial" here see J. Licht, *T[...]
in Post-Biblical Judaism (Jerusalem, 1973), p[...]
6. A play on the proper name; as a noun or[...]
"he who bestows love," hence perhaps, "affe[...]

The be[...]
87b. It[...]
from th[...]
publish[...]

7. D. G[...]
into seven[...]
(1961): 40[...]
8. See M[...]
of Samuel,[...]

2 אתה חופש כל חדרי בטן / רואה כליות ולב //
3 ואין כל דבר נעלם ממך / ואין נסתר מנגד עיניך //
4 יהי רצון מלפניך / ה' אלהנו //
5 שתמחל לנו על כל עונותנו / ותכפר לנו על חטאנו //

1 You know the secrets of eternity / and the hiddenmost things of all that live //
2 You search all the chambers of the innards / seeing kidneys and heart //
3 Not one thing is hidden from you / and nothing is sheltered from your sight //
4 May it be your will / O Lord our God //
5 That you forgive us all our sins / and pardon us for all our transgressions //

8. Two Alphabetical Praises

These two compositions, of similar theme, both show the alphabetical acrostic construction known from the Psalter and extremely popular in the early period of *piyyut*. In some biblical alphabets such as Psalm 119 one may observe a marked weakening of semantic parallelism and even the blurring of the pause-sequence—presumably, the existence of one lineating system allows the loosening of another. Nevertheless, many postbiblical songs, despite their alphabetical structure, are strikingly traditional in their use of parallelism and the maintenance of two-clause sentences. The following excerpt is as it appears in the order of prayers of R. Amram Ga'on (ed. D. Goldschmidt, Jerusalem, 1971), p. 71:

1 אל אדון על כל המעשים / ברוך ומברך בפי כל הנשמה //
2 גדלו וטובו מלא עולם / דעת ותבונה סובבים אותו //
3 המתגאה על חיות הקדש / ונאדר בכבוד על המרכבה //
4 זכות ומישור לפני כסאו / חסד ורחמים לפני כבודו //
5 טובים מאורות שברא אלהנו / יצרם בדעת בבינה ובהשכל //
6 כח וגבורה נתן בהם / להיות מושלים בקרב תבל //

1 God, Lord over all creation / blessed and praised in the mouth of all that breathe //
2 With whose greatness and goodness the world is filled / knowledge and discernment surround him //
3 He who is exalted above the heavenly beasts / and magnified in glory upon the chariot //
4 Merit and right are before his throne / with love and mercy his glory is filled //
5 Goodly are the luminaries which our God created / he formed them with knowledge, understanding, and science //

6 Power and might he invested in them / that they act as governors in the world's midst //

This second alphabet, of more exacting construction, is taken from Sa'adya Ga'on's collection, *Kitāb Jamiᶜ al-ṣalawāt waᵓal tasābīḥ*, p. 36:

1 אל ברוך גדול דעה / התקין ופעל זהר חמה //

2 טוב יצר כבוד לשמו / מאורות נתן סביבות עזו //

3 פנות צבאות קדושים / רוממי שדי תמיד / יספרו לאל קדושתו //

1 Blessed God, great of knowledge / prepared and wrought sun's brilliance //
2 Formed skillfully glory for His Name / placed luminaries about his Might //
3 Chiefs of holy throngs / praising God endlessly / recount to God his holiness //

9. An Abodah of Yose b. Yose

The following excerpt, the first two stanzas of a long alphabetical Abodah prayer by Yose b. Yose, was written for the Day of Atonement liturgy. (The author's dates are not even approximately known, estimates varying from the third century to the sixth.) It, like indeed many pieces like it, provides valuable evidence of the persistence of parallelism in the evolution of early *piyyut*. Along with the alphabetical arrangement, the two-clause structure and some semantic parallelism are apparent throughout.

אתה כוננת עולם ברב-חסד / ובו יתנהג עד קץ הימים //

אשר לא ימוט מעון יצורים / ולא ימעד מכבד פשעים וחטאים //

אדמה בעודה ציה וצלמות / באור דת שעשעת, ואצלך שחקה //

אמרת לתתה מרפא לכל-אנוש / טרם תפעלנו חייו הכינות //

בררת שחקים למכון שבתך / ורוחת עליות לכם הדרך //

בם תסתר בלי תשורך עין / ומשם עיניך משוטטות בכל-פעל //

בנתה לקרות ארץ על בלי-מה / להדם רגליך, ולמושב יצוריך //

בתהו ובמסערה יסודותיה תלית / ועת תשגיח בה עמודיה יפלצו //

You established the world with abundant love / and (established) that it continue in it to the end of days //

That it not be shaken by creatures' sins / nor totter from the weight of transgressions and faults //

While the land was yet waste and gloom / with Faith's Light [i.e., the Torah] you took pleasure and she sported in your company //

You vowed to give her as a cure to all mankind / Before you made him [i.e., man] you had prepared his life //

You chose the Heavens as a place for your dwelling / and set off the heights for your glorious throne //
Wherein you might be hidden, that no eye see you / but whence your eyes might range over all that is done //
You built the rafters of earth on the abyss / as a footstool for you, and dwelling-place for your creatures //
With chaos and storm you hung its foundations / and when you gaze upon it, its foundations tremble. //

10. Moses b. Asher's "Song of the Vine"

This poem, discovered by M. Zulay and published by B. Klar in *Tarbiz* 15: 43 (1944), is an alphabetical acrostic modeled on biblical examples. It is the work of the Masoretic scholar Moses b. Asher (ninth century): the text and a translation are found in P. Kahle, *The Cairo Geniza* (Oxford, 1959) pp. 83–86. Despite the biblical idiom, the composition as a whole is striking by its unusual, repetitive style. Here are the opening lines:

אתה נטעתה גפן שוריקה / משובחה היתה מכל הגפנים //
במגדל דויר היתה נטועה / וארז מלבנון היה בתוכה //
גפן ה' שבטי יעקב / ואיש יהודה נטע שעשועיו //
דליות הגפן הם הנביאים / ומגדל דויד הוא הר ציון //
היתה שתולה על מים רבים / ותגבה מאד בין העבותים //
והגפן החיא כפנה שרשיה / ועל מים רבים שלחה קציריה //

You planted the stock of a vine / praised it was over all other vines //
In the tower of David it was planted / and a cedar from Lebanon was in its midst //
The tribes of Jacob are the Lord's vine / and the man of Judah is his favored plant //
The branches of the vine, these are the Prophets / and the tower of David is Mount Zion //
It was rooted beside mighty waters / and grew most lofty among the bushes //
And that very vine stuck its roots / and sent forth its sprigs beside mighty waters //

11. From a Prayer of R. Sa'adya Ga'on

The following is excerpted from one of many parallelistic prayers by Sa'adya Ga'on. For this text and its recent history, see M. Zulay, האסקולה הפייטנית של רס'ג (Jerusalem, 1964), pp. 211–19.

אתה מרום לעולם ייי / גבור מני עד ועדי עד /

ומעולם ועד עולם אתה הוא אל //
בהשמים חסדך / ועזך בשחקים //
הודעת לבני האדם גבורותיך / ועל ישראל גאותך //
מכנף הארץ זמירותיך / ובקצה תבל מילי שבחך //
אתה הוא חי העולמים / וחיי כל החיים מלפניך הם //

You are forever exalted, Lord / mighty from eternity to eternity / and from everlasting to everlasting you are God //

In the heavens is your love / and your strength is in the clouds //

You made known to men your mighty deeds / and your majesty is upon Israel //

From the edge of the earth [extend] your songs / and at the world's border are words of your praise //

You are the one who lives eternally / and the lives of the living are all before you. . . . //

Sa'adya was certainly not the last to compose such free parallelistic prayers. Interested readers are referred especially to the compositions of R. Hai Ga'on (eleventh century), published by H. Brody in ידיעות המכון לחקר השירה 3:5 (1937). On Hai's experiments with off-rhyme and parallelism see B. Harushovsky in הספרות 2:742 (1971), and E. Fleischer, עיונים בשירתו של רב האיי גאון in Z. Malakhi, (ספר הברמן) שי להימן (Jerusalem, 1977): pp. 239–74.

APPENDIX B: ON SYNTAX AND STYLE, WITH SOME REFLECTIONS ON M. P. O'CONNOR'S *HEBREW VERSE STRUCTURE*

Among the studies of biblical poetry that have appeared during the time the present volume was in preparation,[1] one differs sufficiently from the contemporary approaches surveyed above to merit some special mention. It is M. P. O'Connor's syntactic study of the problem of biblical prosody, *Hebrew Verse Structure*.[2] At this late writing and in the present format, I will not be able to review all his arguments, but it may nevertheless be worthwhile to discuss briefly his book's overall method and its relationship to previous studies, as well as to this one.

O'Connor's is certainly a fresh approach and one that has already won high praise.[3] With a broad knowledge of contemporary linguistics, he reexamines much of the standard wisdom on Hebrew verse and strikes at its salient weaknesses. The metrical hypothesis, insofar as it aims at strict numbers, he judges doomed to failure: attempted scansions over the the last "two and a quarter centuries" only prove the weakness of the traditional metrical approach. (He is somewhat more tolerant of the "descriptive" approach cited above in chapter 7.) Similarly, he argues that parallelism *per se* is not linguistically definable; nor, indeed, is it a single feature, but rather a "congeries of phenomena." With a few deft strokes he dismisses synonymity, antonymity, and Lowth's whole categorizing method. The force of his

---

1. There are dozens of new articles and books, but I will limit myself to a single work that ought to be added to the references in the foregoing chapters, A. M. Cooper's *Biblical Poetics: A Linguistic Approach* (Yale Ph.D. diss., 1976, soon to appear in the Semeia Supplements series), which studies the phenomenon of parallelism in detail and, in an appendix, collects some of the material about medieval Jewish writings presented above in chapter 5.

2. M. P. O'Connor, *Hebrew Verse Structure* (Winona Lake, Ind., 1980). All subsequent references will appear in the text.

3. D. N. Freedman's appreciation appears on the book jacket; he describes it as "a great leap forward in the analysis and interpretation of early Hebrew poetry. . . . Much of the debate of the past century is thereby rendered both moot and sterile."

argument in this "negative" part of his exposition is, I think, overwhelming, and deals a severe blow to what O'Connor somewhat airily styles the "Standard Description" of Hebrew poetry (i.e., meter plus parallelism).

If meter is a chimera and parallelism a congeries, what then remains of "biblical poetry"? It is here that one wishes O'Connor had strayed to our question, to the very idea of biblical poetry. Instead, he seeks to redefine the components of the "Standard Description" in such a way as to salvage the concept of poetry, albeit with radical alterations. While strict numbers do not govern the length of A and B, something nevertheless seems to impose broad limits on their length; and that something, he urges, is a matrix of syntactic constraints, constraints that are visible in the "base" and "surface" structure of the line. His analysis of a corpus of 1,225 lines of early biblical poems produces a range of maximums and minimums at three levels of analysis: "clause predicators" (roughly, most verbs, vocatives, and "focus-markers"); "components" (each verb and each noun-phrase, along with the particles dependent upon them); and "units" (verbs and all "nomina").

Clause predicators	0 to 3
Components	1 to 4
Units	2 to 5

These ranges constitute the basic rules governing what can or cannot be found in a line of biblical poetry (like Lowth, he uses "line" to refer to A alone; B is not part of A but the next "line"). Here, then, are the makings of a new solution to the problem of biblical poetry: the metrical component is replaced by a system of syntactic "constriction," and parallelism, the structural constant of many a "Revised Standard Description," is demoted to a series of "tropes" (O'Connor *dixit*) that bind together lines into groups of twos, threes, or more.

Much of this is extremely suggestive. It would be helpful to be able to pin down some of the present study's remarks about the "syntactic simplicity" of A and B to some more precise formulation and to isolate clause- and sentence-types unacceptable to the terseness of the Bible's loftiest expression. O'Connor makes some progress in this direction, but he is hampered by his own particular aim: for in seeking to use observations of syntax to derive a set of quasi-metrical prescriptions, he skews somewhat the focus of his inquiry.

One might begin by noting in this undertaking a major (though not, as it turns out, the *most* troublesome) problem: the very numbers O'Connor comes up with, it seems to me, argue eloquently against the use he wishes to make of them. His claim is that syntactic constriction functions as a kind of meter; the first question one might ask is whether a line of three clauses in fact has very much in common with a line of no clauses. How are they comparable to two lines written in the same meter? Only in the fact that neither of them has *four* clauses? How is a line of two "units" in any way equivalent to one with two-and-a-half times that? Or, to use examples from O'Connor's own lineation, how can one believe that *yārâ bayyām* (Ex. 15:4) jingled in its hearers' ears as a coin of the same value as *umibḥar šālišāyw ṭubbĕʿu bĕyam sûf* (Ex. 15:4)? Can *middam ḥallālîm* (2 Sam. 1:22) be the "constrictional" sibling of *šāʾûl wîhônātān hanneʾehābîm wĕhannĕʿîmim* (2 Sam. 1:23)? The very fact that his attempt to create syntactic categories expressive of the basic terseness of all lines has produced such broad ranges only indicates to me that the categories are not very useful—that, indeed, other attempts to express broad limits on lines, such as contemporary syllable- or letter-counts or even Azariah's "ideas" or "items," are, crude as they may be, no less precise an index than O'Connor's. Moreover, the basic feeling of regularity produced in Hebrew songs derives, as we have seen above, from the recurrent sequence _____ / _____ //, an abstraction of the "seconding" assertion "A is so, and what's more, B." This patterned regularity arises from the conjunction of a host of factors, syntactic, semantic, and phonological. By separating the last two from the first, and by limiting the syntactic analysis to an inventory of possible components for each half-verse as a concern separate from the interrelation of consecutive clauses, O'Connor has lost most of the pattern. (This is an important point, to which I shall return presently.)

Such is not to suggest, however, that even if O'Connor's matrices cannot be used to demonstrate what he wants, they nevertheless have some descriptive validity. They do not, because the "line" that they chart proves to be a somewhat protean entity (only sometimes does it correspond to what we have been satisfied throughout to call, with some imprecision, the "half-verse" or "clause"). For what is the reality underlying O'Connor's line? His line is not, as he points out, a grammatical unit (i.e., not necessarily a "clause" in the grammatical sense); and, because "parallelism" has been redefined as a series of optional and multi-layered tropes, "line" is free from "parallelism's" lineation. Nor need the line be defined by any particular syntactic parsing one might be inclined to perform on longer units—the sentence, A + B, etc. It is thus a potentially arbitrary entity which conforms to O'Connor's constraints because these alone define it in the first place. While many of his lines do correspond to the traditional "hemistich" (i.e., A or B), a great many will be found to be shorter, indeed shorter by half. For should a line be in danger of exceeding O'Connor's limits, he always has the option of dividing it into two, provided that neither of the new entities violates his minimums. Herein lies an unfailing flexibility in his system, yet one which forces the question of where, besides the "matrices," a line actually lives:

עורי עורי דבורה / עורי עורי דברי שיר //

Arise, arise, Deborah / arise, arise, sing a song //   Judges 5:12

O'Connor divides B above into two (lest it violate his stipulation that no line of three major clause predicators contain anything else, p. 315). Yet this subdivision splits the juxtaposition *ʿûrî dabběrî* in B, which seems the whole point, the punning echo of *ʿûrî děbôrâ* in A; his lineation stops just where it should continue. This matter aside, one must raise the larger issue: if the second *ʿûrî ʿûrî* is sufficient to constitute a "line," why was not the first? And the answer, obviously, is that if the first *ʿûrî ʿûrî* were considered a line, we would be left with the extra *děbôrâ*, which has too few "units" to be a line on its own. The same phrase is thus treated two different ways depending on whether the word or words that follow it can stand alone as a new "line." In other words, lineation here (and elsewhere) is determined by the very rules that were supposed to have been deduced from it!

Expediency alone does not explain all the questionable lineations. (It is not clear what does.) Why, for example, make one line of

יהודה אתה יודוך אחיך

when it is clearly of two parts, in which B wittily draws the conclusion from A's assertion:

Judah are you / let your brothers give you homage //   Gen. 49:8

or perhaps more in keeping with the spirit of the original:

Judah's your name / let your brothers *judge* you well //

Why treat as one line

נאם בלעם בנו בער

Oracle of Balaam son of Be'or   Num. 24:4

and as two its answering half-verse

ונאם הגבר
שתם העין

Oracle of the man whose eye is perfect   Num. 24:4

Why two for

אנכי לה׳

אנכי אשירה

I of the Lord, I shall sing   Judges 5:3

and one for its fellow

אזמר לה׳ אלהי ישראל

I shall sing of the Lord the God of Israel   Judges 5:3

One cannot but feel that lineation in this system is entirely *ad hoc*, a bit reminiscent of the fellow who first shoots the arrows at the barn door, then draws the targets around them. Even so, were the corpus of examples expanded a bit, the matrices would run into trouble. By O'Connor's definition of poetry, Psalm 34:8

חנה מלאך ה׳ סביב ליראיו / ויחלצם //

The angel of the Lord stays about his worshipers / and he saves them //

must be prose, because the second "line" (i.e., B) is only one unit long, *wayyiḥallĕṣēm*. The same is true for Psalm 119:46, 55, and others. The maximum limits would be violated still more often but for the option of division.

But in general the difficulty with O'Connor's grid will not be exclusion but inclusion. For if conformity to its constraints will equal poetry, what will not be poetry? (This *is* the great problem.) Certainly "Let there be light," "And God spoke to Moses, saying," "These are the generations of Noah," "This is the ordinance of the burnt offering," and a thousand other "little poems" will emerge from the Pentateuch—indeed, whole passages such as those from Exodus and Numbers cited above in chapter 2 and a good many more, are capable of being divided in conformity to O'Connor's constraints. His definition of biblical poetry, in seeking to be purely descriptive, does not try to distinguish poetry from prose. Wherein that distinction may lie is a subject that, extraordinarily, does not interest this study. *Et pour cause!* For O'Connor has strung his net far too tightly to snag only poetic mackerel while letting prosaic minnows swim free. The inability of this description to describe any difference between poetry and prose is far from an irrelevancy or a minor defect: it calls into question the entire undertaking.

It seems to me that this error is fundamental to a kind of "Uniformitarian" presupposition such as that described by O'Connor in connection with his linguistic axioms. All languages are basically similar; surface differences in grammar conceal "deep" similarities. As a corollary, all languages have a "sub-system" called poetry. If the language inconveniently fails to divide itself along recognizable prose-and-poetry lines, it will be necessary both to redefine poetry so as to embrace the variety of subsystems encountered and to try to strip poetry of generic and other implications, which will, nevertheless, cling to it and so distort perceptions, as we have seen. Moreover, when the segregation of one sub-system from another becomes troublesome, one will have to assert, as O'Connor does, that ordinary prose contains here and there "little poems" or, on the other hand, that the trappings of poetry also mark "Levantine literary prose" (p. 27). In other domains biblical scholarship seems to have learned to be wary of universalism. Few people nowadays take seriously the great universalist rumblings of nineteenth-century anthropology—Sir James Frazer explaining Genesis through an inexhaustible and ever-convenient supply of Bushman and aborigine myths that contain "the same idea" as the story of the Garden of Eden or of Cain and Abel, for, after all, are not people (especially primitives) the same the world over? There is a useful limit to generality, which such universalizing quickly exceeds: this is as true of language as of any aspect of culture. Given the axiomatic existence of biblical poetry, every researcher will go astray. For it is "biblical poetry," and not merely parallelism, that is the "congeries of phenomena."

The most "poetic" aspect of the Bible's high style, its "physical and immediately perceptible recurrent quality,"[4] is not to be found in the (wide-ranging) brevity of short clauses strung together but in the semantic–syntactic–phonological complex of the "target form" A + B. That is why O'Connor, with his exclusive focus on syntax in lineation and his somewhat capricious and incomplete "line," is off on the wrong foot from the start. A study of syntax must concern itself with the sequence A + B as a whole, and particularly with the articulation of the medial and final pauses, an articulation which is, of course, not merely a matter of syntax. To deal with only half the true line is to overlook a good deal about syntax and to join as equals highly dissimilar elements.

About the other half of O'Connor's analysis, his remarks about parallelism, it is to be noted that his study has not a little in common

---

4. O'Connor uses this phrase to describe the role of meter in poetry, p. 60.

with the pre-Lowthian tropes-and-figures approach. He breaks down (with admirable clarity) this "congeries of phenomena" into different categories and shows them operating at different levels: the word, the line, and the supralinear group. At the word level he speaks of "dyading," which he conceives as a range of phenomena, with actual repetition at the one end, and at the other, different forms of "coloration," including "binomination" (Balaq / son-of-Sippor, Jacob / Israel), coordination (Moses and Aaron; heaven and earth; three and four), and "combination."[5] After treating such word-level tropes, O'Connor moves to the clause level, where he finds "matching" (described above as syntactic equivalence) and "gapping," i.e., ellipsis.

As with the matter of constriction, the absence of the semantic element here is crucial. Clearly, what is going on in matching and gapping is not only going on at the syntactic level, e.g., O'Connor's example

שאל אביך ויגדך / זקניך ויאמרו לך //

Ask your father and he will tell you / [Ask] your elders and they will speak to you //   Deut. 32:7

To limit the discussion here to syntax is, obviously, to misrepresent.[6] Moreover, the futility of this analysis as a description specifically of poetry is inescapable: dyading, matching, gapping, and so on are phenomena general to Hebrew style. Some of this O'Connor concedes

5. This last category is, however, ill-conceived; its evils have been described above under the rubric "distribution." No more need be added here, save to observe that the existence of this category seems genuinely to have confused O'Connor in his translations, often grotesquely so. Thus for Psalm 106:16

They acted jealously toward Moses in the camp / and toward Aaron, the Lord's holy one //

O'Connor splits B into two parts, "Aaron" and "the holy one," (i.e., the holy shrine). Then, via distribution, he comes up with the composite, "They vexed Moses and Aaron in the camp of the shrine of YHWH."

6. R. Austerlitz's *Ob-Ugric Meters* (Folklore Fellows Communications No. 174.8, Helsinki, 1958), which O'Connor praises highly and which apparently served in some measure as his own methodological model, was criticized on precisely these grounds by J. L. Fischer in his review of the book, *Journal of American Folklore* 73 (1960): 337–40. R. Jakobson apparently endorsed this criticism: see his "Grammatical Parallelism and its Russian Aspect," *Language* 42 (1966): 404 n. 23. Moreover, Fischer's reaction to Austerlitz's metrical theories has a familiar ring: "If one thinks about this a moment it becomes clear that this is a considerable extension of the useage of the concept of meter. . . . Using the author's definitions, metrical analysis is equally applicable to a prose text."

(pp. 101–02); but he is curiously emphatic that verb-gapping is simply not to be found in biblical prose. This is unfortunate, because he will then be stuck with such two-line "poems" as

ונתן לי לחם לאכל ובגר ללבש

And give me bread to eat and [give me] clothing to wear   Gen. 28:20

ונתתי את שמיכם כברזל ואת ארצכם כנחשה

And I shall make your skies as iron and [I shall make] your land as brass   Lev. 26:19

יד הערים תהיה בו בראשנה להמיתו ויד כל העם לאחרנה

The witnesses' hand shall be upon him at the start to kill him, and all the people's hand [shall be upon him] at the end [to kill him]   Deut. 17:7

וסלחת לעמך אשר חטאו לך ולכל פשעיהם אשר פשעו בך

And you shall forgive your people that which they transgressed against you, and [you shall forgive] all their transgressions that they sinned before you   I Kings 8:50

This whole section on gapping is oversimplified: the line between gapping and apposition needs to be addressed, and this in turn points to the necessity of taking on the issue of syntactic and semantic boundary-markers for A and B in cases where lineation is relatively determinable. Furthermore, this should be done in the context of a corpus of examples far broader than the "poetry" chosen here.

But there is a more general objection to be brought to this naming of parts. Whatever distortion the notion of parallelism introduced into biblical scholarship, it did correspond to a reality perceived beneath the surface differences outlined here by O'Connor. That reality was the role played by all these phenomena in establishing the pause-sequence, both the articulation of its boundaries and the connection of B to A. The regularity of this sequence, as noted, *is* the regularity of the Bible's high style. On the one hand, its constituent elements are far more varied and complicated than those presented by O'Connor; and on the other, their underlying functional similarity (see above, chapter 1, section 10) is obscured through the distinction of word-level and line-level phenomena, as well as through the separation of different categories of effects at each level. O'Connor's approach to parallelism, enlightening as it is, thus succeeds in obscuring the one thing that was most valuable in Lowth's "parallelism"—its grouping of a variety of procedures under a single rubric because of their basic effective similarity.

If my reaction to O'Connor's approach has been harsh and if I have not dwelt sufficiently on its merits, no doubt the blame lies in part with my own researches into the history of writings on biblical poetry, which suggest the potential use to which his book might now be put. Superficially, of course, O'Connor's flair for taxonomy might remind one of the great Gomarus's *Davidis Lyra*, in which almost anything can be made to fit some metrical prescription or other; this is unfair, though perhaps not quite unfair enough to be ignored. In a deeper way, however, his book bears some resemblance to a more substantial work, Lowth's own *Lectures*, whose parallelism and irretrievable meter distilled enough truth and fancy to keep the idea of biblical poetry on its traditional axes for some time. So here, it seems, the substitution of "constriction" for meter and the assimilation of retropified parallelism to various effects found elsewhere in "world" poetry is in danger of effecting a similar salvation, at least in some quarters. What is of undeniable value is the standard of precision and clarity set by this volume. If this standard is emulated in subsequent approaches to Hebrew syntax and style, its contribution will have been ipso facto substantial. Beyond this, its rigorous treatment of previous approaches to biblical meter and to the confusions surrounding "parallelism" are, as noted, to be applauded.

General Index

O'Connor, M., 315–23
omnisignificance, midrahsic doctrine of, 104–05, 107, 138
Origen, 133–34n, 138n, 145–46; attributed meters to Bible, 147–48, 149, 152, 154, 163, 169, 222, 228, 281
Orpheus, 145

Pagis, D., 198n
Pagninus, Sanctes (Xantes), 227, 232, 279
Parḥon, Samuel b. Abraham, 131n, 191
parallelism: misleading name, 2, 7, 57, 59–63, 70, 95; morphological, 2, 49–50, 55; emphatic character of, 8, 49, 51–54; Lowth's categories of, 12–14, 57–58, 281; other categories, 14, 15n, 42–44; in other literatures, 23–40, 70, 96; binariness of, 26–27, 51, 85; repetition in, 35–40, 55, 306; *the* trope, 86; in post-Biblical Hebrew, 96, 305–14; described by early Christian writers, 156–59, 162, 165–67; in medieval Jewish exegesis, 173–80; in Flacius, 229–31; in Fleury, 233n; Schoettgen's treatise on, 266–73; Lowth's exposition of, 277–82; as substitute meter, 282, 286. *See also* Lowth; pause sequence
Paul, Saint, 139, 149, 161, 165
Paulinus Diaconus, 157–58
"pause sequence," 1–2, 51, 56, 59–61, 64, 66
payyetan, early meaning of, 129–30
Pellicanus, C., 207
Pembroke, Countess of, 244
Petrarch, F., 212–16, 221, 224, 233
Philo, 117–18, 128–29; used metrical terms for Hebrew, 135, 140, 141, 146, 154, 163, 171, 200, 248, 281; allegorical exegesis, 135–36, 139
Pherecydes, 168
Pico della Mirandola, 211
Pindar, 152–54, 170, 222, 234–35, 256–57, 274
piyyut, 129–30, 131n, 132n, 188n, 191; origins of, 130n, 305, 311–12
Plato, 143, 178n, 188n
poetry: no biblical word for, 69; distinguished from prophecy, 151–52, 158,

204, 280; in medieval Spain, 181–82; includes prophecy, 182n, 280–82; falsehood best part of, 188, three classes of, 193n; theology a kind of, 211
— biblical: idea of, 73, 86, 115, 127; Hellenistic origin of, 85, 127–33; lacking in rabbinic texts, 129–30
Politian (Poliziano), A. A., 217
Pomeranus, I., 224n
Poole, Matthew, 264n
Pope, Alexander, 233
Portaleone, Abraham b. David, 203, 210, 238, 240
psalmody, 110, 113
Puttenham, George, 221–22

Qalonymos b. Qalonymos, 182
qaṣīda, 134
qtl-yqtl alternation, 17–19, 20, 23, 50, 55, 77
Quintilian, 189, 235, 276
Qumran: *hodayot* from, 57, 108n, 140, 287n, 305–06; community of, 120
Quntrus bediqduq Sefat 'Eber (anonymous), 196, 238
Qur'an, style of, 25, 185

Rab, 122, 306
Rabanus Maurus, 167, 169
rajaz, 25n, 133
Rashbam (R. Samuel b. Meir), 35n, 174, 176–77, 179, 204, 207
Rashi (R. Solomon b. Isaac), 35n, 173–74, 176, 204, 207
Reuchlin, Johannes, 206–07, 279
rhyme: introduced in Hebrew, 130–31; found in Bible, 222, 233–51
rhythmus: distinguished from *metrum*, 164n, 233–36, 242–44, 256–58; and rhyme, 239
Rivet (Rivetus), André, 264n
Rossi, Asariah dei. *See* Azariah dei Rossi
Rufinus (trans. Origen), 134n

Sa'adya Ga'on, R., 25n, 110n, 130n, 131, 175, 184, 206, 308, 312–13; *Sefer ha-Egron*, 131, 133n, 183n, 238; did not find "poetry" in Bible,

Scriptural Index